THE SIN OF HENRY R. LUCE

CHOICE   MAY '75

Communication Arts

CORT, David. The sin of Henry R. Luce; an anatomy of journalism. Lyle Stuart, 1974. 481p 73-90774. 12.50.   ISBN 0-8184-0201-6

This rambling, self-serving, and bitter memoir of 14 years (1932–46) with *Time* and *Life* apparently struck someone as raw material that could be packaged and promoted as a searing exposé. Within a loose format shaped by a retrospective leafing through and commentary upon back issues of *Time* and *Life*, Cort offers interminable evidence of the corporate infighting, personal rivalries, and nasty status struggles which seem to have been particularly rife in the Luce organization. Long lists of staff members are mulled over with an obsessive fascination that would do credit to a Kremlinologist. Despite the title, Luce rarely appears directly, figuring mainly as a Zeus who occasionally fires down a thunderbolt memo upon the hapless Cort. Luce's "sin," according to Cort, lay in the lust for power and in favoring mediocrity over talent — particularly the talent of David Cort, whom Luce fired in 1946. Cort shows no familiarity with W. A. Swanberg's major (though hardly unflawed) biography, *Luce and his empire* (CHOICE, Feb. 1973). Sad and embarrassing, Cort's "book" stands as a monument to the lengths to which cupidity can carry a publisher.

By DAVID CORT

THE SIN OF HENRY R. LUCE

An Anatomy of Journalism

LYLE STUART, INC. / SECAUCUS, NEW JERSEY

by David Cort

ONCE MORE, YE LAURELS

GIVE US HEROES

THE GREAT UNION

THE BIG PICTURE

THE CALM MAN

IS THERE AN AMERICAN IN THE HOUSE?

THE MINSTREL BOY

SOCIAL ASTONISHMENTS

THE GLOSSY RATS

REVOLUTION BY CLICHÉ

THE SIN OF HENRY R. LUCE

Copyright © 1974 by David Cort

Library of Congress Card No. 73–90774
ISBN 0–8184–0201–6

Queries regarding rights and permissions should
be addressed to Lyle Stuart, Inc., 120 Enterprise
Avenue, Secaucus, New Jersey 07094

Published by Lyle Stuart, Inc.

Manufactured in the United States of America

Introduction

IN ANY great affair, such as the one here studied, two kinds of men must work together: the talent, defined as "glory men," and the executives, defined as "power men." The latter tend to ally themselves with a third kind, the mediocrities. The bias here is that the glory men are the true value in a society, and the power men its latent enemies. The conflict is always kept as invisible as possible, as will be seen. Sometimes an avowed glory man, scenting the rank spoor of power, turns into a power man, and the virtue mysteriously ebbs out of the creation. This is merely a classic form of the tragedy, for it is common to all human enterprise.

The commodity for sale in this case was history, as seen through journalism. It will become apparent that history is less what *actually* happens than what people *think* has happened or should have happened.

The difficulty is in cutting through all the favorable appearances to the graceless truth which, while more complex and disorganized, is also more interesting than the best of appearances.

Section I

THE GHOST OF HADDEN

IN April of 1932, a hard month in a hard year, a hard loser in a love adventure was looking for a job. Because my career until then had been exquisitely literary (my second novel was about to be published), I wanted a nonliterary or even antiliterary job. Because I had led a self-indulgent life which had trapped me in the reckless love affair, I wanted a hard, exacting, nonpermissive job. I also thought the time had come to inform myself of what was going on in the great world, of which I had been contemptuous until then. In short, I wanted to escape completely from the world of *Vanity Fair*, *The New Yorker*, and *The Bookman*. I was in fact neurotic.

Precisely the job I wanted existed, and I soon realized where it was. It had to be on *Time* magazine, then nine years old. But nobody I knew knew anybody on *Time*. The *Time* people, though literary, existed outside the literary world. In this impasse my former editor, Frank Crowninshield of *Vanity Fair*, gave me a letter of introduction to John Stuart Martin, then managing editor of *Time*.

I presented this to Martin and was hired for the usual six-week trial period. It was so easy that it occurred to me, in my neurotic state, that Martin intended to prove, at the end of the six weeks, that what was good enough for *Vanity Fair* was not good enough for *Time*. I concluded that I was not to exhibit any literary bravura during those six weeks. Later events indicate that I was not paranoiac but correct.

The routine was to put me on Milestones—births, deaths, weddings—to discover whether I accepted this hack work with humility. I did, with pleasure. From this I graduated to Miscellany, a column of oddities in the news, requiring some minimal felicity with words. At the end of the six weeks I was still on the payroll.

I did not know it, but the status of John Martin was central to the evolution of Time Inc. He and Noel Busch were first cousins to the real creator of *Time*, Briton Hadden, who had died in 1929, possibly from an infected cat-scratch, certainly from streptococcus. Hadden had been the editor over the years while Henry Robinson Luce had covered the business end. Hadden had invented the tone, in style and personnel, of blatant virility, factuality, and snap judgments on anything under the sun. With a system of (usually) male writer and lady checker (finding a source for every word), he aspired to being invariably right and, within mortal and journalistic limits, nearly succeeded. "Curt, clear, complete." He did not shrink from boasting.

So Hadden was dead. Martin, his cousin, was a slightly deformed version of Hadden; he was the most naturally gifted journalist I had ever met; he tried to run an absolute tyranny which enraged some men, made others laugh; and his was the last reign of the Hadden dynasty and temper.

Before Hadden died, he had written into his will that none of his 3,361 shares of *Time* stock were to be sold for 49 years—that is, until 1978. His heir was his mother Bessie and his executor his half brother Crowell Hadden who, together with the lawyer, a Mr. Carr, was a friend of the *Time* crowd. The official Time Inc. story was that Mrs. Hadden needed immediate income (she could have borrowed at least half a million on her shares). The actual story was that Crowell Hadden and Carr told her, on the urging of Luce and Roy Larsen, that she should diversify her holdings. John Martin may have added his voice and got some of the stock. The real motive was that Luce and Larsen objected to working to make Mrs. Hadden rich. In sum, the will was ignored and 2,828½ shares were sold at $360 a share, for something over a million dollars. Today they would be worth—what figure do you want? $100 million?

Luce took the largest cut, 625 shares; Roy Larsen, 500. When Luce borrowed on his own stock to buy Hadden's shares, the amiability of the bank made him realize for the first time, it is said, that he was a rich man.

His situation in 1929 was peculiar. He knew that he owned and controlled something big, profitable, volatile, and unpredictable. And he was terrified that without Hadden he could not manage it. With his courage and composure he never revealed this. But he acted on it.

Hadden's cousin, Hadden's admirer, and Hadden's mimic, John Martin became managing editor of *Time*. Luce's attitude toward Martin in 1932 was respectful, perhaps grateful. In later years Luce gave this same love to any editor or writer who seemed to have journalistic secrets he did not know. Hadden was dead but he never died in Luce's subconscious, reminding him that he was an incomplete journalist. As will be shown, eventually he lost this image of himself.

The peculiar approach of Briton Hadden, whom I never met, was indicated in 1971 in a report by the Yale class of 1920's secretary, John M. Hincks, in the Yale alumni magazine, of a trip to Houston, Texas, to serve at a wedding of one Peavey in December 1920: "In those days it took two days and two nights by train to travel from New York to Houston. All the way down and all the way back on that trip, Brit was dodging off the train at every fair-sized city to buy the local newspaper. His idea was that each paper had something of interest which was not carried by any others and that these facts could well be of interest to people everywhere. This was the real genesis of *Time*, the weekly newsmagazine." In this naïve observation we can see that Hadden's objective was a national (and international) newspaper, without regional bias, and intensely condensed. He was possessed by the desire to learn and to tell. And he had the ability to interest, even to astonish.

Luce was not this kind of man. He was burdened with an acute sense of responsibility for the effects of what he did or published, which developed into a consciousness of power. For though it is often said that power should assume responsibility, it is less often remarked that a sense of responsibility tends to decay into a sense of power.

The catch was that the only way to understand Hadden's invention was to be irresponsible—as I was and am by instinct. I accept the truth that the facts of any situation are more important than any doctrine. I have a fiendish need to know the truth, none to conform it to any plan. Luce carried the world on his back; I travel very light.

Luce found the ideal people to corrupt Hadden's creation, which he had never understood. This may seem a small sin but in its development by Luce, a man of religion and superabundant conscience as well as ambition, it became "persistent rejection of grace, light, or truth," defined as the Sin against the Holy Ghost, while the "grace, light, or truth" resided in people like myself, without conscience except toward "grace, light, or truth," not toward responsibility or power or money. Circumstances and personnel delayed Luce's completion of the sin for about twenty years after my arrival at Time Inc.

Anyone curious about Hadden might read his cousin Noel Busch's book, *Briton Hadden of Time* (New York: Farrar Straus, 1949), commissioned by Luce. Busch regards Hadden as the epitome of the 1920s and describes a vital untrammeled young man worth $1,100,000 at his death and quickly forgotten by the public.

In 1932 Martin was one-armed (a childhood hunting accident), beetled, and exercised extreme rudeness and a wolfish sense of humor. John Shaw Billings was National Affairs editor (since 1929) and Laird Goldsborough Foreign News editor (since 1925). Billings was a most capable journalist and later editor. Journalistically, he became the most important man in the organization but he was not the kind Luce admired. I gathered that he was terrified of Luce, for I never heard him disagree with Luce on anything. Goldsborough was a lame, humped, semideaf Southerner with aristocratic pretensions. He was capable of writing the whole Foreign News section with perfect ease and cynicism. He was the kind of writer Luce admired in the thirties.

At that time I did not know that my problem was to be admired by Luce, whom I rarely saw; I wanted only to be admired by Martin. I soon realized that here, far from the world of *Vanity Fair*, *The New Yorker*, and *The Bookman*, I was in a company of talented respectable young writers. Certainly they worked under an unremitting discipline (nowadays it would be called Fascist), but it was a purposeful discipline to transfer facts from the sources to the pages of a magazine in a way that would interest a hurried, preoccupied, and indifferent reader. The objective was easily understood; the facts were in front of one; only the conventions had to be learned.

The stages of my assimilation into this team may be instructive. As recorded in a scrapbook, they are quite different from what I "remember." For April there was nothing; Martin was evidently patient with me. Finally, in the issue of May 9 which had gone to press May 2, my debut is two columns of Milestones, with such eloquent passages as:

Born. To Novelist Louis Bromfield (*The Green Bay Tree*, *A Modern Hero* et al.) and Mrs. Mary Appleton Wood Bromfield; a daughter (third child); at Senlis, France.

Died. Harry Kelsey Devereux, 72, Cleveland socialite, onetime president of the Grand Circuit Racing Association and of the American Association of Trotting Horse Breeders, model for the drummer boy in A. M. Willard's° painting *The Spirit of '76*; at Thomasville, Ga.; of heart failure.

I had caught *Time*'s predilection for businessmen, and mastered semicolons.

The next week I did both Milestones and Miscellany, a peculiar art form to which I contributed this item:

In New York, on trial for his life for murder, William J. Turner, 21, pulled out a deck of cards, began playing solitaire. The judge stared, sent the jury out of the courtroom, protested. Attendants confiscated the cards. The judge spoke briefly on courtroom conventions. Said Defendant Turner: "What do you think I am going to do—sit here all day and cry?"

My recollection was that I was restricted to Milestones and Miscellany for about a year. The record confutes me. As of May 23, I

° Uncle of President Theodore A. Willard of Willard Storage Battery Co.

did about five columns on Art and Cinema, the latter permitting a little literate ridicule. Then ensued two weeks of Cinema and Sport, and back to Miscellany and Art.

My recollection was that I was relieved of Milestones in the spring because another cub, Hubert Ames Kay, arrived. But Hubert tells me he did not join until September 1932. He has remained my companion and friend for many decades. Whether everybody came to Time Inc. for neurotic reasons is unknown to me but Hubert did. While he was teaching elocution in college, he developed a stammer. He was of the Billings type, a thorough and indomitable worker. And of course he was first put on Milestones.

Despite my five-month seniority, Hubie Kay and I remained equals in the hierarchy for many years, two reliable producers.

We each had a decision to make, however, one that would control our careers at Time Inc. and perhaps, in a peripheral way, the history of the United States. We had to decide very soon which *Time* department we wanted to specialize in.

Hubie chose National Affairs. It was the tough sensible choice. The United States, in the Hoover Depression, had apparently insoluble problems. Its agony was the greatest event in the world. The 1932 elections were approaching. National affairs was the No. 1 ring.

It was not clairvoyance that made me choose Foreign News. It was a kind of dilettantism, a preference for telling about the faraway and unknown. I had been to Europe twice. At *Vanity Fair* I had dealt with the affectations of England, France, and Vienna. I was fascinated by European history. Foreign News appeared fun. Certainly, I had no premonition that for the rest of the century Foreign News would be the No. 1 ring. At the time it was difficult to get readers to look at the Foreign News department, for Hitler was not yet master of Germany. It was my luck, my destiny, to choose this area.

The luck was mired for four years in the fact of Laird Goldsborough. *Time* tyranny I had come to accept, but Goldsborough elaborated it with Byzantine meanness. He would assign his subordinates a dozen minor stories a week and, if they were well done, slide them into a desk drawer. If the writer, resigning himself to this, wrote a sloppy story, he would send it in to the managing editor.

His No. 2 writer was Francis de Neufville Schroeder, a delightful joker who was more aristocratic than Goldsborough. No. 3 became myself. Evidently, we were the only two who could put up with Goldsborough's satanism year after year, and we had the field to ourselves when he went on vacation.

Retrospectively, I am complimented by Martin's putting me in Goldsborough's stable, for he must have recognized some psychic toughness or masochism in me. My first Foreign News story appeared in the August 15 issue, about the Gran Chaco war between Paraguay and Bolivia, a subject on which Goldsborough evidently did not want to brief himself. My next Foreign News story, September 26, was on Chile.

Meanwhile, I made another lifelong friendship on an Art story (August 22) on Buckminster Fuller's model of a dymaxion house and his ideas: "a whole new order of society, based on function rather than property . . . money ('credits') would bear no interest; the State would guarantee 'primary survival' (food, clothes, shelter) to the lazy, and reward individual energy and enterprise with increased latitude for play and amusement." It struck me then, as now, that the publication of one such story makes ephemeral nonsense of all the periodicals, such as *The New Yorker*, which had the insolence to degrade *Time*. For the date was 1932. And his guarantee is realistic: not to "the disadvantaged"; more honestly, to "the lazy." No healthy person under the age of sixty can possibly be so "disadvantaged" as not to go out and do a job, if jobs exist, unless he or she is lazy or responsible for children, who can be given to day care centers today. "Disadvantaged" can generally be taken as synonymous with "lazy." But Mr. Fuller accepted the lazy, without the ignorant and guilty liberalism that must call them "disadvantaged" to cover its eyes from the vision that people are people.

I think the fact that I was assigned to do a three-column obituary on Edith Rockefeller McCormick (September 5) marked my final acceptance, for *Time* and Martin were impressed by Chicago society and would not have let a novice hand profane it. The story was in National Affairs, not Milestones.

Who comprised this brilliant company of which I was now an accredited member? In the Christmas issue of 1932, when my name finally entered the masthead, that roster listed the following after Luce and Martin. Associates: John Shaw Billings, Laird S. Goldsborough, and Myron Weiss (Science and Medicine). Weekly Contributors: Elizabeth Armstrong (Music), Carlton J. Balliett, Jr. (Religion and Education), Noel F. Busch (Cinema and Sports), David Cort, Washington Dodge II (Business), J. T. Everitt, Mary Fraser (chief of checkers), Albert L. Furth (Press and Aeronautics), Allen Grover (assistant to Luce), David W. Hulburd, Jr. (first full-time correspondent at Chicago), Hubert A. Kay (People and Animals, later Education, then National Affairs), E. D. Kennedy (transferred to *Fortune*), Peter Mathews (an imaginary whipping boy), T. S. Matthews (Books), Frank Norris (National Affairs and Theater), Ralph D. Paine (understudy on Press and Aeronautics, later Business), Francis de N. Schroeder (Foreign News and Art), Cecilia A. Schwind (Foreign News researcher), Charles Wertenbaker (Animals), and S. J. Woolf (cover artist).

Later, Manfred Gottfried and Kay and Sidney James were in National Affairs and, when Noel Busch under protest became National Affairs editor, he came to Kay on *Life* and asked: "Say, Hubie, what's a primary?"

The most brilliant journalist was Ed Kennedy; the most amusing, to me, Busch. Genuinely literary, one way or another, were Busch, Cort, Kay, Kennedy, T. S. Matthews, Norris, Schroeder, and Wertenbaker. Most were recent arrivals.

Another magazine, *Fortune*, was Luce's invention. Larger than life, beautifully illustrated, ponderous, and grandiloquent, it had begun its career in February 1930, in the first backwash of the Wall Street crash (Hadden had probably discussed it before his death). Its staff, who considered themselves superior to *Time*'s staff, at this time included Ralph McAllister Ingersoll, Russell W. Davenport, Manfred Gottfried, Archibald MacLeish, Dwight MacDonald, and Wilder Hobson. *Time* writers, if I am an example, hardly knew *Fortune* was there and did not read it. For Luce, the gamble on *Fortune* expressed a mania; it ennobled Business, in which he believed; it implied that an American Depression was impossible and impermissible; it repudiated the muscular brevities of *Time*, Hadden's creation; and Luce gave his love to its editor, Parker Lloyd-Smith, who went out the twenty-third-floor window in September 1931.

The people at Time Inc. hardly knew there was a Depression. To some extent this was because the company was doing wonderfully well in the Depression. In 1930 *Time*'s circulation was over 300,000, its advertising at 2,353 pages (just behind the *Saturday Evening Post*.) I believe we were adequately paid, though Kay remembers getting $25 a week. There was, however, a sense of elitism. But in a subtler, more pervasive sense, Luce's dementia that an American Depression was inadmissible (symbolized by *Fortune*) had penetrated the organization. I may be embarrassed now at having been so insensibly brainwashed, but it is so. Just before I arrived *Time* had moved to the fiftieth and fifty-first floors of the Chrysler Building, where it was hard to be proletarian, and I have never since tried.

The Depression, and also Prohibition, were the chief relevancies in 1932, as the elections approached. The question arises: What was the attitude of Luce, and *Time*, toward Franklin D. Roosevelt? Early in the year the adjectives for Roosevelt were "ambitious, young." May 9, Walter Lippmann was quoted: "The people of the East . . . have detected something hollow in [Roosevelt], something synthetic, something pretended and calculated." This was a reflection of Roosevelt's one-to-three loss of the Massachusetts primary to Al Smith, and his fairly narrow victory in the Pennsylvania primary. A curious social note was slipped in: "During the Wilson era the Hoovers and Roosevelts were fast friends." This was clever but perhaps too clever.

As a Roosevelt-lover, I understood perfectly that *Time* was against him. The same cautious "factual" snideness continued through the campaign.

But the important thing is that during this period Luce was serious about ideas and principles. The character of Herbert Hoover, his ideas and principles, genuinely appealed to Luce. Even if, in clinging wistfully to them, he estranged his magazines from the great mass of the desperate American people (excluding his own employees), even if he had totally misread the past, present, and future, this was a serious intellectual commitment which one had to respect. Of course, he always misread Franklin D. Roosevelt, a phenomenon he could never accept or understand. And how could he? Roosevelt was an opportunist, but he was also an aristocrat; Luce was a religious bourgeois. Luce was gropingly doctrinaire; Roosevelt was not. Roosevelt was for the whole society; Luce was for Business. Finally, Luce was born in China; he looked at America as would a man from the moon. Roosevelt was feudal, of the land, with an ancestral stake in the land. Luce was a rootless careerist, as indeed I was myself.

In the last month of the campaign, *Time* was making much of Huey Long's support of Roosevelt, accusing Roosevelt of coyness about the veterans' bonus, ridiculing his claim of being a farmer. Hoover was seen as "harassed and long-suffering." *Time* reported, however, that Walter Lippmann finally decided for Roosevelt.

The official Time Inc. history, *Time Inc.*, makes the preposterous assertions: "Luce had no particular reaction to the nomination of Roosevelt. . . . *Time* reported the campaign with no bias. . . . Luce felt personally relieved by Roosevelt's victory." Luce voted for Hoover. Since he was not made of mush, the detachment could not have existed. The writer had overdone the lie. A year later (April 1934), in Scranton, Pennsylvania, he made a speech asking Roosevelt: "Mr. President, do you hate Big Business as I hate Al Capone, and do you propose to teach the American people so to hate?—that is the question I raise." There spake the founder of *Fortune*, and he was very far from "no particular reaction" to Roosevelt.

A practical *Time* reaction to Roosevelt's election was an investment in $150,000 in gold on the London market and the laying in of $50,000 in cash. During 1933 the company, under Stillman's direction, largely switched from high-grade bonds to common stocks, anticipating inflation.

Time and the American people were not fully aware that more portentous events than Roosevelt's inauguration were in course.

Roosevelt was inaugurated on March 4, 1933, and slept soundly on the eve. On March 5, 1933, the German people went to the polls and gave Adolf Hitler an absolute majority in the Reichstag. On March 24 the new Reichstag voted Hitler absolute powers over the German people. Many people in Germany never slept soundly again.

Time's handling of this enormous event cannot be charged against *Time* or Luce; it was strictly Goldsborough's affair, for this was, by the definition, "Foreign News."

In January 1933 three issues of *Time* made no mention of Hitler, one gave the movement two paragraphs, another two sentences. In February, Hitler smashed his way into *Time*.

For President Hindenburg had named him chancellor of Germany with limited powers. *Time* expressed no particular alarm. "The Nazi party is pledged to so many things that it is pledged to nothing." It also had the merit of persecuting Communists (as well as Socialists and Jews) and of imitating Mussolini's fascism, which was respectable to Goldsborough. The word "ludicrous" was used several times and Hitler was "a pudgy, stoop-shouldered, toothbrush-mustached but magnetic little man." A trial joke was to call him "Der Osaf," formed from *Oberste Sturmabteilungenführer*, but this did not catch on.

During February, *Time* dutifully reported Hitler's dissolution of the Reichstag, the calling of new elections, and some Nazi hoodlumism, with the explanation that in any revolution the lower orders get out of hand. It was noted that several of the Kaiser's sons were pro-Nazi, a further sign of respectability. March 6, the Reichstag Fire was noticed in three inches of type, with no recognition of its probable effect on the elections.

March 13, a flattering picture of Hitler and a dog was the *Time* cover, for Hitler had won the election and been accorded tyrannical powers by President von Hindenburg. The Reichstag Fire is now presented as either a Communist or a Nazi plot. March 20, the Storm Troop gangs were let loose on the Lucullan customers of the Berlin night clubs; March 27 under the title "Scared to Death," on the opposition politicians. But it was all very far away and odd and unimportant. April 3, *Time* concluded: "Few if any Jews had been killed. Physical violence was on the wane." But on May

22 it noted the ceremonial burning of books all over Germany.

Goldsborough's tone on other nations can be sampled in this period. In every story about Mahatma Gandhi, he is described as a lemur. On Russia, "like a bee on a bear's nose, the Communist Party is a little group of 3,200,000 from all Russia's 164,000,000," and everybody in the south of Russia is recorded as starving. Of England and France, they ought to pay their war debts, but they weren't doing so. The English appear quaint and aristocratic, the French amusingly mad. Mussolini is a reputable statesman and political genius. That spring he was promoting a four-power peace pact that would have accepted the principles of treaty revision and German rearmament. It withered into a vague "collaboration for peace," of course, but the Romans were rapturous over their leader's statesmanship. One explanation for the mishandling of the Hitler story was that Goldsborough had earlier decided that Hitler was a false alarm, and had to defend his status as a forecaster. Another may have been that *Time's* pervasive business bias convinced everybody that the German story was money—reparations. This was developed in a March 27 story about Hjalmar Horace Greeley Schacht, new president of the Reichsbank and a perpetual *Time* favorite, describing him as "genial, kindly, twinkle-eyed among friends" and gifted with "iron nerve, bold acumen, acute intuition." His brilliant intuition had been that Germany would never be able to pay reparations. *Time* liked people who were right. But Hitler had been right, too, and Goldsborough was wrong.

Another explanation may have been that Martin, a far better journalist than Goldsborough, was losing his grip. He had always lived hard, prided himself (with one arm) on his golf game and his shooting, and gloried in his consumption of hard liquor. He may have been only overdoing his role as the second Hadden, and overdramatizing the plausible idea that some version of Hadden was indispensable to *Time.* But the observable result was that Martin was sometimes in a state of dissolution Saturday at noon—a very important time, because the work week was Thursday to Monday, and a flood of copy reached his desk on Saturday. Occasionally, Mary Fraser, a hardheaded Scotswoman whom everyone swore by and who could have run the magazine on instinct, tried to cover up for Martin by editing until he recovered. The tact and discretion required for this endeavor were nearly superhuman.

It became the rule for Luce to edit on these occasions, and later for John Billings to take over under Luce's nagging supervision. Billings is quoted as complaining that he did not find "a strong staff"; even now I resent this. At all times, the *Time* staff was trying harder, by far, than anybody else in American journalism.

But perhaps Billings was right. Whether the staff was strong or weak, the earnestness of the effort under discipline gave the writing a certain brittleness of inhumanity. Looking at my own contributions during 1933, I find them mechanical, bloated with facts insufficiently digested, full of substance and yet jejune.

For example (April 10, 1933), a most interesting and important fact is presented in this way: "Few of Mexico's leaders are white men. Calles is the illegitimate son of an unknown and a peasant woman. Ortiz Rubio is reputedly three-quarter Spanish, one-quarter descent of Michoacan Indian kings. President Rodriguez is a halfbreed, speaks Yaqui fluently. Both Cardenas and Amaro are pure Indian. Observers have long noted the virility of the Mexican Indian blood, the emergence of an Indian dynasty in Mexican politics." The approach to the great subject, which dominates Mexican society today, is ungainly. The word "observers" means the writer, and the evasion could have fooled only the most besotted *Time* reader. (A year later I was doing better than this.)

The difficulty was that a *Time* writer was rarely able to get on top of his subject. He had perhaps four or five hours to identify, approach, and master it. Writers who could do this were not very common. I could have been worse and still held the job—but only by trying hard.

I remember 1933 very pleasantly. I was publishing a fair amount of foreign news, though chiefly when Goldsborough was on vacation or floundering with his German stories. A group of writers—varying among Balliett, Busch, Dodge, Hulburd, Kay, Paine, sometimes Wertenbaker or Norris, and myself—ate lunch at Child's, half a block north of the Chrysler Building. Balliett was Religion (one of

Luce's two favorite subjects), Dodge and Paine were Business (the other), Norris and Kay were National Affairs.

Busch had best mastered the *Time* attack, adding something to it: a precise hauteur and an assurance that he knew what proper human deportment was in any situation. Applied to the movies, this attitude was devastating: "a morose and timidly salacious picture," "All this is fundamentally as absurd as it sounds but much less vicious," or "Lionel Barrymore acts all through the picture without belching once." Its flaw was that the reader had difficulty believing that the picture had attracted Busch's attention. In person, Busch was like his prose: the best of credentials. I was (and still am) an admirer of Busch and his style, both literary and personal. He and Norris were both Princeton and close friends. Norris' snobbery was less convincing. Kay and I were quite deficient in snobbery.

Midst all this camaraderie, the masthead in mid-1933 split the writers into two castes. Associates: Billings, Busch, Fraser, Furth, Goldsborough, Manfred Gottfried (from *Fortune*), Norris, Schroeder, and Weiss. To the "Weekly Contributors" was added William A. Lydgate who joined our poker game and became the close, ambiguous friend of Francis Sill Wickware, who committed suicide. (The wives participated in the poker game.) Only the elevation of Bill Furth mystified me, for he had very little beyond decency and sincerity, but this may have been a forecast of things to come. I hardly aspired to being an associate nor did Kay. I was undisturbed by Martin's malign rudeness; Kay was not; he wanted to kill Martin. I wrote a Milestone about a gangster on which Martin scribbled, "The greatest Milestone ever written." The gangster had been shot, but neglected to die, and my little masterpiece died instead. His word to me in these petty enterprises was "All right, Dave, carve me a walnut," and I tried, but today the walnuts do not seem to me carved. But Martin, with any encouragement, was a romantic. And I believe that such a man is good for journalism, though Martin was certainly not good for himself. I regret his decline and fall.

One writer was assigned duty on Monday night when the magazine closed, primarily to read the early *New York Times* and tell the printer by teletype what late additions should be made in major stories. Usually, Mary Fraser made a point of being present when a fairly new man was night editor. On one such might I drank a little too much and discovered to my amazement that I could not type. Miss Fraser took care of it, but let the lesson come home to me. Fra, as she was known, seems to have been the sole surviving essence of Time Inc. in this period. She deserves immortalization in Time Inc.'s annals, far above any executive, including Henry R. Luce. For she magically indoctrinated the people who were to create Time Inc. for the next decade or so (including me).

The last-minute additions to *Time*'s copy may seem trivial but they represented that last extra spasm to convince the reader that the magazine had been written five minutes before he got it. They also forcibly reminded the staff that *Time* was in fact dealing in time, an insubstantial passing commodity which had to be snatched at the instant of passing. Time, like electricity, could not be stored; it had to be consumed on the instant if it was to be consumed at all. I believe that Luce never grasped this simple fact and that Hadden did. Whatever anyone may think of this philosophy, long subjection to it made me very comfortable with time. I am still grateful. Others, such as Charles Wertenbaker and T. S. Matthews, have expressed their resentment, and for this I consider them fools and ingrates.

Busch made the same point in a very different way, saying that at Time Inc. his tenure lasted only for the current week and had no validity for any subsequent week. (This would horrify the "responsible" men such as MacLeish, Matthews, and Wertenbaker.) True, it has something of the tone of Roman gladiators or of British second lieutenants in World War I, but I set my nervous clock to Busch's synchronization from then on. I existed solely on what I produced in the current week, not at all on past or future. For a young man this is an exhilarating philosophy, though it is fallacious in the long term, but it was widely shared by the real writers on *Time*, and separated them from the executives, the time-servers, the careerists, devoid of talent or pride in self. These latter were humble with the writers; they were lying in wait, as the company prospered; they knew their time would come.

The bruited brashness of *Time* was the disciplined obligation to seize the day (*carpe diem*), to say something positive on the instant. That week, that day, that hour would never return; we were wolves dining on time. Of course, a fact of time was that various events were happening simultaneously, and these had to be synchronized. Thus President Roosevelt (October 2, 1933) held a conference on inflation reported in National Affairs, and again in Business and Finance, "While President Roosevelt conferred and cogitated about currency inflation . . . the dollar hit a new low of 63.71 cents gold on international exchange." This was followed by a story on the New York Stock Exchange's moves to resettle in Newark, New Jersey, doubtless as a form of blackmailing Roosevelt. The American people smiled.

To accommodate these simultaneities, there had to be a fragmentation into discrete categories. Thus, in National Affairs (October 9, 1933), the sections were the Presidency, Judiciary, Communications, Transportation, Crime, Labor, States and Cities, and finally a grab bag, Political Notes.

Naturally, there are also serial stories, sequences in time. Thus in my scrapbook comes (May 22, 1933):

Each time the storm of a great Japanese offensive breaks in North China it is preceded by a gentle shower of propaganda leaflets. Month ago the shower fell in Miyun, 50 mi. northwest of Peiping (*Time*, May 1). Last week a Japanese plane zoomed through a wild anti-aircraft barrage over Peiping itself. U.S. Minister Nelson Trusler Johnson hopped out of bed to . . . examine one of the first leaflets:
"Fellow-Asiatics: Since we all speak the same language (*sic*) and belong to the same race, we should live and prosper together. Why should we slaughter each other? . . .
"Your soldiers will be exterminated. Good and evil alike will come to harm. You will lose your stupid heads due to the failures of Chiang.
"WILL NOT THAT BE SAD?"

This story was, as usual, checked by a young lady who had to find a source for every word and put a red dot over the word. No imagination was permitted. And so, when the writer found in the material such a subjective revelation as the very tone of voice of the Japanese invasion of China, he leaped on it. The average newspaper reader would not have noticed this quotation, or would not have correlated it with the serial story. *Time* made a pattern, a plot, a pointed story out of at least one week's facts.

On the other hand, it was usually impossible for the reader to tell at a glance what a given story was about. The circuitous approach was the *Time* art form, though I tried to avoid it. This is the opposite of the newspaper format where the headline signals the subject, so that the sophisticated reader can skip the story. *Time* did not propose to be skipped.

The operation was stimulating to the writer and useful to the reader.

As against this performance, we have such comments on *Time* as: ". . . strutting little venture . . . scarecrow style . . . snook-cockery . . . ludicrous, exhibitionistic but arresting dialect of jour-nalese . . . slickness, smartness, bluff." This is more shocking than it sounds for it issued from T. S. Matthews, who became managing editor of *Time* from 1943 to 1949 and included the lines in a book, *Name and Address.*

In reviewing the book for *The Nation,* I commented:

He tells us that at every stage of his career on *Time,* he blushed, flinched and held back, hating each more elevated prostitution while bowing to his shameful fate, like a character in *Candide.* . . .

Time was directed at the literate Philistine reader, who was assumed to be in such a hurry that only great charm and provocativeness could stop him long enough to read anything. The reader's attention was all-important; the subject quite secondary; and it was best if the writer, until just before he read the research, had been as ignorant as the reader. The success of this method derives from the psychological truth that the first impression of information on any mind is more vivid than any follow-up.

I must interject that to be T. S. Matthews or his like must be a horrible experience. His self-cleansing has nothing to do with *Time.*

I was mystified by the hirings and firings on *Time.* Matthews' hiring was understandable because he was Princeton and the issue of a bishop and half of Procter and Gamble. But John O'Hara was fired. I ran into him and he was furious, asserting that John Martin didn't know the difference between the D.S.C. and D.S.M. and he, O'Hara, did. That seemed to be the reason he was fired. Another able man, Max Wylie, was hired and promptly, but too promptly, wrote the best story on the circus *Time* had ever had. He was then fired. My suspicion was that the man had exhibited too much sophistication too soon.

A kind of naïveté, or appearance of naïveté, seemed required. (I had the latter.) Luce, Hadden, Larsen, Davenport, Grover, C. D. Jackson, and most of the others might all have been choirboys, and were handsome, or at least distinguished, men. But their characters were built on an original innocence of the upper middle class. One had to be clean all the way through, or at least look and sound clean.

I imagine this was Luce's doing. Hadden had represented the older code that the aristocracy is virile; Luce stood for the missionary idea that the better elements are moral.

It can be argued that though an initial innocence about a subject is enlivening to the writer, at first, he must subsequently become sophisticated about it. That is, the originally new truth must become a cliché to the writer, as well as to the reader.

The *Time* attack—which had to be repeated week after week, year after year—was carefully edited to avoid this dead end in communication. New facts were injected into old situations—as, for example, during the rise of Nazism the theme of the various colors of the flags of the Empire, the Weimar Republic, and the Third Reich.

The book *Time Inc.* reports that in November 1933 Luce solved the problem of John Martin by creating an Experimental department "to be headed by John S. Martin, who thereby ceased to be managing editor of *Time*," John Billings taking his place.

The facts are remarkably different. On *Time*'s masthead, Martin remained the sole managing editor until May 7, 1934—that is, for six more months.

From then until June 4 the masthead read, Managing Editors: John S. Martin, John Shaw Billings.

On the latter date, the format was changed to:

Managing Editors: $\begin{cases} \text{John S. Martin} \\ \text{John Shaw Billings} \end{cases}$

This remained the form through 1934, 1935, 1936, and well into

1937, when Billings' name, not Martin's, was dropped, because Billings was by then managing editor of *Life* and Martin was again managing editor of *Time*. For three years Billings had produced *Time* without ever being listed as sole managing editor. This was a form of cruelty inflicted on Billings that matches the more obscure cruelties of Goldsborough.

I believe the reason was that Luce still saw Martin as the indispensable ghost of Hadden. Billings was merely superbly capable; he was definitely not a genuis. Luce found nothing in Billings to be in awe of. Martin, drunk or sober, awed him. Luce still had the grace to know that the writer, in a medium for communication, was supremely important, and that different writers communicated at different levels. Some had bugles, some had tin whistles, some might even have violins and know how to play.

In the Experimental department, Martin was given the assistance of Dwight MacDonald, a Trotskyite, and Natasha von Hoershelman, a White Russian, both highly verbal. The new department was perfectly designed to accomplish nothing, and this it did. It put together several dummies for a picture magazine and talked about a sports magazine. It also responded to the writers' belief that there was a lot more to *Time* stories than ever appeared in *Time*, by inaugurating a little magazine called *Letters*, which started with the readers' corrections, objections, and amplifications and affected a modest air of scholarship. It reached a circulation of 35,000 and was dropped in 1937. The Experimental department had then long since been dissolved—in June 1934. The ghost of Hadden waited to make his next appearance.

With Billings as managing editor, some of the élan went out of the operation. He could never have told me, "Carve me a walnut." In fact, I recognized at once that he was not my type (I thought of him as "The Fat Boy"), and so it is odd that under his auspices I reached my peak in the organization. My friend Hubert Kay *was* Billings' type and was perhaps the only writer to receive his confidences, a few of which he passed on to me. But Billings was an honorable and fair man, dedicated to producing a magazine that would satisfy Luce. I imagine that he cared less about my personality than about my work. In any case, I became the all-departments writer for *Time*, the hack who could be inserted into any slot when the writer was sick, drunk, or on vacation. This role delighted me. Doing Science, and meeting a story on colloids, I had to look up the word in the dictionary. At least the impact of the final story was fresh and, if I could understand it, anybody in America could understand it. I think there was one department I never handled; it was Religion, reserved to Balliett, a tall proper gentleman who liked to quote the line about "a life of quiet desperation" and ultimately killed himself in his quietness.

But, essentially, the *Time* writers were quiet. When Luce held one of his staff meetings of minds, nobody responded, except Myron Weiss, who was considered somewhat of a joke. Busch's hauteur had spread to the whole staff. Even Wertenbaker, who later wrote a book on the subject, only stared back at Luce's naïve avowals. There was, in short, not one politician in the carload.

Almost immediately Billings had trouble with me. The play *Mary of Scotland*, with Helen Hayes, was to open on a Monday night when *Time* closed. Perhaps because I had long been a fan of the subject (though not of Helen Hayes), Billings made the exception of allowing me to review the play and insert it in the issue of December 4, 1933, without any editing. All week I researched Mary and had written my lead before I saw the play. Helen Hayes as Mary of Scotland was a travesty. I wrote: "Nearly 400 years after her birth, any new play or book about Mary Stuart, Queen of Scots, is news in the hope that it may explain why Mary is still potent to make historians and poets weep. She was Queen of Scotland a few days after birth, Queen of France at 18, true Queen of England according to Catholic Europe. She was tall, slim, dark, with an oval plump-cheeked face like Film Actress Diana Wynyard's. She had beauty, brains, charm that she never turned off. She had little Scots patriotism, no bigotry, a great gift for hatred and revenge, a warm and grateful heart. . . . Mary was alone in a country too cold for her. . . . Author Anderson's plot makes more sense than history. . . . Helen Hayes, back to the stage from suffering in cinemas like *Farewell to Arms, White Sister*, gives to

Mary little but these same brave, little girl accents . . . just a Hollywood actress."

All the other reviewers gave Helen Hayes glowing praise, so that when Billings saw the *Time* review on Thursday he was dismayed. As far as he was concerned, *Time* was wrong. Some months later other critics, headed by George Jean Nathan, reconsidered and came around to my point of view.

However, I redeemed myself (December 18, 1933) with *Tobacco Road*, which everybody else had reviewed badly. The veracity of the production came through to me and I wrote: "Even the smell of hot dust, of unwashed bedding and dried food leavings seems to drift out over Manhattan audiences. In this unhurried shiftless atmosphere the events of *Tobacco Road* stretch themselves with lazy brutality . . . it moved Manhattan reviewers to call its characters 'livestock,' 'pigs,' 'guinea pigs,' 'weird savages,' 'the primitive human animal writhing in the throes of gender,' 'foul and degenerate parcel of folks,' 'the hangdog and hookworm set.' "

Since *Tobacco Road* became a success in spite of the critics, this unorthodoxy, in contrast to the one two weeks before, was applauded. The difference in Billings' mind between the two reviews may have been that in the first I had asserted some personal eccentric power of opinion, while in the second I had submitted myself to documentation. Or, better, in the first I had abused my unfettered freedom, while in the second I was supervised. Actually, I don't know what went on in Billings' mind.

The first big story under the Billings regime was a natural for Martin—the repeal of Prohibition December 5, 1933. Since the final news came in at the end of the work week, the story was told in one sentence (December 11).

In Billings' issues, National Affairs, which had been his department, seemed more knowledgeable. Foreign News seemed more subdued and artfully written. The "Man of the Year" story (January 1, 1934) went through two columns of discarding eminences abroad and in medicine, sport, theatre, movies, literature, and finance before it lit on Hugh S. Johnson of the National Reconstruction Administration. This seems fairly dull. But under Business an investigation of Detroit banks was treated as another St. Valentine's Day Massacre. And under Insull was the sportive pun, "Insullated."

In that issue a new name, Maurice English, appeared under "Weekly Contributors." I remember him as a tall, soft-spoken, cultivated young man, but he disappeared from the masthead in two months—I don't know why. During 1934 three other new names appeared—Paul Husserl, Walter Stockly, and Joseph J. Thorndike, Jr. The first two were capable journeyman journalists, the third became a figure in American publishing, a choirboy type with an icy brain. As a newcomer, he made a point of snubbing the man, C. D. Jackson, who had gotten him his job.

By this time Time Inc. had several other media, which ought to be listed.

Roy Larsen's enterprise, the radio "March of Time," ran from 1931 to 1939, took a vacation, and ran again from 1941 to 1945.

Luce's hobby, *Architectural Forum,* was published by Time Inc. from 1932 to 1964.

Another Larsen enterprise, the movie "March of Time," began in late 1934, and absorbed the full time of Larsen and Louis de Rochemont, whose brother Richard had taken on the radio "March of Time."

The two "March of Times" were considered marvelous advertisements for *Time;* doubtless they were, but they introduced into the basically truthful concept of *Time* a meretricious (and inevitable) counterforce of all-out showmanship. A radio program or a movie had to say one simple indubitable thing, and say it loud and hard. At first, Luce had held himself apart from the "March of Times," but slowly he responded to the power of their effects, particularly that of the movie. In contrast to these bludgeons, *Time* seemed pussyfooting and epicene with its claim to objectivity. But this infection, if it had in fact taken hold, had not swayed Luce from his allegiance to *Time,* to ideas and principles, and to writers.

Billings sent me over to the radio "March of Time" to monitor and edit the compositions of the hard-working radio writers. It was easy to point out items of importance omitted from each script, for I had read the *New York Times* from front to back. We would rewrite the script with the added material. It was then timed with the actors, and so many seconds of talk had to be eliminated. I agreed to eliminate precisely what I had put in. For I had been indoctrinated in the finitude of time; I accepted it as a non-negotiable fact of life; and, if there was no time to say something, it *would* not get said and *should* not get said. I went back to *Time* and reported to Billings what I had discovered: it was not feasible for the "March of Time" to approach telling the whole truth about anything. In the years since I have never heard anything on radio that would lead me to change this opinion; and the judgment on television must be even bleaker.

The point I am making about the "March of Times'" decadent effect on Time Inc. is so subtle that I do not think Roy Larsen can be blamed for failing to anticipate it. He was not, after all, a *Time* writer.

In 1934 Billings may have had a slight bias against Foreign News, for the section grew shorter and was run in among the advertisements. Goldsborough continued his propaganda for Mussolini as the respectable Fascist. A story of Mussolini's meeting with the premiers of Austria and Hungary (March 26, 1934) "served notice on Germany that Italy would brook no further interference with Austrian affairs—or with Hungarian affairs for that matter." Again, when Hitler visited Mussolini in Venice (June 25, 1934), the host was described as "the world's No. 1 Fascist." This version of the *Realpolitik* prepared nobody for the future of Europe.

Nor elsewhere in the magazine would one have been prepared for the later glorification of Marcus Garvey by a story (May 14, 1934) describing him as a swindler with the titles of "Provisional President of the African Republic, Imperial Potentate of the Valley of the Nile, Emperor Marcus I of Ethiopia, Admiral of the Black Star Line, President General of the Universal Negro Improvement Association, Commander of the Nobles of the Sublime Order of the Nile and Knight of the Distinguished Service Order of Ethiopia." Obviously, he had no intimation of what was in store for Ethiopia the following year.

Time dead-panned its amusement in telling (May 21, 1934) how

Russia had offered the Jews a national home in Biro-Bidjan in farthest Siberia, where the only policeman had been eaten by a Siberian tiger.

A now-forgotten irony which will amuse some but did not amuse *Time* at all (May 21, 1934) was a federal charge of income tax evasion brought against Andrew Mellon, formerly "the greatest Secretary of the Treasury since Alexander Hamilton." The grand jury refused to indict.

A supposed body blow to Hitler (July 2, 1934) was a mild criticism of Nazi tactics by von Papen, and Hindenburg's immediate congratulations to von Papen. "Enthusiasm for Nazism was some-what on the wane" was the thoughtful conclusion. Two weeks later (July 16, 1934) Hitler bloodily purged some of the Nazi leaders. But a trace of nervousness was read into his having all the bodies cremated, leaving no trace. This was followed (August 6, 1934) by seizure of the Austrian chancellory by Nazis and the murder of Chancellor Dollfuss. A week later (August 13, 1934) Hindenburg died, as Hitler was arranging to assume all the president's powers. One way or another, the obstacles in Hitler's path were disappearing.

Any misappraisal by Goldsborough of the *Realpolitik* was rela-tively inconsequential. For *Time* was reporting the events; the reader saw the play unfold; the violence of the action itself made its impression. Such asides as "enthusiasm . . . was somewhat on the wane" could hardly blunt the impression. Thus, the formula of the magazine justified itself across the months and years, and the reader could properly be described as "well informed." After all, it would still be five years before Hitler would career into World War II; there was still time to be supercilious.

I would even offer the writers' superior detachment from the news as a virtue. A lot of hysterical heresies were abroad during the Depression. In the pages of *Time* one found oneself in a solid stable world again; change was regarded with disdain. For in any changing society more will remain the same than will change. The revolutionist is nearly always (Lenin and Mao may be exceptions) what a happy man would call a "jerk"; he has a personality only so long as he thinks about the revolution. Most American radicals during the Depression handsomely fitted this description, and vanished like May-flies when the thought had gone. *Time* remained sure of itself.

Subsequent history has shown that *Time* was right not to lose its nerve. America was improved by Roosevelt's New Deal but not revolutionized. Indeed, Roosevelt strengthened capitalistic democracy. Since *Time* writers were generally pro-Roosevelt, the magazine covertly gave a favorable picture of him.

I remember Sunday as the pleasantest day, Lexington Avenue being empty as we strolled up to Child's for the frugal lunch. On one beautiful Sunday toward the end of that 1934 summer, we saw on Forty-third Street the unnaturally splayed body of a suicide who had just gone out a lower Chrysler Building window. His shoes, worn but well made, impressed me as heightening the tragedy, for everything could have been useful a little longer. By a fortuitous piece of research, I can report that he was Jerry Faulkner, a copywriter for the J. Stirling Getchell advertising agency, working on the great new 1935 De Soto account; he left a note saying in substance, "So long, guys. Can't take it any more. Sorry I won't be around to see the Yanks take the Series." Then he launched himself out the window. (The Yankees were not in the World Series in 1934.)

That year the Democrats won the elections and in the same issue (November 12, 1934) the British Labour party's clean sweep of the London County Council elections was reported.

Time may be said to have popularized the blind anecdotal lead, now the refuge of every untalented journalist, as in the *Reader's Digest*, as in this (October 1, 1934): "At 10 o'clock one morning fortnight ago a man in a black Dodge sedan drove up to the Warner-Quinlan filling station on Manhattan's Lexington Avenue at 127th Street" (now one of the most murderous Negro areas in the world). A full two columns later the man's name is first given—Bruno Richard Hauptmann, the kidnapper of Charles Lindbergh's son.

In this case a hint of Luce's sharpening interest in news pictures was given by a spread of Hauptmann photographs. Later (October 29, 1934), two pages were given to the famous pictures of the assassination of King Alexander of Yugoslavia and French Foreign

Minister Barthou, for assassination closes the generation gap. Because of the size of the *Time* page, the pictures were small and the captions were not skillful. But the fascinating discovery of what pictures could add to words had burst on *Time* and Luce, and the future was pregnant with the revelation.

At about this time an ominous figure moved onto the scene, Daniel Longwell, formerly a promotion man for Doubleday publishers, a man I had known contemptuously at Columbia College. Luce had been bewitched by him. The gap between Luce and myself was widening. Anyone who believed in Longwell had to be a fool. He was named as picture assistant to John Billings on *Time*. His name did not reach the masthead until April 22, 1935, half a year later, as one of the "Associates," and this must represent the period of Luce's indecision between truth and power. He had had no *Time* training. He represented a philosophy the exact opposite of mine: the instant impact, Fourth of July fireworks, parades, colored balloons, exhibitionism, infantilism, shock value, hurrah, hurrah, hurrah. A very likable man, he was my antithesis for the next decade. I believe that he was that novelty among *Time* editorial people, a man without character; he had invented himself out of whole cloth. But he was adept in the ways of corporations, having been blooded in the Doubleday-Doran wars, and quietly he built himself a little empire of photographers—Thomas McAvoy, Peter Stackpole, Alfred Eisenstaedt et al.—who specialized in the candid camera. He was an hysteric but not at all stupid. Since I am an hysteric under control, I am unreasonably irritated by hysterics, so that my opinion of Longwell is not objective, but absolutely sincere.

The power of pictures which Longwell had discovered (and the discovery was to be highly contagious) is easily explained. Everybody goes through life looking at people and things, not at words. Thus everybody sees his world as scenes (pictures). The seen is virtually the whole substance of reality, with small supplements from smell, sound, taste, feeling. Words are an arbitrary, learned, inadequate shorthand for the seen reality. The word "slack-jowled" is feeble beside a picture of a slack-jowled man, for the reader relates the picture to all the slack-jowled men he has known, compounding an impression out of his most personal and valuable possession, his experience of people. The impression may not be valid, but it is immediately the reader's own. The word "slack-jowled" relies on the reader's unreliable talent for visualizing and relating. Therefore, the prevalence of pictures presents a perilous challenge to democracy, on the faith that the people's judgment of appearances will be basically correct for democracy. It is possible that such belief will prove more reliable than belief in words, but this is not certain.

The new hidden interest in pictures at *Time* was not noticeable after Longwell's arrival, for most *Time* stories were word stories. A beauty (December 3, 1934) was Smedley Butler's fantasy of a Fascist plot to march an army into Washington and depose President Roosevelt. No fantasy (December 17, 1934) was Stalin's blood-bath in reprisal for the assassination of his friend Kirov. *Time* complained that the American press, outraged by Hitler's earlier purge, remained unmoved by Stalin's equivalent. When the Italians arranged a border incident with the Ethiopians (December 24, 1934), *Time* correctly called it "just possibly the overture to Il Duce's long postponed symphony of colonial conquest." In this issue was another prophecy that has become obsolete: "Negroes . . . are the Black Hopes of Communism in the U.S. . . . Nowhere else in the world is a Negro so pampered as in Russia."

The "Man of the Year" (January 7, 1935) was Franklin D. Roosevelt, presented with some admiration. The story was illustrated with lesser figures of 1934 captioned, respectively, Rich Man, Poor Man, Beggar Man, Thief (Dillinger), Doctor, Lawyer, Merchant, Chief (James Farley). This was amusing. Elsewhere, a gaggle of college professors was quoted as sweeping the New Deal into oblivion.

The Treaty of Versailles began actually, not verbalistically, to slide into oblivion (January 21, 1935) when, in supervised elections, the Saar voted by over 90% to return to Germany. The League of Nations fidgeted and whimpered over this stony fact and adjourned in its usual way, while Hitler assumed that the Saar was now his—and so it was. As between the talking League and the acting Hitler, *Time* was halfway sympathetic to Hitler.

The new picture phase of *Time* appeared (February 18, 1935) in three pages of photographed diplomats engaged in "Pact Making" or the web of post-Versailles treaties. The subject was far too conceptually complex to be explained by pictures of statesmen talking, sitting, or standing, plus brief captions. Dan Longwell was finding, as the "March of Time" movie had found, that it was awkward to present a complex word story of ideas in picture form. Photographs of morning coats and high collars do not explain diplomacy.

What pictures can do was shown (February 25, 1935) in three pages of candid shots of President Roosevelt at his desk, captioned "Mn Mn," "Tch, Tch," "Eh?" "Hah!" "Hey, Hey!" A picture can indeed say "Tch, Tch" or "Eh?" as idea content. It can also (and probably did) convey the quality of Roosevelt with his composure and skepticism and smilingness, as impression content. Appearances thus supersede ideas, whatever the facts.

Mussolini sent three Italian divisions to Italian Somaliland to close in on Ethiopia. Whether he did it with an expression of "Mn Mn" or "Hey, Hey!" was not recorded in *Time*, but it would have been interesting.

In periods of change, it is natural to describe the world as "mad." *Time* (March 11, 1935) characterized bar gold as "the only absolute in a now definitely mad money world." And again (March 25, 1935), with a note of horror, it was pointed out that all Europe was frankly rearming. This was translated into American rearmament with two pages of pictures of the military high command in the United States, as ineffective as pictures as the earlier display of diplomats. But America, as it painfully discovered a few years later, was not rearming. This peculiar naïveté about the nature of war as a fact of life dominated *Time* for some further years. An example of the naïveté was the statement in *Time* that French General Weygand had won the Battle of Warsaw against the Bolsheviks, whereas in fact Pilsudski had won the battle by ignoring Weygand's advice. But this Weygand reputation had something to do with the later fall of France. Though little wars by other people seemed romantic, the idea that the United States might some day have to fight for its life was not acceptable. There was still time to be supercilious.

The future is frequently foreshadowed in these old pages. A Negro riot in Harlem (April 1, 1935) over the supposed shooting of a shoplifter opened an accurate exposition of the degradation of Harlem where Jews owned everything and were opposed by an "extraordinarily feeble collection" of black politicians. Next came a story of the official end of the Seminole Indian war of the 1830s in which the whites had treacherously, under a flag of truce, seized the Indian leader Osceola. Finally, there was a "Nudist Theatre Guild" in Mount Vernon, New York, whose performance was voted "depressingly modest" (shorts and aprons).

A remarkable proof of the superiority of the amateur over the professional (April 22, 1935) was the prediction of the columnist Viscount Castlerosse: "Of course London will be bombed in the next war. . . . London is not going to be wiped out nor is the civilian population going to be exterminated." This infuriated professional airmen, one of whom replied, "One third of London's population would be wiped out by morning. Lord Castlerosse is talking through his hat." Thus the enthusiasm of airmen for their arm, to this day not supported by their achievements except with the atom bomb, brought the aviators well past defeatism and close to treason. This sort of propaganda helped prepare for Munich.

The picture campaign went on, giving a page to Hermann Göring in this issue, three pages to the Silver Jubilee (25th) of King George V of England, who was also on the cover (May 6, 1935), pictures of Secretary of Agriculture Henry Wallace (May 13, 1935), and candid pictures of Father Charles Coughlin, the rabble-rouser (May 20, 1935). Ostensibly an added value in *Time*, these picture acts may have begun to dissolve the reader's faith in the periodical as seriously truthful. For pictures are like music: they say something, certainly, but it is a something that cannot be defined accurately in words— that is, cannot be learned and used. Pictures convey an impression, an appearance. And it was precisely to probe beneath impressions and appearances that Hadden had created *Time*. To some extent Luce understood this, but it was not bred in his bones, as it was in those of a real *Time* writer. He was too easily seduced, probably by the lesson of the "March of Time" movie, into seeing that pictures were power over people. Is it too subtle to suggest that anyone who begins to believe in pictures is ceasing to believe in words? Not, I must emphasize, "ceased." At this time Luce was still a word journalist. But he was being closed in on by people who believed in pictures: Larsen, Longwell, Louis de Rochemont, all honorable men.

Longwell's chief contribution here was the candid photography of Thomas McAvoy, usually of American politicians. A variant was the two-page picture act (June 24, 1935) of conditions in the Gran Chaco war between Paraguay and Bolivia, then coming to an end, but the pictures were the drab product of the agencies.

I was given some important Foreign News stories—doubtless Goldsborough was on vacation and Schroeder was running Foreign News. I note also that I never used the "blind anecdotal" or roundabout lead, but got immediately into the story. Thus (May 27, 1935), under "International": "Which Capitalist European Power would be the first to swallow its hatred of Communism and make an ally of Soviet Russia?" It was France, whose Pierre Laval then went to meet Stalin " . . . in whose face Laval saw much the same calm, woodchuck cunning he sees in his own mirror. The two got along famously, two born listeners who knew what they were doing. . . . France has checkmated Germany for the present."

Back in America, *Time* pointed out (July 8, 1935) that the New Deal, after spending $9 billion to lower unemployment, since 1933, saw the total of unemployed slightly higher at 9,711,000 in 1935. The week before it had analyzed Roosevelt's attempt to create 3.5 million new jobs with $4 billion as coming to $1,142 per job.

Mussolini's projected war on Ethiopia had gained respectability as an attempt to impose civilization and the abolition of slavery on the Ethiopians. Haile Selassie was always translated in *Time* into Power of Trinity I. Later (July 15, 1935), Roosevelt answered an Ethiopian appeal with the evasion that he "would be loathe [*sic*] to believe 'that either nation would resort to' other than pacific means." The shocking contrast between Mussolini's approach to conquest and Hitler's only four years later in Poland is evident. Hitler made an agreement with Stalin, and immediately rampaged. Mussolini was to go on talking for three more months; however, his delay may have been merely to wait for the Ethiopian rainy season to end.

It does not suit my present theme of dignifying the *Time* writers but another remarkable error appears in this issue. Of the murdered Austrian Chancellor Dollfuss, he was "just the right size to sit beside a cherubim." *Time*'s function was to show that cherubim is the plural form; not to take advantage of an obsolete usage (cherubim sounds more important than cherub). It was a mistake, an illiteracy, and one may laugh if one likes. Remember, everything in *Time* was read carefully by four or five people, at least.

Suddenly (July 22, 1935), one is alerted by a *Time* cover on Joseph Kennedy of the Securities Exchange Commission. What does it say of his historic family? It is a clumsy story in Business and Finance, probably written by Paine, and part of a sentence is devoted to the family: "He manages to weekend with his wife and as many of his nine children as he can collect"—this of Rose, Joseph, Jr., John F., Robert F., Edward, and the girls, a whole generation or more of spastic American history. But the writer cannot be faulted for this lack of clairvoyance, John Kennedy then being eighteen years old, and all of them alive.

The Nazi persecution of Jews had to be recognized (July 29, 1935) in the mob beatings of Jewish men and women, particularly if blonde women were accompanied by "Jewish-looking" men, whatever that may have meant. On a very different level, the American persecution of American Negroes was reported (August 12, 1935) with a visit of Negro Elk officers to President Roosevelt. It was noted that a Pennsylvania law against segregation and discrimination against Negoes in stores and restaurants was ignored by the whites.

Goldsborough revered George V and his Queen Mary, but felt a peculiar revulsion toward their children. The word "fairy" had been elliptically used against the Prince of Wales. Now (August 19, 1935) the Duke of Kent was described as "the youngest and willowiest son" of George V. His bride was called a "clever, ambitious minx." In other words, with no discredit to the father, we are to understand that all his sons are probably deviants. The complications in

Goldsborough's psyche that produced this fantasy are beyond me, but they led him a year later to his greatest coup, though not on the lines he had laid down. And I would think that this very coup led, in a way he could not have expected, to his downfall.

But he was preparing his downfall in other ways, virtually authorizing Italy's invasion of Ethiopia (September 2, 1935) by announcing that Haile was "a usurper, the rightful Emperor of Ethiopia being dusky Lij Yasu (Child of Jesus)." (This was a cull from old encyclopedias, Lij Yasu having been born in 1896.)

The picture theme was developed (September 9, 1935) with two pages of bucolic pictures of the Iowa State Fair and the first picture ever taken of the U.S. Senate in session (by Thomas McAvoy), during a Huey Long filibuster. This was marked "Copyright Time. Reproduction forbidden."

This was made still more historic the following week by the assassination of Huey Long. Oddly, Robert Cantwell appears in the masthead as an associate (September 30, 1935), is demoted to a Weekly Contributor (October 7, 1935).

When Roosevelt took a cross-country train trip (to return by navy cruiser via the Panama Canal) (October 7, 1935), *Time* was sarcastic—". . . as an Oriental potentate uses his viziers to scatter cumshaw to the multitude" (cumshaw is Chinese, vizier is Turkish) ". . . before a station crowd of 15,000 (expected: 100,000)."

I have an idea that Luce was editing.

The *Komsomolskaya Pravda* was eloquently quoted: "Among the noble qualities of the Soviet citizen is class hatred . . . organic hatred toward all the filthy, abominable remnants of the old world, its wolfish laws and fetid life. . . . Irreconcilable, inflexible, untamable hate should be nourished." This iridescent beauty of hatred has done well in the ensuing years.

The next issue (October 14, 1935) was notable in several ways.

First, I know Luce was editing. Second, Herbert Hoover was the cover, and the story considered as Republican candidates in 1936 Frank Knox, Landon, and Hoover, the last seeming best. Third, in the baseball World Series, the Detroit Tigers won their first Series.

But the Series was swept out of the news by Mussolini's

long-advertised invasion of Ethiopia from both Eritrea and Italian Somaliland. *Time* had found its war, though the Japanese had been fighting in China for years, but this was a white man's war. In view of subsequent history, it is amazing to see that *Time*'s second department was now "THE WAR," given six pages, while Foreign News followed with seven columns, or 2⅓ pages. The indicated hysteria must have come from Longwell, who had wanted to start a picture magazine solely to sell copies on this long-projected war. THE WAR started with the admission that no war had been declared, and then moved on to "THE FRONT" (echoes of World War I) where some Italian bombers were taking off to bomb Aduwa, scene of the 1896 massacre of an Italian army by the Ethiopians. As usual, the coverage was excellent, but the idea that this was *the* war must in retrospect seem hilarious, a further revelation of the innate naïveté, but a welcome accretion to Goldsborough's department.

THE WAR was preceded by the first full-page map *Time* had ever used, the work of the official cartographer, Richard Edes Harrison. Working under pressure for both *Fortune* and *Time*, nearly without sleep for a week, Harrison was near exhaustion when he was summoned to Luce's office Sunday afternoon. Goldsborough was opposing the map. Luce finally agreed, "All right, no map." Harrison fell into a chair and lowered his head to let the blood run into it. Mary Fraser ran to his aid. Luce then said, "All right, map." As seen now, the map was indispensable. But Harrison had involuntarily done the right thing.

To my surprise, I was given "Ethiopia: Mobilization," as follows:

At the south entrance of the palace, a huge young Galla lifted his open hand and struck the great dull-brown Negarit (Emperor's) war drum. OMMMM . . . OMMMMMM. Forty smaller kettledrums from the palace answered, rommommommommommomm. The booming throbbed, swelled, seemed to shake the air. On each of the mountain tops that hang over Addis Ababa, other drummers smacked their drumheads. The monotonous, terrible call to war spread out from the capital, from mountain top to mountain top, across the wild gorges, jungles and plateaus of Ethiopia, until it rolled into the capitals of the six great rases (princes), whose war drums took it up, passed it on to the great chiefs and the little chiefs. To the farthest nomadic tribes, foraging no one knew where, couriers rode out by mule and camel. *"Kitet!"* was the word the couriers gave, "Close ranks, unite!"

The congested rage of six long months of restraint boiled up out of one of the world's most naturally savage peoples. Mobilization means nothing in Ethiopia. When the drums sound, the men go to their chiefs, the chiefs start for the enemy and the war is on. In Addis Ababa the 5,000 in the Emperor's courtyard heard the order out, solemnly applauded three times, then went into a fit. They brandished their swords, accidentally slicing off some of each other's ears and noses, spotted a nearby huddle of white newshawks and had almost mobbed the white men before the Emperor's guards ran in between. . . .

Out of this half-insane killing rage of a people, observers last week asked, how much of a fighting force would meet the factory-made modern Italian army? . . . But far beyond all these, he had Ethiopia's eternal defense, one of the most tortured and inhospitable terrains on the face of the earth. On that his throne last week rested.

How I knew all this I have forgotten. Even if it were not in my scrapbook, the piece is not in Goldsborough's style, or in Schroeder's. I was exhilarated by the ignominious war. I had three pieces in the diminished Foreign News. Mussolini had slightly advanced my career—very slightly.

In Goldsborough's mind, but not in Luce's, the overemphasis on the Ethiopian war was, perhaps almost subconsciously, a way of obscuring the real center of fascism: Hitler. Propaganda can indeed be achieved by mere journalistic format—THE WAR. The magician diverts the eye with nonsense while the business is done elsewhere. But I do not suggest that Goldsborough was covering up for Hitler; he honestly preferred Mussolini. The effect was the same.

The validity of THE WAR format is revealed by its history.

October 21. THE WAR: six pages. Foreign News: 3⅔ pages. Here we also see the death of Briton Hadden's executor, Crowell Hadden, at 40 of pneumonia, and a favorable review of John O'Hara's *Butterfield 8.*

October 28. THE WAR: four pages. Foreign News: four pages. Under the latter heading was a logical defense of Mussolini, as not the bluffer everyone took him for, to support the cover of Il Duce with two sons. There was jubilant notice of a *Literary Digest* poll (which later destroyed that magazine) showing that 62% of Americans disapproved of Roosevelt and the New Deal.

November 4. THE WAR: four pages. Foreign News: three. There are two pages of pictures of the followers of Roosevelt's handout rival, Francis E. Townsend, and a story suggesting that Austria-Hungary's Crown Prince Rudolf was murdered by a homosexual lover at Mayerling.

November 11. THE WAR: two pages. Foreign News: 4⅔. The stories on Roosevelt are getting more bitter. The League of Nations stories on sanctions against Italy develop a subtlety that may have influenced British and French policy in Italy's favor.

November 18. THE WAR: two pages. Foreign News: five pages. THE WAR has now changed to "dreary little war."

November 25. THE WAR: two pages. Foreign News: four pages.

December 2. THE WAR: two pages. Foreign News: six pages.

The collapse came (December 9, 1935) when "THE" was removed from in front of "WAR." Now, as "WAR," the department could also cover the Sino-Japanese war, and pointed out the much greater scale of that war over the "dreary little war."

The experiment, which I believe sprang from the "hurrah, hurrah" promotional instinct of Dan Longwell, was proved a fiasco based on an hysterical approach to the news—sans perspective, sans morality, sans sophistication, sans composure, sans everything. Doubtless, the readers hardly noticed the embarrassing retreat from "THE WAR" to "WAR." The Gran Chaco war had by then ended. At the time I noticed none of this, or at least it left no impression. I would assume that the abandonment of THE WAR was the doing of competent John Billings, stuck with an atrocity. I would also assume that this was another blow to Goldsborough's journalistic credibility. For no magazine prospers by backing down on a format, while apologizing for adopting it in the first place.

In this awkward episode we see the intrusion into *Time* journalism, which I respected, of a philosophy of impressions and appearances, of flamboyant selling, of psychedelic lights and balloons, and hurrah, hurrah. This grand intuition is hindsight. But a primary requisite of journalism is to distinguish between large and terrible events and nongigantic events, even if the latter can be turned to journalistic profit. And I suspect that profit was the motive for the egregious THE WAR.

WAR was a vulnerable vermiform appendix of the initial error, which Billings could not excise, for Luce had bequeathed it to him. In listening to Longwell, Luce was not betraying word journalism; in his humility, he thought he was learning something. And I doubt whether he ever realized the kind of error he had committed in grooving his magazine into THE WAR, on such a foolish errand.

In the December 23 issue, there was a masthead change of the guard. Ed Kennedy and T. S. Matthews, who had disappeared, returned and James Parton, a later colleague of Thorndike's on *American Heritage,* appeared. Cantwell and Furth were dropped, probably to go to *Fortune,* and Husserl left forever, probably to go to a better job, for people quit Time Inc. and went on to fame.

Section II

TEMPTATION ON
THE MOUNT

AT this point things were coming to a head—at Time Inc. and in the outer world.

While Luce was editing *Time* in October, with Billings presumably on vacation at his Carolina plantation, his wife was getting a divorce. (She is described as a lively and attractive lady.) In the December 2, 1935, issue, Luce's remarriage was announced to "Clare Boothe Brokaw, 32, playwright . . . onetime managing editor of *Vanity Fair.*" There was a weaseling review of her play, *Abide with Me.* Several versions of the review were written, the final one describing the "most gilded opening of the week," presenting the murder of a scoundrel, "which brings relief from much tedious psychiatry." That was the best the editors could bring themselves to give the new Mrs. Luce.

Mrs. Brokaw had been on *Vogue* while I was on *Vanity Fair;* she had been doggedly courted by Donald Freeman, managing editor of *Vanity Fair* and my managing editor on the *Columbia Jester* where he had expertly toadied to Alexander Woollcott and H. L. Mencken. Clare was obviously beyond poor Don Freeman's reach. At a party at his house I had insulted her. Next day she demanded from Freeman that I produce a formal apology. Naturally, I refused. This went on for about a week. Finally, to Don's pleadings, I signed a note saying that I commiserated with her for her misfortune in meeting David Cort. She marched in to my desk, asked, "Is that all you have to say?" and tried to outface me for five minutes that seemed like sixty. Long later, after Freeman drove his car at speed into an abutment, almost certainly as a suicide, she became managing editor of *Vanity Fair*, and *Vanity Fair*, supposedly a men's magazine, vanished in 1936.

Probably in December, at lunch at Child's, I confided this anecdote to a group that included Del Paine, concluding, "I expect to be fired." At a later lunch with another group that included Del Paine, I repeated the story, and he snapped, "I don't want to hear that story again." This irritated me then, and it irritates me now. But it is not beyond belief that the new Mrs. Luce may have been my champion with Luce.

Her story, which she has frankly avowed, is that her life began in what she considered humiliating poverty, doubtless exaggerated. Her father can be described as an itinerant fiddler but was actually a violinist in a touring symphony orchestra, and rarely at home. Her mother's second marriage to a Dr. Austin financed an ocean voyage, on which Clare was spotted by Mrs. O. H. P. Belmont, who was delighted with her. Under Mrs. Belmont's sponsorship, Clare was given other social opportunities, none of which she bungled. In this way she gained the rich socialite husband, a Brokaw, divorced him, went on to *Vogue* and *Vanity Fair*, and to writing plays which were botches until Luce's money could engage George S. Kaufman to restructure them without taking credit. The rare combination of real beauty, a cold brain, and character account for her remarkable versatile career.

But greater things than her career were afoot. It was inevitable that Luce would try to produce a picture magazine. Everybody in New York and perhaps the country assumed it.

The project that would become *Life* began strictly as a series of executive decisions. If we are to believe the official history, *Time Inc.*, the printers, Donnelley of Chicago, came to New York immediately after Luce's marriage and discussed the printing of a picture magazine. Mrs. Luce was in favor of it, but the printing process wasn't ready. In February, back from his honeymoon, Luce proposed it to his fellow editors, got a mixed reception, and asked Donnelley whether they had solved the printing process. They had.

Now at last the idea of the magazine could be approached. John Martin was called back in February 1936 from the "March of Time" movie to head a new Experimental department including Longwell, Thorndike, Kurt Korff (of whom I had never heard), and other people not mentioned in the *Time Inc.* book. In March 1936 Time Inc. created a subsidiary, Pictures Inc. (no comma here either?), and contracted for the picture services of the Associated Press. In June Luce presented the idea and a tentative unenticing budget to the directors; the decision was to proceed. Advertising salesmen went out to sell before there was even a dummy. Test mailings in May indicated a circulation guarantee of 250,000, and an advertising rate of $1,500 a page. Fourteen budgets for magazines of various sizes and circulations were developed. Stillman and the assistant treasurer, David W. Brumbaugh, took charge of production. The decision was to settle on a 10½-by-14-inch page size, suitable for advertising plates made for either *Vogue* or the *Saturday Evening Post*. Stillman persuaded the paper suppliers to perfect rolls of coated stock in sufficient quantity. The printer, Donnelley, began to convert its equipment to a gas-fired drying process. Construction was begun on new presses.

Decisions. Decisions. Doubtless, all were essential and brilliant. But there was still no magazine, no idea, except the phantasm of pictures, hurrah hurrah.

Oh yes, there was an idea: a prospectus by Luce produced in June saying, "To see life; to see the world; to eyewitness great events; to watch the faces of the poor and the gestures of the proud; to see strange things—machines, armies, multitudes, shadows in the jungle and on the moon; to see man's work—his paintings, towers and discoveries; to see things thousands of miles away, things hidden behind walls and within rooms, things dangerous to come to; the women that men love and many children; to see and to take pleasure in seeing; to see and be amazed; to see and be instructed."

This may have been the best paragraph Luce ever wrote, but a more revealing point was made in the introduction to his book about the "March of Time" movie, *Four Hours a Year*, describing pictures as "a new language, difficult, as yet unmastered, but incredibly powerful."

Powerful. That is the word not confided to the customers. The *Time* process of investigating and describing the manifold kinds of power and their practitioners may have inevitably given the managers of Time Inc., but not the writers, a slowly infiltrating power envy and obsession. I suggest this, not with venom, but with sympathy and even pity. For the power obsession (as distinguished from power) is a subtle sense of self-aggrandizement in the physical body, a stiffening in the legs, a boldness in crossing the street, a choice of the time to talk and the time not to talk, a skilled distinction between useful and useless people, a demand for the best of everything.

I viewed with suspicion this prospective picture magazine, which still did not have a name. At that time, the newspapers had rotogravure sections. Their extermination was one of *Life*'s functions.

The concept of power was exquisitely appropriate in 1936, for two kinds of power were about to express themselves: the one communism, invented by a German who went to England; the other fascism, invented by an Englishman who went to Germany; and both infecting the world of decent free men who began to lose their sanity on this lunatic division, forgetting the vast magnanimous mercy of the U.S. Constitution in this delirium. Of course, both fanaticisms were the same thing, in the sense of the state's infallibility and power, and the individual's impotence and fallibility. But even decent Americans believed that there was a chasm between the two European manias, and chose sides.

To look ahead, the essentially Fascist revolution of the Spanish army against the elected government in 1936 reduced to farce the Europeanized thinking of Americans, and notably of the Time Inc. people. *Fortune*, loaded with liberals who still believed communism had some of the colors of nobility, thought Goldsborough's Foreign News was Fascistic. The smug pomposity of Archibald MacLeish of *Fortune* thus ran head on into the smug pomposity of Goldsborough.

I cannot be accused of partisanship for Goldsborough, but in the exchange, I endorse his memorandum:

According to MacLeish, "*The* issue" in Europe and perhaps the entire world "used to be between Communism and Fascism, but is now between Democracy and Fascism." [Author's Note: where has commusism gone? Ostensibly into democracy, actually into fascism. Wait just three years.]

It is immaterial to Goldsborough, who tries to form his own judgments independently and assumes that MacLeish does the same, that this thesis matches word for word the official thesis of the Soviet Union's Ambassador, Mr. Troyanovsky, in Washington and that of the leader of the United States Communist Party, Mr. Browder. This is in fact the official thesis of the Komintern. To uphold it . . . makes the question of definition arise as fundamental.

Goldsborough told MacLeish that, in his opinion, the *Fortune* series— which must necessarily be much concerned with Communism, Socialism, Democracy, National Socialism, and Fascism—should contain at the outset a brief series of definitions of what *Fortune* means by these terms. . . .

To this MacLeish replied warmly that he is altogether opposed to defining any such terms. . . .

In Goldsborough's experience it is only in extreme pro or extreme con circles that the very mention of defining fairly and squarely the terms one intends to use, touches off anger.

For all his errors elsewhere, Goldsborough had eviscerated the paratreasonous sophistries of MacLeish before the bar of eternity— and with an admirable courtesy and precision. I am not so courteous; MacLeish was the worm in the apple of democracy, with many companions: the intellectuals, ha-ha. I am an intellectual but I do not speak to my company. And poor Goldsborough, who committed suicide, was also an intellectual. MacLeish did not commit suicide; perhaps Goldsborough was the more real, even as he is the more dead. MacLeish in a rather overextended *Who's Who* entry records no connection with Time Inc. at any time whatsoever. That is, he, like Tom Matthews, does not know who he is. And I don't know who he is either.

The *Fortune* (MacLeish) heresy that Roosevelt Democracy was merely a mask for a noble socialism or communism (which the Roosevelt-haters received with joy) attracted to Time Inc. a minor swarm of Communists of various dye, who certainly did not get their views into print, but demoralized the organization, as is their wont. Whether this was an instinctive gravitation or a Muscovite drill I do not know. But in terms of the shifting European politics, I found that in a day or two of casual conversation I could identify a Communist, a hazy fellow traveler, a Fascist, or an American. A certain sort of statement would make the other's eyes widen or narrow. As time went on, I polished these litmus-paper techniques. (I have never publicly accused anybody of being a Communist, up till now, but the mortal vulnerability of democracy makes this no virtue.) Of the yawning differences between any communism and American democracy, MacLeish was insufficiently aware.

Haile Selassie got a favorable story (he was definitely not a Negro but a Semite, somehow a better thing) as "Man of the Year" (January 6, 1936) with two pages of pictures.

WAR dwindled to one page (January 20, 1936) and the China war was back in Foreign News.

The end of something came when (January 27, 1936) King George V died, and in the same week Rudyard Kipling. The former was worried about the latter but was not told of his death. George V's honor is considerably compromised by the story he told his heir that he must postpone his shenanigans to his own reign. Edward VIII did precisely that.

The compromising of the new king was to become Goldsborough's primary objective in the year ahead. In terms of world realities the whims and passions of the new king of England were of marginal concern, but they became Goldsborough's major obsession, as if he had a blackball on who should be king. History and Gossip are not mutually exclusive. Edward VIII's love life began as Gossip and ended as History. This led to the description of Goldsborough as having a "chambermaid's mind," a stupid slander, but it described *Time*'s reputation, at least in England, for this period.

WAR as a department vanished (February 3, 1936). Foreign News had eight pages, mostly on the obsequies of George V. Edward VIII was revealed as "known to be pro-German" and attracted to "snappy" women. In the U.S. Congress a motion to adjourn in respect to George V was opposed by a single Irishman from Cleveland.

A businessman (February 10, 1936) wrote and signed a letter to

Roosevelt—"You _____, I warn you, if you destroy my business, I will strangle you with my own hands"—and got only 90 days. There was no WAR. Foreign News was interested in how English papers (except the Communist) avoided identifying King Carol's (Rumania) masseur in the funeral procession. And, again, "King Edward emphasized his pro-German leanings." He became the first king to receive the Soviet ambassador and asked the Russian "why we had to execute the Tsar and I explained why. He impressed me as a mediocre young Englishman who reads one newspaper a day." (Edward was 41. And probably he knew that the czar and his family were not executed, if more recent research is correct. The ambassador might better have explained, in view of the Treaty of Brest-Litovsk, why Lenin could not have dared to kill the imperial family, cousins of the German kaiser, whose armies held Lenin by the throat.)

I remember envying Busch's good fortune in being sent to report on the German Winter Olympics at Garmisch-Partenkirchen. His report (February 17, 1936) treated the Nazis with his usual hauteur, as in "the Nazi hand-wag." His captions on two pages of pictures included a diagram of the required figure-skating "school figures" and explained that the skaters must execute "the above curlycues without falling down," endorsing the American athletes' omission of the Nazi-like Olympic salute. ". . . in competitive ill-will . . . the Winter Olympics of 1936 would outclass all their predecessors." In this issue, a salt-water canal across northern Florida was begun by the Corps of Engineers, indifferent to its prospective and almost certain ruin of Florida's fresh-water table and has not yet, thirty-five years later, completed it, but has otherwise gone far in devastating Florida's ecology.

Billings achieved the perfect compromise on "The War" by making it a subheading of Foreign News (February 24, 1936), noting an Italian victory in Ethiopia. Under "Eastern Asia," another shooting war, between Communists and Japanese, was described at length on the border of Outer Mongolia. The story expressed Luce's faith in China, not a combatant in the war. The Olympics story used a quote from Westbrook Pegler that the American athletes "did not deserve so much as a nickel ride on a street car, much less a voyage de luxe to the Old World," which in fact Pegler—and Busch—had enjoyed with far less outlay of energy. The Americans had placed fifth in the unofficial standings.

As a Belgian politician (March 2, 1936) expected a European war at any moment, the Spanish contentions began to justify him. After the election victory of the Left, 30,000 leftist political prisoners were released from jail and proceeded to raise hell, especially in Catalonia, the well-to-do fleeing over the French border. In fact, said *Time*, "the election was a draw." As Carnival Week interrupted the uproar, "Spain's crisis was snowed under with confetti."

The Spanish lunacy appeared (March 9, 1936) with a law compelling all employers to rehire every employee fired since January 1, 1934, *for whatever reason*, including murder of the employer. Granted, Goldsborough's opinion that the Republican government was operationally not quite sane had some basis in fact. The idea that *any* budding of democracy should be encouraged with indulgence had not occurred to him, and perhaps democracy never had a chance in Spain. A man more or less in the middle was the French Socialist Léon Blum, shown on the cover bandaged and bedded (allegedly fraudulently), whose obsession was to ally France and Soviet Russia. He was given the attention of "that exquisitely cultivated Jew and famed rabble-rouser" and "painstaking Marxist style." Another style of the time was the slaughter of the leading Japanese statesmen in one holocaust (two made miraculous escapes) by a small cadre of young army mutineers. Japan remained unoutraged. The violence was having all its own way.

Next (March 16, 1936) Hitler marched his army into the Rhineland demilitarized by the treaties of Versailles and Locarno. While the French became verbally hysterical, England remained remarkably unmoved. The League of Nations' absorption with Mussolini's minor adventure was a great help to Hitler. *Time* thought Hitler's oration was "of definite greatness" and in fact it was a pretty good résumé of postwar history. It included the line, "We have no territorial demands to make in Europe."

The League of Nations (March 23, 1936) exhibited every

symptom of not *doing* anything about the occupation of the Rhineland, while British public opinion was polled at 55% pro-German, 24% pro-French.

On whether Germany had violated the Locarno Treaty, not Versailles, the League Council at last voted "Guilty" (March 30, 1936).

The violence of the present can thus be seen as not unprecedented. The supposedly base human instinct to meet force with force is vindicated. For a mild show of force by France at this moment would, we are told, have led to Hitler's suicide, and possibly (but not probably) the avoidance of World War II and the death of perhaps 55 million people. In fact, Hitler's suicide promise was a bluff, and not known to the chancellories. Naturally, Hitler talked and acted with resounding confidence, and the chancellories talked and acted with recessive uncertainty, comfortable in the illusion that talk was the civilized substitute for action. In any such conversation, the act will always win.

At Time Inc. too the executives were making grand decisions. The circulation guarantee for the new picture magazine was set at 250,000 and the advertising rate at $1,500 for a full page. Advertisers who contracted before publication were guaranteed the rate calculated at a 250,000 circulation, for the first twelve months, *and renewable*. Since the magazine had 235,000 charter subscriptions before publication, this brilliant executive decision was not virtually, but literally, suicidal. And how could these bright boys be so stupid? Because they did not believe in the magazine as idea content. They were in a game of chess, not in an act of communication. *Life* began, betrayed by the executives, and it ended that way. After all the apologias, the chief executive was Henry R. Luce, pyramided by Roy Larsen and Charlie Stillman.

In contrast, the Cowles brothers of Des Moines, planning their picture magazine, refused advertising the first year until they knew their circulation. Everyone thought then that the Cowles magazine would be a mass magazine, *Life* a class magazine (probably because the boss's wife had worked on *Vanity Fair*). The Cowles executives, however, made the Time Inc. executives look like the idiots they were. They could distinguish God from Mammon, as Time Inc. never could.

Some idea content had to be provided for the executives' puppet creation. Inevitably, John Martin, the resident Hadden, was put in charge. The first dummy in the spring was dreadful. The second, put to press on a deadline of twelve days, was not much better. An advertising man, Paul Hollister, was enlisted to improve the dummy and nominated his assistant, Howard Richmond, as art director. Richmond, with a mustache, was faceless but competent, as were most subsequent art directors. It is my observation that all art directors are in some degree impostors.

Billings said he had recommended me to Luce as foreign editor and art editor of the new magazine, asking me to show Luce examples of my recent work. Billings must have thought of himself as managing editor of *Time*, and of me as quite expendable. I gave Luce half a dozen of my longer pieces in *Time* and, with the comment, "You seem to have written everything except Foreign News," to which I agreed, he accepted me as Foreign News and Art editor of the new magazine. I take this now as a sign of his relative indifference to the idea content of *Life*, not as a recognition of my coruscating talents. He revered Goldsborough. If he had taken *Life* seriously as idea, he would have conscripted Goldsborough. Without Hadden, he was not sure he had a real magazine at all. I was a cheap facsimile of a foreign editor—or so I now believe. (Unless Clare was telling him how great I was: doubtful.)

I was to report to *Life* in early September; the first issue was scheduled for early November.

Meanwhile, Billings was getting the "war" subheading lost. During February and March, five issues had no war, two had THE WAR, three had "War" as the Foreign News subhead. In Spain (March 30, 1936), "the Left mobsters of the Socialist and Communist parties" had burned 17 churches, 11 convents, 33 Rightist political clubs, 10 newspaper plants. In America things were better (April 6, 1936) for the "Marxist Mayor" of Milwaukee, Daniel Hoan, had not yet turned Milwaukee Socialist. Two pages of pictures illustrated H. G. Wells' movie, *Things to Come*, by which World War II was dated 1940, followed by total barbarism, and the first moon-shot was dated at 2036. Hitler made the cover again, captioned "99%" (April 13, 1936), to mark an election where the ballot showed only *"Ja."* The story said that "the Treaty of Versailles all but wrote into its text the eventual arrival of Adolf Hitler upon the world scene." England seemed to accept this as fact. A Communist party official delighted Republicans by endorsing a New Deal tax proposal.

Southern whites disapproved of the Roosevelts' Negrophilia and distributed pictures of them with Negroes (April 27, 1936). The rumor now went that Saar coal-mine galleries ran underneath French fortifications, and the Maginot line was manned. General Gamelin boasted that France was impregnable and Britain need only defend Belgium and provide air power. In the event, the Germans struck at the hinge and the British did not dare commit all their air power to a collapsing cause. Gamelin had succinctly diagrammed the fall of France. The British editor of *The Aeroplane* ridiculed the French air force and, gratuitously, "the little dark scum of southern France," by which he may have meant Pierre Laval. Such talk did not cement the alliance. Hitler's people surely informed him of these details. And they may have decided certain of Hitler's courses of action in World War II.

The WAR subheading gave its last flicker (May 11, 1936) as, under the title "Empire's End," Haile Selassie, his family, and gold bullion treasure escaped by train to Djibouti in French Somaliland, while the deserted troops rioted in Addis Ababa. This, said *Time,* "has wrecked the League of Nations and given British prestige an enormous black eye." In the southern United States there were three lynchings of Negroes. And Roosevelt was tactfully advised by *Time* that he "needs a friend with the gumption to remind him that he cannot always be right." Since Luce had such associates, he felt that Roosevelt too deserved them.

The burgeoning campaign for a Republican president (May 18, 1936) put Governor Alf Landon of Kansas on the cover (it just "happened"). And the king of Italy became "the first Roman Emperor in 1,460 years"—a fairly awesome observation. The premier of Spain, Azaña, who believed communism "impossible" in Spain, was moved up to president of the republic. There was still a thin chance for democracy in Spain. The issue noted that Eskimos are impervious to cancer or diabetes, but did not mention communism.

The Negrophile tendencies of the Roosevelts were confirmed (May 25, 1936) when Mrs. Roosevelt entertained at the White House sixty delinquent girls, mostly Negro and all venerally diseased, from the District of Columbia penitentiary. Guards patrolled the grounds to prevent the guests from escaping Mrs. Roosevelt's party.

The state of Texas, complete with history, was the focus (June 8, 1936) of the point that Texas had declined its right to become five states, with ten U.S. senators, in order to remain just big. Since Palestine was being subjected to Italian-inspired Arab riots against Britons and Jews, England was cold to Mussolini's sudden discovery that he wanted only to be friends with England. But this was trivial beside a simple *Court Circular* announcement of a dinner party of the king of England's at St. James's Palace, at which the guests were (according to Goldsborough, not the *Court Circular*) "Mrs. Ernest Simpson, the former Wallis Warfield of Baltimore, Md., known to the world press as King Edward's favorite dancing partner, his companion on numerous holiday excursions" ("known to the world press" was a Goldsborough device to outflank the checkers, for "world press" might mean anything), Mr. Ernest Simpson, Prime Minister and Mrs. Stanley Baldwin, the Mountbattens, the Duff Coopers, the Charles Lindberghs, Lady Cunard (mother of an eccentric American daughter), and the former king's most proper friend and secretary, Lord Wigran.

For all his royal-imperial status, Edward VIII was brazen in giving official cognizance to this guest list. Certain members compromised others. The Lindberghs were an innocent American camouflage for Mrs. Simpson and for the American Lady Cunard. The guests described an extraordinarily wide, but blending, spectrum of international society. Socially, it was far too cute. In practice, it did not matter that Stanley Baldwin may not have forgiven King Edward VIII; what mattered immediately was that Goldsborough did not.

Nor do I criticize Goldsborough for his persecution of Edward VIII, culminating in the abdication, though it would not be my style.

The Ethiopian war had died on him; the Spanish hoodlumism had not yet come to a climax; he still thought Hitler was just another rabble-rouser, to be overthrown by the aristocrats and generals and bankers in due time. The Simpson scandal was opportune. He had first spotted Mrs. Simpson in 1934 dancing the rumba with the then Prince of Wales at Cannes, and he had not forgotten her.

On Goldsborough's annual trip to Europe that year he arranged audiences with King Edward VIII, President Lebrun of France, French Premier Léon Blum, and Spanish Premier Manuel Azaña, and was received. Goldsborough, unlike myself later, had the corporate wit to majesty himself into huge expense accounts for his Grand Tour. Goldsborough, wrote C. D. Jackson, "has whittled, wheedled, chiseled and frowned his way through an expense account which has finally assumed almost laughable proportions." I can look at this sentence only with admiration and drooling envy, while recognizing my lack of the requisite presence and gall. In fact, the intent of this inquiry into journalism is to separate the talent for the art from the mean adroitness of achieving intramural prestige, power, and pay. As for separating the men from the boys, the "men" are the executives who feed off the talent of the writers—the "boys" are the talent.

Goldsborough was asserting the power of the talent, as if the men were the talent. He could do it for himself for a little while; he could not institutionalize it. Institutions in general do not surrender power to talent. Talent is too involved in being talented to think about power, much less to connive to gain it. The writers risked their power in every issue of the magazine, and risked it again, with no accretion of power. The executives watched this naïve exercise, like weasels in the underbrush, and made their safe executive decisions, acquiring prestige, power, pay, and fringe benefits.

Goldsborough was risking his power (June 15, 1936) in virtually urging Britain to compromise with Mussolini in ending the League sanctions against Italy. Coming events are signaled with the revelation that there were 3.5 million of Hitler's Germans in Czechoslovakia, as Blum became premier of France and strikes paralyzed his country.

Next week (June 22, 1936) the French Chamber confirmed the

40-hour week for French workers (which also confirmed the Fall of France four years later). In America, at a Republican convention demonstrating that everybody loved Herbert Hoover, Alfred Landon was nominated for president.

Ten pictures were shown (June 29, 1936) to illustrate the movie *Green Pastures*, with the notation that the movie might have made—but did not make—the mistake of improving the Negro version of heaven too much. There were also five pictures of a Hindu fakir levitating himself beside a stake, with his hand languidly on the stake, for four minutes. The scientific explanation was catalepsy plus enormous physical strength. Well, all right.

When Roosevelt was renominated (July 6, 1936), he was perfectly understood by most of the nation with "divine justice weighs the sins of the coldblooded and the sins of the warmhearted in different scales." This must have thrown Luce into baffled fury but *Time* reported it. The honor of Luce must be adduced thereby, scattering the rabble who would discredit it. That week Turkey graciously invited the Powers to nullify the Treaty of Lausanne (one of those popularly lumped under the title "Treaty of Versailles") which had forbidden Turkey to fortify the Dardanelles (already fortified). This was allowed but the Powers got hopelessly mired in the argument over who should have free transit (which Turkey controlled). In this issue a movie of the San Francisco earthquake (and fire) of 1906 (with pictures of 1906 versus the movie) was dismissed by Noel Busch with his habitual detachment: "makes it plain that [the earthquake's] real cause lay in the fact that Clark Gable did not say his prayers at night." This seems admirably relevant criticism, on a satirical level far above the contemporary, crude, and famous satire on *Time* and Luce by Wolcott Gibbs published in *The New Yorker* which caused Luce and Ingersoll bottomless agonies. I knew Gibbs—a second-rater, I would judge. But the executives were always amazed by what a writer could do to them. After all, I had worked with a really capable satirist, Corey Ford (John Riddell), on *Vanity Fair*. To me, the Gibbs thing seemed inapplicable and amateurish. To tell the truth, it sounded like Gibbs. The seriousness with which the *Time* executives took the piece began to tell me something. At a party

Gibbs was good for about two hours; after that he didn't fight, he dissolved, and had to be carried. The detachment of Time Inc. from the literary world of America made it incapable of forming a judgment of Gibbs or of levels of satire. (Nobody asked for my opinion, but at about this time I began to lose contact with my former friends on *The New Yorker*. I think I had expressed my disdain of Gibbs's famous job, possibly even to Gibbs.) The celebration of this piece tells more about the intellectual world than about Luce. Sadly, intellectuals love a cheaply won opinion, if it is fashionable. Since I abhor being in fashion, this fact almost makes me abhor being an intellectual, if that is what my company is. But these people are mob-men, not intellectuals. And Gibbs knew what he was doing, in speaking to the ready mob in the vulgar idiom.

As strikes racked Spain (July 13, 1936), an American labor story noted that Alexander Berkman who had half assassinated Henry Clay Frick with knife and pistol in 1892 had died by his own pistol in Nice, France. The following week (July 20, 1936) T. S. Matthews is dropped from the masthead. Robert Cantwell returns, probably to the Books department. Mussolini was on the cover and his fascism was glorified with the endorsement, "A scant 14 years ago the Kingdom of Italy was as confused, irresolute and radical-ridden as are France and Spain today." Here Goldsborough expressed his foreign policy in one crystal formulation. This same prejudice against confusion made him gloss over *Time*'s troubles with British censorship of the earlier story about Mrs. Simpson by noting that the British magazine *Cavalcade* had given five columns to Mrs. Simpson. The *Court Circular* noted another of Edward VIII's dinners for Mrs. Simpson, this time without Mr. Simpson. And there was a page of pictures of Mrs. Simpson and her home.

A farmers' poll favored Landon for president (July 27, 1936) and the Republicans charged that the Democrats were exploiting the anti-Semitism issue, accusing Landon of being both Jewish (middle name Mossman) and anti-Semitic.

And now there tiptoed rather nonchalantly into *Time* a war that might legitimately have been christened THE WAR, for it has occupied most of the twentieth century. According to Goldsborough, it began in Melilla in Spanish Morocco when some Socialists leaned out their windows and booed a regiment of the Spanish Foreign Legion returning to barracks. The Legionnaires broke ranks and threw the Socialists out their own windows. Miraculously, garrisons in Morocco and Spain rebelled, Francisco Franco opportunely appeared, the ports of Cadiz and Malaga were overpowered, and troops landed at Algeciras "in high good humor." The government's arming of the "Red militia" "was what definitely took this week's revolt out of the traditional formula of Latin *coups d'état* and put it into the class of Russia's revolution of 1917." Goldsborough's revolution was therefore defined as the elected government's resistance to a Latin *coup d'état* by the generals. His grounds were that the government forces were disorderly, the rebels' orderly.

The next week (August 3, 1936) the revolution (meaning the army's revolt) was "absolutely Grade A." Most of the story was given to the troubles of foreigners trying to get out and to the "Red militia's" atrocities. The sort of attitude that Goldsborough was reacting against was revealed in the fact that U.S. Ambassador Claude Bowers, a liberal academic, had written home earlier that reports of "dangerous" conditions in Spain were "mostly pure propaganda inspired by the old regime that hates democracies and republics." In this context, Bowers was a fool. Charles Lindbergh was seen inspecting the German air force with great admiration, showing realistic acumen but political foolishness.

The Spanish government became "the Red cause" (August 10, 1936) as Italian planes brought help from Sardinia to Morocco, and Russian ships were reported on their way to help the government. A page of pictures showed "War Women of Spain." Goldsborough's other aggravations were that England had made a £10 million loan to Russia at 5½ percent, instead of the usual 11 percent, and that Mrs. Simpson had been invited on a yacht trip by King Edward VIII.

Spain still got only two columns (August 17, 1936) as the pope protested "the slaying, sacking and burning in Spain" and German warships arrived in Spanish ports.

But it got ten columns and the cover (August 24, 1936), as the rebels tried to take Irun and San Sebastián on the French border and besieged Badajoz, while the Loyalist northern miners besieged Oviedo. These agonies did not deter *Time* from noting the shocking waste of King Edward VIII in driving thirty-five-cent golf balls in great numbers into the Adriatic on his yachting excursion with Mrs. Simpson, who did his shopping for him along the Yugoslav waterfront.

My recollection is that my vacation, then due, was truncated, because Ed Kennedy, doing Business and Finance, had disappeared on one of his drinking exercises. Looking at this issue, I feel a dim familiarity with the stories on Charles F. Kettering of General Motors, A. P. Giannini of Bancitaly Corporation, the Province of Alberta's "prosperity certificate" money, and the troubles of Pacific Mutual Life Insurance Company, and assume that I wrote them—or some of them. I accepted the deprivation with the usual soldierly *Time* phlegm, for it was to be my last week on *Time*, the next stop being the new still unnamed picture magazine after my vacation. But I held no resentment against Ed Kennedy, for he was my kind, the archetype of the producing writer, when he felt like it, the indispensable man.

It may be well to examine the pro-Loyalist point of view which later overwhelmed Goldsborough's position. The "Red" gangs (meaning Socialist, Communist, anarchist, or anybody) had destroyed a great deal of property and human life in Spain before the rebellion. This sort of mass murder is roughly individual, spontaneous, and crudely doctrinaire; it is communal but not official. The liberal position would be that these mass murders are less wicked than such official but limited and selective killing as that of Nazi Germany or Communist Russia (or now China or Vietnam or Korea). The disorganized killing may be described as "democratic," since it is by the will of individual people, without orders from above, and this was true of the killing under the government before the rebellion. If a minority of people in a town burn down the church, that too may be described as "democratic." At least, without orders, it is not totalitarian. If the majority then kill the minority that burned down the church, this is even more democratic than burning down the church. Obviously, this sort of "democracy" will soon vanish. For everybody killed had relatives and friends, and the murderers become their blood enemies. The Spaniards were (and are) peculiarly susceptible to this sequence.

Goldsborough had no power to halt the sequence, but he was not wicked because he could not countenance it. In a sense he was right, because the Fascist dictatorship is still in force in Spain as I write this. He did not share the liberal view that amateur violence, however bloody it may be, is preferable to professional, orderly, selective violence, even if less bloody—perhaps because the amateur violence is inefficient and senseless. Symbolically, politics separates the chaotic children from the punitive parents.

But for Time Inc. there were now far more important things than amateur and professional violence. Before I went on my postponed vacation, I wrote Luce a memorandum on the picture magazine dummy, showing my lack of interest in a picture magazine:

May I submit my reactions to the Picture Magazine Dummy?

It seemed to me to prove that there is a possible Picture Magazine and that this is not it. The proof lay in its very excessive readability. I reached a spread, took a quick look over it and started reading at the upper left. The excellent, simplified, quick-reading writing led me across the page. I glanced briefly at the pictures and was shortly down at the lower right corner, where I was invited to turn the page. It was all over like that. When I had finished, I found that I knew no further facts nor had I added to my visualized sense of the scene. I had seen another and, of course, infinitely improved, rotogravure section of a newspaper. I think any reader would finish the Dummy in half an hour or less.

The reason, I believe, was that the editors, far from being overconvinced of their magazine's importance, were continuously by implication apologizing for it, trying to make it completely effortless, on the assumption that it had nothing really worth telling and that the reader was unwilling to make any effort, did not really want to look at it.

The trap the Dummy fell into was the sacred convention of the picture-with-caption. I submit that this is the world's worst way of conveying information, excitement or anything whatsoever. It seems to require two kinds of mental effort to *read* and to *look* and the two do not mix. After doing one, nobody wants to do the other. Either the reader looks thoroughly and reads not at all or he reads thoroughly and glances at the picture. In any case the effort to read and look at a rotogravure section is a wearying, profitless affair. The Dummy proves this. A page with a minimum of type is astonishingly satisfying and comfortable, like the Townsend Convention spread. Even pages that are solid text, like the Cleveland Art story, are a relief. The broken pages, with their old-fashioned movie captions, are extremely uncomfortable.

There are two obvious solutions to this difficulty.

1. You have a swell picture. Stake everything on it. Slap it on a page without any headline overhead. Only the looking eye is engaged. The very absence of words would, I think, incline the reader to ask what the editors meant by putting it there. He would get the idea that they thought it was good, worth being there by itself. He *looks*. Probably he begins to identify things about it, a prominent face, a street sign, a uniform. He figures at least that it's in the U.S. or Russia, winter or summer, a parade, a party or a nudist wedding or a girl in a lion's den. Giving him a chance to do that all he wants, give him then a long, solid legend. Give the story in which this picture is a moment or the climax as glibly as you like, but refer it to the picture. Go even to the limit of saying "Note this" "Note that." Go all out to sell the picture, for what you see in it and know about it.

2. You get a swell story. Since the reader does not know the story and cannot get excited about it until he does, tell him the story precisely as *Time* would. No pictures in sight to distract him. If it's a good story, he gets interested and wishes, as perhaps some *Time* readers do, that he could be there, see the hero and his landscape or the machine or the flora and fauna. Then he turns the page and there are the pictures. When he looks at them then, he doesn't need to be told about them. They satisfy a demand that already exists. They need have only labels, JOE SPINK, HIS HOUSE, HIS WIFE. Of course you may sometimes get on such a page a picture which is also a swell picture, in which case start NOTING again to the limit.

This was returned to me with Luce's scrawl: "Yes, there is much truth in what you say. HRL." It had been forwarded by his secretary Corinne Thrasher with a request to see him. I do not think I saw him, and small wonder. Certainly the functions of looking and reading work very differently on the human brain, but I was still looking over my shoulder at the primacy of the word in the *Time* sense of hard-working exposition, and Luce had had a brief unfocused peek at the vision of power through pictures. I think my memorandum was intelligent, but it was no help in the going crisis.

In the early fall of 1936 the "editors" were assigned a long hall with picture bins on top of which, perched on stools, they manipulated such illustrations as the picture department had provided, and

occasionally got sets of pictures turned into photostated layouts by
the layout department. John Martin was officially in command, but I
do not remember him. Martin is described as expressing openly his
contempt for Dan Longwell (though I do not remember it), probably
for the same *Time*-indoctrinated reasons that alienated me. These
frictions expressed in a quite conscious way the realization that the
new picture magazine was to be a heresy against the holy canon of
Briton Hadden. The employment of such *Time*-trained people as
myself tended to bridge the heresy, but Longwell was too much for
Martin to take. Once again Martin had exaggerated his symbolic,
cognate indispensability. In intracorporate wars the Longwells
always win.

Through September and October, the "editors" rooted around for
ideas that would still be timely in several months. I have an "art-idea
list" of this period:

Olof Krans, U.S. Primitive; Miss Scott's suggestion of spread on Milliner
Mme. Talbot, now in N.Y.; Surrealistic show (Nov. 25) Museum of Modern
Art, followed (Dec. 10) by Salvador Dali show at Julien Levy; Degas and
Picasso Nov. 7—Philadelphia's Penn. Museum of Art; Show of Glass at
Metropolitan (Nov. 1) from 1500 B.C.–1935 A.D. perhaps combined with
modern glass for sale; Sir Robert Mond's toy Napoleonic Army, now being
looked into, in London. There is also another 20,000-piece army in London;
Manet—Nov., Wildenstein; Treasury Dept.'s mural paintings, Oct. 6,
Whitney Museum; Carnegie Exhibition of moderns, Oct. 15, at Pittsburgh;
Winslow Homer, Dec. 15, Whitney; Page in color of fine jewels; or of
gardens (pix available of Jap garden); add Carl Milles.

I also produced a two-page list of the works of Rembrandt, with
their resident museums, in the dim hope that somebody could get
color reproductions of them. These operations were of the nature of
seeming to do a job while hoping someone else would make a
decision.

I remember fiddling endlessly with Spanish war pictures around
Irun, San Sebastián, Badajoz, and Oviedo, trying to make a sequence,
in vain. I remember Luce looking at some of these, hopefully. Out of
all this came such a memorandum as the following, which will be
gibberish to the modern reader:

Laid out: German women, Ambassador Bonnet, Kilns in The Potteries,
Libya, Sark, Mongolia lassoing, Hindu god-maker, German Navy's mine

salvaging, Little Princesses at Glamis Castle, Iran veils, Genoa cemetery, Anti-Jew signs and anti-Russian show, Quetta rebuilding, Kemal Pasha, English model village, South American Indians, Inner Mongolia, Degrelle, Duke of Richmond's plane, Sellier (French Public Health), Iron Mountain, Habsburgs.

Holding: British Army posters, Liberia, Second Internationale leaders (Jouhaux), Mme. Brunschwigg, Philibert Besson, Louis Fischer's Spanish pictures, 145 Piccadilly, Balearics, Palestine, German colonies, English dog hospital, English mushroom tunnels, Kenya skiing, strange horns, Manchu Cabinet faces, Chinese mt. shrine, Rome College of Propaganda, Chengtu (Chiang's and PanAm's base), Mosley, Heligoland, old English footballers, Hitler Jugend, English dukes, English milk bars, Oxford, Hyde Park, Ambassador Dodd, Funny Japan, Jacques Doriot, Norwegian shipping, Russian Arctic development (for spring), Russian bathers (summer), Renoir model & daughter, Czech Army, Jap wedding (Funny), Crusader castles, Monastery of St. Wandrille, Vilna corpses, Japs in Shanghai, Boy Kings, Jap lady wrestlers, India untouchables etc., French academicians, English gardeners on horizontal ladder (summer), Valentino Shrine, German roads, early Edward VIII, early Hitler, Capetown, Siberian civilization by Julian Bryan, Chile, Spanish Treasures, Ethiopia conquered, Ankara buildings, shooting seats, English party people, Edda Ciano (for May), Campbell's bomb dugout, Abd-el Krim & Annamite at Reunion.

This list, each item of which had a hot relevance for me at the time, must now provide a wholesome perspective of journalism. Some are intelligible and even eternal; most were ephemeral. Who was Philibert Besson (eccentric French politician), what was 145 Piccadilly (Duke of York)? The Annamite exiled at Reunion Island was a Vietnamese. One of the "Little Princesses at Glamis Castle" became queen of England.

But such a list was hardly doing a job of selling. I also tried writing copy. Since we were likely to do an act on the Kansas painter John Steuart Curry, I provided text for expanding this into the story of Kansas, as follows:

This is Kansas. It lies dead center in the U.S., a flat rectangle of wheat and corn, grasshoppers, 2,000,000 descendants of Yankee pioneers and the Republican Party's 1936 nominee for President of the U.S.—Kansas' Governor Alf M. Landon.

More than any other state in the U.S., Kansas is all alike. Most Kansans are "typical." One Kansas farm is much like another. Only in the western counties does the land get a little higher, drier, poorer. But Kansas is entirely different from all its four neighbor states. Colorado is definitely the Mountains. Nebraska is the Northern Plain. Missouri is a Mississippi River state. Oklahoma is the South. In the middle is Kansas, with a character all its own, the character of being the Middle of Everything.

The Kansas character was set when the pious, self-disciplined Yankee settlers, bred on barren New England hillsides, found themselves on the rich flat Kansas plain. Out of the Yankee's soul-searing struggle to relax in a land of Plenty grew the soul of Kansas. Kansans still feel a moral uplift in any disaster to their Plenty, fondly recall the great grasshopper Plague of 1874, pooh-pooh this year's mild drought and picayune scourge of grasshoppers.

Kansans are born fighters. Their ancestors found a frontier perilous with some of the American Continent's toughest, hardest riding Indians. Forts went up. The buffalo were slaughtered. The frontier vanished westward into the mountains leaving Kansas a conservative agricultural democracy with a declining birthrate. The forts remained, leaving Kansas, 000 miles from any coastline, the most-fortified state in the Union and its greatest wheat-producer. Its specialty is red winter wheat, planted in October, harvested in early summer. Crop this year was 150,000,000 bushels, best since 1931, 50% of the entire U.S. crop.

Despite this Plenty, 70% of Kansas farms are mortgaged. Before the Civil War, Kansans hated Slavery and the South. After the Civil War, they hated the railroad-building money barons and the immigrant road gangs. Today they suspect the banker East. Though 90,000 of Kansas' 166,000 farms get Government aid, Kansans temperamentally dislike Government spending, Government charity. In the heart of the U.S., a state without very rich or very poor men, self-respecting, hard-handed Kansas sincerely believes in the gospel of Rugged Individualism.

Another Cort-Longwell memorandum presented a theme pursued now and also in 1938:

Mr. Luce wants a letter written to Mills in England, saying:

1. Get a good London *Illustrated News* artist to draw a preview of the coming opening of Parliament, perhaps at the moment the King is taking his oath as a Protestant, on Nov. 3. If this moment involves everybody standing up in such a way as to make a poor picture, choose another moment. I like to see Members with their hats on and their feet up. We certainly want to see all the newsworthy people and get a clear conception of the Government and Opposition benches and the organization of the House. You are to fix a maximum cost for this.

2. Mills is to tell us by return mail what the laws and penalties are against taking photographs inside the Commons and Lords while in session.

He is to inform us what the chances are of our pulling a fast one and getting such good pictures anyway, and if the chances are fair to go ahead at once on the opening of Parliament Nov. 3. Obviously, he should do this without compromising himself or *Time*. Meanwhile he is to send us everything at once available (in pictures) of the Houses of Parliament: lobbies, Thameside porch, bar, washrooms, Members arriving and leaving, Lords arriving and leaving, etc. The idea is to catch the first issue of the magazine.

Around 1938 the same request was repeated in more detail.

I find another list of picture ideas and feel baffled.

Dec. 1: Pan American Peace Conference. Pictures: Argentina's Saavedra Lamas (?), President Monroe, Britain's George Canning who proposed Monroe doctrine, leaders in the Bolivia-Paraguay peace negotiations, some white South American Presidential faces, typical Indians of Argentina, southern Chile, Central America, the Chaco, etc. representing the South American majority.

Jan. 1, 1937. Naval building race starts. Diagrams of Jap, GB and US pet ships. General ideas:

1. Palestine. The Husseini and Nashashibi leaders. Spic & span Tel Aviv. Lousy Jaffa. A surviving Crusaders' citadel and one of the Assassins'. Wailing Wall, cause of the last troubles. Iraq's Ghazi and Transjordania's Emir. Turtles carrying tapers into grain. Irrigation project. Wauchope and the British Commission. Pontius Pilate.

2. Chiang Kai-shek's war force, against a possible 1937 war with Japan. The Szechwan base and the Honan pillboxes. Crack troops and war lord irregulars.

3. Adolf Hitler's day. The glass and steel Reichskanzler office, the nearby hotel dining room where he walks for his cup of chocolate, the Bavarian retreat, if possible the door before which his chief bodyguard sleeps at night, his plane, car, etc., the handful of men he sees without appointment and especially the faces of his bodyguards.

4. A social stratification of France. The hermetically sealed old nobility. The Bonaparte nobility. The very rich men of good family. The modern tycoons. The Jews. A concierge, a shopkeeper, a farmer, a southern cowboy, a worker and a beggar.

5. Pan-Arabia, separate from Palestine. Some of its old heroes, Saladin, Baibars, etc. T. E. Lawrence. What killed it for 500 years: the Turkish and Egyptian ruling classes. Kemal Ibn Saud, and Shah Rezi. The importance of what the Crusaders brought back from the Saracens to the birth of the European Renaissance and the rise of Europe. A typical Arab small farmer, enemy of the nomads. Probability of a Fascist Arab set-up. Ibn Saud's tanks and Black Maria of wives. At the contact point with Europe: Palestine and the Jews planted by canny Britain.

6. Biro-Bidjan, another Jewish haven, planted by canny Soviet Russia in the path of Japan.

7. The underground Communist movement in Germany, Poland, Yugoslavia, Rumania, Austria, pictures to come obviously chiefly from Austria. (New book on this.) Pre-Nazi leaders of the great German trades unions and what they are now. Thalman, Dmitrov, et al. A hard one to get.

8. A great Indian prince, whoever can be gotten, Patiala, Hyderabad, palaces, jewels, ceremonies, hunt, landscape, preferably a charming one such as Kapurthala.

9. The fabulous Bagdad Jew family of Sassoon, now only one generation away from Assyrian beards and prayer slippers. Ellice Victor, Philip, Siegfried, the late incredible Flora, Founder David and his four sons, of whom one was Edward VII's friend, while Philip now rates as Edward VIII's friend. Ellice Victor is a photography fiend and might part with some of his own. His doings and remarks are first-class copy. I think the whole family is the most astonishing above-race-&-country family in the world.

10. Takeouts of such remarkable cities as Bombay, Shanghai, Hongkong, Ankara, Angkor (under Art), Hue in Annam, Peshawar, Quetta rebuilding, Bolivia's La Paz, Iceland's Reykjavik, trying to improve on the *National Geographic* Magazine handling.

Other memoranda:

To: H. R. Luce
From: D. Cort
Subject: Exceptional pictures

German colonies: (1) German boys on floor around big relief map of the world, showing location of Germans with flags. (2) 8-ft. African negro with two six-foot women. (3) air view of hippos in river.

Catalonia: (1) Barcelonia street scene, very clear and natural; (2) militiaman asleep in chair at the Generalidad; (3) elderly, coquettish nurse and officer.

Argentina: (1) the oldest church in Western Hemisphere, air view of Lujan, (2) Christ against the Andes.

Chile: (1) mountainside of guano birds (an industry), (2) beach view of Vina del Mar resort, (3) southernmost city, Punta Arenas.

Palestine: (1) lazy Arabs sitting around, listening to phonograph and bargaining over mutton.

Gwalior: half a dozen beauties of fort and palace.

Manuel Quezon of Philippines: looking astonished at desk with Frank Murphy looking severe, after Tydings independence bill had been passed.

Paul Hoeffler Indian expedition: four pix of tiger killing Indian.

Norway: (1) fishing fleet, sails up, in harbor of Hammerfest; (2) liner in impressive fjord.

Pictures in foreign magazines:
Illustrated London *News*, Oct. 17, p. 684: Scotsmen marching in Jerusalem with bagpipes (sent for).

Same, Oct. 3, p. 591, flamingoes and eggs on nest-mounds; p. 592, iguana's paw looking like a dead hand in chain mail (not sent for).

Same, Sept. 26, p. 509, King Edward playing whip & arrow in Vienna (sent for).

Le Monde Coloniale, Oct. No. 159, p. 203, Negresses standing around, virile maiden with tattooed chest and breasts (sent for, German col.) p. 198, fine air view of River Jordan and Hahalal Colony (sent for).

Sphere, Oct. 3, p. 12, crater of White Island, Australasia, very striking and British Empire's only big sulphur deposit (sent for).

Same, Oct. 10, p. 45, Hoare and admirals (sent for).

Same, Sept. 26, p. 499, owl with rat (not sent for).

VU, Oct. 21, p. 1250, a crazy palace built by a Frenchman in his backyard (referred to Eggleston for art horror).

I remember seeing pix of British Justices kneeling in prayer, I think in recent London *Illustrated News*.

We now have pictures of a fair-looking Spanish church (Barcelona's Maria del Pino), intact and destroyed; also a plain church (Seville's Omnium Sanctorum), intact and destroyed; also ordinary churches that have been destroyed. Some experts, however, list them all as "treasures."

I asked for research on the "ancient Near East race that used a symbol like the swastika that they called the gammadion." The race turned out to be the early Christians who combined four gammas into either a swastika or a voided Greek cross, the gamma standing for a cornerstone. This was at least a good try from ignorance, but I could have done the research myself by opening a dictionary.

The memoranda asking for impossible pictures now depress me, as one demanding photographs of Goyas, Velásquezes, El Grecos, Catalonian twelfth century frescoes, the Romanesque cloister of Santo Domingo de Silos at Burgos, the Mozarabic chapel of San Baudelio de Berlanga (tenth century), San Miguel de Escalada near León, Oviedo's San Miguel de Linio, and so on.

Again, I asked for "a picture of Toledo as seen by the Rebels entering, showing the Alcazar destroyed, much as El Greco's Toledo in a Storm (Metropolitan) shows it." *Life*'s foreign news was to vary from *Time*'s in that it regarded the Loyalists as representing a democratically elected government (echoes of the American Civil War), hence innocent until proved guilty. Thus, I was asking for pictures of treasures that the rebels, not the government, had destroyed. (My copies of memoranda are undated, so I do not know exactly when they were issued, except by the internal evidence.)

In fact, much of this early accumulation appeared later in the magazine. Visual oddities, of course, were more likely to appear in foreign news than in American scenes, and the magazine wanted the striking oddity.

Meanwhile, the executives were making grand decisions. The Chicago printer, Donnelley, had two converted presses with which they would try to print the new magazine, with misgivings. Besides these, they were prepared to use "a rotogravure press and outmoded sheet-fed presses." Ideally, the decision should have been to defer publication until new presses could be produced. But the decision was to plunge ahead at full speed. Another problem was an adequate supply of coated paper in rolls. The supplier produced a paper at a suitable price but with limited production. If more were needed, the executives gambled that somehow more could be found.

Another dummy was issued in September, including my Irun, Nürnberg rally, and Stalin biography pictures. Unfortunately, my copy was thrown out long ago by my maid. By this time it was definite that the new magazine's name would be *Life*, the old humorous *Life* having agreed to disappear from view.

In late October Luce told Billings he was to be managing editor of *Life*, informing Martin he would be managing editor of *Time*. Longwell had won his battle and, with a discretion learned in earlier Doubleday-Doran wars, chose the moment to retire from the field. A novice would not have known enough to play it this way. But of course Billings had to realize how indispensable Longwell was to the magazine, for Billings knew nothing.

The magnificent simplicity and good sense of Billings took command. The first issue, dated November 23, 1936, was assembled,

96 pages of it, and printed with difficulty to the number of 466,000, making all executive decisions idiotic.

The issue represented, under the circumstances, a magnificent job by Billings.

It began with a newborn baby held upside down by a doctor—"LIFE BEGINS": undoubtedly a Longwell idea. Then there was a friendly full-page "introduction to this first issue of *Life*."

Margaret Bourke-White's coverage of a work-relief project in Montana made the cover and the lead. "Life on the American Newsfront" (4 pages) used small pictures, as did "The President's Album" (2 pages). Then came Chinese schoolchildren in San Francisco, perhaps a sop to Luce's Sinophilism.

Next, the Republican candidate for president being from Kansas, came an American painter, Curry of Kansas (4 pages), into one of whose paintings I wrote, "Wet skunks move in on an already overcrowded island refuge to the obvious dismay of one hog," because, without that, most people would have missed the skunks.

Brazil (5 pages): "Brazilians are charming people but incurably lazy . . . a colossal human failure." There was a wonderful noonday picture of a frontier town, for which I fought. I added life to it by noting, "The dog in the foreground has fleas." Again, a troop of Brazilian cavalry entered a farmyard, and I pointed out that the family (left) leaning on the fence were having the thrill of their lives, though the three people were barely detectable. A picture of a dance specified dark-skinned individuals as being, in Brazil, "white."

Fort Knox (1 page). Edward VIII's residence, Fort Belvedere (1 page), again, specifying the pool, the tennis court, the rose garden.

The Camera Overseas (6 pages) included Italy's Ciano aping his father-in-law, Mussolini; identified wigged English justices at prayer in Westminster Abbey.

Besides some visual oddities, there were also a black widow spider's romance (2), a section called "Private Lives," and "*Life* Goes to a party," in this case a French hunt.

I had produced about 16 pages in the issue. A crucial point is made by references to the nature of my text. Longwell took the picture seriously, not the scene. I did not take the picture seriously, but I took the scene very seriously. As an amateur, I was applying the *Time* respect for facts and people, and I examined every picture for anything it had to reveal, no matter how trivial, if the reader could confirm it with his own eyes. My intuition would be that this procedure, faithfully pursued, would convince the reader that he could trust and benefit from the writer. The above examples are remarkably petty but the communication is not petty at all.

In the years since, to my amazement, very few picture magazine editors have grasped this simple point, which is to observe it even to the length of absurdity. The fact is there in the picture, staring at you; you cannot lie about it or misname it, and you must not ignore it. This obvious truth, as expressed in *Life*'s foreign news, was part of what won *Life* its fantastic reader allegiance for at least the next ten years. And it is a truth so small and practical as to be laughable.

The masthead of the first issue of *Life* is historically significant. Editors were Luce, Billings, and Longwell. Photographers were Bourke-White, Eisenstaedt, McAvoy, and Stackpole. Associates were Rachel Albertson (probably head checker, Mary Fraser evidently having refused to allow her name in the masthead) David Cort, George T. Eggleston (soon gone), Geoffrey T. Hellman, Dorothy Hoover (picture department, a fixture), Joseph Kastner, A. K. Mills (soon departed to foreign offices), Willard D. Morgan (soon gone), Paul Peters, Sherman Raveson (no recollection), Howard K. Richmond (first, useful art editor), and Joseph J. Thorndike, Jr. For Luce to have committed the idea content of his great gamble to this academy must reveal either his contempt for the writer or his belief that his inspiration could inflate any carcass into the writer he wanted. (The latter, in my case, is the more preposterous.) This was not even the junior varsity, but the 150-pound crew, except for Billings, who was varsity.

During this period of gestation, other stories were coming to climax in *Time*, notably the presidential election. Westbrook Pegler was quoted: "Considerable mystery surrounds the disappearance of Alfred M. Landon of Topeka, Kans., who has been missing from his regular haunts for some time." The Missing Persons bulletin:

"everything average." "Roosevelt luck" brought rain as he toured the Western drought areas. "U.S. Communists . . . hoping and praying for the re-election of Franklin Roosevelt." The *Literary Digest*, alone among five polls, predicted Landon, 54.8% (370 electoral votes), Roosevelt, 40.7% (161 votes), and soon afterward the *Literary Digest* died. The election results (November 9, 1936) were Roosevelt, 523 electoral votes; Landon, 8.

In the great Spanish war, the rebels (called the Whites) captured Irun, put to the torch by the Anarchists. In Madrid, Loyalist "class justice" was executing 250 people per week, though "Red" atrocity stories were debunked. Already, 100,000 Spaniards were reported dead. The defense of Toledo's Alcazar by rebel cadets became a heroic "farce" of opposing claims. Next week a rebel relief force saved Toledo. A real death picture of a Loyalist by Robert Capa was accompanied by a quote, "The apparently innate tendency of the press to fake." The Spanish story was left till last in Foreign News, noting that Franco was given "full power over the Spanish State" and that the "Radical Government [of Madrid] was digging trenches . . . for the bloody last battle with the Whites which was coming as inevitably as Death." (Whether or not this was bad politics, it was naïve military prophecy.) The rebels approached within sight of Madrid, and first President Azaña, and then the cabinet got out of sight of Madrid. The fall of Madrid (November 9, 1936) was estimated as "a matter of hours."

Far more space was filled by the matter of Mrs. Simpson. Her new quarters in London, a veritable palace, were shown. It was admitted that references in *Time* to Mrs. Simpson had been clipped by the British distributors. The king showed movies of Mrs. Simpson on their yachting cruise, and it was noted that American newspapers were now selling papers by blowing up Goldsborough's discovery. It was pointed out that the king had already legally committed adultery by traveling with a married woman and staying at the same hotels. Mrs. Simpson now filed for a divorce in Ipswich, on grounds provided by Mr. Simpson. A story of seven columns noted that her London moving firm was named Trollope. The divorce decree (November 9, 1936) occupied five columns.

As seen today, the king's conduct was incredibly brazen for anyone in a public position, especially so in the England of 1936. He can only be judged a weak, infatuated, drunken idiot. Goldsborough's gloating but perfectly correct emphasis on the affair worked as a distraction from what was going on in the world—communism, Nazism, and the arena, Spain—much as he had earlier used the now forgotten "Stavisky Affair" in France. Goldsborough intended primarily to keep himself amused. More to the point, he wanted to keep his readers amused, at a moment when the time for amusement had almost ended.

Another enormous story in this period was Stalin's trial and execution of the Old Bolsheviks, "the Founding Fathers" Kamenev and Zinoviev (both identified as Jews), and fourteen others, which was fully reported (August 31, 1936).

The issues of *Life* immediately after the first were conspicuously less effective. Mrs. Simpson was shown once with Turkey's Kemal Ataturk. Of Hitler it was said, unamusingly, "Adolf Hitler is the fulcrum on which peace or war in Europe rests." Mussolini was seen as funny in an unamusing way. The Spanish Loyalists were regarded as government troops, and *Time*'s "White" troops as the rebels. The foreign policy of *Life* began to take form as a recognition of the obvious. Good planning, probably by Longwell, showed up in a movie, *Rembrandt*, followed by color pictures of Rembrandt's painting. *Life*'s greater freedom to go into history was shown in a Communist picture history of the life of Stalin (both on November 30, 1936).

It is amazing that the whole country went on being excited about *Life*, as these fairly idealess issues followed one another. My suspicion is that Luce had expected the magazine to stabilize at this mediocre level, with the staff he had hired. He had intended a magazine of appearances, not of idea content. A symptom of this is that theatre and movies were the lifeblood of every issue, plus some art works in color. Luce was delighted by the discovery that young Argentine society looked elite and formal, insisting on a spread of pictures, even though they had to be blurred reproductions from an Argentine magazine. Appearance was all. Mrs. Simpson's fairly squalid birthplace cottage at Blue Ridge Summit, Pennsylvania, was played opposite the magnificence of Windsor Castle seen from the air (December 14, 1936). The text read: "His Majesty's dogged devotion to this American-born commoner was about to precipitate one of Britain's gravest constitutional crises. . . . But a King's job remains the same. He is not required to be an able King. His duty is simply not to be a bad King." Finally, "almost inevitably the dark-haired little girl at the left will some day be Queen-Empress Elizabeth." (Correct, except that she was denied the empress.) Here was idea content, virtually smuggled into the magazine.

As if recognizing that *Life* was a godsend to press agents, a new department called "Released for Publication" appeared, and readers were urged to send in pictures, especially high-speed ones, for "Speaking of Pictures." One sent in a picture of the sixth newsstand at which he had failed to find a copy of *Life*, and was answered: "The special presses on which *Life* is printed are now running every hour between issues. . . . Each week the present presses are delivering a few more copies per hour." The executive miscalculations underpinning *Life* had now become a national scandal and a corporate calamity.

Edward VIII's abdication took place December 11 after a reign of 325 days and *Life* headlined (December 21, 1936) "The Throne of England Has a New Heir" over Edward the Confessor's throne, followed by 1935 pictures of Mrs. Simpson bathing with Edward at Cannes. As if confirming the apocalypse, the issue had a full coverage of Queen-Empress Victoria's Crystal Palace burning and destroyed. In a play with appearances, a line of noble British children were shown at play, over an infra-red airview of the English Channel. But these were welded with the text: "Their children and their Channel are what Englishmen worry about when their talk turns to air raids." (I think I had to fight to get the Channel airview.)

Another recourse for *Life* was to compile heavily researched acts. Thus we have pictures of all 66 members of the College of Cardinals, Pius IX being 79, "The Pope's Choice" for next pope knowledgeably defined as Pacelli. This too was good idea content.

The brutal events abroad compelled me, in full awareness of my nonpower, to offer values and idea content. Thus I described the rebels' bombing of Madrid as their "worst mistake" which "won many middle-class citizens to the Government." The pictures were the tomb of the great Cardinal Jiménez de Cisneros (bombed and also, by good research, before) and the bombed palace of the Duke of Alba and a subway shelter which a bomb chanced to penetrate. This story probably convinced the Leftists in the organization (suddenly numerous) that I was not a Fascist, since I was describing "Fascist atrocities." I am happy to say that their good opinion of me did not last.

Since Billings had to accept any such idea content before it got into print—and also Luce—any singular merit or demerit of mine must be disavowed.

In the same issue, the celebration of the new Soviet constitution noted that it "would in no way interfere with [Stalin's] present monopoly of the practical governance of Russia." This did not bother the *Time* Communists, since Stalin's rule was perfectly splendid. In this strange fact, one can see that the most deadly indictment of Communists will be taken as hearty endorsement, for a Communist's secession from imperfect humanity has always taken place long before, and black night is high noon (I have plagiarized a famous title).

For the Christmas issue (December 23, 1936), the reliance was again on the visual realities of the movie *Gone with the Wind*, an American artist's work, and ten great paintings on the life of Jesus Christ, with a thousand words by a Presbyterian minister (Luce's denomination). "The Cruel Chinese" showed executions of Chinese Communists.

A Luce concept, "Roosevelt Rule," got 20 pages (January 4, 1937) and a cover of Roosevelt's eyes, nose, and mouth. Of TVA, it was said, "Its chief product has been costly lawsuits with private power companies." But the lead glorified the House of Orange-Nassau (whose Juliana was about to marry) whose brains and character I had long admired. The reason the current members were "perfect rulers of the Dutch" was "their pure instinctive Dutchness," not exactly the quality that had informed the great stadtholders. A caricature of

Léon Blum composed of vegetables was captioned: "No cabbage-head is Mr. Blum, but the best-educated and most exact-thinking of France's recent premiers." There went another of *Time*'s whimsies.

A Japanese army essay (January 11, 1937) exemplified a central problem with pictures. If one showed a photograph of a tank, a range-finder, a rifle, it was obligatory to say exactly what it was, preferably with name of manufacturer. Word stories about war could say anything with impunity but, when the picture was looking at you, the identification had to be correct. I had been sending the checkers all over town to get such identification—there was, for example, a Japanese War Office listing in the New York telephone book—and various military attachés had been authoritatively "identifying" the weapons, almost invariably with ignorance. Not even officers knew anything about weapons, but *Life* was compelled to know. So we did the best we could.

I acquired as researcher Ruth Berrien, who turned out to be a very rare woman, representative of the highest type of Time Inc. employee, incapable of lie or evasion or cowardice. Ultimately, she left me to marry Henry Fox; she died quite recently. Her interest in these later years was poetry. Ruth would go on these frustrating trips with a photostat of the weapon. If she were alive today, this would be a better account of the history.

The recourses of *Life* in this period tell the story: Margaret Sanger; *Tobacco Road* after a three-year run; Sonja Henie the skater; Mrs. Luce's play *The Women*, partly in color; a picture biography of Hermann Göring; Darryl Zanuck of Twentieth Century–Fox movies; women bathing in foam, milk, and hot wax; 100 hippopotami swimming in panic; 200 elephants stampeding in panic (both frightened by planes); a hippopotamus seen both fore and aft (the latter opposite an advertisement for Campbell's Soup, to its great distress); and "Britain's Noble Beauties." This last, showing some very handsome young ladies of blood, satisfied Luce's illusion that there was still something admirable in the world. And the readers too may have been ennobled and educated by the recognition (jargon word: anagnorisis) of this desirable and unattainable society, with its historic names pinned on cuties. This is also idea content.

But in solider ways Billings was beginning to grope his way into the function of *Life* that Luce had never anticipated, for Billings was a truly professional journalist. Thus he displayed a sit-down strike (January 18, 1937) and at great length the floods sweeping the country (February 8, 1937). Such stories must have consolidated the whole society, identifying the flooded with the nonflooded, the consumers as either for or against the striking workers. These stories opened the door to the real exercise of power. The waterlogged farmer was told that his tragedy was shown in *Life*, and visually known to millions (far more moving than learning one has been merely written about). If he ever saw the story in *Life*, he felt that his tragedy had been even more dramatic than he had thought. The nonflooded reader had *read* about the floods, but had not *believed* in them until he saw the *Life* pictures.

If Luce saw this first intimation of power, he never, so far as I am aware, made the smallest attempt to cheat with it. This alone is a testimony to his honor and patriotism.

A truly historic set of pictures (January 25, February 1, 1937) were the first pictures of the Chinese Communists, brought back by Edgar Snow. The photograph of a young Mao Tse-tung was the frontispiece. With dull pictures and long captions, this story was a documentary of doubtful fascination, but it conveyed the impression that the magazine felt a duty to the reader—perhaps even to bore him if necessary. And in this case, the magazine seemed to say, it was necessary.

Meanwhile, the executives were at work. Stillman's original contracts for coated paper were one third the requirement within six months. He began buying any paper he could obtain at any price. Having sold advertising at a cut rate geared to a low circulation, *Life* now had to print the advertising in four times the number of copies promised the advertisers. This incredible bonanza for advertisers was costing Time Inc. $2.5 million a year, and Time Inc. was not quite that rich.

Prepublication advertisers had the right to buy more space at the original insane rates (and did so). The Time Inc. executives had the lunatic notion that Madison Avenue would be grateful, an hallucination that did not materialize. The loss that year is given by Time Inc. as $5 million. This figure is a lie. Financiers say that it was $10 million and that if it had reached $12 million Time Inc. would have vanished. The power men—Luce, Larsen, Stillman—were the disaster. Bailing them out of bankruptcy were the glory men, those who believed in telling the truth and maintaining the whole communication with the reader, not to make money but for the sake of the truth. Finally, these clever little executives were bailed out by the very people they despised, the contemptible people with talent.

But that Stillman did not lose his executive bravura is attested by his writing Larsen (on the back of a Hollywood place mat): "We should have a set statement which we all make about the money we are losing and why we are losing it. Then we should proceed to lose it without hysterics in an atmosphere of *complete and serene confidence* that we know what we are doing." What a comfort a Charlie Stillman would have been on Napoleon's retreat from Moscow, except that Napoleon might have resented getting his grand strategy on the back of a Moscow place mat.

The nonsense bandied by executives is further seen in Larsen's demand to Luce for "recognition of necessity for leadership in weekly mag field once we pass 1,500,000. Leadership can ask and get highest price; runners-up take lower than leader's price. 1938 must be another stepping-stone year."

Apart from the crass insolence of calling a magazine a "mag," I think one must read into this a prematurely gluttonous greed, afflatus, and foolishness, to which Luce sensibly responded: "As a matter of fact, *Life* has to be defined editorially before it can be defined advertisingly." He had begun to sense that *Life* might have an idea content that the executives did not understand or evaluate.

As for editorial content, the book *Time Inc.* says, "The marriage of words and pictures required the evolution of a *Life* writing style quite different from that of *Time*." This is not true except for such trifles as changing "famed" to "famous." Billings is quoted as saying that "most of the first editors and writers on *Life* had worked on *Time*." This is not true, as the *Life* masthead given earlier has proved. Billings thought he was developing a "fresh, clear, simple, factual" style for *Life*, but his many virtues did not include any great sensitivity to style. Certainly, I did not change my style. Furthermore, *Time* style had straightened out considerably from the early eccentricities with which Briton Hadden, and later Wolcott Gibbs, amused themselves. Not until mid-1937 did Billings bring Hubert Kay up from *Time* to do National Affairs, probably because Kay could not put up with John Martin on *Time*. The other nominal *Time* writers besides myself were Kastner, a drudge from *Fortune*, and Thorndike, a neophyte. That's it.

A small point about *Life* style. Since the first few words of any caption were printed in bold face, they had to give the basic subject of the picture. This is elementary good sense, and hardly constitutes a style. The rest of the copy was in standard *Time* style, as "curt, clear, complete" as possible.

The arrival of Wilson Hicks as picture editor ushered in an expanding staff of photographers: Carl Mydans, Hansel Mieth, John Phillips ("admiral's aide"), Robert Capa (hero), Fritz Goro ("scientist"), Walter Sanders, Wallace Kirkland, William Vandivert ("admiral's aide"), and Bernard Hoffman ("invisible man"), a former office boy who had discovered this new road to fame.

As indicated, their techniques at work broke them down into three groups: "scientists," "admiral's aides," and "invisible men." Necessarily, photographers had to infringe on the rights of strangers, adopting personal social roles to do so effectively. Their habit of assuring their subjects that *Life* would make them famous backfired when the pictures died in some editor's bin. In consequence, the world began to fill with sullen, skeptical subjects when another *Life* photographer appeared with a new set of promises. One photographer was so "invisible" that a famous lady was amazed to discover him in bed with her. The moment of visibility had come.

The enormous flaw in photographic reporting is that, when the photographer snaps the shutter, somebody should immediately begin researching the facts about everything in the picture. But the photographer moves on to another picture, and another. Until they are developed, he won't know all that they show. By then it is too late; the moment has passed; the people have gone in various directions. The captions are nearly always inadequate (the team of Carl Mydans and his wife, Shelley Mydans, provides an exception) so the editor, in a state of relative ignorance, is obliged to do a deductive job on the finite picture. He is lucky if the photographer's notes disclose its place and time. If he knows which way is east, he can deduce the time by the shadows, if the picture is outdoors, but he can't tell the day.

These details did not matter if the picture was only a symbol picture—as, for example, in showing Britain's frantic rearming, especially in the air, a photograph of any warplane would do. But my own instinct, forced on me by the medium, was to find out exactly which plane it was and how good it was, as compared to the probable enemy plane. On such a fact the reader could not check my information to see whether I was being truthful. But if *Life* told him a mother duck with ten ducklings was crossing the street, and the reader counted the ducklings and there were ten, a strange human perhaps naïve kind of credibility accrued to *Life*, as distinct from any word magazine. And I submit that this honorable approach to pictures in *Life* derived directly from Briton Hadden's conception of *Time* and that, though Luce welcomed and supported it, he had not envisioned it and for some time did not understand it. He thought it was frivolity when I pointed out that "the dog in the foreground has fleas." It was not. It was a statement that the reader could check with his own eyes, which he had come to trust. In this preoccupation with the obvious and provable, I may mark myself as a dull boy, a hack monotonously writing down what he sees. Yes, but that was the true simplicity of the business I was in, and not many people realized it. I have long suspected that the recognition of the obvious is not given to the generality of educated people, with whom we were richly endowed at Time Inc. "Ten ducklings"; yes, it's ten. Somebody one could trust. If this childish trust is not present, the picture magazine must become a carnival spieler, or something like it.

As compared with the above modest but sensible criticism, I now succumbed to the Time Inc. mania for memoranda, in which the champion was Luce himself, followed closely by Ralph Ingersoll. Addressed to Luce, this was titled "Redefinition of *Life*" (my copy is undated) and is worth including for its effect of groping in a dark room. For we were all uncertain about what we were doing, and aware of many possible (perhaps preferable) ways of doing it. The insubstantiality of the *effect* a magazine, or any other communication, is making on the recipient is as indefinable for *Life* as for the effect the actual readers (not the critics) receive from the works of Marcel Proust. The sales of the communication show that the readers like something about it. But the uncertainty of what the something is puts editors into a state of terror in which they tend to do the same thing over and over. The best editors are therefore bold and successful mass mind readers, simply by producing something *they* like. Herewith, my memorandum:

To: Mr. Luce
From: Mr. Cort
Subject: Redefinition of *Life*

Telling stories with pictures presents at least one special problem in FN.° Beyond the immediate action of the news story, *Life* must convey to the reader that all this is happening, not in the country he knows but in a country he doesn't know. I think it is reasonable to say that *Time* is written on the basic premise that foreigners are funny. The Swiss are always stingy. South American politicians are all children. Pictures rarely make such clear-cut journalistic points. I feel the pictures that we have shown have not added up to the fact that foreigners are funny. Perhaps that is all right. Pictures make all peoples look nearly equally important. It is usually only in the captions that you can say some are heels.

FN is definitely a luxury. Anything that shows the U.S. may have a practical value for the subscribers. But only in case he has some wider curiosity and imagination, if he realizes that his country is subtly tied up with the other countries, that what happens outside may some day affect him seriously, does he get interested seriously in FN. One way of appealing to disinterested readers is to be frivolous about it. But I wonder whether *Life* couldn't afford to throw FN solidly at the reader. That is, to run all pictures of foreign countries in one part of the book. The reader certainly must change his point of view when he looks at an FN picture and it might be more comfortable for him to find that all together. I make this suggestion for what it is worth, realizing that other factors in the makeup of the whole issue may be more important.

° FN refers to Foreign News.

What kind of stories should we hit? Theoretically there are pictures for every news story. If we give up trying to tell picture stories, we can run pictures of people who have made the week's news. We did a little of this at first and then gave it up. Do you want me to make an effort at this kind of coverage? The faces are often interesting, the captions give weight to the section but it is true that such stories are off the picture-magazine track.

In FN we must often come up against this situation, of trying to use a picture to make a point not specifically shown. Example: the German boys and girls exercising together, with a caption on bastardy. Do you want that continued?

Looking through past issues, I had a feeling of dissatisfaction. There is one good excuse for that. *Life* is still at the stage of making in pictures the large, simple generalities about foreign countries. In a sense we will always remain at that stage. But we can feel more comfortable after we have told people about the Japanese Army, the central European situation, Brazil, Barcelona, the British Navy, the Palestine situation, Chinese Communists, et al. Perhaps we can then get more sophisticated about some of these things, having drummed home first principles. But I found thoroughly satisfying the takeouts that took their time at making a simple point about a country. I still like the Brazil act. Nothing is easier for pictures to do than to take people on a leisurely foreign tour, without too heavy an emphasis on the politics. This kind of thing is in marked contrast to our political acts. A lot of newsworthy peoples' faces are in the end confusing, I think, when each one is presented to the reader as being important. Thus, the Diplomats Over Europe act struck me as a failure, interesting as it was editorially. One head man is all right. A lot of unimportant people are better than all right, because you don't have to worry about whether you notice them or not and so the reader tends to look at them pleasurably.

The foreign pictures that seemed to have lasting value, some of them, were the Accession Document, Northwest frontier, Finnish logs, Mr. and Mrs. Baldwin, Ordzhonikidze funeral, the infra-red air view of the Thames, Calais and London. These were all fine pictures, they had a lot of detail, they made a single unified impression and they hit the exact center of a point about the places and people shown. Notice that three of them are air views. They gave the impression that they were showing everything. (Not all air views do.) None was a candid camera shot.

This brings up the fact that we seem to be specializing on anniversary celebrations, funerals, formal parties and dinners. Certainly we are not then showing the transaction of Big News. We are only showing bigwigs, at possibly the least significant moments of their lives (except funerals). However, the best photographers are then on hand and the best decorations are out.

I wonder whether our readers will not rapidly acquire emotional impressions or prejudices about given peoples, based on our pictures. Pictures certainly give them. Such impressions are hard to dislodge with more pictures showing the other side of the case. I submit that it is the job of the captions to keep people from forming these hard-&-fast judgments that would tend to log-jam all our future acts. This is the queerest fact yet about good pictures. They bring out in the reader a like or a dislike that no amount of further propaganda or fact is able to affect. Our pictures of Lucy Baldwin and the Archbishop of Canterbury have undoubtedly made many people absolutely deaf to anything good that may be said of them. Because people are most jealous of their judgment of people, of faces, and never give up or apologize for their prejudices. . . .

This was inferior to the memorandum style of Luce, Stillman, and Ingersoll, but it was trying.

The magazine too was trying, but floundering, relying heavily on Movies and Art (Carl Milles sculptures, Thomas Hart Benton paintings of Missouri, Joan Crawford, etc.). I think I had gotten rid of the title of Art editor by now.

Life seems to have felt that it should be fair to the Left, possibly to offset *Time*'s policy. The lead (February 22, 1937) was Leon Trotsky, the most unwanted man in the world, in exile in Mexico with Diego Rivera and a heavy police bodyguard. And the art was some Spanish Loyalist paintings of heroic proletarians, with the Loyalist captions, such as "overpowering enthusiasm of a people fighting for a Cause." The following *Life* photographs of Barcelona told a corrected story that here "the church-burning and aristocrat-killing of the Spanish Civil War reached its height." The story was padded, as was then our way, with panoramas and tourist views of Barcelona, and such statements as that the "Cathedral is rated an unfinished atrocity" and "Catalan has more obscene words than any other [language] in the world." A Hitler story showed an almost empty street during one of his radio speeches, pointing out that "four Berliners shown above are taking a substantial risk of arrest" (for not being indoors listening). A page of twelve "Great Nazi Street-Fighters," just twelve faces.

Under the Longwell-Larsen-Hicks influence, Billings was running to startling visualities: a hundred laboratory mice on the cover (introducing a story on cancer research), fine airviews of contour strip planting, and airviews of what looked like islands (actually Finnish log jams bound by a chain boom) being towed by a tug. A picture of Queen Mary's secretary stepping on her hem, a sequence on German U-boats, and a collection of aristocratic babies, "The Belgrave Square Club," managed to make it.

But Billings' journalism reasserted itself (March 8, 1937) with a story on strikes and the murder of a union leader and, again, Chief Justice Hughes and the Supreme Court, then under attack by Roosevelt. The odd sights were incidental—"14,000 [?] bats hanging head down," Cambodian pirogue racing, and, lamely illustrating the anniversary of Strauss' "Blue Danube," his home, violin, grave, and the Danube River. This last hardly carried its weight as either idea or picture, except as sly propaganda for Austria, a very hot subject in Europe.

The next issue (March 15, 1937) was dominated by a steelworker lead and an Eleanor Roosevelt album. Six pages of color were given the regalia of the coming British Coronation, with an explanation of the sanctity of the ceremony and the importance of legitimacy: "To Britons a bad king is better than a wrong king." A grim dark spread was the funeral of Soviet Commissar Ordzhonikidze, possibly poisoned, supported by a fully captioned lineup of the Soviet high command, with Stalin in the second row, a young Khrushchev in the front row.

Now Austria came into view (March 22, 1937) with a five-page lead saying, "Sooner or later Nazi Germany will take the Austrian trick unless the ace in the hole is played: the restoration of the Habsburgs to the throne of Austria." (Almost exactly a year later, Hitler took the trick.) Pretender Otto was shown wearing his Orders, correctly identified. The story ended, "Instead of the one Bosnian terrorist society" (which started World War I) "there are now five active terrorist societies operating in southeastern Europe. . . . For pictures of those assassins and the men they are out to kill this year, see next week's *Life*."

Next week they were shown and identified as Rumania's Iron Guard, Bulgaria's IMRO and Sveno, Yugoslavia's Ustashi, and Hungary's TESZ. However, in America, the department name was changed to "Death on the American Newsfront," as a gas explosion under a Texas school killed 400 students. More terror to come was epitomized in a faked picture of London's proposed balloon barrage against air attack, and a map of England's defense network, as it was producing a total of 6,000 fighters and bombers. "England is an island," said the text, but no longer. The pictures virtually forced me to discuss the weapons—"the new antiaircraft gun which can throw 1,000 shells a minute up 18,000 feet . . . almost never score direct hits, trust to exploding shrapnel within 50 yards."

Curiously, such information was not to be found in *Time* for several more years. Luce is reported at this point as saying, "Though we did not plan *Life* as a war magazine, it turned out that way." What he meant was that I turned out that way. Again, it was obvious that since war was coming the most important facts in the world were the characteristics of existing weapons. The obvious was still majestic and, when *Life* said that Italy and Germany "treat the Spanish Government as rebels against General Franco," it exploded Goldsborough's foreign policy, which agreed with Italy and Germany.

To the editors of *Life* on the masthead had been added John S. Martin, in one more obeisance to the ghost of Briton Hadden. Billings, Longwell, Thorndike, and myself were still on the *Time* masthead. Wilson Hicks had been added to the *Life* masthead, along with two names that mean nothing to me: Charles Breasted and Alan Brown.

Life's superiority to *Time* in making a single strategic point (what Luce called an "angle") was obvious to everybody by now, as in the sit-down strike, Austrian, and British antiaircraft stories. It was an unfair advantage. The strategic point might be in *Time* (but often wasn't) but buried in words; in *Life* it was headlined and given a perhaps factitious reality by the massive impact of pictures. The Austrian story was a perfect example and I think the strategic point was sound, at worst compelling an earlier revelation of Nazi violence. *Life* editors also acquired a kind of sophistication denied anyone who had not seen a lot of pictures. Thus, *Life* could toss off the trivial fact that Libyan Spahis rode Arabian horses, while the Sahara Patrol rode cream-colored camels. Most people are impressed by such useless information.

Billings was overwhelmed by the Longwell influence into printing pointless covers of "terrier barking up tree," a hundred-year-old lady holding a cigarette in a pipe, and the head of a rooster. This sort of thing could have destroyed *Life*. But inside the magazine Billings had stories on sit-down strikes historically traced to the dancing mania of the thirteenth century, Gandhi, and the French Popular Front, Hershey Chocolate strikers routed by farmers and nonstrikers, the Wagner Act ruled constitutional by the Supreme Court switch of Justice Roberts, and the military defenses of Hawaii.

About now Luce evidently changed his mind (April 12, 1937) about the ignominy of the *Life* staff, for the masthead and table of contents, hitherto slipped into the back of the book, were now printed in the front. I would interpret this as a sign of Luce's renewed compact with the writers as valuable people.

An unexpected feature (April 19, 1937), probably not my idea, probably Luce's, was nine pages on England's Queen Mother Mary as the one member of the royal family on whom the English knew they could rely. Breaking all precedent, she was scheduled to ride in the Coronation procession, ahead of King George VI. This expressed Luce's theme that pictures could show decency, dignity, even majesty, and helped remove the aftertaste of Edward VIII.

In *Time*, Goldsborough was continuing his theme that the Spanish government were Reds, but sometimes radicals, and that Britain and Italy were "natural friends" and should never have quarreled over Ethiopia. At last (January 18, 1937) the Spanish war was the "Little World War," as it had always been. His philosophy petered out in a quote from Masaryk, the creator of Czechoslovakia, that the Machine Age had made it possible for One Man to win the loyalty of nearly all his countrymen, hence that the new style of government was simultaneously a democracy and a dictatorship, to which Goldsborough appended, "A mystery potent enough to recall the Trinity." An inner exhaustion, which wins my sympathy, is discernible.

There was a convulsion in the masthead of *Time* (March 1, 1937), Billings remaining as the second managing editor behind John S. Martin. Hubert Kay and Ralph D. Paine, Jr., were promoted to associate editors; Longwell, Cort, Thorndike were dropped; also Elizabeth Armstrong, Robert Cantwell, E. D. Kennedy, and S. J. Woolf; and the new recruits were Finis Farr, Robert Fitzgerald, Reuben Frodin, Walter Graebner, Newton Hockaday, T. S. Matthews (again), Arthur Ogden, Russell Olsen, and Robert Sherrod. Olsen I remember admiringly because he described me later, in the Newspaper Guild wars, as "the parlor fink." Finis Farr was a friend to Busch. Fitzgerald was talented. Graebner and Sherrod became correspondents. I think Hockaday was involved with pictures, but he was also in the weekly poker game and insisted on betting when drunk.

Time reported that World War I veterans meeting in Berlin felt Hitler was "simpler, more attractive and more sincere" than they had expected. Of course. Mussolini and Stalin were attractive too. Success, as they say, cures all neuroses, nor would the man get to be dictator if nobody liked him. Propaganda addressed to an intelligent audience is wise to acknowledge that the devil has charm and a raison d'être, but that he is nevertheless the devil. I never acquired any interest in arranging personal interviews with these charmers.

On *Life*, invisible to the reader but indispensable, wind drifts of memoranda whistled through the organization, trying to convert ideas into pictures in hand. The first set went from the editors to the picture department. Ultimately, the results enabled the editor to give Billings a memorandum for the week's issue.

I have a typical one for the May 3, 1937, issue—Subject: Features.

1. Japanese elections, April 30. The Army and the high bureaucrats *v.* the politicians. We have pictures of both, the new Diet building, the Diet

meeting, the Labor Party, and Natori's pictures may add to it. The issues are being left pretty much unspoken.

2. The Duke of Windsor's romance becomes legal April 27 when Mrs. S's decree becomes absolute. We have a fine set on his life-long grooming as Prince of Wales.

3. "The Outburst of Goodwill" in the Non-Intervention Committee, when the Italian and Russian delegates (Grandi and Maisky) began talking soft. A takeout of this outfit?

4. Japan's Mt. Asama erupted Apr. 16. How about our four pages on Japan-From-the-Air, in which Asama shows?

5. The second branch of the Moscow Subway was opened in January; the third is now being rushed. It passes close by the Kremlin walls and there is a station nearby but no Red Square Station. In its present state of activity, this is good any time this year.

6. British coal and shipyard workers are threatening a series of strikes on Coronation eve. We have pictures of Depressed Areas (some of which we used with Edward VIII's visit to South Wales), also of the Tolpuddle Martyrs, founders of the British labor movement, now heroes of a play that annually tours the country.

7. Indian Nationalists. Dissatisfaction with the new Constitution is now festering underground to make Neville Chamberlain's first "crisis." We have air views of places, Gandhi, Nehru, elections, woman suffrage, etc. Also the Kadir Cup finals with Linlithgow and an Indian ferris wheel.

8. The Grain Race contestants are heading for England, the winner to reach there some time in May. We have a good set.

9. To go with Hyde Park Coronation sheep, making way for tourists, we have a spring-like set on Rotten Row riders and gardeners on a ladder.

10. The U.S. is really French. To kid *L'Illustration*'s America-pandering, with pictures of Chicago's Marquette Building, 17th Century Nouvelle France, and French-named U.S. cities. *L'Illustration* gave this a whole issue.

Most of this memorandum did nothing for the issue. No. 9 contributed to the lead on pre-Coronation England, the "gardeners on a ladder" propped across a garden, whose flowers were carefully identified as Hens and Chickens, Ageratum, Vinca, and periwinkle. No. 1 also contributed a short political essay, dressed by pictures of top-hatted Japanese fishing with long bamboo poles for the emperor's carp. An act on the Indian northwest frontier, previously touted, also made the issue, as did German illegitimate babies and Soviet churches still in business. The northwest frontier was becoming an exotic *Life* specialty in this period. In factual terms, it documented Rudyard Kipling, while presenting an esoteric "scoop."

The turmoil on *Life* meant that everybody was becoming more sophisticated about existing pictures than the most worldly traveler. The value of the scenes varied, and the best were symbolic of more than they showed.

An example for people who had not read the famous book *Middletown* was a lead on the real town, Muncie, Indiana (May 10, 1937), showing both the poor and the town's rich family, which had its own fox hunt. As the Coronation approached, there was a story on the Coronation scene, Westminster Abbey, with a drawing showing where everybody would sit in the Abbey. As a side in the Spanish Civil War that "the British could love," the Loyalist Basques were presented, "who are both pro-Liberty (which the Rebels are not) and pro-God (which the Loyalists are not)." A true symbol picture was magnificent Marienburg Castle, once the center of the Teutonic Knights fighting eastward, now a rally for the Nazis, again looking eastward to Poland and Russia. This sort of significance might have been dismissed by serious historians but, as of the present date, it cannot be debated. It was a gamble, a bold risk of credibility. Close readers of *Life* were getting the truth about coming events. In this issue the masthead added the name of Francis E. Brennan ("Hank"), of whom I can say only that I never knew exactly what he did except be affable.

Several trivial issues followed, two including pictures of the Coronation which, I suspected, had begun to seem like a hollow mummery to the reader, a great deal of trouble over little or nothing (the definition of aristocratic ritual). The horror of the zeppelin *Hindenburg*'s explosion at Lakehurst, New Jersey, was curiously ineffective in a series of still pictures in black and white (May 17, 1937). The first airmail pictures of the Coronation came next week.

That issue (May 24, 1937) would have closed on Saturday, May 15. I was, I think, ordered to take a vacation, since the next two issues anticipated very little foreign news except the Coronation and the next was to be devoted wholly to American colleges. I do not remember my replacement, but anybody could interpret Coronation pictures from the acts we had done.

And so I was given a most peculiar revelation, integral to my story.

Section III

SUDDEN GLORY

AS indicated, I had been a contentedly humble worker on *Time*. I had been published in *Life* for just over five months, not producing any miracles of journalism, so far as I was aware. I thought I was fairly solid in the job, partly because Billings hated to deal with new people and partly because of Luce's compliments.

But my distinct recollection is that I was treated, as I was about to embark on the *Normandie* for Europe, sailing Wednesday, May 19, 1937, as Somebody of Importance. Chronologically, this is ridiculous and impossible.

The reason was that anything and anybody connected in a key capacity with *Life* was then and for long afterward bathed in the magic aura of incredible success and profits—money. *Life's* ads always referred to the "incredible" demand for the magazine. "Incredible," meaning "magical," was the word, even as the enterprise was losing $2.5 million in 1937, for that too was "incredible," given our brilliant executives. I must admit that being a central figure in such an all-conquering thaumaturgy inflated me, so that I was not surprised by my new status as Somebody of Importance, even though it now seems preposterous. Similar feelings must have inflated various Yankee baseball teams or the Met team of 1969 or Hitler's armies from 1939 to 1941 or Patton's army or the team inventing the atom bomb or Charles Dickens. The individual on such a team always feels that he has been both lucky and clever to get on the team.

A trivial indication of my importance was A. K. Mills' arranging that on the *Normandie* I should look up the wife of John Martin, traveling with the singer Libby Holman. I did so on the first afternoon, heard Miss Holman say that she was *"enervé,"* saw the prizefighter Tommie Doyle, called the Irish Thrush, enter, and soon departed, sensing that I was out of my class. I was received in the Paris office by Richard de Rochemont's wife. The Paris Exposition was not yet open. Therefore, I went on to Vienna, where I was received by our correspondent, Robert Best. I have described him elsewhere: "He was fleshy, rumpled, and dilapidated and he somehow reminded me of the strange characters who haunt American public libraries. [Oddly enough, this description fits another traitor I knew at the time, Whittaker Chambers.] I soon noticed that he was guilty of small crudities of manners, an uncoordinated brusqueness, but these lost their offense by the curious and friendly gleam in his eye [Chambers to the life, again]." Ultimately, Best broadcast for the Nazis, and died in an American prison. At the time, he only championed Mussolini's corporate state. I liked him, and I liked the Viennese women even better.

I went on to Budapest, where I took our correspondent to the Prince of Wales nightclub on Margareten Island, only to discover that he felt too inferior to associate with the lovely girls. I went on to Prague, where I noticed the uniquely American feel of democracy, but also the statutes of a police state against anybody not a Bohemian. Then I took the train for Paris, passing through Nazi Germany. The train stopped and I got out to buy cigarettes, passing a group of Nazi officers. When I returned, they stopped me, demanding my ticket. I burst into curses, luckily in English, but showed my ticket. One of them stamped it, and I was allowed to return. At 4:00 A.M., the porter woke me up at the French border to tell me that I had no French visa, and should alight at Kehl to get one from the consul. I sent him away twice, insisting that I had a French visa, for the idea of stopping in Nazi Germany horrified me. At last, the

French official arrived in my stateroom, and somehow I understood that I had exhausted my French visa by passing through France. I sat up in my berth and delivered the speech, *"Alors, monsieur, je suis venu à France pour voir l'Exposition. Mais l'Exposition n'était pas ouverte. Ainsi, je suis continué à Wien, à Budapest, à Prague, et maintenant je reviens à France encore pour voir l'Exposition."* Miraculously, this schoolboy French persuaded the official, and I was allowed to continue, providentially since I was out of money (and on the Gestapo black list, I had been informed). The postponements in the opening of the Exposition were a sensitive point in France just then. At our Paris office I refreshed my finances, cursorily saw the Exposition, and went on to London where I was welcomed by Dick de Rochemont, Erland Echlin, and, I think, A. K. Mills.

The contrast between this self-paid pub-crawling and Goldsborough's subsidized Grand Tour would have been leaped on by the executives, and not to my credit. I was a bargain counter foreign editor.

I have a record that Hubie Kay sent me $200 at Budapest, on which is noted the hotels I stayed at—the London Savoy; Vienna, Graben; Budapest, Szent Gellert; Prague, President Wilson—but not the one in Paris. In Paris I found a beautiful girl who would have nothing to do with me, to the outrage of the other older whores who sympathized with me. I had the same experience in London but without the sympathy. I have found only one such girl in America but she was a gangster's moll and untouchable (during Prohibition). (Of nonwhores, there are many more beautiful, but a truly superb whore is a miracle. I have met three.) On a tax return I find that the government would not allow me even $1,000 for the expenses of my professionally educational trip to Europe (not substantiated). I have long regarded the various American taxing agencies as more subversive and patriotism-eroding than any imported subversion. I also find that Time Inc. paid my boat fares. Not as handsome as Goldsborough's expense account but better than I had ever remembered.

Around the time I got back, Billings brought Hubert Kay up from *Time* to do National Affairs, to my great satisfaction. (Breasted now disappears from the masthead.) Kay was a man who plodded his way to the truth and presented it with crystalline honesty. He thought heavily but purely, though with an unnecessary anguish. His brain is like his body—heavy, bulldoggish, looking right at you with no more than curiosity. *Life* began to take on a character. Immediately (July 5, 1937), the lead was on the difficult subject of the right to strike versus the right to work. This was tightrope work but Kay was getting the feel of the big-impact medium. The essay was six pages on Palestine: "The Arab-Jew vendetta is racially absurd, because both are Semitic. The Jews have already raised the standard of living of Palestine Arabs." Of Tel Aviv, "Murder is almost unknown. There is some larceny and a great deal of usury. . . . Picturesque Arab oldsters, among the world's most warlike and murderous people, dislike civilization's effect on Arab laborers." My position was cruelly basic, expressed in the statement, "The Jews stand for Occidental civilization." I was pulling out no chestnuts for the Jews. I was merely expressing my article of faith that Western civilization is a good thing.

The Jewish Agency for Palestine, while aware of my position, presented me with a case of Palestine white wine—the only "graft" I received in fifteen years at Time Inc. It was very good. I told Billings about it and got a dubious look.

In this issue was a piece on the French Bastille Day, which I cannot see myself writing. It said that "social democracy" had not been invented by the American Revolution but by the French Revolution, which failed, and that American democracy arrived only with Jefferson in 1801. What in hell the writer, probably Paul Peters, thought the American Constitution of 1787 was, I cannot imagine. The story was obviously a maverick Communist ploy but, remember, it was passed by Billings and Luce who, I can only conclude, did not know what they were doing. For certainly they were not Communists.

A subject I had requested arrived—the meeting of the Order of the Garter in St. George's Chapel in Windsor Castle—"the most exclusive club in the world." The twenty-six members' banners above their stalls showed only their edges, but this was the sort of identification I felt was obligatory. With much nagging of London and study of Burke's Peerage, we were finally able to identify half a dozen or so. In my opinion the picture compelled us to try, if not fully succeed.

A frontal attack was made on Goldsborough's bias on Spain (July 12, 1937) with a lead, "Death in Spain," frontispieced by a since-famous Robert Capa picture of a Loyalist soldier dropping with a bullet in him. This emphasized Spain's oversized and overpaid officer corps and its topheavy hierarchy of 100,000 priests. "The ruling classes of Spain were probably the world's worst bosses—irresponsible, arrogant, vain, ignorant, shiftless and incompetent. . . . The people of Spain had fired their bosses for flagrant incompetence and the bosses had refused to be fired." This evaluation of Spain—in terms of efficiency, not political philosophies—probably got the story past Billings and Luce, but its effect on Goldsborough must have been brutal. This was followed by a movie of the civil war with captions by Hemingway who must have signaled the respectability of the Loyalist cause even to Longwell. This was followed by an impartial account of the prewar two-sided "Terror in Spain," which may have made inevitable the eventual rebellion. In effect, the Spanish Civil War was the classic and eternal war within society, fought by extremely courageous and uncompromising people who did not run away. It had not yet been wholly corrupted by the Communists. Goldsborough had picked the winning side; I had picked the losers.

Life, unlike *Time*, permitted a large philosophical view of its subjects. Thus (July 19, 1937): "One of the most powerful dreams of mankind is to find a supreme judge as lofty, well informed and disinterested as God"—this in a story about the International Court at The Hague.

The sit-down strikes had magically transposed to Americans the Spanish Civil War's practice of using the purely European epithets of "Communist" and "Fascist." Confronting this disease (July 26, 1937), Hubie Kay with magnificent phlegm wrote: "Non-alarmist, democracy-loving citizens have scratched their heads. Thoughtful ones recalled that real Communism is an arduous discipline which has only 45,000 adherents in the U.S., that prerequisites of real Fascism are usually a genuine proletarian menace, a middle class driven to despair by disorder and want, and a leader. None of these has yet appeared convincingly in the U.S." The healing effect of this simple lead seems to prove the value of Time Inc. writers' calm and objectivity in the midst of national uproars. This was a true exercise of power, from which the writer accrued no added power. A failure of nerve was not a characteristic of the writers I admired, but it was rampant in America then, as since in some quarters.

I asked Billings for a raise. He told me, "I never give a raise to anybody who asks for it." Since I liked my job, I accepted this as part of the routine tyranny at Time Inc. A few months later, Billings having made his point, I got the raise. The thing was to accept this sort of obscenity without blinking. Having started with Martin, and regarding Billings as a crude understudy, I had this faculty.

It was probably the preceding Christmas that, misreading my relationships in this peculiar organization, I had sent Billings a Christmas present of a Finnish salad bowl. Billings was John Shaw Billings. Martin was John Stuart Martin. Billings' reaction was to show me that I had addressed my sycophantic gift to John Stuart Billings. At the time I did not understand such churlishness but now, knowing that Martin's name was always above Billings' on the *Time* masthead, I see that the foolish slip was a dagger in the Billings heart. I am surprised he did not fire me. I never sent him another Christmas present.

Of great interest to the executives, and no interest to the writers, had been Luce's appointment of independent publishers for the magazines: Larsen for *Life*, Ingersoll for *Time*, Eric Hodgins for *Fortune*. In the summer John Martin as managing editor of *Time* was again not managing. It was decided to give him a long rest.

The *Time* issue of September 7, 1937, gave the managing editors as { John S. Martin / John Shaw Billings. The rest of the masthead is worth mentioning. Associate Editors:

Busch, Fraser, Goldsborough, Gottfried, Hulburd, Hubert Kay, Norris, Paine, Schroeder, and Weiss. Contributing Editors (some novelties): Balliett, Robert Fitzgerald, Reuben Frodin, Walter Graebner, Newton Hockaday, Peter Mathews, T. S. Matthews, Arthur Ogden, Russell Olsen, James Parton, Daniel Rochford, Robert Sherrod, Henry Robert Stimson, and Walter Stockly.

But on the masthead of September 13, 1937, the managing editors were
⎰ John S. Martin
⎱ Manfred Gottfried and Hubert Kay had been dropped from Frank Norris
the associates.

The executives jiggered the advertising rates in such a way as to produce financial losses for another year. But Luce was still the champion of his magazines' idea content and of his editors. *Life's* fascination for the readers was the primary *fact* in his mind; the executives' decisions were still secondary to the writers' decisions.

Of the new publishers, Larsen was harmless to *Life*, Hodgins was probably fine for *Fortune* (though, as I have indicated, *Fortune*, while a central balm of conscience to Luce, was peripheral to Time Inc.), but Ralph Ingersoll, who did not understand the idea of Briton Hadden, was a mistake for *Time*. A former *New Yorker* editor, he liked to edit, to manage, to disgorge attitudes, opinions, philosophies, and he could never see that the magical secret of *Time* was to be amateur. He was that abomination, the truly creative and manipulative editor, trying to change fact into something else existing in his mind, called "the Scientific Principle" and "specialists": a frightful misjudgment.

He had got rid of Martin. His next objective was Goldsborough. As an intracorporate killer, he deserves ranking with Longwell, for he had been through a similar bloody school.

Oddly, the promotions on *Time* meant that Noel Busch, the perfect and magnificent amateur, editor of Sport and Cinema, was obliged, over his haughty protests, to become National Affairs editor. Gottfried wrote that *Time* was always "skating on thin talent ice." I once reviewed a book of his on Genghis Khan, favorably, but I do not think that he was thick talent ice. The denigration of the writers seems to have come easily to Time Inc. editors but, remember, it was always in the closet.

We see here the institutional progress toward blurring the stark reality that the true communication is between writer and reader, one human being to another, the only communication a human being will accept, particularly when he also gets the venal institutional communication in the advertisements. The reader does not want, and does not believe, a corporate communication. Nor does the human communication have to be signed with a name; the individual communication telegraphs itself. On *Life*, I think Hubie Kay and I achieved this some of the time.

Luce's desire to prove that *Life* was not a sophisticated, big-city magazine was indicated by repeated farm stories: (1) the grasshopper plague on the Great Plains; (2) a scholarly study of the various U.S. wheat belts and their product; (3) an Iowa corn-and-pig farm.

A new name appeared in the masthead, Maria Sermolino, for Fashion (August 16, 1937). Robert Capa's wife, the Communist Gerda Taro, a photographer, had been accidentally killed in Spain, and this was memorialized. Madame Chiang Kai-shek and her illustrious family got the lead. There was an attempt to explain with pictures and diagrams "how to fly an airplane."

A characteristic of my style was to try to find the expression "the most ——— in the world." This is far more available than the amateur would think. A variant came (August 23, 1937) with "Egypt gets its first king in 1,990 years," since Cleopatra's brother, a Ptolemy. This would be Farouk, called by the English "the most perfectly brought-up boy in the world," but not for long. The attempt to make every *Life* reader an airplane pilot was continued with a DC-3 panel board identifying ninety-six instruments, a staggering research job.

In the next issue (August 30, 1937) were seven pages on the Japanese in various quaint practices, "the world's most conventional people," accompanied by an anthropology I would not wish to defend today.

Hubie Kay's sanity again informed the lead (September 6, 1937) saying that the National Labor Relations Board (under the Wagner Act, by now declared constitutional by the Supreme Court) "is indisputably the ablest agency yet created to settle U.S. labor disputes by law and reason, instead of by clubs and tear gas." This was the hearing in progress versus Weirton Steel.

In the next issue (September 13, 1937) was an essay on Weir's Weirton, showing the satisfaction of prosperous workers under unbridled but benevolent capitalism. The possibility of this sort of capitalism under founder or family ownership, if labor had been polite, must be considered. The possibility vanished as nonfamily management, responsible to the stockholders, took over. One man may be decent; a corporation cannot be. Labor never considered the possibility that the one man was decent; it wanted its benefits by force, not by favor. Given the nature of man, a self-policing capitalism is not probable, but I must suggest that it might have been possible for a little while longer. The Wagner Act made it impossible, on the instant. The question then became whether labor could police itself.

An inconsequential name appears (September 20, 1937) in the masthead, Andrew Heiskell, later chairman of the board of Time Inc. And here is a very thorough account of the Battle of Antietam, for which Lincoln had waited to issue the tabled *Emancipation Proclamation*, hoping for something better than Antietam.

The peculiar meaninglessness of 1937 was expressed (September 27, 1937) in the lead: "Ever since the last War, Europe has been waiting for that set of unpredictable events that would march it, as in a dream, into the next War." This disbelief in war was due to the fact that the threat was Italy, suspected of launching "pirate submarines" to sink ships bringing supplies to the Spanish Loyalists. A conference was called at Nyon "to shoot a mad dog." The "threat of war" seemed a mere diversion. Again, it was taking our eyes off Hitler and Stalin. And so we showed the Nazis' annual Nürnberg congress. In a story commemorating Masaryk's death, we said his creation, Czechoslovakia, "theoretically a democracy, has its own dissatisfied minorities of Germans, Hungarians, Moravians, Poles, Ruthenians, Rumanians." Thus early, *Life* policy was to be that Czechoslovakia was not exactly an impeccable democracy, and indeed could not afford to be, an insight that my European excursion had given me.

Magazines such as the *Reader's Digest* try to solve people's problems; others such as *The New Yorker* and *Playboy* tell them they have no problems. *Life* did both simultaneously. Billings, with his clear-eyed unobsessed simplicity, had the naïve genius to achieve this result.

The hand of Luce is seen (October 18, 1937) in the lead claiming that Roosevelt had changed "the whole course of U.S. postwar foreign policy" (the use of "postwar" instead of "prewar" is interesting) in saying, "Let no one imagine that America will escape [war], that it may expect mercy, that this Western Hemisphere will not be attacked . . . no escape through mere isolation or neutrality." Luce overlooked what Roosevelt saw plainly: that America was also composed of Irish who hated England, Germans who revered Hitler, Italians who loved Mussolini (an incomplete roster), and also of native Americans who thought that Europe had made its own mess and wanted no part of it. Roosevelt knew he represented these people too. His problem, which he could never avow but which I sympathized with, was to wait for these people to see what was really going on. To help enlighten them was part of my job. Luce was perpetually out of step.

One signal that Roosevelt had this awareness (perhaps possible only for an aristocrat) was provided later when he named a troublesome Irishman, Joseph Kennedy, as ambassador to Great Britain, a subtle reminder to the English that America was not entirely English, even though it spoke the same language, and a semaphore for the alert of future American policy, contrary to Luce's "responsible" faith. Anti-Rooseveltians call him an opportunist—of course he was—and I loved him for it.

A surprising social note intrudes. Mr. and Mrs. Luce invited me to dinner at the Waldorf. In the elevator, Mrs. Luce, whom I had not seen since *Vanity Fair* days, says, "Oh, you're the fey one." I reply, "You've got me mixed up with Corey Ford" (my close friend, now dead). "Oh no, you're fey." This must have bewildered Luce. At dinner I was seated next to a beautiful lady, Dorothy Hale, widow of the painter Gardner Hale, killed in a California automobile accident. Since I did not envision a social life as extra man at Mrs. Luce's parties, I accepted Mrs. Hale's suggestion that we leave early and go to a night club. I admired her but was married soon after. Later, she became engaged to Roosevelt's assistant, Harry Hopkins, but somebody gave the news to a Broadway columnist and this seems to have broken up the engagement, possibly because she had been involved with a Japanese. Dorothy then leaped out the window, somehow landing without impairing the beauty of her face, I am told.

An example of truth telling was a story on Spanish propaganda pictures (October 25, 1937) calling both sides liars with the obvious statement: "If a man is mad enough to fight, he is mad enough to lie."

As the American stock market was crashing (November 1, 1937) and *Life* was telling Roosevelt in effect (November 29, 1937), you got us into this, now get us out, the first anniversary issue (November 22, 1937) carried 72 advertising pages; the next had 35 pages. In the first, the total number of pages was 132; in the second, 96. This stayed (December 6) at 96, dropped (December 20) to 80, (December 27) to 68, and leveled off at 64 pages—a diminution into less than half its size in just over a month. This remarkable shriveling was hardly noticed; it saved the company a great deal of money. And of course it was at the dictation of the executives.

Gerry Piel's science was, as usual, excellent: four ways for the "world" (meaning only this planet) to end; the Mount Wilson Observatory and the universe it was watching, with a prediction of the Mount Palomar telescope by 1940. There was also another Czech story (November 8, 1937) pointing out that Woodrow Wilson had hoped that Europe as well as America could maintain societies combining traditionally hostile races, but in Europe the flaw was that the homelands of the hostile races were nearby. The first Nazi demonstrations having taken place, it was asserted that "experts have long felt that Adolf Hitler must get Austria before he takes on Czechoslovakia." This forecast does not appear in the current issues of *Time*. By this time Martin had vanished from the *Life* masthead, but not from *Time*.

The totalitarian societies begin to look like one another (November 15, 1937). Of the first secret ballot in Russia since 1912 (only one candidate on the ballot), "a 60% victory in a really free and secret election is a 'landslide.' But the 1,800,000 Communists in Russia will smell treason in anything less than a 99% victory." The results will have "no executive significance under Stalin." In Italy, "the words of Mussolini tell the grown children (as Mussolini considers Italians) how to feel and think." The Italian wall newspaper tells all the news most Italians get—"nearly in words of one syllable and always in thoughts of one syllable."

It may have been here that Luce protested my giving the Japanese "case" for invading China: that an offshore island nation must have the cooperation of the adjoining continent. I answered that we must assume the enemy had some sensible theory, and that our duty was to give it if we knew it. "O.K., you're right," he said immediately.

Two brilliant predictions by Joseph Kennedy (November 22, 1937) were that the United States would desperately need an efficient merchant marine in case of war and that, soon after, air transport would obsolesce large passenger ships. The collapse of the Chinese defense of Shanghai, emphasizing three heroic months, is noted.

Hubie Kay has (November 29, 1937) a tremendously informative chart identifying all 96 U.S. senators as New Dealers, coattail riders, mustangs, politicians, conservatives (the last three bracketed as "unpredictable"), anti-Roosevelt diehards, and one hell-raiser. An ad in this, the first birthday issue, gave circulation as 1,600,000, without noting that advertising rates were in frantic debate.

After an innocent lead on American hunting (December 6, 1937), all of 14 pages were given to Japan's incursions into Asia, with a color foldout of prints of the forgotten Sino-Japanese War of 1894–1895 pointing out the historical errors in each scene. Since the Chinese emperor never received the Japanese ambassador, the war was regarded as an impudence. The story described the Japanese soldier as "one of the world's best marchers, smallest eaters." On a Moscow balcony, appears with Stalin his daughter, "bright, serious, 11-year-old Svetlana, now in the fifth grade of a Moscow school where teachers are instructed to allow her no favors."

In this issue and the next (December 13, 1937) were scoop essays of a massacre of Haitians by Dominicans and of Haitian voodoo, engineered by a talented mountebank named Alexander King. As an idea man, he was competitive with Longwell and not destined long to survive that competition. I enjoyed arguing with him until I discovered that, when cornered, he always said that nothing was true. Billings destroyed him, when King claimed he knew just what was going to happen in Europe, by having him seal his prediction in an envelope. Billings then tacked it to his bulletin board, and it stared at King as events went another way. I think the envelope was eventually destroyed, unopened. Later, King became famous in the less skeptical world of television.

The lead (December 20, 1937) was on the new pneumonia serum, for lack of which my mother had died in 1936. In contrast to *Time*'s earlier scamping of Joseph Kennedy's family, *Life* gave them a two-page spread, when John was 20, Robert 12, and Edward 6 as father Kennedy left to become ambassador to the Court of St. James, his capital then assessed at a mere $9 million, a frightful insult, at which he must have smiled. At this point Colette, as unique as Joe Kennedy, became the first woman admitted to the quaint French Academy.

The Christmas issue (December 27, 1937) showed the magnificent Frick collection in eight pages of color. It was pointed out that television, mechanically perfected, was useless until television programs were developed, and hence that as yet there was no point in trying to sell television sets. Almost parenthetically, there was diplomatic uproar, enjoyed by Luce, over the Japanese sinking of a U.S. gunboat, *Panay*, in the Yangtze River.

A touching note from Luce must be given in full, in view of my lack of importance just over a year before.

December 24, 1937.

Dear Dave:—

I can't let this year's end go by without telling you how much personal satisfaction your work has given me.

I say personal for several reasons—not least of which has been the fun of working with you. I think you have still to work out some more satisfying method of what I might call coverage of Foreign News. But you have certainly put into picture-journalism a tone and color which I could never have "prescribed" but which would have been just what the doctor ordered had he known how to order it.

We spoke several months ago of a five—or was it a ten-year plan. I have had to table that subject for various reasons but I hope to take it up again in January.

With all regards,

Sincerely yours,

HENRY R. LUCE

Some idiot announced (January 3, 1938) that Marlene Dietrich's career was finished because "the age of Exotica had ended." (The Time Inc. ukase was never more neatly travestied.)

My memorandized theory of telling a Time Inc. story at length, before showing the picture, may have surfaced (January 10, 1938) with a full column on the Chinese refugee story, preceding a large picture of Chinese boarding a ship from sampans. "The Panay Incident" documented by a movie was blown into seven pages, and the Japanese were also shown looting Nanking, with the sober judgment that this disciplined army permitted it because "its supplies are getting low."

At this point *Life* was hurting *Time*, and Ingersoll was screaming at the top of his memorandum form, and so *Time* was given the inside back cover of *Life*.

A perfect example of my journalism (January 17, 1938) was the headline "The Greatest General of the War" describing the funeral of Ludendorff, one of Hitler's first supporters. The assumption was that his being a Nazi did not make the slightest difference in his proved distinction as a figure in military history. The disdain of the doctrinaire anti-Nazi position was obvious. He was given full honors in *Life* though it was added, factually, that he was not a real Junker and was "an hysterical man who fell apart in defeat." The other kind of reporting, the litmus-paper evaluation in terms of the mob's current fashion, seems to debase the mind of our species. A further defect is that it soon loses the belief of an intelligent audience. If the reader knows that one will always abuse any German, he has no need to read the magazine. Such stories kept open *Life*'s communication to such people, including many Germans, Irish, Italians et al. and perhaps in the end made the American decision nearly unanimous. But this was easy enough to do; one told the obvious truth about Ludendorff, a great man at his business.

Evidently, readers had been objecting to our war news. For a reply was forthcoming (January 24, 1938) in the lead on "The World's Two Wars": "Obviously *Life* cannot ignore nor suppress these two great news events in pictures. As events, they have an authority far more potent than any editors' policy or readers' squeamishness. . . . The important thing that happens in a war is that somebody or something gets destroyed. Victory comes to the side that destroys the greatest number of somebodies or somethings. . . . America's noble and sensible dislike of war is largely based on ignorance of what modern war really is. . . . Dead men have indeed died in vain if live men refuse to look at them."

This last sentence I recognized as the one sleazy sophistry in the whole lead. But Billings, and probably Luce, remembered it then and for years afterward, as a classic epigram worthy of Socrates. It was of course a self-serving lie. But I had to defend a picture of Loyalist dead on the field at Teruel in Spain, and the Chinese "scorched-earth" destruction of Japanese-owned factories at Tsingtao. War, it said, was an acceptable form of human behavior, and here it was accurately shown.

More to the current point was a story describing Austria (contrary to current journalistic opinion) as "a third Socialists and Communists . . . a third Nazis whom he [the Premier] suppresses half-heartedly and perhaps a sixth monarchists." *Life* readers were getting the idea that Austria would not last much longer.

This was emphasized in a subsequent lead (February 7, 1938) saying, "A new and pregnant stampede seemed to have started, away from the democracies and the League of Nations and toward the great Fascist Powers of Central Europe. . . . France and Britain are far away; the League of Nations has failed to defend Ethiopia, Spain and China; and Germany is near." This calling of a massive shift in the balance of power was taking a fixed risk, which could not be washed out or hedged in later issues. I was on record. But Billings and Luce had accepted the point. Balancing this story was one on Boss Hague of Jersey City (8 pages), and another on Russia's Supreme Soviet, elected in "the only democratic election in the world" (all "good" Communists), in which the times on two clocks were noted as 11:40 and 11:45.

Readers' letters (February 14, 1938) swooned over the "Two War" lead: "Lincoln himself could not have phrased the truth about war more tellingly." The lead told of small businessmen in Washington—"the working of pure democracy, as opposed to representative government . . . surprisingly sensible program with which the little businessmen emerged after only two days." Coincidentally, there was a picture biography of Lincoln (his birthday).

The next issue (February 21, 1938) was a breathing space with a lead on the birth of "one of the rarest animals alive—a member of the Dutch royal house of Orange-Nassau."

Goldsborough's answer to *Life* came (*Time*, February 21, 1938): "Mussolini, who is not anxious to have Germany swarm into Austria, and thus jostle Italy, had inspired Dr. Schuschnigg's hurried visit to Herr Hitler. . . . Chances brightening for a British-German-French-Italian understanding to uphold Europe's territorial status quo." Austrian Nazis felt " 'Hitler has betrayed us' laid the larger issue of merging Austria with Germany on the shelf . . . pledge by Hitler to squelch Austrian Nazis' violence."

What were the reasons for this colossal gaffe? First, Goldsborough was committed to the idea that Mussolini was the No. 1 Fascist. Second, he was temperamentally more interested in the subtleties of diplomacy than in raw power plays, and believed in the former. (This does him moral credit.) Third, he was on the side of law and order. But he was finally undone by his compulsion to try to make *Life*'s lead look foolish; in the end, he was not serious about world affairs, though he was probably more scholarly than I. But in my reading I was always looking for The Point; Goldsborough was looking for the complexities. I was the more superficial. But, as things turned out, I was also right.

For Luce to allow both *Life*'s lead and Goldsborough's undermining of it reveals his distinctly peculiar, or perhaps admirable, ambidexterity, often apparent in the years to come.

The argument continued (February 28, 1938). *Life* said flatly that Hitler had taken the Austrian trick by forcing Premier Schuschnigg to take on a Nazi minister of the interior. In *Time*, Goldsborough countered in a kind of frenzy, "While the world's blatant headlines were yammering as though Germany had already swallowed Austria politically . . . a customs union is now highly probable."

The *Life* focus turned (March 7, 1938) to Neville Chamberlain and the British cabinet split: "If either of those powers [Germany and Italy] fight England this year, their chances of winning would be better than in 1940. . . . Chamberlain would rather wait until England has its usual 60–40 chance of winning any fight it gets into." With this one obvious fact, any *Life* reader could safely predict the history of the next three years and win all his bets with *Time* readers. Elsewhere, it was pointed out, "Most of Europe believes that the next move in Fascist Germany's long projected drive to the East will be an attempt to gobble prosperous Czechoslovakia." *Life* had assumed that Austria was lost.

Meanwhile, *Time* had a story that Schuschnigg was defying Germany, and in the next issue (March 14) *there was no Austrian story at all.* For the following issue Schuschnigg supplied *Time*'s cover.

Against an American background (March 14, 1938) of New Orleans Mardi Gras and the insane (9 pages) and an utterly unfair description of the great circus gorilla, Gargantua, as "a murderous paranoiac," *Life* had more on fascism: "It is not hard to start a Fascist movement in Europe"—fourteen nations had them, and Belgium had three. The leader must find people with a grievance and tell them that "life is hard and heroic and they are heroes. He makes them look more or less heroic by putting them in uniforms. . . . What America cannot realize is that Europe's rages are almost always 'justified' by things that happened centuries ago."

The German army and Hitler entered Austria on Saturday, March 12, the *Life* issue closing date (March 21, 1938), so that *Life* gave it only two pages: "Austria Goes Nazi and Hitler Follows the German Army into His Native Land." But how would Goldsborough in *Time* cover his tracks? It was easy. First, he blunted the point with a story of German Ambassador Ribbentrop lunching with British Prime Minister Chamberlain, saying that it was "hours before incredulous official London believed the occupation of Austria was taking place." In that case, Goldsborough had been no more wrong than the British Establishment. Furthermore, everything had been as Goldsborough had said until Schuschnigg had called for an Austrian plebiscite on whether to join Germany, and Hitler, having one of his sudden intuitions that Germany might lose the plebiscite, invaded Austria. All that is omitted from this perfectly plausible story is the mind of Hitler.

Luce had an enormous respect for success and so *Life* (March 28, 1938) took full overweening credit for its correct prediction of the death (temporary) of Austria, with all of 17 pages of the lead. My copy on this inflated funeral exhibits a certain fatigue; my emotions were the opposite of Luce's. The headline said: "The Austrian Corporal Who Went On Fighting and Finally Won the War." This was followed by a brief picture biography of Hitler and the history from 1870 on of the shift of German power from Vienna to Berlin. As for the Axis plans for the future, with map, I am revealed as having forgotten my sound predictions and drifting into a fantasy scenario: "Hitler's next large objectives are Hungary and Poland, surrounding Czechoslovakia. . . . By this time the realistic Czechs would probably have joined a German customs union and perhaps even given Germany the border strip of Germans. . . . The next step would be war with Russia."

The naïveté of this, especially as regards Czechoslovakia, cannot be excused. There were pictures of Goebbels who "honestly believes . . . the democracies 'are stupid cows going to the slaughterhouse' " and of the German road system: "Action and talk are the twin screws of Fascism . . . toward that day, Germany's great highway system." There were also pictures of the sinking of a Spanish rebel cruiser with this snub to the press: "(*Life* prints the actual photographs, not the phoney retouched versions which were widely printed.)"

The proof of Luce's enlightened generosity (though in the long run not fulfilled in my case) had come in a letter dated March 10, 1938:

March 10, 1938.

Dear Dave:—

On Friday, March 17th a proposal is being submitted to the Annual Stockholders Meeting by which you may be given an opportunity to acquire 100 shares of Time Inc. stock on a special basis.

Pending final adoption of the plan, I would like to give you a rough idea of what it is all about.

First, what is a share of Time Inc. stock? Altogether there are about 237,000 shares. In a year when the net profits of Time Inc. are $2,370,000, then—in the language of finance—Time Inc. has "earned $10 a share." Shares of stock in this company or other companies are often valued roughly at "ten times earnings." On that basis, when Time Inc. earns $10 a share, the market price of a share would be $100. On the same basis, if Time Inc. should earn $4,740,000 in a year, the stock might sell for $200 a share. If the stock should sell for $200 a share, that would place a value of 200 x 237,000 or $47,400,000 on Time Inc. That seems a fantastic valuation for our products. But all things are relative, and such a figure does not seem fantastic when it is noted that a socially insignificant soft drink called Coca Cola can have a stock valuation of over $400,000,000. (And in order to be worth that, Coca Cola has got to advertise!)

Actually, Time Inc. stock has sold at a much higher ratio than ten times earnings. This has happened when there is optimism in the country and when the prospects seem bright for Time Inc. to increase its earnings. On the other hand, Time Inc. stock could sell for less than ten times earnings. This presumably would be when general pessimism prevailed and/or when a number of people thought that Time Inc.'s earnings were more apt to decline than to increase.

Actually, Time Inc. stock has sold as high as $260 a share (a year ago) and in the last six months the price has averaged about $130 a share. (In the last year the tremendous speculation called *Life* has been, of course, the big factor in the market's guess-work about Time Inc. stock.)

Well, what is Time Inc. stock worth?—which is practically the same as asking what will it be worth in some future time? I don't know—nobody does. What do I *think*? I will tell you what I *think*—and I do so only as a senior partner who is willing to make himself ridiculous in the interests of candor among the number of partners. I *think* Time Inc. stock will again sell at $260 a share some day. This opinion is, of course, based on the assumption that America will once again, within five years, achieve a degree of what might be called prosperity. As to whether or not this country is going to hell before it recovers—your opinion is as good as mine.

About the only definite way of saying what a share of stock is worth is to look up today's market quotation to see what you can get for it. The market tells us that Time Inc. stock is worth $130. But this information is not nearly so valuable in the case of Time Inc. as it would be in the case of, say, General Motors, because the market for Time Inc. stock is a "very thin market"—that is, there is not much actual buying and selling and hence the market reflects the opinion of only a comparatively few people and, secondly, it does not tell us what anybody would pay for a large amount of Time Inc. stock.

Now, roughly, the plan proposed for you is that you should be given a chance to buy 100 shares of Time Inc. stock for $100 a share, in easy instalments of a period of *five* years. The plan is that you should pay for this in the following instalments by salary deductions:

1st year	$500
2nd "	1,500
3rd "	2,000
4th "	2,000
5th "	2,000

Ah, but that only adds up to $8,000 whereas 100 shares at $100 a share equals $10,000. What about the other $2,000? Our idea is that it is not necessary to lay down any definite schedule at this time for the payment of the last $2,000. In general, it is thought that if you proceed toward the purchase of the full 100 shares, and if Time Inc. enjoys the prosperity in which it is desired that you should share, you may receive salary raises or bonuses which will enable you to make payments on the additional 20 shares,—whereas if Time Inc. does not enjoy prosperity you will probably not want to complete the purchase anyway.

I will not attempt to make a technical explanation of the plan. Your publisher will answer any questions as to detail after consent of the stockholders is obtained and after the actual purchase agreement has been submitted to you for your consideration. But here are some of the proposed provisions: (1) You can cancel this agreement as to future payments if the market price of the stock goes under 100 and stays there for some fair period of time to be specified. (2) If you leave the employ of the company at any time you can take with you the stock you have actually paid for (at $100 per share) but you are not entitled to purchase any more. (3) During the five year period, if you stay in the employ of the company, you will be required to keep the stock deposited with the company and therefore cannot sell it or borrow on it. (4) After five years, the stock is yours outright without strings.

This offer will be made to about 50 people. With a few exceptions they are:

1. People (not in the Advertising Department) who are getting $10,000 or more salary and who have been here two years.

2. People in the Advertising Department who are getting $12,000 or more and who have been here two years.

(This difference reflects the fact that in this business advertising men seem to have a higher rate of pay than others for what might be regarded as equivalent seniority.)

In conclusion, let me tell you not what I think and certainly not what the company promises, but what our hopeful intention is regarding this plan. We hope that Time Inc. stock will deservedly go to $250 a share and stay there (or higher) for a while. We hope it will be there, or higher, five years hence, however it may gyrate in between. That would mean that your 100 shares would be worth $25,000. That is not a fortune, but it is a substantial lump of capital—it is something for you to show financially for your labors over and above a good living during the next five years. Lots of things can happen in five years. Some of you, if we have prosperity, may make and put aside more either in salary raises, bonuses or even other stock offers. But $25,000 is the least which we hope everyone will have, who has contributed an important amount of creative or managerial or selling effort to publications which have the profit possibilities which ours seem to have.

Sincerely,

HENRY R. LUCE

A revolution in employee policy, recognizing the lower echelons, appeared (April 4, 1938) with a listing of editorial associates in the masthead. Including those added in the next issue they were: Rachel Albertson, Margaret Bassett, Ruth Berrien (my assistant), Alan Brown, Judith Chase, Mary Fraser (evidently an emeritus listing), Frank Hall Fraysur, Dorothy Hoover, Sally Kenniston, Alexander King, Dorothy Jane Larson, Margaret MacFarquhar, A. K. Mills, Willard D. Morgan, Helen Robinson, Roxanne Ruhl, Bernice Shrifte, and Margaret Varga.

At the same time the hierarchy was formulated. Editor: Luce.

Managing Editor: John Shaw Billings, for the first time in his career sole managing editor of a magazine. Associate Editors: Longwell and Hicks. Assistant Editors: Howard Richmond (Art), Hubert Kay, David Cort, Paul Peters, Joseph J. Thorndike, Jr., Joseph Kastner, Geoffrey Hellman, Andrew Heiskell, Lincoln Barnett, Maria Sermolino.

The nonalphabetical listing indicated a pecking order in which I am subordinate to Kay. This was proper. *Life* lived primarily on its American news; Foreign News was still a spectacular, often horrifying extra. America, I recognized, had not entirely accepted the fact that Europe existed.

The celebrated "balance" of the issue combined a family on relief, the circus, France's Devil's Island, and Eton.

An irrelevancy added to *Life*'s fame (April 11, 1938) with pictures from "The Birth of a Baby" movie, which some cities wanted to censor. *Life* played the martyrization to the hilt. In the same issue was "The Nine Kennedy Kids Delight Great Britain"—Bobby and Teddy being the most conspicuous. A story on the Rebel bombing of Barcelona added, "France . . . dares not risk expensive weapons for what her staff officers now feel is a cause already lost" (the Loyalist cause). Of a German-aggrandizing map distributed by the Nazis, it was said, "Much more immediate and ominous is the German tide lapping the Western boundaries of Czechoslovakia . . . of which Bismarck said, 'The master of Bohemia is the master of Europe.' "

A fine piece of sanity (April 18, 1938) was Kay's lead reporting that Congress, fearful of Roosevelt dictatorship, voted down his reorganization bill. In a democracy, it was observed, "The difference . . . is not in the leader, but in those led." A spread showed Roosevelt and the dictators doing many of the same things (such as being nice to babies), but explained that the new dictators had learned to mimic standard democratic practices for propaganda purposes.

A company statement was made (May 2, 1938) on the attempts to censor "The Birth of a Baby" issue, which had aroused "more controversy than any magazine article had ever before aroused."

Various executives had offered to be nailed on the cross in various cities. The thing had a meretricious nobility about it, for its idea content was invisible to me, but the executives felt wonderful. They had invented childbirth; unfortunately, none could achieve parturition at the moment.

The lead noted that General Pershing was still alive, and Jewish veterans were shown trying to break up an American Nazi meeting. Hitler had provided a ship to let German servants of Englishmen vote in the plebiscite on the absorption of Austria. They voted 99.4% *Ja.* "These amazing percentages, largely honest despite proved examples of false returns, show the real effectiveness of Nazi demagogy. . . . Its secret is to deal with the people not as individuals but as crowds. The message to the crowd is a series of simple, basic, memorable words—nation, people, blood, family, comrade, friend, home, soil, bread, work, strength, hope, life, fight, victory, birth, death, honor and beauty. The Party is set up as having a monopoly on giving the people these virtues and good things. To a people whose immediate past has been hard, muddled and apparently irremediable, simple emotional words have an immense, reverberating authority."

Billings had three prejudices: one against Indians (shriveling *Life*'s coverage of most of Latin America) and others in favor of pigs and railroads. The last produced an essay here on the Southern Railroad (8 pages).

The next issue (May 9, 1938) gave 12 pages to summer fashions and 10 to Italy's version of Fascism—the Corporative State. I think this was not by me, perhaps by Paul Peters.

As this issue went to press, on the last two days of April 1938, the editorial offices were moved from the Chrysler Building to the so-called Time-Life Building, in Rockefeller Center between Forty-eighth and Forty-ninth streets. For, since the founding of *Life*, 229 new hands had been added to the 650 of 1936, and Time Inc. badly needed the top seven floors of the new building.

Not the worst way to see into a journalistic operation is to study the arrangement of offices. Thus, the floor plans of the editorial departments of *Life* and *Time* are inserted on the following pages.

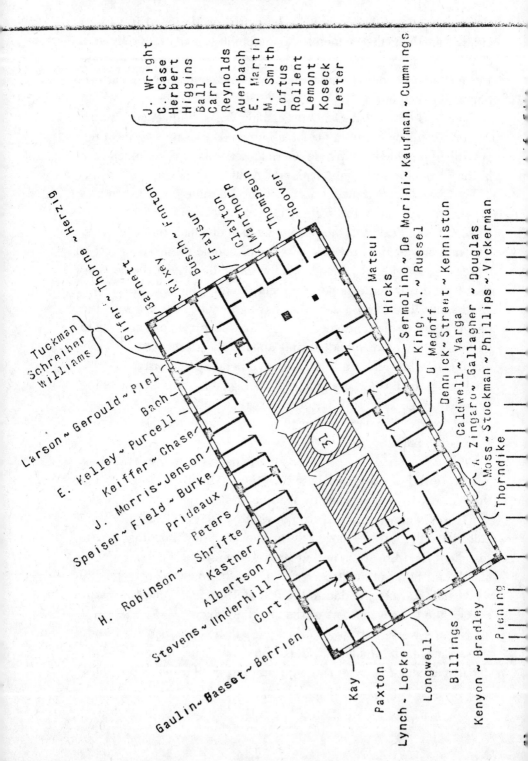

Duffy ~ Ffann
Bauer ~ Garrison
Dieman ~ Barrett
Jewett

Borgida ~ Jackson F. Pratt
North ~ Holsworth ~ McCreery
Stevenson ~ Lincoln
Bigman ~ Marx
Sacartoff ~ Lent
Durand ~ Baker ~ deBlasio
Peckham ~ Norden
Orthman

McCullough
Wertenbaker
Bayles
Hersey
Calliett
Swados
Svirsky
Sargeant
Peyton
Taylor
Osborne
Olson
Cantwell
Ach ~ Best
Hind ~ Mickey

J.S. Martin
Hamburger
Scott
S. Welles
Kroll
Stockly
Hyman ~ Sundholm
Darling ~ Chapin
Lowe
Solberg ~ Krug
Fogel-Ryan ~ Mackenzie
Kimmerle ~ Hulburd
Kellam ~ Budelman
Merz ~ Tasker
Fones - Boyd
Terzo ~ Hopkins
Shor ~ Stover ~ Hanley
Plaster ~ Lewin ~ Weigel
Arrigoni ~ Stearn ~ Saul
Vogel

TELEPHONE ROOM
MORGUE
29
MORGUE
TELGEL
MORGUE

Gottfried
Norris
Matthews
Kronenberger
Chambers
Goldsborough

Time Edit.

29th Floor

Billings and Longwell are at the hub. Hubie Kay is still National Affairs editor in a corner office. Piening is still art director, with his successor, Paxton, already on the scene.

There was good news for Luce (May 16, 1938) in the lead, "China Puts the Japanese Army on the Run"—a victory at Taierhchwang. With pictures of atrocities, these had "(1) solidified China . . . (2) demoralized Japanese military discipline." Billings at this point evolved, out of his reporter's need to blanket the week's news, an editorial page condensing the week's events into the shortest possible space. Probably Kay and I wrote it; certainly we wrote all subsequent ones.

The lead (May 23, 1938) was "Two Little Men Meet in Rome": "Adolf Hitler (5 ft. 8) and Benito Mussolini (5 ft. 7) . . . the tiny dictators were only distinguishable by the khaki chauffeur's cap that Hitler affects, the black Shriner-type fez that tops Il Duce's official uniform . . . the fascist dictatorships, if pressed too far, can present to the world the greatest military machine now in existence, . . . a most unofficial promise from Il Duce to give Adolf Hitler free rein in Czechoslovakia." On the editorial page this was backed up by "Czechoslovakia was still the nation with most to fear immediately from any strengthening of Hitler's hand by Mussolini." An attack on Roosevelt was a revealing chart of the amounts spent in each state and per capita of population. "If [the figures] mean what they appear to mean . . . then the charge that the New Deal has spent and lent its Relief and Recovery billions in the way best calculated to keep itself in power is true. If there is a more convincing explanation, *Life* will be glad to hear and print it." For another dictator, here came Franco on a throne—"a pose no other fascist dictator has assumed . . . he will set up a totalitarian state differing from Germany's and Italy's."

The next cover (May 30, 1938) was of the eye-patched Czech General Syrovy, and *Life* began to apply its enormous power for emphasis to the endangered nations of Europe, *before the event.* The title was "Czechoslovakia: *Life* Presents a Pictorial Survey of a Democracy Defending Its Life." Numerous memoranda had gone to Margaret Bourke-White and John Phillips, the photographers, who received Czech cooperation. This essay ran to 16 pages.

"Czechoslovakia," it began, "born of the last war, and liable to perish in the next, is today the tinderbox of Europe. Already the iron jaws of Greater Germany surround it on three sides. . . . The conglomeration of peoples . . . the Germans of Bohemia . . . the Slovaks of Slovakia . . . the Ruthenians of the East who are Slavic, rural and very poor. . . . President Benes has never been known to tell a joke. He converses in numbered paragraphs, but he is the shrewdest little statesman in Europe. . . . Under the Habsburgs, the Germans had a favored economic position which has since been taken from them by the Czechs. . . . Altogether, Bohemia is a mighty tempting morsel to be left around in the middle of Europe."

My policy, accepted by *Life*, was to cross-examine the supposed innocence of this prospective victim democracy. Thus, of the Sudeten Germans, "Most of them are anti-militarist and Catholic. They would make poor soil for Hitlerism were it not for the fact that they have a genuine grievance—unemployment." Then under Nazi pictures of the Sudeten slums: "These are propaganda pictures. As such they are suspect, but no neutral observer denies that the condition that they represent is largely true." Furthermore, since most Czech exports went out on German rails, Germany "can strangle Czechoslovakia to industrial death." Furthermore, Czech industries "parallel almost exactly those of Germany."

Prague was shown as "not only one of the oldest capitals in Europe but one of the most beautiful," with "an ancient and honorable reputation of liberalism . . . kept its Jews in a ghetto, the Josefstadt, but they were not molested."

After such an act, *Life* could not return at length to Czechoslovakia for some months. This meant that the story must predict Czech history for that period; *Life* was in the business of soothsaying, at least in foreign news. Clearly, the story said that Czechoslovakia's case was far from perfect and would probably be lost. Since it was not guaranteed by England, but only by France and Russia, and readers had been told how England felt about fighting in 1938, the destiny of Czechoslovakia had been indicated correctly. My phrase, about perishing in the next war, was sloppy thinking and writing in the attempt to make an effect.

I must think that Luce saw the leverage such a story gave him on world politics, if he had a writer who sounded honest and even-handed, speaking credibly to the reader in terms of the latter's grasp of reality. I am sure he recognized the supreme value of honest writers. This story gave the reader the feeling that *Life* was working hard to give him solid value, whatever his prejudices.

The real blame for Czechoslovakia, as I once developed in a novel, *The Minstrel Boy*, must be laid on, first, Clemenceau, who fiendishly carved it out, and, second, Henry Cabot Lodge, who prevented the United States from taking responsibility for Woodrow Wilson's creation. Neither had envisioned Hitler. And their grand-sons were to pay the price. (This could not have been expressed at the time, though it was my point of view.)

Pathetically, in the editorial notes of this issue, is a reference to Harry Hopkins, WPA Administrator, "who was last week reported engaged to marry a pretty ex-actress named Dorothy Hale, whom he had met a few weeks before" (presumably through the Luces).

Though I have no dates, I might introduce the matter of the Newspaper Guild's intrusion into Time Inc. The original idea was that everybody would automatically become a member of the Guild. My usual claustrophobia closed me in, I began circulating a petition to the management demanding that we not be locked in any guild or union. Now that I think of it, this happened about six months earlier, but the date is not important. I asked a friend on *Time*, Helen Vind, to spread the petition among the checkers. I had collected almost unanimous signatures among the writers, and Helen had given me a good list of the checkers' signatures when she pleaded with me to have her name stricken from the list, which was done. The Guild had terrorized her. Its president at the time, I believe, was Cameron Mackenzie, of an aristocratic family some of whom I had known socially. It was my understanding that he was a Communist, of whatever status or degree of commitment I did not know. The Communists at that point had managed to capture the Time Inc.

Newspaper Guild, and I still find this a reason for hilarity since, if all the writers on *Life* had gone on strike, I was confident that Hubie Kay and myself could have produced the written part of the magazine unassisted. Without checkers, I would have had to write more cautiously, but I knew I could have done this for months on end without straining. This was my opinion of the Newspaper Guild.

Cameron Mackenzie invited me to a Guild meeting to make my point, and I accepted. I was labeled a "Fascist." Since the exact words were of the utmost importance in Communist circles, I typed my speech and went to the Guild meeting. All sorts of parliamentary nonsense dragged on, and I sat holding my speech. Finally, as I remember, Mackenzie introduced a subject to which my speech was vaguely tangential, and I stood up to begin reading from my paper. Mackenzie interrupted to say that it was irrelevant. I countered feebly that I was building up to a point. My nervousness and anger were making my hand shake so that I could hear my papers rattle. Another interruption, and I answered with more violence and my hand stopped shaking. I was suddenly happy.

I think the speech I delivered was the following:

To the leaders and members of the Time Inc. unit of the Newspaper Guild:

My signature to the petition against a "closed shop" in Time Inc. represented my opinion, which must necessarily be valuable to an organization that pretends to the moral right to speak for me and asks now for the empiric legal right. Naturally I do not want an organization of which I am not a member to ask my employer to fire me unless I join the organization. The fact that my opinion is contrary to that of the leaders of the Guild and the unanimous vote of the Guild does not make me a pawn of The Interests nor make me an enemy of the Guild. As for my ignorance of "the issues involved," the issues involved are as follows:

1. The "Guild Shop" is an absolutely open shop, as the Guild claims, to anyone not now employed by Time Inc. In speaking of it in the newspapers, one might perhaps use the term, open shop. It is, however, a closed shop as it affects all people now employed by Time Inc., in other words, the parties to the transaction. In speaking of it among ourselves, no other term but closed shop is possible. (Whatever the reputation of the term, "closed shop," has nothing to do with the principles involved.)

2. The closed shop principle was determined by what the Guild describes as the normal "machinery of democratic institutions." The method

was to hold local unit meetings, listen to speeches by leaders largely forwarding one side, elect one representative to a central convention, listen to more similar speeches and vote by acclamation immediately after the speeches were over. This method violates the democratic dogmas of free electioneering for and against, free deliberation before balloting, elimination of mass feeling, and the secret ballot. It is based on the Russian method of representation by soviets which elect to superior soviets which elect to superior soviets and so on, a method based in turn on the "cell" organization necessary in Tsarist Russia to outwit the Cheka secret police. It is somewhat similar to the American nominating convention which nobody has ever suggested is really representative of the people but which is based on the Founding Fathers' idea of a congress of the "best men" who would pick one of their own for the presidency. Anyway, by this method, the *Time* Guild unit voted *unanimously* for the closed or Guild shop. Since the voters were no more unanimous than the signers of the anti–closed shop petition, it may be assumed that they really voted to discard their personal opinion in favor of immediate efficiency.

3. Efficiency is the first and sole count in favor of the closed shop. The efficiency is naturally and rightly directed against the employer but to get it, it seems necessary to slap down individual workers' freedom of decision and action (for their own good). The principle behind this is that the employer can indefinitely bully or cozen the divided workers, i.e., that the worker is not individually sane, trustworthy or responsible. This principle does not apply at least to Time Inc. *Time* employees are perfectly capable of judging the employers by their acts and acting on their decisions, possibly flocking to the Guild. In the meantime, they may honestly be unwilling to have decisions made for them by any representative agency other than the U.S. Government.

4. The Guild's claim that they are a U.S. *in petto* is a laughable metaphor. The sovereign nation of the *Time* Guild unit bars from citizenship certain residents of the premises, namely, those people rated as "employers," and is in fact in a declared state of civil war with those people. It is thus a nation founded on a fixed policy of civil war, representing some people more, some people less, some people not at all. The Guild is more properly a Tammany or Republican Party or Self-Help Society for People With Ash-Blond Hair. I am no more bound by the Guild than by such a society as the last-named whose majority decisions could not possibly persuade me to dye my hair black. I am already a citizen of the U.S.A. and that finishes my citizenship affiliations. If the Guild, quite properly, dislikes getting benefits for people who did not work for them, let it make its benefits apply only to Guild members and dues-payers. Then nonmembers would join quickly enough.

5. The civil war conception of the labor movement in the U.S. does not

seem the inevitable or desirable one. There is no reason for anybody getting seriously mad, particularly since labor in its fight with capital for management and perhaps eventually ownership holds all the cards, in such a country as the U.S. It does not need moral force to win, or any force except the overwhelming persuasiveness of the greater good of the greatest number. (This omits another story—what happens when labor victorious begins to run as afoul of the consumers, the bystanders, as capital now does.) The main issue is that a labor movement invites all of us to grow up a little by joining in management and government. That means that all of us throw our weight, not pass the buck to hard-working leaders who will grow up 100 times as fast while we grow up $\frac{1}{100}$ as fast. The Guild, given pause by its first setbacks, might well now consider seriously whether it is really so frightened that it must resort to questionable means of getting phony unanimity for obviously glorious ends. History cynically shows us the graves of the glorious ends while the bad means, used to get them, remain and prosper.

I think it is now clear that the writer was stupid to allow himself to be unionized. For example, in New York City, the neanderthal unions have destroyed a large number of newspapers that gave a voice to writers. I don't give a damn about how typographers or mailers or truck drivers support their appetites. In destroying the newspapers, they destroyed their jobs, but they could do something else. The writer could do nothing else. His vocation was solely to write, and suddenly there was no medium. Heywood Broun, the figurehead of the Newspaper Guild, was a fool. He was a charming man, but he was also a slovenly untalented writer; certainly he could feel, but he could not think very well. That recurrent clown of world history, Philippe Egalité, is seen again in Heywood Broun. In his kindly maunderings, we can see the first intimations of the demoralization, and perhaps the eventual dissolution, of America.

I feel the need for a sort of apology, for saying that Luce *did not* understand Time Inc., Roosevelt, Hitler, or the imminent World War II, and that I *did* understand them all. These were new phenomena that a "responsible" man such as Luce was baffled by, but a fluid irresponsible man such as myself took them into himself without difficulty. (Yes, I even had a partial empathy with Hitler. I missed his signals several times, but he and I were both glory men. Hitler created a total madness, but based on eternal human instincts, and he had the loyalty of the German people to the end. Only the aristocrats planned to kill him. This says something about a society's need for an aristocracy to defend it against blackguards.)

On the subject of blackguards, there is in my files another document on the Newspaper Guild; I have no recollection of its purpose. Here it is:

I should like to begin by saying one thing you already know very well. It is that, by right, wages are not a favor done the workers by the management, any more than our work is a favor done the management by us or, indeed, than the commodities we help produce are a favor done the consumers by Time Inc. The Guild has done well to assert in this organization this primary social principle and to put that principle in contract form. Everything else anyone can say is supplementary to this fact.

One other basic fact I want to add to the frame within which we all have occasion to be sitting here. Who owns the company that pays us the wages for our services? It is not, I submit, the officers or the stockholders or, even, we, the workers. It is of course the consumer, the people who buy *Time*, *Fortune*, *Life*, and the *Architectural Forum* who give them a reason for surviving and us a reason for helping to produce them. This is important in the large view. It means that the stockholders' rights and the officers' rights and our rights do not really amount to much except to us. The paramount right is civilization's right to the best possible magazines it can get. We are all consumers in far more roles of our lives than we are producers. It is important to remember that our aspirations as producers are primarily a selfish, although just, grab for more of the dough involved in this act of production.

If the labor movement in this country and this organization is only a grab, the only gauge of an admirable labor organization is effectiveness. Then I can see the desirability of a strong unified fist of guild with strong authoritative leaders speaking for totalitarian groups of workers. On that line, anybody who speaks a word to disrupt a united front is a class traitor and anything but a closed shop is inconceivable. I admit that there is something very tempting, very relaxing about the emotional conviction of people who propose this. On that line it is reasonable to suspect the solidarity of anyone like myself who criticizes Guild policies and methods, anyone who does not join the Guild. For on that line you are in a fight and who is not for you is against you.

I do not believe that that future is the only possible choice for the Guild. It ignores the most effective tactic in the whole book, the tactic of seeming to be calm and just, of making a good impression on the bystanders. And it is the bystander who decides all fights. Labor and the Guild can impose on itself of its own free will the disciplines based on the hard realities of its part in society. I am not speaking here of its first obligation to the consumer and its corollary obligation ultimately to take a part in management. I am speaking of its secondary obligation to its fellow workers.

For hitherto mysterious reasons, some Time workers have declined the opportunity to join the Guild. The Guild now proposes that they be permitted to stay out of the Guild and that new employees be compelled to join the Guild after three months. This proposal suggests that I will give up the principle of an open shop willingly in exchange for not being bothered. The preferential shop, so-called, seems to be a bribe offered a few eccentrics in ivory towers to forget the world entirely. The question now asked is whether these men of whim will accept this bribe.

Is not the way to find out to ask why they have not already joined the Guild and why they opposed the Guild Shop (which, for reasons inherent in the past history of the union movement, must not be called the closed shop)?

I think very few workers oppose the Guild. Unions are a little step toward bringing the little men into affairs, toward making them think and grow a little older. The Guild justified its existence in Time Inc. solely by raising the pay of researchers. But the role of the individual in the Guild is an individual problem. The Guild can do nothing for one individual; another individual just does not join clubs; still another, already controlled by the orders of his business superiors, does not wish to add to his compulsions the orders of his fellow workers. Nobody gives up a liberty without a substantial reward. Some workers say, in effect, that in the long run the Guild will be too big to buck or too little to bother with. Some workers believe that the Guild's procedure is not democratic.

I understand that votes here have been taken by secret ballot. But I know that the Guild frequently votes by show of hands. Pathetic as it may sound, the average man is not ordinarily willing to back up his opinion to the extent of being unpopular with his fellow men. It is a hard man who will raise his hand alone. Nobody wants to be conspicuous, to be out of step. Few are able to get up on their feet and say, coherently and convincingly, why they think their way is right, and keep on saying it. There are relatively few hung juries. And yet the Guild, if it is to keep its conscience and resilience, must find and cultivate contrary opinions.

For today the Time Guild is a club, subject to the familiar vices of clubs. It is not a democracy. For democracy means putting one's vote silently in a ballot box without explanation. It does not mean being as expert at debate and parliamentary procedure and log-rolling and back-slapping as a Republican national committeeman. The Guild has no claim to the analogy of corresponding to the whole body politic of the United States. It is, more exactly, a national convention. And it is a permanent convention, representing just one set of interests, one place and one party line, going on year after year, collecting dues, giving a workout to professional leaders who like the hobby of leadership. Meanwhile, the workers, who the world over are just guys trying to get along, come to fewer meetings, come to no meetings. But still the club goes on. This seems to some Guild spokesmen a highly desirable arrangement, for they feel that this club will still be mobilized to repel a double-cross by the management.

It might be put in here that the Time management has thus far made no attempt to double-cross the workers, largely because the workers' value in this organization decreases sharply if they come to distrust the management. In fact, the Guild has not needed 100% membership to get its present contract. This management seems anxious to keep the confidence of its workers. We are asked to believe, however, that at some future date this attitude may change. But we are told that the workers' conscience and common sense will by then have atrophied so far that, without a neat little club with all dues paid up, the workers will be lost. I have no such pessimism about the intelligence and courage of Time workers, nor has anyone else. I certainly am not so pessimistic about my own conscience and common sense. And I find myself extremely reluctant, on such a story, to surrender my conscience and common sense to a formal hierarchy of club leaders, who are answerable to other super-club leaders I never heard of.

The unit is not the Guild. The unit is the total of Time workers. Whatever clubs exist within that unit, we are all Time workers. And all our voices have merit.

These perorations convinced the "Popular Front" at Time Inc. that I was a company stooge or Fascist; I suspect that I had also convinced management that I was their boy. Hubie Kay had told me that the Newspaper Guild was either too little to bother with or too big to buck. But I had an emotion which nothing could prevent me from expressing. Since I knew myself, and had for some years, I did not even react to the idea that I was a management stooge.

Being misunderstood at Time Inc. was nothing new to me. I had concealed the fact that I was a published and talented writer before I came to Time Inc. I never referred to my previous career. My role at Time Inc. was always a sort of masquerade of pretendimg to be less than I was. Some people thought I was a Communist; others thought I was a Fascist. It was all one to me.

A little more authority in the military captions around this time makes me think of something else.

An important event in *Life*'s history was the appearance at the reception desk of a slightly cross-eyed young man with a scrapbook in which *Life*'s military captions were pasted, followed by statements about the weapons. (We were usually wrong.) As soon as I saw this work, I demanded that John Garrett Underhill, Jr., a Harvard man, one of the *Harvard Lampoon* crowd that raised the Soviet flag on the White House lawn, be put on the payroll. I do not know when this took place. I suppose that he was first hired as a consultant, and later full time.

My dream of being infallible about the weapons shown in pictures suddenly became possible. Probably Underhill was already the world's No. 1 expert on comparative weaponry but, with the benefit of *Life*'s pictures, he soon became so. His grandfather had been a general and founder of the American Rifle Association, as I recall. Billings never accepted him but I cherished him. With him, *Life*'s Foreign News department became one of the most knowledgeable centers of military intelligence in the world. All my subsequent feats of military reporting owe 60 percent of the credit to Underhill, and I think my retention of even 40 percent is pure conceit.

After Pearl Harbor the army grabbed him for G-2. Interrogations there were by five colonels and one sergeant (Underhill). A colonel would ask a stupid question. The sergeant would add, "What the colonel wants to know is . . ." I lost touch with him after I left Time Inc. Much later, I discovered that he had committed suicide in Washington, D.C., lying in bed, shooting himself behind the ear, the pistol dropping beneath the sheet, so that a friend looking in on him on two separate visits did not realize he was dead. For his peculiar specialty had gone out of fashion; his kind of thinking (and to some extent mine) had become anathema. I am sure that his execution of his own murder was ballistically perfect, with consummate awareness of what the weapon could perform. Anything less would have shamed him. For both selfish and patriotic reasons I revere his memory. In his function on *Life*, he helped steer America into the correct courses of rearmament. At least in one magazine, the intuitions of the German and British general staffs were available to any American who would trouble to read.

A truly queer thing is that, for some years after I began using his services, *Time* ignored Underhill and took on an amateur military expert or so. At long last—I don't remember when—*Time* borrowed his services and bent beneath the shock of meeting the pure military classicist. This was part of what was wrong with *Time*.

Life continued with its refinement of the art of emphasis. A whole issue (June 6, 1938) was given to the youth of America, except for pictures on the childish behavior of two French playwrights, Henry Bernstein and Edouard Bourdet, in fighting a duel, with Paul Morand as a witness. Bourdet was pinked; both stayed mad.

The Japanese bombing and shelling of China (June 20, 1938) promoted the line, "Dead Men Have Indeed Died in Vain If Live Men Refuse to Look at Them," to a banner headline. Some weapon details—"Divisional artillery does not exceed 6-in. and consists chiefly of 3-in. (75 mm.) fieldpieces for general service"—show the hand of Underhill, I suspect.

A dividend from *Life*'s increasing prestige came (June 20, 1938) with the first pictures ever permitted by the U.S. Senate to be taken from the floor during a session, these by Thomas McAvoy. One of Alex King's gags was a midget shown lifesize across two pages. A long essay was given to Congo Negroes, including the eight-foot-tall Watusi aristocrats, with a court etiquette as strict as that of Louis XIV. There was not even discussion of whether such people should govern themselves, as they were doing a generation later.

An intrusion here is part of the contract expressing in hedged terms the generosity of Time Inc. to selected employees. It can be skipped, or it will inspire various feelings in various readers. One of the liabilities of getting rich, I suppose, is that one must read such documents as this carefully. I don't believe I read it.

Agreement dated June 21, 1938, between Time, Incorporated, a New York corporation (hereinafter called Time), and David Cort (herinafter called the Purchaser).

Whereas, for the purpose of strengthening Time through the acquisition by its employees and employees of its subsidiaries of a proprietary interest therein, Time has determined to sell to such employees shares of its Common Stock without par value (hereinafter called Time Stock) on the terms and conditions hereinafter set forth; and

Whereas, the Purchaser is one of such employees, and is willing to undertake to purchase the shares of Time Stock hereinafter referred to on the terms and conditions hereinafter set forth;

Now, therefore, Time and the Purchaser hereby agree as follows:

1. Time agrees to sell to the Purchaser and the Purchaser agrees to purchase from Time, at $100.00 per share, in the respective instalments and upon the other conditions hereinafter set forth, an aggregate of 100 shares of Time Stock.

2. 80 of such shares (hereinafter called the First Shares) shall be purchased in the following instalments:

      On July 1, 1939.. 5 Shares
      On July 1, 1940 .... 15 Shares
      On July 1, 1941.. 20 Shares
      On July 1, 1942.. 20 Shares
      On July 1, 1943.. 20 Shares . . .

My career compels me to find this sort of thing very funny.

The great question of who should govern themselves (still far from solved and certainly not interchangeable terms for lawyers or politicians) was raised (June 27, 1938) in a story on the Slovaks, demonstrating against the Czechs, like the Germans. "In 1918 they were hardly competent to govern themselves. Since then the Czechs have spent vast sums on schools and roads for the Slovaks and Ruthenians. The Slovaks are now ready to govern themselves."

Both Hitler and I understood that gratitude is not a human emotion. The Slovaks, even more effectively than Hitler, destroyed Czechoslovakia, even as Tito's Croats destroyed Yugoslavia. (Today in America we have the Negroes, the women, the children, the Chicanos, the homosexuals, and, I would hope, the dogs and cats, most enslaved.)

The "*Life* Looks Back" feature also looked to the "birth of Czechoslovakia" in the United States in 1918 with old pictures showing Masaryk's map that did not include the Sudetenland in the nation its founders envisioned. The lead proposed, on the basis of opinion polls, that a majority of Americans disapproved of the New Deal (worse than Czechoslovakia) but that Negroes liked Roosevelt the best (interesting in view of the recent Negro discovery that both Lincoln and Roosevelt were racists—and why not Jesus Christ?).

Most of the magazine was given to a tourist look at America. This included the field of Gettysburg, which I had just visited with my wife and, I think, the photographer Carl Mydans. I described the battle, noting that "European military observers . . . had never seen or heard of anything in European history to match [Pickett's] charge or the ferocity of the fighting on both sides." (Hitler seems to have missed this issue.) I had just read Freeman's *R. E. Lee* and was the local authority on the event.

A fascinating memorandum went from me to Hicks (8 copies), to which Hicks replied apologetically.

Some modification must be made in the present Picture Department system of showing all choice Foreign News pictures directly to the Managing Editor. Without grudging Mr. Hicks his personal satisfaction, it is apparent that the Picture Department is not adequately selling Foreign News pictures to the Managing Editor. The pictures are not getting into the magazine. They are now being "sold" with about the degree of knowledge that the *New York Times* rotogravure section has at its disposal. The Picture Department, despite valiant effort at omniscience, cannot know why the Foreign News Department asked for a particular set of pictures, hence cannot often properly "sell" them. The Suez Canal stockholders meeting, a priceless pair of pictures taken at the specific request of the Foreign News editor, is a case in point. The Canton bombing pictures, pre-sold by the Foreign News Department, which was then ignored as later pictures came in, is another example of scandalous lack of cooperation by the Picture Department.

Standout pictures may well be shown the Managing Editor by the Picture Department directly. The Foreign News department will willingly continue to show the rest of the pictures that do not rate the Picture Department's attention. But a strong request is hereby entered that the Foreign News Editor be personally informed hereafter, by memorandum or word of mouth, of any and all Foreign News pictures that go directly to the Managing Editor.

After a lead on the stock market boom (July 4, 1938) an odd interjection was on Sweden, irrelevant to the European crisis but obviously intended by Luce as a reproach to the New Deal: "supremely a democracy, a land of private initiative, a society midway between private initiative and iron Socialism . . . on the Swedish principle that the consumer has rights fully equal to those of either Capital or Labor." This last, I think, echoes my remarks to the Newspaper Guild. Contrary to Time Inc. practice, credit is given a book, Childs' *Sweden: The Middle Way*. A pun was illustrated with a picture of Shirley Temple before the Lincoln Memorial and the inscription, "In this temple as in the hearts of the people . . ." Anyone is allowed his opinion of this atrocity. But there it is.

Luce produced a memorandum on "Redefinition of *Life*," dated July 8, 1938, possibly based on my earlier written "Redefinition of *Life*." He too wanted more emphasis on word exposition of stories. He also recognizes "the far-planning essay" without being aware of the need for correct prediction. The dullness of pictures of important people is acknowledged. But, written in the months leading up to Munich, all omission of a grasp of the international situation is striking. (Luce believed that the Czechs would fight, while I hardly think *Life*'s readers thought so.) His memorandum tries to be an outline of a doctoral thesis on what *Life* was all about, or should have been about. Thus, Foreign News is put on the same level as Sport and Personalities competing for two issues a month. And the memorandum ends with the colossal fallacy, "the magazine is the sum of its parts."

The order of the list of people to whom it is addressed may have some significance: "Hicks, Kay, Thorndike, Cort, Heiskell, Kastner." Thorndike's preceding me, Heiskell's preceding Kastner, were at the time peculiar. Some dissatisfaction with the layout department may be read into the piece. A drift toward downgrading of the writer, the word talent, may be suspected. The analysis does not even notice the factor of credible communication with the reader, or the reader's growing trust in the writer, but instead is deeply concerned with the cumulative credit the magazine gets for its allocation of pages to various departments. It is the approach of a banker to how hard his money is working. Here is the memorandum:

July 8th, 1938.

Memo to: Messrs HICKS
              KAY
              THORNDIKE
              CORT
              HEISKELL
              KASTNER

Herewith a *strictly confidential* document called "Redefinition of *Life*." It is *not* intended as a piece of coherent literature—merely notes to focus practical discussion and practical *decisions* by the editors.

It has been read and discussed to date by Messrs Larsen, Billings, Paine and Dreyfuss.

First discussion resulted in general agreement, except:

1. Pictures to the Editor was loudly voted *in*.
2. It was felt that cover policy developed within the last few months was properly reflecting character of magazine—in contrast to year ago.

Chief departmental discussion turned on Movies and Art. Re Movies it was variously felt (1) that *Life* had not lived up to its original early enthusiasm for movies (2) that there should be more movie material in addition to Movie of the Week—or Movie of the Week should be handled with more angles and (3) in general *Life* had still not adequately succeeded in being that much-desired thing—the middle-class movie-fan magazine.

I send this to you to keep you up to date. A general meeting will be held next week. Meanwhile communicate your points to me now or at any time.

HENRY R. LUCE

Redefinition of *Life*—Part I

First let me define *Life* for today and tomorrow in terms of specific editorial problems which we now recognize. These problems are (not necessarily in order of importance or logic) as follows:

1. *Making the Text Inviting.* The text in *Life* can be improved but it is already extremely good. The trouble is the text doesn't *look* inviting. The problem is to overcome the resistance to reading the text in *Life*. The problem is to get readable text read. It is partly a writing-problem—i.e. headlines, leads, etc. must be more provocative, amusing, what not. But the problem is mainly, I think, a problem in lay-out.

2. *Flip-through.* Advertisers question *Life*'s value because they think people don't spend enough time on it. This is a bum argument but let's grant it. It may be that even some readers feel they don't "get enough out of

Life." Actually, if a reader reads all the text (he does, of course, look at all the pictures—though perhaps with insufficient care) he will get plenty out of *Life* and it will take him a good solid hour or two or three shorter readings. The answer is to get him to read the text (see above). But the answer also is to provide the reader with a few places to settle down. Development of a few more predominantly text-pages is indicated—(such as Traffic or Sweden)—as part of regular pattern. Danger here is that we go too stodgy, high-brow. Being highbrow, our common denominator with low-brows is pictures. Must develop the common touch in word-material. Does not mean writing down—nothing worse. Means dealing vividly, intelligently with facts and subjects of broad interest. Remember Franklin Roosevelt and Captain Patterson, God bless them.

3. *Humor. Life* lacks humor. Photographs reveal the ridiculous. But the ridiculous is not the same as humor. Don't know the answer. Probably must develop humorous drawings. But meanwhile we can stand more humor in the text.

4. *Beauty.* Even when *Life* runs beautiful photographs, they don't always look beautiful. A make-up problem. Beautiful pictures probably need more staging. Also we should be more economical in the matter of giving space to pictures which are either not beautiful or not significant. My hunch is that many of our "gag" pictures would do just as well in smaller space—thus leaving big space to emphasize beauty or significance.

5. *Big Subjects.* In the last few months all of us in various ways have stressed importance of making our take-outs important. There is here a natural but by no means insuperable difficulty. Simply means that *Life*, from Managing Editor down, must be organized to function on two rhythms—the rhythm of the nervous alert news-magazine and *also* the rhythm of the far-planning essay—topical-magazine. In learning this syncopation, we create a great new thing in weekly journalism.

6. *News-coverage.* This is the problem into which we have put most effort with least cheers to date. But again, after solemn re-examination, I, for one, still believe in the news-picture magazine. And I believe results will begin to show from here on. Main thing now is, I think, to stick to it doggedly—and not to be seduced, in the news-parts of the magazine, by the superficial effectiveness of "smash" or "charm" or "flow" or whatnot. Not that it isn't a make-up problem. It is plenty. And any week that the Art department does not contribute at least two useful solutions for effective use of the available news-pictures, it is not doing its part. But, in the words of Mr. Cleveland, the way to get news-coverage is to cover. If we are going to have a non-news or merely topical picture-book, then why a weekly? With a fast printed weekly, the one thing we can capitalize above all other mass magazines is news.

7. *Distinction between News and Feature.* Put Item 5 and Item 6

together. They don't conflict with each other; they help each other. Danger is that we go fuzzy in confusing them. Each is a different kind of pictorial journalism. Together they make a great weekly. Any issue which has a strong popular take-out and swell nervous exciting intelligent news-coverage is an issue we don't have to worry about!

8. *Beginning and Ending.* How to make it clear where one article or section ends and another begins?

9. *Proper Intermingling of Advertising with Editorial Matter.* With relatively little advertising this problem is not acute. With a lot of advertising, perhaps it doesn't matter what we do. But last year it did matter. The fact that the editorial department was swamped with a lot of ads before it was properly geared to handle it did, in my opinion, definitely slow up our editorial development. Every hour that the Managing Editors had to fuss and fume with the exigencies of make-up was an hour taken away from the true functions of editing. And those hours were legion. And even more were the hours wasted by the editorial staff while Managing Editors tried to get things to fit.

10. *Number of Pages.* Whether *Life* should publish 25, 50 or 100 editorial pages an issue, or more finely whether it should publish $48\frac{1}{2}$, $50\frac{1}{4}$ or $51\frac{3}{4}$, is a problem which is more important to *Life* than to any other magazine. *Time* and *Colliers* have a base minimum of, I suppose, about 30 pages,—and a page in either *Time* or *Colliers* is a much cheaper proposition than in *Life*. With those few cheap pages those magazines not only maintain their circulations but are also prepared to support 50 or 60 pages of advertising. *Life* is prepared to publish 50 editorial pages to support only 20 or 25 pages of ads. Let us face the fact frankly that on the face of it, a really good picture magazine appears to be an economically unsound proposition because a really good picture magazine needs: (1) a big page (2) of fine paper and (3) a great many of these pages (4) at a low price to meet the pocketbooks of a wide audience. Should we: (1) reduce the page size? (2) use cheap paper? (3) use fewer pages? (4) raise the price? I still don't quite understand how we have managed to establish a reasonable break-even point despite carrying all these economic burdens. There must be something awful screwey about the economies of all other magazines! Or is *Life* screwey? . . .

Also dated July 8, 1938, another Luce "Strictly Confidential Memorandum" was worth noting. Recognition of the new possibilities of treachery within the organization, inspired by the Newspaper Guild and the Communists, is avowed. The list of assigned photographic essays for the following issues had virtually nothing to do with the magazine as produced, as can be checked in this review of the issues. The Munich crisis made its own rules for coverage of "Germany." "Mexico" was covered in due time, but not on September 19. The suggestions for other essays could have been invented by anybody who read the newspapers, perhaps Mrs. Luce.

Strictly Confidential Memorandum

Herewith the beginnings of an attempt to plan the Photographic Essay further ahead than we have ever done hitherto.

A prime requisite for the Photographic Essay now is not only good photographic material but also a strong editorial point. In most cases a layout and first-draft of the article should be made at least two weeks in advance of going to press.

Incidently, this method of editing involves a problem which we have hitherto ignored—namely the problem of keeping our plans to ourselves. Every editorial worker on *Life* is in a confidential position. But until this idea gets thoroughly understood, the senior editors must take special care to keep our plans confidential.

The following list is, of course, tentative. But it is not only tentative as to subject—it is especially tentative as to angle. In most cases we must have more study before we can settle the angle. What I want to emphasize is that, with some exceptions, an idea for a take-out is not acceptable until the angle has been developed and accepted by the Managing Editor.

The list:

August 1st: *Garment Workers.* A great and famed Trade Union headed by a now near-famed man. *Life* invites you to meet this union. In this case, this itself is probably the angle.

August 8th: An Exploration or Archeology or Natural History act to be discovered. I suggest Archeology in the manner of *Time*'s occasional reviews of Diggers. Modern Man is a great digger-up of his past. He is currently engaged on digging up what? This should take us to strange places, give some beauty, and give us a check-up on man's recent knowledge of his past.

August 15th: *Vivisection. Life* is for it. A highly controversial subject.

August 22nd: *New York Times.* Angle: The U.S. Press is now a great subject of debate at the White House, in the Newspaper Guild, and elsewhere. The issues will be stated in words—and then we show you in words and pictures the finest achievement of the U.S. Press—*The New York Times.*

August 29th: *Housing.* A very special act being developed by Larsen.

September 5th: *Trade Unionism*—its history in the industrial age and particularly in America, story coming to a climax in its almost breathless development in America in the last few years. Angle: Evolution. Subsidiary (and perhaps highly opinionated) angle: to show from the point of view of a Liberal those evolutionary developments which are good or necessary and those which are bad and unnecessary. "Cooperation between Business and Labor" versus The Class War.

September 12th: *Germany:* Scheduled to come out week of the Nuremberg party. Dictators build—what has Hitler built? The new Germany (what there is of it) in stone and plaster. Perhaps Berchtesgaden in color.

September 19th: *Mexico:* Whither is Mexico tending and don't we give a damn—or do we?

September 26th: *The President's Intimates.* The People (*Fortune's* Surveys) don't like the President's Intimate Advisers. Angle: here are the people you think you don't like and maybe you shouldn't.

October 3rd: *Cooking. Life* has never gone into food—food on the plate. Here it takes a big jump into the subject. Angle: Americans don't eat well because they don't cook well. Many subsidiary angles. The Kitchen. Chefs. Canned food.

October 10th: *The American University.* Picture Angle: The spires of learning in America. Carrying on the great tradition of Lux et Veritas. If "the lamps are going out in Europe," how are they faring in America's mass-industrial age? Development of story possibly by A. MacLeish.

October 17th: *The Voters Guide.* Pre-election special issue. Not so much folk-lore stuff about how elections are fought, but news-coverage of how the election situation stands in various states, how the issues shape up, etc. & etc.

October 25th *The Automobile*—the great American dream & gadget.

November 7th: A Hollywood story.

November 14th: A football story.

November 21st: *The South and the New Deal.* The South looked at from the point of view of the present and future impact of the New Deal upon it.

November 28th: Japan—China.

December 5th: Open

December 12th: Music Students in U.S. with special reference to Curtis Institute.

December 19th: Open

December 26th: *Theatre* (color & general estimate of season).

January 16th: *Radio.* Candids of the leading performers.

۰   ۰   ۰

Until further notice, Luce will take principal responsibility for getting these futures set. So it will be my worry. But all who receive this are earnestly requested to suggest alternate ideas for any or all issues. Please send ideas in writing.

Paine will work closely with Luce on these projects. Of course, the usual delegation of responsibility will occur as soon as projects are assigned and under way.

HENRY R. LUCE

July 8th, 1938.

The Canadian Fascists of Quebec (July 18, 1938) provided the lead, as the issue pilloried Barbara Hutton who had "'robbed' the U.S. of $45,000,000, though it is still invested in American securities" and "has probably won the New Deal more votes than Jim Farley." Surely this is rabble-rousing, at least for Republicans.

In the lead "a poet's face" (July 25, 1938) was ascribed to Howard Hughes who had just flown around the world and was shown with seven girls, including Katharine Hepburn. This may have made him a recluse. A comedy bit was added with Mussolini ordering his Fascist leaders to spring over bayonets and through blazing hoops. "No democracy's leader would dare ask his subordinates to put on the absurd performance shown on this page." In contrast, a dignified story on England's Queen Elizabeth said, "Just now the chief requisite for being Queen is not to be Wallis Simpson, Duchess of Windsor. The second is to look and act British. The third is to be as much as possible like Queen Mother Mary."

This is fairly trivial stuff, but Larsen came out with a statement that the "big editorial features" had "established in people's minds the fact that *Life* is 'important.' Before that, *Life* was a sensation, yes, a novelty and interesting—but not important." He added that *Life* would still lose money because of new editoral (dwindling to 64 pages an issue, and my raise was not ruinous) and promotion expenditures. A *Life* group of pollsters found that *Life* readership was 17,300,000, surpassing every other mass magazine. That is, the talent was "important." And it must have occurred to Luce that *he* was "important." He had to accept that the magic power of pictures, as emphasis, had been proved beyond a doubt, beyond his wildest dreams, and that he was about to get rich and powerful in the same measure. And he began to ascribe the fulfilment of this power not to the talent, but to himself and his executives and their brilliant decisions, as in ordering this gratifying poll of the "pass-along" readership of *Life*. But the unseen secret of the power was still the modest direct communication between writer and reader, and the ensuing credibility.

The hidden heartbeat of the magazine was the constant communication between the editors and the picture editor, Wilson Hicks. I have a cumulus of these which a historian may wish to examine some day but they need not burden the reader. As seen above, I had criticized Hicks' procedure and his reply came back in due course:

> You certainly should have been called in on the Chinese pictures week before last and I shall see to it that on "direct passes" you are not again left out. You are quite right that the Picture Department should see that the writer gets the rejects and most assuredly he should be informed of the available pictures in advance of their being made up.   W.H.

Amiable as this is, it reveals the executive's inexorable compulsion to try to extend his leverage, to move in on the function of the creator, the editor, and the writer (here the writer). Hicks' reaction to the universal situation is Pavlovian; because he was unimportant, he had no hope of real power, he just wanted a little more power. His maneuver was in a sense pitiable, and his memorandum implies that he intends to continue it. But I think he understood something of what *Life* was all about.

As an example of my memoranda to Hicks, for transmission to the available photographers, I submit one on Mexico, dated August 9, 1938:

> On Mexico: We did not get what we asked for last October: what has happened to the old white ruling class in Mexico: the pure whites of Spanish descent. Could a photographer get into the house of some well-to-do aristocrat, take old style Latin American luxury, into some aristocratic city and country clubs, getting names and ancestors of denizens and some Indian-blooded parvenus, if any? Take a rich bachelor's typical day and night—expensive night clubs, centres of Rightist agitation (Confederation of Middle Class and Employers' Confederation). Where the rich foregather and talk like Republicans.

We have only poor pictures of labor union headquarters—CTM and CROM. Fair pictures of Lombardo Toledano, poor of Luis Rodriguez. We want fine candid shots in the National Congress as well as in some state legislature like Puebla or Vera Cruz. The Federal Board of Conciliation and Arbitration. The Supreme Court. A takeout of the Partido Nacional Revolucionario and Portes Gil. . . .

A glance at floundering *Time* will be useful. The masthead had changed. Ingersoll is publisher; Gottfried, Norris, and T. S. Matthews (not Peter Mathews) are managing editors. Associate Editors: Balliett, Busch, Cantwell, Goldsborough, Hulburd, John Stuart Martin (thus demoted!), Fanny Saul, Stockly, Dana Tasker, and Myron Weiss. Contributing Editors: Roger Butterfield, Robert Fitzgerald, Calvin Fixx, Graebner, John Hersey, Sidney Hertzberg, Sidney James, Pearl Kroll, Louis Kronenberger, Thomas K. Krug, John T. McManus, Peter Mathews (imaginary), Allan A. Michie, Robert Neville, Russell Olsen, John Osborne, James Parton, Winthrop Sargeant, Robert Sherrod, Leon Svirsky, and Robert Terrall.

In the astonishing demotion of Martin we see the beginning of Luce's escape from the ghost of Briton Hadden. It is natural to suppose that the success of *Life* had freed him, and that in his own mind he was now bigger than the ghost of Hadden. (*Fortune*, "March of Time," *Architectural Forum* had failed to achieve this purging.) This is a subtle matter, but the evidence in the masthead is conclusive. The subtlety comes in whether he had begun to free himself from allegiance to the talent, which Martin and the ghost of Hadden had represented, had identified himself with the executives, and was now, as a businessman, merely manipulating the talent to exploit the base of power. In my opinion, on all the evidence, not yet. He was still an editor.

Leading up to an important *Life* story, went a memorandum to Hicks:

July 19, 38

To: Mr. Hicks
From: Mr. Cort

1. Could we get a photographer into, say, Bulgaria to take pictures of the way German goods have changed the way of life of Bulgarians. This naturally calls for research by the photographer on whether the thing

shown, as a taxi, a vacuum cleaner, a paper napkin on a cafe table, a readymade dress on a streetwalker, a threshing machine, a machine gun, comes from Germany, who was the manufacturer, what was the price to the Bulgar purchaser, does the user like the thing, has it stood up under use, is the thing better than what he used before, etc., etc. Germans have subsidized Bulgar soya bean and tobacco crops. Pictures of such.

2. Could we get a photographer in Germany to do one of our typical U.S. takeouts of one German family—a man who is not a Storm Trooper but is a Strength-Through-Joyer, who was not employed for a while but now has a job, is a competent mechanic anxious to support his family. We would want also his relatives and in-laws, a whole series of stories, all thoroughly researched. This could be done with official permission but the research would have to be unofficial, written after the photographer got out of Germany. We have to get in a few unfavorable facts. Let's see him on an excursion, at work, at dinner, at a mass demonstration (mob pictures plus close-up of him), hiking, eating his monthly one-dish Sunday dinner, paying his taxes, contributing to Government panhandlers on street, his cousin in the Storm Troops, his nephew in the Army, his daughter in the Hitler Girls, his boy in the Hitler Youth. An examination of his larder and icebox if any, his clothes closet, his garden, his wallet.

Goldsborough (July 25, 1938) was still missing the point. By loans and trade agreements, Chamberlain and Daladier were trying "to win over to the side of Democracy . . . those countries which, impressed by Adolf Hitler's adroit bluffing show of power, last year decided, or almost decided, to line up with Nazi Germany." Here Goldsborough is mumbling to himself.

The crisis leading to Munich was better reported by the newspapers, with their black sensational headlines, than by *Time*, where one could hardly find the story. Through August, Goldsborough adequately reported the events, but not until very late (September 12, 1938) was the opening FN story on the threat of war. At the ostentatious mobilization of all Germany (consider what the total mobilization of Russia or China would convey to you now), Europe had "refused to be personally alarmed." British fiscal experts thought "the peril of war is acute," but Joseph Kennedy thought, "No war is going to break out during the rest of 1938." Mr. Kennedy, not I, was fey.

As against this, *Life* made the lead (August 1, 1938) the king of

England's visit to France: "The No. 1 political fact about Europe is that England and France are still friends." Recalling 1914, "France might be in similar trouble any time now." The editorial page said that the king's visit had so alarmed Hitler that he had proposed a "non-violent solution of the problem of Czechoslovakia . . . a dismemberment of Czechoslovakia into nearly autonomous states." The democracies rejected this peculiar definition of nonviolence. A long essay on the International Ladies' Garment Workers Union faintly suggested that the tide had turned against organized labor. Great tides always turn, and the tide was about to turn on Hitler.

Something was happening in *Time*'s foreign news, for the delightful "Bunny" Schroeder, No. 2 man under Goldsborough, had come to *Life*, probably because Ingersoll did not approve of him. His talent was for amusing details and ironies, and should have made him the ideal writer into pictures. Billings did not like puns, however. Schroeder did not last long. Faced with a picture of an Eton bedroom with a chamberpot under the bed, "Bunny" captioned it "Generations of British Peers." Billings did not catch the pun and, when it was pointed out by readers, he was furious. Bunny did it once again, a little later, and that was it. He went on to become editor of *Interiors*, not a medical magazine, where he was, as he said, Oberon, King of the Fairies. Our pasts had earlier coincided on *Vanity Fair*.

The continuing Hitler tantrum, comparable to, but much more carefully calculated than, the current youthful demonstrations in America (August 8, 1938) had brought England to send a Viscount Runciman to "investigate" the Czech case. This was noticed only on the editorial page. I was not at once aware of what now seems the major purpose of Hitler's Czechoslovak tantrum: to rupture the French-Russian alliance by showing that it was impossible for France to be allied to both the British and the Russians at the same time. Elsewhere, the issue pointed out that Czechoslovakia's anti-Semitic interior minister had pigeonholed applications from 50,000 Austrian refugee Jews. A story on the Chinese Communists explained that Mao Tse-tung's "only vices are cigarets and a love of pepper."

Oddly, the Yellow River flooded the Japanese offensive (August 15, 1938): "It was not surprising that the Yellow River broke its dykes [*sic*]. . . . But it was a little odd that it did so exactly where it could do the invading Japanese Army the most damage. Most experts decided that the Chinese Army, despite denials, had arranged it." This was developed with fine airviews, a map of five East Asian wars in fifty years, and a "*Life* Looks Back" at the Russo-Japanese War. Europe's crisis was covered by "Europe's Four Best Reporters Interpret the Continent's Bluff and Guff": "The greatest chance a newspaperman ever had exists right now in the chancelleries of Europe. . . . Will France let the Spanish Loyalists lose? Need Hitler fight for Czechoslovakia? Will Rightists or Leftists win the underground struggle for Poland? . . . The trouble is that European journalists are lazy, opinionated and corrupt." The four were then quoted with ridicule.

Undoubtedly, Bunny Schroeder's work was a beautiful analysis of the foods and wines served at the king of England's luncheon in France; it was another indication of what he could have contributed to *Life*.

I was not unaware of the Russian factor in the Czechoslovak crisis and so (August 22, 1938) the lead was Russian belligerency and Stalinophilia: "Just how good this army is is one of the world's most anxious mysteries. Certainly the high officers are now unreliable, for recent Soviet purges are reported to have taken off two out of five marshals, 12 out of 15 army commanders, 43 out of 57 corps commanders, 122 of 186 generals of divisions." I would think these figures came from Underhill. The editorial page said, "Headlines briefly screamed that Hitler planned to march on Monday, August 15, against Czechoslovakia. . . . Where this well-planned scare was designed to take effect, however, it did—in London, in teetering Poland and Hungary and in the capitals of the Balkans." Czech army officers declared they would give up "not one step, not one foot, not one hand's breadth."

I sold Billings on a strange aberration: an essay on Poland (August 29, 1938), not in the news at all. I suppose Billings sold it to Luce on the grounds that "Dave says Czechoslovakia is gone. The thing to think about now is Poland." The journalistic sense in running this story a full year before Poland was destroyed is debatable, but it was part of the soothsaying responsibility *Life* had taken on, and in this case the prediction was probably timed a little too soon. I suspect that Billings frequently thought so.

The lead said: "The standout fact about the Poles today, as in the year 1000, is that they live between the Germans and the Russians. Their character has been undermined by trying to support two great fears at the same time. Shifty with fear, Poland now finds itself almost friendless in Europe—a pushover. . . . A jackal to Germany's lion has lately been the policy of the Polish Government.

"The late French Marshal Foch predicted that Europe's next great war would start in Poland. If Hitler decides that his first job is to isolate Soviet Russia from Western Europe by taking Leningrad, Foch will be proved right. Poland was in fact intended to be a buffer State by the peacemakers who seem today to have broken Europe into pieces small enough for Hitler to swallow easily. Poland's sole hope is its oversized Army. . . . It is exactly as behind-the-time as Poland . . . 40 cavalry regiments. . . . Just as few Americans can conceive of the poverty of Polish peasants, few Americans can imagine the splendor of a rich Pole's establishment." Finally, "And intervention by Germany and Russia in Poland would make the intervention in Spain look like a game of marbles."

I have never forgiven myself for failing to take the one very small logical step that would have revealed the future. I had never believed there was much difference between communism and fascism. I had thought through to the fact that both wanted Poland, recognizing that Russia had been snubbed by the West over Czechoslovakia. I think I was suckered by the claims of the Fascists and the Communists that they hated one another, notably in Spain. In any case, I did not predict the August 1939 alliance of Nazi Germany and Bolshevik Russia against Poland. If I had omitted the words "by taking Leningrad" above, I might have sounded smart. Almost alone, I had come to the threshold of Hitler's thinking, stopping there.

The next lead (September 12, 1938) showed Hitler receiving Hungary's Regent Horthy. As Colonel House had told Woodrow Wilson in 1914, "The situation here is extraordinary. It is militarism gone stark mad . . . the biggest war games since 1913. . . . The

Nazi press had discovered that Hitler, the Wartime corporal, is now a 'military genius.' . . . Disarmed until 1935, Germany finds itself behind France in trained reserves, in regimental officers and in general experience." The editorial page added: "Beneath the scarehead stories of Europe's war itch last week rarely if ever mentioned was what all the shouting was about—the postWar partition of Central and Eastern Europe by the treaties which the U.S. Senate emphatically refused to ratify. Those treaties are based on the un-American principle that nobody can get along with anybody except his own kind. Yet Woodrow Wilson's own Fourteen Points were repudiated by nearly everything the postWar treaties did. . . . Beside Hungary's claims, Adolf Hitler's much-advertised claims in Czechoslovakia are laughable." The essay (12 pages) was Hungary, "The Kingless Kingdom Clamors for Lost Lands." This began: "The postWar peacemakers carved off a peel more than twice as big as what they left. . . . [Hungary's] claim is political dynamite because it is amazingly reasonable. . . . With half a chance Hungary would march tomorrow. . . . Their old country was a natural geographic unit. The rivers they lost to Rumania and Czechslovakia flow . . . right back into Hungary. If they strip off the trees, Hungary gets the floods."

C. D. Jackson told me that a Prince somebody from the Polish Embassy had complained about the Polish essay and wanted to send somebody to talk to *Life*. C. D. foisted this man off on me, not one of the aristocrats I had praised, but a slimy parvenu, with whom I went to lunch in the Rockefeller Plaza. Returning, I told him the time of day. I said that America by winning one war had made possible the rebirth of Poland, and that the American people might be asked to win another war brought on by Poland. It was therefore necessary that the American people be kept informed of the kind of job the rulers of Poland were doing with what had been handed them. At this, I left.

C. D. Jackson told me, grinning, that the man had quoted me as saying that all American magazines were obliged to be Communist. C. D., whom I always liked, did not need a reply. That Polish scum was the reality behind the façade of the handsome aristocrats of

Poland. The word, however, had gotten around and the Hungarians were very nervous about the treatment they were getting.

Howard Richmond was dropped from the masthead and Charles Tudor, Peter Piening (Art), and Bunny Schroeder added (September 19, 1938). I have the pleasantest memories of Charlie Tudor, as I have for the whole layout department, with whom I frequently lunched. Hitler kept giving me the lead, here "The British Cabinet Rush Home from Vacation to Play Poker with Hitler." "Chamberlain, like Hitler, was trying to play his joker as though he would fight, without running a serious risk of actually spilling English blood on the Continent's battlefields. Whereas Hitler could play his cards without showing them to anybody, Chamberlain, as the leader of a democracy, had to have the whole British Empire kibitzing over his shoulder." I noted that Ambassador Kennedy had called on Chamberlain and, in my opinion, had to tell him not to count too much on America. The issue had another Schroeder pun. When the American Pratts rented a Scottish grouse-shooting, he described the retreating family as "a field of Pratts." Billings was annoyed.

The next lead (September 26, 1938) was "The Fate of Europe Turns on the Bavarian Terrace of Reichsführer Hitler," showing that terrace. "With Europe whirling on to what looked like inevitable war, a new and utterly unexpected figure stalked onto the Hitler terrace." (Picture and words were working perfectly together, enabling the reader to imagine the "unexpected figure" entering the explicit scene before his eyes.) "It was Britain's elderly, sobersided Prime Minister Chamberlain come to talk the whole thing over with the Reichsführer 'to try to find a peaceful solution.' " The next spread showed nine closeups of each man on opposite pages. There followed a general view of Berchtesgaden: "When Hitler is at Berchtesgaden, his favorite retreat, uplifted by the rarefied air and the view, he feels nearly omnipotent. . . . And Russians know that a peace in the West means eventual war in the East, for a finish fight between Fascism and Communism." A strange device was a spread of quotes from Hitler's Nürnberg speech, illustrated with small pictures: "full of superficial, simplified history." Then came a spread on the Czech army.

The next lead (October 3, 1938) opened with seven pages on France's Maginot line (in exclusive stills from a "March of Time" movie) and Germany's Siegfried line (glimpsed from France). "The 20-year-old boundary of Czechoslovakia had collapsed under diplomatic pressure from Germany, England and France. Many another frontier was trembling violently." A sequence of maps showed the World War I secret treaties, the Brest-Litovsk treaty with Russia, Versailles (five treaties), the postwar rearrangements, the Rhineland occupation, European minorities, and German export business. "The arbitrary redrawing of the map of Europe by Chamberlain and Hitler is in the strict tradition of European diplomacy. Nobody thought it important to ask the people living on the land in question what they wanted. A plebiscite, said Chamberlain, would have been 'objectionable.' Even the Czech President agreed. . . . At this time (1917) the principle of 'Self-determination' was just a German Socialist phrase, *Selbstbestimmungsrecht.* President Woodrow Wilson borrowed it. . . . Wilson knew about the secret treaties as early as April 1917 but felt that U.S. entry in the War had made them all null and void, since the Allies by themselves seemed to be losing the War." On the editorial page: "The Czechs asked France and Russia for immediate military support, got a flat No from France, a hedged No from Russia. . . . At last, on September 21, the Czechs capitulated. The danger of war, instead of diminishing, straightway heightened. Hitler, sure he was on the right track, began having his famous hunches thick and fast." Everybody began mobilization. The text piece was "The Rise and Decline of Mussolini," ending Goldsborough's image of him as the No. 1 Fascist.

After pictures of the hurricane damage in the northeastern United States came the essay (12 pages): "Negroes—The U.S. Also Has a Minority Problem": "These 14,000,000 colored people make up the largest and most indissoluble minority in the U.S. They are also the most glaring refutation of the American fetish that all men are created free and equal. The Negro may be free but in no way—economically, politically, socially—is he the white man's equal. . . . The white man will, however, be surprised at the achievements of the Negro in America, some of which are set forth in the following

pages"—colleges, artists, high society, "20 of America's most distin-
guished Negroes." The consultant on this story was Time Inc.'s only
Negro, Earl Brown, a politician whom I learned to trust, and whom
Malcolm X later trusted.

An ad called *Life* "the most eagerly read magazine in the world
. . . the most *wanted* magazine . . . satisfies a peculiarly modern
hunger and longing . . . a source of knowledge that's important and
right." This was not meant as a compliment to talent; it was directed
at advertisers.

The lead (October 10, 1938) is "Hitler Listens to Reason" under a
picture of the back of Hitler's head at the rear of an empty hall. "If
Hitler does not doublecross Britain now, Germany's future looks
brighter than ever before in modern history . . . a relieved world
looked around for a goat and, ironically, settled on Chamberlain. Yet
Chamberlain had got a considerable backdown at Munich from
Hitler. . . . The much-debated right of Britain and France to take
Sudentenland away from Czechoslovakia is considerably influenced
by the fact that they gave it to Czechoslovakia in the first place at
Versailles in 1919."

A headline noted, "World Force Replaces World Law." The
League of Nations was impotent and the areas given Germany "are
primarily important because they are the mountain bastion of
Bohemia." A picture biography of the Chamberlain family was
appended. In this issue, John W. Field is added to the editorial
associates.

Life shook off the European nightmare easily. The next lead
(October 17, 1938) was "Republicans Sing with New Zip and
Zing"—this sounds like undiluted Luce, and Roosevelt must have
smiled. On the editorial page: "The victor in a holy war against
Fascism would be Soviet Russia. After that Peace, German and Polish
soviet states would also look to Moscow." (This is certainly long-term
soothsaying of a very high order.) "Anybody can join the game of
guessing Hitler's next move. Chamberlain's move is to speed up
rearmament, to make a fight for the air and to hold the sea." (This
describes the Battle of Britain less than two years later, under
another prime minister.)

Roosevelt would have smiled again (October 31, 1938) at the lead "America Gets Ready to Fight Germany, Italy and Japan"—for this again was pure Luce—and about as far from Roosevelt's intention as one could get. This was not my story; it concerned the need for a bigger navy.

Ingersoll sent Luce a memorandum blaming *Time*'s troubles on the "Roosevelt Depression," *Life*, and Laird Goldsborough—"a tired, tired Jesuit—'Jesuit' in the philosophical sense. And a tired, tired Jesuit is Laird Goldsborough," recommending a leave of absence for Goldie.

Luce agreed to a leave of absence for Goldsborough, while testifying properly to his "brilliant and tireless work during the thirteen long years. . . . No writer has contributed more to *Time* than Laird Goldsborough." The Jesuit stuff is pure nonsense and expert in-fighting in the world of memoranda communication. *Jesuit* means "(**2b**) A casuist; hence, a crafty person; an intriguer." Personally, he was that; but his foreign news was not crafty, it was simply wrong. He had held on to his old hero, Mussolini, too long. And his gift for intrigue might have let him smell the Nazi-Soviet pact, as I was unable to do. *Casuistry* is defined as "**2.** Sophistical, equivocal, or specious reasoning, or false application of principles, esp. in regard to law or morals." Applied to Goldsborough, the use of "Jesuit" or "casuist" is a handy insult, with a note of frenzy.

In effect fired, Goldsborough fell sick, was given a few chores, retired in 1941 with a lifetime pension (which, conspicuously, I did not get, though my active tenure was nearly the same), hung around, and in 1950 went out the window of the Time-Life Building, complete with gold-headed cane. To the degree that Time Inc. was a true Cause to its devotees, it seems to have occasioned suicide. Of course, this does not apply to the hack inheritors. The power men rarely put their lives on the line but, like everybody else, they die.

This man was able and, I thought, indomitable. His fault seems to have been that he identified himself totally with Time Inc. as a majesty, suddenly deposed and dishonored. The Communists at Time Inc., in a newspaper secretly distributed in 1938, rejoiced at his departure. I discussed with colleagues getting out a fake issue of their paper, *High Time*, in which we would viscerally and plausibly insult everybody, as in ascribing bad breath to a member of the picture department, and the suspicion of hemorrhoids to others, making the Communists sound like what they were. I was advised that it was too risky. We would have listed the editorial staff as the suspected Communists, who were pretty well known to all, clearly a nasty lot. Though perhaps not quite as nasty as I, with cause.

The firing of Goldsborough further dissociated Luce from identification with the founding talent (though Goldsborough had arrived in 1925). It was also part of the dissatisfaction with *Time's* current performance. Ingersoll had set up a structure of senior editors who edited writers' copy, Gottfried alone to read every word in the issue. Ingersoll had also decreed that *Time* would "make each department so sound that it can stand the test of the expert's microscope." With this brilliant editing, it turned out that the resulting magazine was mysteriously uninteresting. Luce wrote himself a soliloquy on this subject (revealed in the book *Time Inc.*) in which, after endless maundering, he concluded, "If I had to say what is wrong with *Time* in one word, I would say it lacks Unity."

This is incredible. The trouble with *Time* was that it had become a sycophant of the academic community, under the guidance of Ingersoll and Matthews, but not of Gottfried and Norris who did not, however, reassert *Time's* long-term values. The essence of *Time* was always that it affected to be amateur, not specialist. Among these congested groves, *Time's* leadership did not see the overweeningly obvious fact that a war was close, and that weapons and warfare would be the decisive specialty. Any amateur could see that; all *Life's* readers saw it. But these parvenu professors had not seen it. To them I looked like a street hoodlum. However, one very serious type from *Time*, Calvin Fixx (who became a curious *cause célèbre* about four years later), wandered up to *Life* for a while and seemed to be trying to absorb my mystical secret. But I had nothing to teach. To each new story I presented an open mind, with a wind whistling through it. I was only an amateur. Fixx wandered away, later to fall in with the demonic Whittaker Chambers, who in effect killed him. And I mean dead.

The writing in *Time* was not individualistic, opinionated, satirical, with the exception of Noel Busch's Cinema and Sports. The writers sounded intimidated, forced into a recessive detachment, incapable of being dogmatic about anything, leaning on statistics wherever possible. The subjects were often esoteric, as on semantics (always a mud puddle) and on obscure Negro composers of serious music. The Foreign News during October does not sound as if it was written by Goldsborough. It is amateurish, sentimental, and inclined toward the "betrayal" or Popular Front theory about Munich. The whole Foreign News section is given (October 10, 1938) to the Czech crisis. The next issue, with Neville Chamberlain on the cover, almost drops it. One must deduce that, though Ingersoll's memorandum had not yet gone to Luce, he was already cutting down Goldsborough. The extraordinary thing is that Ingersoll did not try to eliminate Noel Busch, producing the only good copy in the magazine.

Luce was happy again with the lead (November 7, 1938): on how to vote to revive the Republican party, whose revival was suggested as essential to democracy. He was unhappy with an essay on the defeat of the Chinese armies. On the editorial page, Hitler now doesn't want to give Hungary the Czechoslovak Ruthenians, but wants to hold them as "the fuse for a great Ukrainian 'self-determination' campaign." This had not been thought through. As a dictator, Hitler knew very well that only democracies had minority problems. Dictatorships had none: they knew how to handle minorities. I was only trying to make Hitler look like still another kind of son of a bitch.

I remember the next issue very well (November 14, 1938) because from midweek on my wife was trying unsuccessfully to give birth to my son. Luce was editing. I had a set of pictures of the Japanese army in China by the great Japanese photographer Younosuki Natori, in which Underhill had spotted indications that the army's morale was in dissolution. I sold it to Luce as a long lead. Underhill and I knew what we were trying to say, and were anxious not to say too much. The picture captions made the point. "The officer . . . slept beside a private—an unheard-of intimacy in any Western army. . . . To military experts, this [beautiful picture] is an object lesson in straggling. . . . House-to-house fighting should never be done this way." Of an old fortress, "Only a fool would defend such a perfect artillery target today." An amazing contrast of two pictures showed a hillside before and after soldiers took cover, the men having completely disappeared in the second, though they were still there. A continuation into the back of the magazine, opening, "An army is a funny thing. . . . Discipline is not an officer's racket; it is an iron necessity for men at war. And military men have an extraordinarily keen nose for signs of discipline-trouble in armies." Thus in 1938 we were telling Americans about the inevitable climate of war. The hardships of the Japanese were given, including "the flies that bite (Japanese flies do not bite)."

The problem became rewriting for Luce the last paragraph of the lead. I did this, I think, four times, after Luce had made another groping speech about what he wanted. Since he was talking about what I had told him of Underhill's intuition, he was actually wandering around inside my mind in a most amateurish way. The paragraph as printed, under a picture of a rest camp tent, heavily described, runs: "The mess of this tent would be a disgrace in any first-class Army, even in a temporary camp. From a mass of such little facts, military observers are beginning to form a suspicion that is of incalculable importance. It is that a great many units of the Japanese Army have suffered an amazing slackening of discipline and morale that, given a hard blow, the Army would be in grave danger of serious collapse."

Whether his editing was sound in getting a judicious distribution of the "incalculables," "amazings," "grave dangers," whether it was toward getting a bolder or a more cautious statement, I do not remember nor can I guess. It was, I thought then, unnecessary and narcissistic and ignorant, obviously. I had said it the first time.

As I was finishing my last version around noon Saturday, November 5, 1938, the hospital phoned to say that I would have to come up to sign an authorization for a Caesarean. I put my copy on Luce's desk, saying, "I'm afraid this is the last rewrite I can do." Luce started to stiffen at the arrant insubordination, when I explained. His story afterward was that "Dave was like ice up to that moment, and then his knees began to knock." This is purely fanciful. The operation turned out well. The editorial page noted that Hitler had given Hungary the Ruthenians and 5,000 square miles of Czechoslovakia. So much for Ukrainian "self-determination." As also for my wife's and my son's "self-determination."

An ad appears (November 21, 1938) that ought to make the reader laugh. *Life*, it said, gives "illuminating and searching picture-word essays on European countries. . . . The whole purpose of war is destruction. *Life* shows it thus . . . though we fully know that realistic war pictures shock and outrage thousands of readers. But the dead of war have indeed died in vain if live men refuse to look at them . . . America's most potent editorial force."

This can be taken as an abdication by the executives before the talent, since it clumsily parrots the editorial line, but it was merely commercial parasitism on the talent. The executives were waiting for their great feed, soon to come. For in 1938 *Life* lost less than a million dollars and was in position to become the greatest money-maker in journalistic history. The executives understood this with razor-sharp clarity. The fresh journalistic creation of the magazine came through to them dimly, but the smell of money was rank and rich.

The issue was primarily American with a lead on the elections which had restored the Republican party "to major status," with 169 Representatives, a gain of 81, and an increase to 18 governors—not good, not bad. The text piece was on "Ickes, Man of Wrath," and the essay on "Cuckooland" (California). A story on Cuba said, "Notice Negro boys. Cuba has probably nearest thing to perfect equality between whites and blacks in the world today."

The lead of the second anniverary issue (November 28, 1938) was unhappily "Nazi Germany Takes an Awful Revenge on Its Jews": "The world discovered last week that parts of it are by no means civilized." One Jew in Paris had assassinated one German attaché. At the instigation of Hitler and Goebbels, the Nazi street gangs burned German synagogues and smashed Jewish stores throughout Germany. And the government assessed the Jewish community a fine of $400 million. The usual Nazi pomp of Nazi officials saluting Hitler with stiffened arms took on a diabolic look, as of mad apes pretending to be human. One old German is quoted as whispering to a foreigner, "Don't look. This is not the real Germany." The story ended with a spread, "The Democracies Pray for the German Jews." But this episode was symptomatic of the psyche of what was the legal government of Germany.

A story of U.S. ambassadors included one who had earned "a reputation which may well carry Joseph Patrick Kennedy into the White House." I don't think I wrote this story. Nor could I have written the essay on Barcelona, in which it was hypothesized that a society could survive without its natural leaders whom it had killed. The writer may have been Paul Peters, and I am reminded of the story on the French Bastille Day, and the myth of "social democracy." In this world Thomas Jefferson's "natural aristocracy" of "virtue and talent" becomes anathema. I think that about then I was telling Billings, "Both sides stink."

On one of these Spanish stories, after I submitted my copy to Billings, he called me in to meet Longwell, who demanded, "Where did you get these facts?" Since I was an indoctrinated Time Inc. writer, not in the business of inventing anything, and he was not, I looked at him for some moments in astonishment. In effect, the whole structure of Time Inc. had come crashing down, and I should perhaps have looked at Billings. "Well, I'll tell you, Danny," I said. "Yesterday I had a lot of trouble with this story. But I went home and went to bed and I had a dream. And as soon as I woke up, I rushed in and wrote it down, and there it is." "Don't take me for a fool," cried Longwell. Instead of answering that properly, I replied with a guttural roar, "And don't take me for a liar." Billings broke it up, but I believe he made some modifications in my copy on Longwell's case. Another time Longwell brought in a parlor Fascist (who later became Rear Admiral de Flores in the U.S. Navy) who had marched into Madrid with Franco and he contradicted my description of Madrid. I think Billings compromised on this one too. Later, Longwell and the Fascist passed my door going out. I leaped up and met Longwell coming back. "Wasn't that your Fascist friend?" No reply. The Fascist was a pet of New York society.

The Spanish affair gave me another jolt from the opposite direction. I had heard that my Columbia classmate, Meyer Schapiro, was an authority on Catalan art, and so I telephoned to ask what were the greatest examples of Catalan art. I did not know he had been a Communist and forgot that he had been a close friend of Whittaker Chambers, also a classmate, in his dubious Communist phase. Schapiro replied with vituperation and contempt for my plot to accuse the Loyalists of destroying the art. Since *Life*'s policy had been the reverse of this, I was astonished, as I have remained on the subject of Meyer Schapiro, a monolith of the peculiar immigrant (born Shavly, Lithuania) arrogance of the rootless.

These episodes—Fascist and Communist—began to give me an intuition that, being just an ordinary believer in people and democracy and the Declaration and the Constitution, I might be in trouble. The Polish emissary had added his own peculiar discordant note. Something very poisonous was running through the veins, not only of Europe, but of America. Since Longwell was also a Columbia man, and another Columbia friend was frankly a Fascist, these poisons were not far away, but right in the family. Insensibly, I began to become a democratic snob, a Roosevelt *in petto*. For the one obvious thing both Fascists and Communists were agreed on hating was Roosevelt. Under the "Popular Front," the Communists pretended to like Roosevelt (the true moment of untruth), but the true fury leaked through, and Whittaker Chambers (involving Nixon and Joseph McCarthy) later revealed it.

I think Luce was bewildered by this sort of thing; he was pure in terms of communism or fascism. But I was down in the snake pit. I can hardly say that I was fighting for my life. In America I had to be on the winning side. Still, I had to realize that the scoundrels were all around me, and closing in with confidence. And they were all in earnest. But so was I.

Suddenly (December 5, 1938), the issue has 92 pages, a harbinger of prosperity to come, though the issues immediately dropped to 80, 68, and 60 pages.

The beginning of an interesting story is a memorandum of December 1, 1938, from Longwell to Cort and Hicks: "I suggested to de Rochemont the other day that we ought to get a series of every day pictures from Germany—the Volkswagon [sic], the hotels, the society people, the schools, etc., etc. no persecutions or pogroms—just people in Germany. De Rochemont thinks he can get Nieholm, a Dane who photos for Conde Nast & *Time* to do such a job. If you are interested, will Cort draw up a list of requests for Hicks."

Promptly on December 3, 1938, I sent Hicks (to be forwarded intact to de Rochemont) the required memorandum, which I follow with another dated January 20, 1939, probably intended to appall Longwell.

Dec. 3, 1938

Let your photographer first take all the things properly that are now legitimately photographed: life in the swell Berlin hotels, a good meal in a fine restaurant, night life, the show girls in a place where the girls sit with the customers—make them pretty and slim, a swell ball, with socialites identified; rathskellers from outside looking in and inside, with singing, beering, and tipsy customers going home along the street; the early morning streets, people going to work; the Germans keeping clean, cleaning streets, windows, railway trains; middle-class social gatherings, singing societies, et al.; some of the great workers' residential districts—airviews, street scenes and inside the houses; the operation of the new canal system—locks, barges, etc.; the one-dish Sunday dinner; the Nazi collections for the poor; some Strength-Through-Joy trips or festivities, preferably of industrial workers; German farms in the eastern hinterland—Silesia or East Prussia; a swell Prussian family at home; inside some independent small shops, the proprietor living in the backroom; the Volkswagen Factory building as far as it has gone; State and parochial schools; inside a few churches if humanly possible, both Evangelical and Confessional for the Protestants, as well as Catholic; don't try for a synagog; a meeting of the Church vestrymen; meetings of SA and SS units, not full-dress meetings but routine business; Hitler Youth and Hitler Girls meetings, camps, marches, hikes, leaders; show workers having lot of fun in entertainment places, etc., etc.; specialize in German children getting trained, educated, taught; good pictures of new German building; the Berchtesgaden govt. offices; clothes, styles; ersatz substitute stuffs in actual use and being manufactured; pictures inside factories in operation and workers welfare work such as workers restaurants, rest halls, games, pools?, playgrounds, housing, etc.; can you get in a govt. radio station, short wave if possible?; people listening to their radios and to street radios; as many street scenes as possible; can you take a govt. broadcast telling about happy factory workers where the workers put on the•

show themselves and pretend to be in the factory at work (maybe they are); collect old pictures of the Koenigsberg Fair; the shipping at Bremen and Hamburg; Hitler's Berchtesgaden hotel for his visitors; Govt. offices where people register for the Volkswagen with lineup, if any; good portraits of bigwigs—Wiedemann, Bodenschatz, Hess, Himmler, Ritter von Epp, Frick, the Kaiser's boys, et al, et al.; vineyards and factory for Rhine wine, also champagne; also beer breweries; Tempelhof airport; interior of the Munich Brown House; organizations to train mothers, colonists, gliders; The Opera; German plays and musical shows.

Then. Try slowly, without giving away your hand, to get a typical American takeout of one German family—a man who is not a Storm Trooper but is a Strength-Through-Joyer, who was not employed for a while but now has a job, is a competent mechanic anxious to support his family. We would want his relatives and in-laws, a whole series of stories, all quietly and thoroughly researched, perhaps kept in the photographer's mind, not written down. This could be done with official permission but the research would have to be casual. Let's see him on an excursion, at work, at dinner, at a mass demonstration (mob picture picking him out, plus closeup), hiking, eating his One-Dish meal, paying taxes, contributing to SS panhandlers, his cousin in Storm Troops, nephew in Army, daughter in Hitler Girls, boy in Hitler Youth, him in church, at work, at dinner, at breakfast, his wife hanging out the wash, at the market, etc., etc., etc. Examine and picture his larder and icebox, if any, his clothes closet, his garden and his wallet, showing all the different official cards he carries.

Jan. 20, 1939

Notes for drawings of Dachau concentration camp:

1. Men marching from barracks to work at 6:30 A.M. They sing "My Heart Is Full of Joy." Separate files of second offenders, old and sick, emigrés and ex-Nazis and homosexuals. In distance, Jews and race-degraders cleaning latrines, one being kicked into the open privy by guard. Men wear black wool caps, fatigue uniforms with black arm bands on forearm, have shaven heads. Put court-plaster patches on left temples of several men, show teeth-gaps. A man is lying face-down in mud. A race-degrader being kicked in the groin. Man tied to post with placard. Three files of priests.

2. The punishment hut. Prisoner with trousers down, being whipped with long, oxtail whip while guards stand around. Might show Commandant Loritz personally lowering man's trousers.

3. Scene on Xmas night, 1937. Naked prisoners doing drill in yard before drunken guards.

4. Small sketches, each showing an individual torture: a man counting his newly-cut hairs into piles of 13 each; man with soles of feet slashed, lips

being burned with red hot wire, pepper and salt rubbed in wounds; man in coffin, water dripping on head; man being trampled on, hit with rifle butts, hit with sandbags; a man being hung in the toilet by SS men; a fight between two prisoners, one with board, one with broom, while guards watch.

5. Interior view of barracks at night as surprise inspection is called at midnight.

The Japanese were seen capturing Hankow (December 12, 1938), and the Chinese had retreated beyond the Yangtze gorges to Chungking. The intrepid photographer Robert Capa produced pictures of the Spanish war that could have got him killed. "Really close to, War does not look like much. . . . There is not much view." There is simply the explosion in which men disappear.

The mysterious Alan Brown leaves the masthead (December 19, 1938), as the lead is on the illegal catches of the whaling industry. The editorial page shows that I was not totally blind to what was going on: "a plot by Adolf Hitler to detach France from its allies in eastern Europe—the USSR, Poland and Rumania." Mussolini was putting on a pitiful burlesque of Hitler's techniques for getting what he wanted. Because Mussolini wanted Italian representation on the board of directors of the Suez Canal, he was "threatening" France by inciting "spontaneous" demonstrations demanding France's Tunisia and Corsica, with some Italian enthusiasts adding Nice and Savoy.

Underhill's enormous value was demonstrated in this issue. The essay (14 pages) was: "U.S. is weak in arms and industry is unprepared. . . . Among the armies of the major powers, America's is not only the smallest but the worst-equipped . . . AND—if America should be attacked it would be eight months before the nation's peacetime industry could be converted to production of the war supplies which the Army would need. Whether there would be any army left to supply at the end of those eight months is disputable.

"These are the facts. There is no cause for hysteria in them. If there were, the U.S. War Department would not have allowed *Life* to take the photographs and print the figures . . . which prove them. . . . U.S. industry sold about $50,000,000 worth of essential manufactured munitions products (excluding aviation) to the Army last year" (a fantastic contrast to the military-industrial complex of recent times). Conclusively, the essay showed the explicit weapons for war and gave the numbers in existence, in one case the only example possessed by the army. When one remembers that four years later this army was facing Rommel in North Africa, the importance of this story becomes majestic. And, without Underhill, it would have been more or less meaningless. I would suppose that Kay wrote the story. I did not. I would think that this story influenced American history, and helped some Americans to survive in North Africa four years later.

The Christmas issue (December 26, 1938) included a life of Christ in paintings and an essay on the Vatican (12 pages). There was also a map labeled "Europe Christmas 1938," detailing the troubles and quarrels of Europe. "The cynical may well conclude that the sooner that continent tears itself apart in War, the better for the world. . . . Two favorite guesses as to Hitler's next victim: Poland or Rumania."

In the next issue Bunny Schroeder vanishes (January 2, 1939), to my great regret. The lead is "Japan Slams the 'Open Door' and the U.S. Begins to Fight." Japan "has asserted its yellow man's superior rights over other yellow men, specifically the Chinese." The United States gives Chiang Kai-shek $25 million in credits. "A spasm of rage and fear passed over Japan." There followed a picture history of the Open Door in China since 1844. On the editorial page, it was noted that the chairman of the Senate Foreign Relations Committee had issued a probably inspired statement:

1. The people of the United States do not like the Government of Japan.
2. The people of the United States do not like the Government of Germany.

This remarkable confession must be construed as, in part, an effect of *Life*'s reporting or, if one likes, propaganda in a form that even U.S. senators could understand. But the *Life* continuation, probably written by Hubie Kay, was: "But moral indignation is a luxury for which a nation must be prepared to pay. Tough talk by a government is not only dangerous. It is worthless unless the government is ready to back up the words with bullets. . . . The course on which America is now embarked may well lead, not tomorrow but in time, to a showdown on that issue." This came to pass "in time," namely December 7, 1941. An act on the air war in Spain noted: "The war in Spain is a poor man's war but it has produced a few huge air battles, prophetic of the air battles in the rich men's war to come. The chief lessons of the Spanish war are that bombers' chief defense is speed rather than gun turrets and that many cheap single-seated fighters are infinitely better than a few expensive ones." The tactics of air fighting were shown in diagrams. I believe that the United States elected to produce a great many expensive, not cheap, fighters. The climate of war was closing in on *Life*'s readers from every direction.

The essay was on hobbies (12 pages) of the famous and humble. This would probably have been a long-term project of Dan Longwell's, and was of value.

The "Speaking of Pictures" (January 9, 1939) may also have been Longwell's idea, or King's. It was on famous people shaving themselves. The lead was on rich girls' debuts and commented, "Except on Union Square, nobody gets very hot under the collar about the 'idle rich' anymore." Brenda Frazier had a head cold at her party and covered herself with a tablecloth. The essay (10 pages), a beautiful picture job on Rumania, was delicately contemptuous of the "Rumans" who became the Vlachs. Finally, "Rumania now can properly be called a civilized nation. . . . It is a waste of time to look for the basic principle behind any action in Rumania. These maneuvers were just maneuvers." Of the late Queen Marie of Rumania: "Her talents, however, did not include that of being a good mother, and a worse-behaved batch than her royal children would be hard to find." It was made clear that Rumania was not anything America ought to fight for, that it was half Hungarian, boasting oil and wheat assets Hitler wanted.

The lead was on Roosevelt (January 16, 1939)—"He Would Save Democracy for the World." With an angle shot from below, he towered on the frontispiece: "As America's leader in potentially fateful 1939, this shrewd, bold, lusty, self-willed man now truly bestrides the world like a Colossus." Luce glorified him because he had misunderstood Roosevelt's statement, "The defense of religion, of democracy, and of good faith among nations is all one fight. To save one we must now make up our minds to save all." Roosevelt was merely justifying his request for more money for rearmament, at which America was disgracefully and almost suicidally laggard. His delay can only be explained by the theory that he had no intention of fighting until he was forced to, as I had always assumed. His timing was not too bad, but he needed a little urging, such as *Life* was giving him. Luce had misunderstood.

I must apologize for the next lead (January 23, 1939): "The noisiest threat of war in Europe was Benito Mussolini's claims against the French colonial empire. . . . France's reply to this yammer was to send Premier Edouard Daladier on New Year's Day on a tour of Corsica and Tunisia. Italy promptly called it 'an act of provocation.'" The editorial page said: "A revealing comment on the kind of democracy Czechoslovakia was before Munich is that since Munich it has relapsed with amazing ease into Fascism."

This produced an idiotic reaction from Ralph Delahaye Paine, Jr., who I suppose was in one of the European offices. Though it may be dull, I will give my reply:

Del Paine asks me to defend *Life*'s text page "crack" at Czecho-Slovakia. Certainly any case against Czecho-Slovakia as a democracy has been snowed under by the violence of Munich. The fashion is naturally now to emphasize the democratic features of pre-Munich Czecho-Slovakia. But when this is used as a proof that other democracies are susceptible to so quick and complete a fall, it is time to examine the differences between the "democracy" of Czecho-Slovakia and the democracy of the U.S., Britain or France, to see whether democracy per se is a push-over for Fascism. (I am speaking of course of internal, not external, developments.) The world's interest is no longer in Czecho-Slovakia, except as a sorrowful lost cause, but in the potency of democracy, elsewhere.

The best statements of Czecho-Slovakia's peculiar kind of democratic (or at least parliamentary—a somewhat different thing) practice plus a race bureaucracy are to be found in Fodor's chapter on Czecho-Slovakia, in the January *Foreign Affairs* (A Turning Point in History) and in Runciman's report, published in the British White Paper of Sept. 28. There was for example the rule that only recognized parties could campaign, that recognized parties must get their party programs accepted by the Government and that no politician not a member of a recognized party could speak for his cause. (This is from memory.) Is it not peculiar that the elections of Masaryk and Benes went off without any material opposition from the Sudetens, Slovaks or Ruthenians, all of whom have since expressed their nearly complete opposition to the program of Masaryk and Benes? The Pittsburgh Agreement had no standing or force except on Masaryk, who used it to sell Wilson on incorporating Slovakia with Bohemia and Moravia. But, at Benes' nudge, Masaryk repudidated it against his own best instincts. No plebiscite whatever was held in any part of Czecho-Slovakia. It was, in a word, the creation of "leaders," of whom the most decisive were the members of the French General Staff. Finally Benes in September was opposed to a plebiscite. What parochial Runciman judged was the Czech performance over a period of 20 years. It was judged not good enough for the world to fight for. Granted, the penalty was far too terrible. But the famous Armstrong piece in *Foreign Affairs* completely fails when it takes up the story in February, 1938. I think in our present sympathy for the Czechs we should not forget the black marks against them.

This sniping from a simpleton doctrinaire liberal was not as crucial as the Fascist and Communist attacks, but it was a further harassment. For I was not a simpleton doctrinaire liberal, nor am I now. This fact appears, oddly, in the essay in the same issue (17 pages) on Mexico, "Life Reports on a Social Revolution in Progress." Since Billings despised Indians and loved only railroads and pigs, it is extraordinary that it got into the magazine, but the explanation will become apparent. "It is a quiet, bloodless revolution, the kind that remakes the world without violence or spectacle. . . . [President] Cardenas says the new Mexico is not Communist. But his plan goes farther toward State Socialism than Sweden's. . . . [This is then demonstrated.] All this naturally makes American businessmen very angry. . . . [Cardenas] is probably the first completely fearless, honest and unselfish politician to appear in Mexico since Madero (assassinated in 1913)." The story showed the expropriation of British and U.S. oil wells, the latter "within five or ten years of running out." This last fact is what made the Mexican Indians newsworthy. Billings and Luce permitted the whole block of copy into the magazine. Roosevelt must have loved it.

The need for new naval bases as demanded by Roosevelt was given (January 30, 1939), with a drawing of a model base.

The "Speaking of Pictures" (February 6, 1939) was on Japanese home propaganda pictures which "make the war in China look playful, even cute. Democratic propaganda is different. In the U.S. during the World War, the Germans were described as superhuman, man-eating Huns. This incited Americans like a challenge. . . . This propaganda in a backward country, however, would have had the effect of terrifying the people into paralysis." The lead was an airplane tragedy, noting heroism among the unterrifiable democrats. The editorial page reported that Barcelona had fallen: "The Catalans of Barcelona are a talkative, frivolous city folk who have a long record of defeat in war. . . . President Companys announced that Catalonia was made of 'granite and flame.' But when the Rebels marched in, they were met by cheering, weeping, saluting crowds eager only for food."

The Senate fight on Roosevelt's demand for rearmament was the lead (February 13, 1939), with the majority of isolationists explicitly identified in a picture of the Military Affairs Committee. On the editorial page the question was whether Roosevelt did indeed "flatly set the U.S. frontier in France." It was noted that, though Europeans did not like to admit that the United States had won World War I, that was the fact. Thus, from the dictatorships, "a cry of genuine anguish." The essay was "The Philippines," quoting its President Quezon, " 'All we have we owe to that starry flag and that great people'—which was the literal truth. . . . The Filipinos are the most fortunate people in all the Orient and one of the least deserving. . . . For all the fond U.S. belief that the Filipinos have learned democratic ways, they will inevitably slide into dictatorship. . . . That the Filipinos are fine fighters and born soldiers is a fact that few Americans know. . . . Much-advertised menace to a free Philippines is Japan, if it conquers China. If not, the menace is China. For both are overpopulated, and the Philippines are notably underpopulated."

That Billings and Luce let slip through "If not, the menace is China," is a testament to their journalistic honesty. Now, over thirty years later, it may begin to be a possibility; the Japanese part of the menace had to wait only a little less than three years. Any great faith in their democratic allegiance is probably still unsound.

This sort of cynicism was documented (February 20, 1939) with the lead on the fall of Barcelona, advertised in the earlier Barcelona essay (not by me) as a proletariat ready to die for antifascism. The pictures showed the people of Barcelona delirious with joy at welcoming the Rebel army. They were smiling and happy. There had been no military resistance. The men had refused to fight. There were beautiful pictures of the flight of Loyalist refugees and a disciplined army into France, in snow and killing temperatures. Though Madrid stood, this was the end of the republic, and it makes one think, as the Barcelona essay suggested, of the power of a people divested of natural leaders. It would seem that the people lacked belief in themselves, as in Barcelona. The text piece was by B. H. Liddell Hart, rating the French military leader Gamelin higher than subsequent history justified.

Life's campaign for rearmament was developed in a lead (February 27, 1939) of Roosevelt reviewing the fleet. A chart of model ships showed the whole U.S. Navy in one picture, as it could never be seen in fact. Unfortunately, this may have indicated American preparedness. The editorial page asserted that "Mussolini's hold on Spain will not get stronger, may get weaker." This was a bold and risky but correct prediction. It was also pointed out that the Croat leader in Yugoslavia looked to the Nazis for help. "The foe of our foe is our friend." Tito's Croats, Communists, ultimately took over Yugoslavia. There was a discussion of the identity of the new Pope, and notice of Pacelli.

By chance, I am able to give the writers and checkers on the stories for one issue (March 6, 1939); many were not yet in the masthead. The lead on the San Francisco Exposition was by Lincoln Barnett and Marion Stevens. The editorial page was by Kay and Cort and, on movie Oscars, by Paul Peters. A story on Harry Hopkins was by Thorndike and Stevens. The pope's burial was by Cort and Ruth Berrien. A Nazi brawl in New York was by Julian Bach and MacFarquhar. A celebration of camellias was by Kastner and Kelly, showing a poetic touch in "By April they will be fading all away" (any English stylist must find this inversion ridiculous). Then came a four-page text condensation of Hitler's *Mein Kampf* (Cort and

Spicer): ". . . the greatest game in the world—guessing what Hitler will do next. His book is the most naive self-revelation by a living Head-of-state written. . . . Hitler's opinions are essentially the cranky, unsound, often brilliant opinions of a lonely, self-educated workman. He suspects conspiracies all around him. He has a romantic admiration for power, courage, efficiency and handsome men. . . . He has an affectionate contempt for the mass of the German people and a bitter contempt for all other peoples except the English. His views on history are a strange combination of brilliant sense and howling nonsense . . . 'the masses love the ruler rather than the suppliant . . . they often feel at a loss what to do with freedom. . . . All propaganda must limit itself to a very few points. It need not search for truth.' " This last strikes me as very knowledgeable stuff for dictators, and I think my criticism of *Mein Kampf* stands up as sound. The text piece was on Heywood Broun by Geoffrey Hellman, the attendant captions by Julian Bach and Ruhl. A piece on a jockey was by John Field and Burke. The movie was by Paul Peters and MacFarquhar. The essay (Kay and Shelley Smith, later married to Carl Mydans) was the celebrated one, "Fascism in America—Like Communism It Masquerades as Americanism." Hubie said that communism and fascism each "wins its converts by summoning patriots to 'save America' from the other, but at bottom they are no more unlike than the red and the black on a roulette board." He advised against smashing either communism or fascism by undemocratic means. This expressed a view that he and I had been coming around to in private for some time. Other pieces were British and German warships (Cort and Kelly), laboratory rats (Heiskell and Lang), theatre (Peters and Lumb), Miami waterfront (Thorndike and Keiffer). I am happy to have these details on what various people were doing. Julian Bach was one of a succession of people Longwell introduced with the intent of displacing me as foreign news monopolist. I always tried to help them displace me, but it never happened. Primarily, Billings was leary of any new face. He had, as he thought, "created" me, and he was not going to liquidate his investment lightly. Bach and the others were doomed. Actually, in this issue Bach was more useful than Thorndike or Heiskell.

The lead (March 13, 1939) was the new pope, Eugenio Pacelli, Pius XII. The editorial page said, "Rebel Generalissimo Franco last week became the legal government of Spain when Britain and France and 35 other nations recognized him, on the ground that, though bystanders may like the loser, they must do business with the winner." The essay (17 pages) was the New York World's Fair. Luce's fondest dreams were reflected in a story that "scientific" polls showed that "the Republican Party appears to have a good chance of electing a United States President in November, 1940. . . . Public opinion as revealed by scientific polls gives President Roosevelt a very slim chance of being reelected to a third term." The possible Republican candidates did not include Wendell Willkie.

A poll of congressmen (March 20, 1939) produced a lead analyzing the ten most effective men in each house of Congress, and ennobling Joe Martin as the "ablest Congressman." The editorial page noted that the Spanish Loyalists were gunning down rebellious Communist regiments, as Franco watched.

The turning point came in Hitler's career (March 27, 1939) with his forcible seizure of Prague and all Czechoslovakia. This was the lead. Noting his earlier talk of self-determination, it said, "Last week Hitler dropped all this mumbo-jumbo and committed his first flagrant act of conquest against a foreign people incorrigibly hostile to Nazi Germany . . . for the fourth time in his role as statesman broke his pledged word. . . . There appeared the naked resolve of Hitler to get what he wants, by any method under the sun."

This was shown (April 3, 1939) in the lead "Hitler Follows the Nazis of His 'Trojan Horse' into Czecho-Slovakia" (we had changed the punctuation of Czechoslovakia—a subtle point). So the Czech Nazis' " 'Trojan-horse' job was to use the democratic practices of free speech, free assembly and free press to destroy the democracy. . . . The Czechs knew that they would have to wait for another World War to get another crack at Republicanism. . . . The best that Great Britain could think of last week was an alliance of Britain, France, Soviet Russia and Poland to 'stop Hitler.' The idea appealed to three of the four but emphatically not to Poland unless backed up by a cast-iron military agreement. The Poles knew that if they sign such an alliance they will come next on Hitler's menu. . . . As stupid and gray and unheroic as any murder were the actual details of the murder of Czecho-Slovakia, shown on these pages." Now *Life* tried a difficult and not successful job of defining in a map and text the mixtures of European races, as explained by a Carleton Coons book and researched by John Purcell. "If all the people of Europe should one day undress, scrub themselves clean, shave their heads and assemble in one place without saying a word, anthropologists could finally separate them into their true sub-races. . . . The Germans think they are Nordic but actually the Russians are far more Nordic (see map)." The text headline was "Europe Is a Shambles of Old Races and New."

After a hard day's work, I was in the habit of touring New York's Latin-American night clubs and clip-joints until perhaps four in the morning. This made it difficult to get up at 9:00 A.M. to be at work at ten. Once, my wife resorted to planting a cold washrag on my face. Without opening my eyes I swung an arm. She declined to try to wake me thereafter. And so one morning at around noontime I had not shown up for work, and Billings was pacing up and down, groaning, "I've got to fire Dave. He's the best I've got, but I'm going to fire Dave. I can't rely on him when I need him. I'm going to fire Dave." Hubie Kay, who heard this recital, telephoned me. I arose, bathed, and shaved carefully, had a good breakfast, and strolled in at about one o'clock. I walked into Billings' office and said, "I hear you're looking for me. I'm sorry to be late. I had to take my brother out to a t.b. sanitarium and I missed the train back." (A brother *did* have t.b.) I am told that Billings knew it was a lie; maybe so. Any idea that it affected my status at Time Inc. strikes me as ridiculous, for I was never absent for illness, while nearly everybody else lost weeks. I would say that I was the only absolutely reliable employee, physically, in the whole organization. But some people think this incident was decisive. Maybe so. From that time on, I assigned the job of waking me in the morning to a servant.

In this period the issues are wavering between 80 and 88 pages, well above the level of 60 to 64 pages. The money smell is beginning to come through, faintly but promisingly.

Spain was finished (April 10, 1939) in the lead showing the fall of Madrid, and Franco as the dictator: "In a country of impatient, arrogant and hot-tempered men, he is slow, thorough and endlessly patient. . . . He notably did not join in the angry political debate which has divided and ruined Spain." But now, with Underhill's knowledge, we showed a Spanish panorama on which a Rebel battalion could be faintly made out (an ostensibly dull picture), and labeled the various deployments in the attack on a Spanish village. Then, pointing toward World War II, came a detailed analysis of the weapons on both sides. "Biggest lesson is that the nation with the best factory workers, mechanics and chauffeurs will probably win the next war . . . sound, well-made models that are easy to use and easy to repair in the field. American method of mass production of standard models is a winner. . . . The Russians had a good idea in tanks but everything they manufacture is likely to have fatal mechanical flaws. . . . The probabilities for the next war are that the totalitarian states will have the advantage at first, because of training and organization. But the democracies have the best mechanics and factories. In Spain the cannon mounted in the Russian tanks was able to drive all the other tanks off the field. (Germany has frantically begun to mount small cannon in tanks.) . . . Loyalist troops were ruined by political interference and atrocious command. . . . France has good tanks. Anti-tank guns: Germans have plenty. Russians have the best. . . . The best truck in Spain was the latest Ford. . . . Russian Chato fighters could outclimb, outfly, outmaneuver Italian Fiats. . . . French multi-seat bomber was a terrifying flop. . . . Czech Mauser was best rifle in Spanish war. Czech 'Bren' light machine gun was mainstay of the Loyalists."

This fairly unpictorial spread, published in 1939, relying solely on John Garrett Underhill, Jr., may have been a fairly important factor in the outcome of World War II, and I do not want to hear any Pentagon donkeys saying they knew it all the time. Perhaps Patton and Bradley did, but maybe they read *Life*. Certainly the Germans knew about the failure of the small fast tank against the big, slow, wide-tracked, low-profiled, heavily gunned Russian tank. In discovering that fact alone, the venture in the Spanish civil war was worth any price to the Germans. They had very little time to apply the lesson, but it explained why they did not immediately go up against the excellent big tanks of France.

Any notion that this information was given *Time*'s readers is too silly to be mentioned. *Time* was still worried about scholarship. And World War II was only five months away.

The military facts known today obsolesce part of the above. We did not know that German General von Thoma never had more than 600 Germans (excluding air and administration) in Spain, and had 12 tank companies, 4 equipped with the captured superior Russian tank, all manned by Spaniards, and 30 antitank companies. The impotence of the Loyalists is not a mark against democracy in a fight but against a rabble, especially one maneuvered by doctrinaires of various stripes.

Poland's reliance on horse cavalry was often ridiculed (and by me) but the German Army kept a division of horse cavalry into the invasion of Russia.

We know now that the deservedly terrible reputation of the SS troops obliterated the fact that the behavior of the German *army* was consistently more honorable in World War II than in World War I. Naturally, this reflected the aristocratic honor of the Prussian officer corps, kept exclusive by the restrictions of the Treaty of Versailles, notably in the persons of von Fritsch, von Rundstedt, von Blomberg et al. We hardly knew that Himmler's accusations in early 1938 against von Fritsch and von Blomberg (the former finally vindicated and permitted to die honorably, on the insistence of von Rundstedt) were part of a plan to replace the army by the SS.

Nor could we have guessed the uniform apprehensiveness of the German General Staff which had not wanted a fight at the time of Munich, dreaded a two-front war, and were sure they could not defeat France. Perhaps we sensed that Hitler's two chief military aides, Jodl and Keitel, were little better than clerks. Much of this we know now from Liddell Hart's interviews of the German generals.

To return to the April 10 issue, the editorial page said: "Poland's

poor roads would . . . delay the German conquest several months."
This error of mine seems to have infected all later military
commentators. The next item reveals a valid but demoralizing vein in
my thinking: "The profound apathy that Central Europe inspires in
the United States was never better shown than by the American
press's snubbing of a real war that raged all last week between
Slovakia and Hungary." I had consolidated the idea that I alone
cared about Europe, thus, that I had a journalistic monopoly on
European events, thus, that I would have a monopoly on the
imminent European war. This was not only my fantasy; I had reason
to believe that it was the fantasy of the whole organization.

There was a story on the Polish Nazis: "If Germany marches into
Poland, it will ostensibly be to save these Nazis above from 'Polish
atrocities.'" There was a story on the French president in London,
trying to cement the Franco-British alliance, but this is not by me.
Billings' prejudice is indicated by "*Life* Goes to a Famous Piggery."

Mussolini's army occupied the Albania it had virtually built (April
17, 1939), and this inspired a spread of maps on the history of the
Balkans. Meanwhile, the lead showed Congress considering how to
stay out of war, with a scrupulously fair description of so-called
"internationalists" and "isolationists," both coming out as patriots by
their lights. The editorial page mentioned that "the issue was
squarely up to Hitler and Mussolini whether they prefer their dreams
of empire or the peaceful survival of their people."

The editorial page (April 24, 1939) echoed Roosevelt's request to
Hitler and Mussolini not to engage in further aggression for at least
ten years. A spread of Europe's leaders and another of U.S.
columnists' predictions of war or peace in Europe referred to the
cover of Neville Chamberlain. The essay, which I had been
requesting for some time, was called "Three Families" and showed
an English, a German, and a French family in detail. The Englishman
had the most freedom; the Frenchman, a farmer, the most security;
the German, the least of either. "Statesmen talk big and make the
news. Headlines proclaim what is done by 'England,' 'Germany,'
'France.' But there is no such thing as 'England' or 'Germany' or

'France.' " This complemented an act of maps giving "a history lesson" on the rise and decline of Europe's empires from A.D. 180 to 1939: "Some nine European democracies have not fought one another in over 100 years. For the little men everywhere are notably lacking in imperial ambitions." The lead showed the prosecution of Kansas City's boss, Tom Pendergast. And a caption said, "In 50 years the picture above will probably be among the most famous in the archives of science," describing the splitting of the uranium atom by Fermi and Dunning at Columbia University. Incidentally, this issue was 100 pages, a high for this period.

A tone of contempt (May 1, 1939) was evident in the lead: "The Italo-Albanian War of 1939 takes its small place in world history." The editorial page described British attempts to get agreement on something with Russia, to the horror of Poland and Rumania. Hitler asked the little nations whether they really feared Germany. With a drawing of the House of Commons (never photographed), a Chamberlain speech was reported. "He did not add that the Russians seemed most reluctant to fight Germany simply for the military convenience of Britain and France."

The essay, properly, was "Russia's Army. Is It Any Good?": "The trouble is that everything in the Soviet Union . . . is hidden in an impenetrable cloud bank of censorship, deception and maudlin propaganda. . . . First of all, big . . . 98 infantry divisions and 32 cavalry divisions, plus artillery and tanks. The high command of the Army has been decimated by Stalin's purge. . . . Most outsiders think the purges wrecked the Army, insiders who know best seem to think they helped it. The Russian Army will be valuable, even if it loses battles. But the nations of the West want to know whether Russia will win a battle or two in the next war. . . . Against the Germans, the answer is in considerable doubt."

On this story I had an entrée to our military attaché in Moscow, Colonel Faymonville, whom I found at the New York Athletic Club. He would not flatly give me any figures on Russian arms. But if I asked, "Have they more than 4,000 tanks?" and "Have they less than 6,000?" he would nod yes or no.

The story continued: "The dream of the Russians is a vast tank attack over the flat plains of West Russia and Poland. . . . Besides heavy tanks for the break-through, they actually have a large quantity of light cross-country tanks to follow up the break-through. . . . Any such attack is doubtful because it rejects Russia's natural strategy of luring the enemy into that country's vast open spaces, breaking his long communication lines and then destroying him . . . at least 4,500 first-line planes and perhaps 6,000 reserves (evidently, Faymonville refused to be definite here); 5,000 tanks (Christie and Vickers copies and the big native Zhdanov); 1,600 pieces of heavy artillery (much of it Czech-designed); 23,000 heavy machine guns; 30,000 light machine guns."

This is not bad prediction; it describes the events of 1941–1945 on the Eastern Front.

The editorial page is fascinating (May 1, 1939), for Hubie Kay condensed Hitler's 25,000-word reply to Roosevelt's suggestion of no further aggression as "Poland, look out! England, take it easy! Roosevelt, shut up! Great going, Adolf!" The Russian position is defined as having "a diplomatic murkiness bordering on genius: 'Our position is perfectly clear. Russia will assist Europe in case of aggression.'" Chamberlain says, "No one can pretend that this is peacetime."

The Letters column (May 15, 1939) called the "Three Families" story "one of the finest things which *Life* has ever presented." "There appears to be not a trace of propaganda and that's what I like." It was also what I liked. The lead was the New York World's Fair. The editorial page noted that Russia's Litvinoff, the last of the "collective security" champions who had engineered the fake identity of democracy and communism, had been "retired" by Russia. A happy poll showed that the American people preferred Dewey to Roosevelt.

An odd diversion from Europe (May 22, 1939) was an essay on Brazil: "So far this racial melting pot has produced a man who is quick-witted, quick-tempered, languid, unambitious, incurious, superlatively good-humored and laughing." The infiltration by Germans, Japanese, British, and Americans is shown, and the peculiar domination of the industrial south by the agricultural north, reversing the North American pattern.

The visit of the English king and queen to North America (May 29, 1939), the lead, dominates the issue. The essay is Roosevelt's Hyde Park in expectation of the visit.

At this point, what did Luce think of his whole journalistic operation? Where was the point at which he wanted the good information to arrive? *Time? Fortune?* We have data on this. On May 27, 1939, he made a speech at Shawnee-on-the-Delaware, Pennsylvania, where he imagined that the U.S. Supreme Court might become the Super Brain Trust of Time Inc. "Well, now that I mention it, I think that would be a hell of a good idea—and maybe we'll get around to doing something like that someday. [Of course, he was being careless and flippant.] It's fun to think of Dave Cort or John Billings, two hours before *Life* is going to press with its lead article, picking up the phone and saying, 'Hughes? Oh, hey, Charlie, what do we do with Queen Elizabeth, give her the big hand, the razz gentle, or the bum's rush?' And not so funny either, since on one kind of treatment or another may depend the balance of power in Europe and therefore the future of the white race." (Elizabeth was George VI's queen, then approaching the United States.) He was thinking of *Life*; he was thinking of power; and at this moment of suspense he was thinking of Billings and me, hoping we would call the shots correctly. But this kind of power is unreliable.

The whole issue (June 5, 1939) was given to "America's Future." The editorial page explained: "The purpose of this special issue of *Life* is to take stock of some of the abiding things which are magnificently *right* about America. . . . Even America's bad headlines looked good beside the headlines which continued to come last week from the rest of the world"—thus, a selection.

The issue paraded the Pacific Northwest and the Grand Coulee Dam (the lead), aluminum versus steel in production, "American Yesterdays" in photographs, progressive education, text "The American Destiny" by Walter Lippmann, U.S. production as compared to other nations' in eleven categories, the "boom" in the arts, scientific farming, urban living, *The Grapes of Wrath* by Steinbeck, television, and pretty girls. My only contribution was the Futurama exhibit at the World's Fair, the text trying to project "America in 1960."

The material in this is far beyond my competence; obviously, it came from Buckminster Fuller, now connected in some way with *Life.* The divergences from the actual 1960, both plus and minus, seem to me fascinating: "The cars, built like raindrops, are powered by rear engines that are probably improvements of the Diesel. Inside, they are air-conditioned. They cost as low as $200. . . . The happiest people live in one-factory farm-villages producing one small industrial item and their own farm produce. . . . Liquid air is by 1960 a potent, mobile source of power. Atomic energy is being used cautiously. Power is transmitted by radio beams focused by gold reflectors. . . . Such new alloys as heat-treated beryllium bronze give perfect service. Cures for cancer and infantile paralysis have extended man's life span. . . . Architecture and plane construction have been revolutionized by light, noninflammable, strong plastics from soy beans. . . . The Lanova cell has made all gasoline motors Diesels. Electronic microscopes literally see everything. . . . Politics and emotion still slow progress . . . a vision of what Americans, with their magnificent resources . . . can make of their country by 1960, if they will." This was followed by a letter from Buckminster Fuller, enclosing little-remarked headlines on recent strides of science.

Bucky's contribution to the issue was, on balance, magnificent. The checkers would have had to work with him, not with me.

The editorial page (June 12, 1939) returned to the failure of British efforts to negotiate a Russian alliance. "Actually Joseph Stalin & Co. look on Britain and France as not only crooked but also weak." A story on the Spanish peace said, "After the parade, the Spanish Peace really got under way. It was announced that 688 Loyalists had been shot by firing squads."

It was a good time (June 26, 1939) to remind people of Sarajevo and World War I on their anniversary (12 pages). Two bullets took 8.5 million lives. Maps showed the history. One picture was captioned "The Russians were all too often seen in this position, their hands in air, their 1891 Mouzin rifles on the ground. . . . The Russian hordes were brave and hardy and they were often deliberately thrown away. . . . The German armies did not break. They retired in good order. . . . But the German home front had cracked months before."

The masthead was revolutionized (July 3, 1939). The photographers, whom I have overlooked since this is a book about writers and their work, had always been listed ahead of the writers. Presumably, this indicated Luce's belief that he was selling pictures. *Life* copy often mentioned the photographer, rarely the writer.

Now, after the executive editors, Longwell and Hicks, came the associate editors, in hierarchical order: Kay, Cort, Thorndike (an elevation here), Kastner, Busch (transferred from *Time* as, I think, text editor), Albertson (head checker), and Richard de Rochemont (a field man). Photographers were divided and scattered among two categories of researchers and junior writers. The first division was editorial associates: Julian Bach, Lincoln Barnett, Margaret Bourke-White, Alfred Eisenstaedt, John Field, Frank Hall Fraysur, Bernard Hoffman, Dorothy Hoover, Harold Horan (a field man, dropped in the next issue), Sally Kenniston, Alexander King, Thomas D. McAvoy, Hansel Mieth, Carl W. Mydans, John Phillips, Gerard Piel, Tom Prideaux, Peter Stackpole, Edward K. Thompson, Charles Tudor, William Vandivert, and Margaret Varga.

Editorial assistants were John Allen, Margaret Bassett, Ruth Berrien, Don Burke, Roger Butterfield, Olivia Chambers, Judith Chase, Diane Cummings, Sidney James, Elaine Keiffer, Will Lang, Dorothy Jane Larson, Margaret MacFarquhar, Richard Pollard, David Ritchie, Helen Robinson, Roxane Ruhl, Bernice Shrifte, Shelley Smith (soon to marry Carl Mydans), Jean Speiser, Marian Stevens, and Lura Street.

Finally came Publisher Roy Larsen, General Manager C. D. Jackson, and Advertising Director Howard Black.

The issue was a diversion: the lead on the admiral of the U.S. Asiatic Fleet (the Japanese were pushing whites around); the Nazi "conquest" of Antarctica; the World's Fair (15 pages); and Nijinsky doing one leap in a Swiss insane asylum.

After a lead on a Louisiana political scandal (July 10, 1939), the editorial page said, "Europe had the jitters bad last week. . . . Hitler was going to move again." A story, "The Threat of War," said: "The whole world suddenly thought it knew the answer last week to the great question of which way Hitler was going to jump next. The world's answer was Poland. . . . Something was about to happen." But the essay switched to Japan and a picture of the emperor: "Readers who do not want to óffend the Japanese will be careful not to hold this picture upside down, to put any object on it, to sit on it, or to throw it away. . . . Every Japanese thinks he is more or less a god. . . . Their fancy history was invented about 700 A.D. . . . completed and codified only 70 years ago." There was a story on the Duke of Windsor's Paris house (not for long), and the text was on Eddie Rickenbacker by Francis Sill Wickware and Charles J. V. Murphy. (Wickware committed suicide about a decade later.)

A brilliant change of pace by Billings was given (July 17, 1939) with a lead on the genius of Leonardo da Vinci, which I wrote, I think, based on my *Time* stories. Contrary to Time Inc. policy, I listed titles of pertinent books at the end. With a cover and story on Britain's Foreign Secretary Lord Halifax went: "Rarely has British foreign policy found itself in a more treacherous quicksand than right now . . . offering Poland a guarantee against any 'unilateral' change in the status of the Free City of Danzig. The assumption is that Nazi Danzig would declare itself in the German Reich. . . . The Polish Army would invade Danzig; Germany would invade Poland; and Britain would declare war on Germany. . . . The solution to all his [Halifax's] troubles was . . . an alliance with Soviet Russia."

The lead showed Roosevelt (July 24, 1939) objecting to WPA workers "striking against the U.S. Government," objecting to the new requirement that they work 130 hours a month. Hubie Kay wrote: "The majority of the American people now unquestionably accept both the necessity and probable permanence of Relief, believe overwhelmingly that the Government should give the unemployed jobs instead of cash." While a bevy of American publishers agreed that "there will be no war this year," the editorial page said that Britain had semimobilized for "possible crisis in August." The essay was, delightfully, on Ireland. I had gotten the photographers to document the ownership of every building and field on an airview of a small Irish village, Quin in Clare. The dominant family was the Clunes. While the Nazi popularity in Ireland was acknowledged, the point was made that "facts are still unpopular in Ireland. Sentiment, piety, a good song or a good phrase, friendship and the past, are what work magic on the Irish."

In the next two issues there was little excitement except for a lead on the FBI's new attention to espionage and notice of Roosevelt's terminating the commercial treaty with Japan as a warning.

On the editorial page (August 14, 1939), after a lead on more union trouble, was a quote from the German chief of staff: "Compared to 1914, we have the upper hand now." An added comment: "If there is to be war this year, Germany and Italy were last week getting ready for it." One British delegation went to Moscow as another "gave up and said he was coming home." Fairly irrelevant were stories on the Alpine passes and a Croat who wanted to break up Yugoslavia, possibly with Hitler's help. Highly relevant was the essay (12 pages) on "The New U.S. Army Division," doubtless with Underhill's help. "In grim earnest America is getting ready to fight a war. . . . By modern paradox a nation makes exactly the same preparations for avoiding war as for waging war." There was full army cooperation to show one streamlined division, which still existed only on paper.

The state of Europe was described (August 21, 1939) after a lead on Saudi Arabia's lease of oil fields to American companies: "In fond memory of these great events there were some 10,000,000 men in uniform last week—2,500,000 Germans, 1,800,000 Russians, 1,000,000 Frenchmen, 1,000,000 Poles, 750,000 Englishmen, 500,000 Italians, 380,000 Turks, 300,000 Greeks, 550,000 Rumanians, 500,000 Yugoslavs, 300,000 Hungarians and 290,000 Bulgarians."

The next issue (August 28, 1939) would have closed on August 19, Saturday, and perhaps I had left on vacation (but perhaps not). The lead was "Germany Uncovers Its Heaviest Artillery to Cow National-ist Poles": "Last week in Europe ten million men slept on their rifles ready for the outbreak of a Second World War. . . . This time it was Poland that was being subjected to the same kind of pressure which eventually obliterated Czechoslovakia. . . . As a deadline for that solution press reports named September 2 when the Nazi Congress opens at Nürnberg." It was observed that the German army was north, west, and south of Poland and that all German weapons were new.

The next issue (September 4, 1939) dated the signing of the Hitler-Stalin pact as Thursday, August 24. It was actually signed by Ribbentrop late at night Wednesday, August 23, but the Soviet News Agency had announced it on Monday. Thus, on Tuesday or Wednesday, I was being driven across the International Bridge over the St. Lawrence River when I read the news and began kicking myself. I had no impulse whatever to rush back to the office—probably I am not a journalist at all. Presently a telegram from Luce, not Billings, arrived: What did I think? I believe I replied that it meant war, almost immediately.

The German invasion began on September 1, 1939, a Friday. Thus, I suspect I had nothing to do with that issue either, though I may be wrong. I could have taken the night train Friday night, arriving on our closing day, Saturday.

Hubie Kay wrote the lead on the "Nazi-Red Pact": "High priests of the world's new political religions make a deal . . . reveal themselves as nothing after all but a pair of hardboiled and practical bosses . . . Stalin stepped neatly out from between the German-Japanese pincers. . . . Hitler nipped the budding British-French-Russian alliance." The map of Germany's invasion lines into Poland was correct; the emphasis on the importance of "General Mud" on Poland's dirt roads became an unhappy cliché; the statement that "modern warfare gives a great advantage to the defense" was contrary to our policy; and the statement that the war might be "but a re-enactment of the long and bloody stalemate of 1914–18" was unfortunate. A nice point made on the editorial page was that Spain's "devout Catholic leaders, who had taken seriously Hitler's attacks on the godless Russians, seemed likely to stay clear of a war." (Since this remained true for six years, saving Gibraltar for Great Britain, this was beautiful prediction, and changed the significance of the Spanish war, if it did not completely justify poor Goldsborough and make a fool of all doctrinaires, for history is notoriously cruel to them.) On this page also appeared the fact that England signed her formal assistance pact with Poland on Friday, August 25, and remember that this is the "Appeaser," Neville Chamberlain. The signing had evidently been held up while the negotiations with Russia went on. After these titanic goings-on, incredibly, the very next story in the front of the magazine is the movie of Clare Boothe Luce's *The Women*.

Hubie Kay, continuing *Life*'s consistent position, had signaled the imminent invasion of Poland (and for good measure predicted Spain's future policy).

What did *Time*'s Foreign News do with this same situation, for their issue (September 4, 1939), closing on a Monday instead of a Saturday, had two more days to work with? The record is preposterous, and one must wonder about Luce's permitting the humbug of *Time* to coexist with the realities of *Life*. The story was a literary orgasm about the crashing of old illusions, and had the curious effect of bedlam. "Poland was not alarmed. Poland had not counted on Russia's help . . . something had shaken Hitler's plan, disrupted Hitler's timetable. . . . He would have had the advantage of war if he had plunged to seize Danzig . . . the Pause of Guilt began." (What in hell does that mean?) The idea of the pact was traced back to January 12, 1939, when Hitler had spoken amiably to the Russian ambassador. The Nazi press is then described as having abruptly broken off its attacks on Stalin! A fantasy of secret contacts is then spun out. Finally, "All the world had predicted it, all the world had known it all along. . . . But the Pact was less than a week old when Stalin surprisingly caused his Congress to delay ratification. By all the omens the Pact had an unhappy life ahead of it."

This is not just wrong, and proved wrong three days later; it is a whirligig of lies. Hardly a word of it could possibly have been checked against any source. "All the world had predicted it"; I had not predicted or heard of it. The story was a total abdication of the whole Time Inc. system. It was a purple fustian of somebody's retroactive nightmare. But whose?

The masthead of *Time* magazine must be given again. Associate Editors: Carlton Balliett, Robert Cantwell, Laird Goldsborough (not foreign editor), David Hulburd, John S. Martin, Fanny Saul, Walter Stockly, and Dana Tasker. Contributing Editors: Roy Alexander, John F. Allen, Robert W. Boyd, Jr., Roger Butterfield, *John Chamberlain, Whittaker Chambers*, Robert Fitzgerald, *Calvin Fixx*, Ralph Getsinger, Walter Graebner, *John Hersey*, Sidney L. James, Eliot Janeway, John Kobler, Pearl Kroll, Louis Kronenberger, Thomas K. Krug, John T. McManus, Peter Mathews, *Robert Neville*, Russell Olsen, Sidney Olson, John Osborne, Green Peyton (a Wertenbaker, and a brilliant journalist), Williston C. Rich, Jr., Winthrop Sargeant, Robert Sherrod, Leon Svirsky, Felice Swados, *Charles Wertenbaker*.

The names in italics wrote foreign news off and on. But there can be no doubt who wrote the above lines. The apocalyptic style of Whittaker Chambers is imprinted all over them. The master of the big lie, thickly lathered with the pretense of culture beyond the reach of his teacher, Hitler, is at work. The intellectuals, left, right, and center, still believe in Whittaker, whom I had known from college on, but here his weird nonsense was exposed in three days. No defense is possible.

Whittaker went on to further heights (September 11, 1939, closing September 4), in which the new department, World War (this time correctly), filled eight pages: "Adolf Hitler, if allowed to take and keep this much [Danzig and the Polish Corridor] might have checked his juggernaut at these lines for the time being. When Britain and France insisted that he withdraw entirely from Polish soil or consider himself at war with them, he determined on the complete shattering and subjugation of Poland." To "General Mud" *Time* soon added "General Snow." It had the main Polish defense line much too far forward. It also described the Mediterranean as "tideless" (poetic license; the tides are feeble except at deep inlets such as the Adriatic Sea).

Poor *Time*, obsessed with cultural scholarship, awoke to find itself mired to its eyeballs in the barbarities of serious war. But, worse, it had Whittaker, who in the above had neatly blamed the destruction of Poland on Neville Chamberlain. *Time*'s foreign news was not only written by a traitorous madman; it was getting into print under the sanction of Luce.

A brief digression on Whittaker Chambers (one of a dozen aliases: his real name was Jay Vivian Chambers) may be helpful. He was not entirely mad. To ingratiate himself with the religious Luce, he decided to be baptized in the Episcopalian Church a year later. This was done. But even here he lies. He has written that he was introduced to the Reverend William D. F. Hughes by Samuel Welles; the minister knows that it was T. S. Matthews who introduced him. T. S. Matthews, who seems in this instance a willing liar, confirms Chambers' lie and later disavows it. But the whole thing is charlatanism, masked by the most beautiful acting, and aimed at Luce. Later, Chambers joined the Quakers: more histrionics. Obviously, Luce was taken in by it: he believed in Chambers. I was at the time unaware of these peculiar gambits in my world. Two sides of my family are Dutch Reformed and Quaker, but I grew up singing in the choir of an Episcopal church. Luce asked me, "What are you anyway, Dave?" I said, "Dutch Reformed." He said, "It figures," a cryptic reply.

I hope to see my view accepted that Chambers was a genius impostor, a congenital liar of such magnificence as to deserve enduring fame, but at present the intellectuals, those eternal suckers for words divorced from truth, do not see it this way. His performance at the opening of World War II may suggest something to them.

Both the Cort and Chambers theories about the Hitler-Stalin pact are brushed aside by history. It had nothing to do with any ideological conjunction of fascism and communism, and still less with a "Pause of Guilt" or anything "the whole world" had known. It was simply what the Prussian officer corps demanded of Hitler, in its horror of a two-front war and indifference to shades of ideology, for most of them were disgusted by Nazism. We know this now, at least to my satisfaction, from Liddell Hart's *The German Generals Talk*.

Section IV

THE HOLOCAUST

THE invasion of Poland on September 1 was a culmination for which *Life* readers were prepared, for I had long since deduced that behind the plausible and even acceptable words lurked a mad dog. The event (September 11, 1939) was, I believe, described by Hubie Kay, closing out any myth that Cort was indispensable. The frontispiece, by a shrewd philosophic indirection, was on the children who would be the casualties of World War II bombing, as they had not been of World War I, but this earlier "lost generation" now had to fight World War II. And "Second Armageddon was on." A history of the progress toward war from 1918 on followed, making the point that it was Europe's mess. But March 15, the day when Hitler seized the rump of Czechoslovakia, "made him an outlaw. . . . It was plain that Hitler could never again ask the world for justice." With maps of the Mediterranean, irrelevant at the moment, it was suggested that Hitler's " 'little war' threatened to spread and spread and spread until it included the Mediterranean," as it did, beginning a year later. The issue, closing on Saturday, September 2, nevertheless included the fact that Britain and France declared war on Germany on Sunday, September 3, at respectively 11:00 A.M., and 5:00 P.M., their time. The text piece was on Göring; the essay on war planes, giving the pregnant facts that at last British plane production was at 1,000 a

183

month and "The German Air Force has 6,000 first-line planes which are easily the equal of the first-line planes of any other power." Possibly on the basis of my reply to Luce's telegram, the issue had been geared in advance to war, for the movie was *Nurse Edith Cavell*, a heroine of the last war, and the "Speaking of Pictures" was on recovery of scrap metal from old battlefields.

The problem of Underhill and myself (September 18, 1939) became Major George Fielding Eliot, called in to write a page of "military analysis" of the war, probably through Dan Longwell. His account was a travesty, which Underhill and I edited, but still this appeared: "A serious battle, the first great engagement of the war, seems now to be developing" south of East Prussia. "Very much stiffer Polish resistance may now be anticipated . . . the Polish Army is still intact and ready to act at the proper moment. . . . Britain and France appear to be mounting an attack against the German western border." The lead made the somewhat different point that "seven-day drive by a mechanized German Army 200 miles northeast to Warsaw showed that once a 'break-through' is made and the enemy's resistance is disordered, an efficiently organized tank attack can keep on driving him over the horizon. This is a potent precedent for the western front." (More prediction.)

Probably later, I asked our London office to see whether Major General J. F. C. Fuller, author of a favorite book of mine, *Decisive Battles*, but unfortunately a British Fascist, would do military commentary. The British government forbade any communication with General Fuller. (His description of the Battle of Warsaw is beautiful.) Longwell was of course defending Major Eliot. One excuse for Eliot was that he was trying to make a suspenseful contest out of the Polish war when the suspense was over.

On the editorial page was the note that Mussolini was still neutral, and that the war might peter out. The text piece was on "The Week the War Began," a delightful assemblage of trivia by Noel Busch. At the end, "*Life* Goes Calling on Winston Churchill"— an early and by no means stupid toadying to the next prime minister, certainly instigated by Longwell, who probably went over to interview him. Here we see at its best the instinct of the political mind, as contrasted with my own, which was not even concerned with Churchill. Like Goldsborough, Longwell believed in politics, connivery, personal relations, the boys in the back room.

Luce's instinct for making things big, big, big exploded in a whole issue of 104 pages (September 25, 1939) on "The War World." Of course it could not be achieved, but he had people who could make a philosophical pretense of achieving it.

The lead on the Polish conquest said, "Nobody can add up all the tears and agony and rage that a people feel when the sovereign nation they live under is destroyed by the brute force of an alien people. . . . The world was getting its first real taste of what war, Nazi-style, was like."

But, given the known fact of the Nazi-Communist pact, why was there no recognition that the pact must have given part of Poland to Russia? It seems that an event obsesses the journalist and inhibits him from speculating on the preceding or subsequent policies of the actor. He has a job: the event. He is so busy telling about it that his generalized thinking is cut off. This is, of course, an alibi for my lack of perception.

Then came Major G. F. Eliot: "The case of the Polish Army as it stands is bad if not wholly desperate. Its first great ally, General Mud, appears on the way. . . . If General Mud can hold Germany up till Poland's second ally General Winter arrives, Germans will not be in a good spot." His story was contradicted by Life's map showing the areas of German conquest. Underhill and I were protesting every paragraph of Eliot's, but in vain. I see now that Eliot was injected by Longwell in an attempt to cut back the monopoly on war held by myself and Underhill. I did not think so at the time.

The editorial page noted cautious fighting on the Western front, the Russian army's entry into Poland, and Russia's truce with Japan. A Fortune survey of public opinion showed that 83% of Americans wanted the Allies to win; 3% "wanted to fight with Allies now."

Then in "The War World" came some maps of grand strategy, pictures of "who's who in the war world," how to force a fortress, a text piece on Adolf Hitler, with an illustration, "he is enraptured by body movements of Broadway dancer Verne." This was one Miriam

Verne, whose lawyer brought suit against Time Inc. I gave a statement to our lawyer on why every interest of Hitler's was of possible significance in world affairs, and the suit was dropped. Then came a story of bombers and maps of logical European target areas, a story on birds of prey which had gone to press six weeks earlier, one on the blockade of Germany with map, a world map of trade routes, giving ship tonnages, "gold hordes" (*sic*, but correctly spelled in the text), short histories (2 pages each) of the British Empire and the German people—friendly toward both—American neutrality founded in "the disillusion of their last crusade," a picture story of U.S. progress into World War I and of the postwar disillusion, exposure of British propaganda in both wars, a "Dictionary of Modern Warfare," explaining infantryman, machine guns, grenades, mortars, light artillery, howitzers, medium and heavy artillery, tank, anti-tank gun, armored car, anti-aircraft guns. The issue was at least sincerely trying to be "The War World."

As for the real facts of "The War World," the Germans used 1,180 bombers, 336 dive bombers, 1,179 fighter planes against Poland's 935 military planes, most destroyed by surprise in the first hour or so. Two German air fleets fanned out at 4:40 A.M. September 1 and hit airfields, rail junctions, bridges, and mobilization centers, preventing the mobilization of any more than 800,000 Poles. German convicts in Polish uniforms "attacked" German outposts, were killed and displayed as proof of provocation. The Germans employed 1.5 million men in 55 heavily gunned divisions, including 6 armored, as against 1 Polish armored division and masses of cavalry. The famous German blitz was compromised when one Polish general (Kutrzeba) counterattacked with 12 battered divisions against the flank of an envelopment, and brought down on himself the German Eighth, Tenth, and Fourth armies—an episode the French General Staff might have noted (but did not). The French were busy delivering a rabbit tap on the Western front with overwhelming superiority. Of the *heroic Poles*—surely the word is not obsolete—100,000 escaped via Rumania to fight again in Western Europe. Poland lost a million men in combat, 1,286,000 in captivity, by both German and Russian hands. The heroism is singular, the black villainy double. At the time we sensed accurately the crude outline, seen in fog, and no more. But not Major Eliot.

A letter in the next issue (October 2, 1939) applauding Eliot's "expert military analysis" seems to me now (not then) an obvious and vulgar Longwell plant, even crassly dictated by him. To the present reader it must come through as sheer historical farce, poor Longwell, obsessed with office politics and his own destiny. The lead noted: "Tidal wave of anti-war letters hits Congress." The editorial page said: "Though Poland's capital, by a strange trick of lightning war, held out, the war in the east was over." There was mention of the death of Colonel-General Werner von Fritsch, ex-commander-in-chief, without knowledge of the officer corps' refusal to accept Himmler's false dossier that he was a homosexual, and the compromise that he be allowed to die in battle. Under a newsreel sequence of a Nazi bombing flight over Poland was the story "A Brand-New Kind of War." "Germany knew before it invaded Poland that Russia was ready to come in the back way as soon as the dirty work had been done. The Germans therefore decided to carry the war of fast mechanized columns to its farthest extreme. . . . This new tactic was simply to strike for the enemy's bases and communications, hell-bent for leather, and largely ignore his armed forces." Obviously, this contradicted Major Eliot's accounts of what had been happening. Reverting to the Western front was an airview drawing of the Saar, noting, "The very first lesson in war is geography. The shape of the land, the course of rivers, impose their shape and course on all armed conflict." The text was Joseph Stalin, by Leon Trotsky, making the point that Stalin could not tolerate losing an argument.

The neutrality point was continued (October 9, 1939) with a lead on the American Legion Convention which significantly voted to stay neutral on the matter of neutrality. The editorial page reported that Russia had virtually seized Estonia. The text was by George Fielding Eliot: "How the Germans seized Poland in Four Weeks." "German object was the destruction of the Polish Army in as short a time as possible." (This contradicted my earlier statement that the Germans had "largely ignored" Poland's armed forces, but was old-style military thinking.) This sort of maundering went on until "a word of

caution is perhaps necessary against overemphasizing the possibilities
of mechanized troops used as the Germans used theirs in Poland in a
swift long-range war of movement. . . . These conditions are unlikely
to repeat themselves in western Europe." Backed by Underhill's
intelligence, I did what I could to tell Billings that Eliot was missing
the whole point of the Polish war, but what I have quoted appeared
in print. It occurs to me now that Longwell had more power than I
suspected at the time, and it was perhaps my innocence of his
machinations that enabled me to overpower him for so many years
(but not, of course, forever). My power was merely the truth, not
political. Longwell's power streamed directly from Luce, and it
intimidated Billings. For in those days the truth was destroying such
mountebanks as Longwell, as with Whittaker Chambers on *Time*, a
destruction in that case delayed by only three days. But Luce, as the
subsequent history proves, did not notice these destructions or, more
probably, did not care, for his attention was becoming fixed on
something more fascinating than the truth—power.

For power was what we were looking at—the power of Nazi
Germany and Communist Russia, the power of a man in a room to
send out an order that would activate tens of millions of other men to
accomplish a coherent end. And then the end was accomplished.
Whole nations vanished like smoke, almost overnight, as if by
pressing a button.

The issue also described "The Low Countries" ("the armies of
both Belgium and The Netherlands are negligible") "And a High
Country": "Switzerland rears out of Europe like a fortress. Its people
have the same fighting tradition as the mountain peoples of Scotland,
Afghanistan and Kentucky. Its Army does not look like much but it is
a bear cat. . . . The Swiss rifle is a beautifully made piece, unlike the
mass production junk used by the Russians, Germans, French and
Italians."

Another problem Underhill and I labored under is indicated by a
memorandum I addressed at about this time to Billings and
Longwell, with copies to Allan A. Michie, Ralph D. Paine, Frederic
Sondern, and Noel Busch:

Mr. Michie entirely demolishes *Time*'s stories on British and German
aviation for 3½ pages, then polishes off *Life* in half a page as "even worse in

its inaccuracies and wrong conclusions." His claimed sources are the aviation editor of Scripps-Howard's Science Series, the U.S. air attaché in London and "officials of the British Air Ministry." The stories were for September 11 and 25.

Life Error No. 1: "The average crew of bombers, none of which are sound-proofed as *Life* says, is three or four men, not five. The radio operator and aft gunner is usually one and the same person." The facts: July 5, 1939, *Aeroplane, Jane's Aircraft, Aviation* Editor S. Paul Johnson, and the U.S. Army agree that the Vickers-Wellington heavy bomber (under which *Life's* caption appeared) has a soundproofed cabin, carries five men normally. Not only are Michie's sources wrong about the Vickers-Wellington *Life* was describing but, in heavy bombers, as well as many medium bombers, of all kinds, five-man crews are common if not the minimum. Examples: Boeing B-17, Douglas B-18, Junkers Ju-89, Italian SM-79 and 81, etc. Furthermore, *Life's* caption specifically states that the radio operator or navigator works the aft machine gun.

Life Error No. 2: "*Time* says the Wellington does almost 300 m.p.h. *Life* says it can only do 180!" *Life* said, to be exact: "When loaded, it has a range of 3,200 miles at a speed of 180 m.p.h." As anybody is supposed to know, a plane's top speed is enormously wasteful of gasoline, only applies to emergency spurts in combat. We were giving its economical cruising speed with a load for distance, as even the uninitiated reader realized. The entire spread carefully distinguishes between top and average cruising speeds.

Error No. 3: "The cut used of the He 11 for a German bomber is not representative, for the Dornier bombers are much more commonly used and much better." *Life* printed pictures of both. (Did this man read the story?) But, even if we had only printed the Heinkel, the Heinkel He 11 is the plane that gets into every day's newspaper, the Do-17 not nearly so often. Probably—though nobody knows—the Heinkels now outnumber the Dorniers.

Error No. 4: "The Hurricane is not the fastest British plane, as *Life* says, nor the commonest fighter. Both distinctions fall to the British Spitfire." *Life* said, "Vickers Spitfire, an interceptor, is Great Britain's fastest plane." Nobody can find any reference at any time in *Life* to the Hurricane as the fastest or the commonest. The Hurricane was laid out on the page ahead of the Spitfire, however, indicating it was then the commonest, which it was, according to Al Williams, Bell Aircraft's Larry Bell, *Aviation* Editor Johnson and all the British aviation magazines for the first half of 1939.

Error No. 5: "Figures on total British production are very much in error. The Air Ministry set 1,000 planes a month as their goal for Oct. 1. They reached this mark, and topped it by almost 200 planes." On this point at last Michie may be right, for *Life* said in the issue of Sept. 11, as of about Sept. 1: "This summer Britain really speeded up mass production. Planes now coming off the line at the rate of 1,000 a month."

I have gone into this criticism of Michie's in such detail for a special reason. *Life*'s military research has put us so far in the enviable position of never having had to back down on important facts.° On some arguable points, probably the writer is to blame for trying to make the facts more effective. Through Underhill we have had contact, directly or indirectly, with the great American names in American civil and military aviation and Underhill seems to understand what they are talking about, unlike many "experts" and nearly all journalists. Americans have had a far better look at German aviation than the British or French. Americans also are in a fine position to get Allied information, since they are supplying Allied planes. The U.S. is right now about as good a place as there is in the world to find out what's up.

As against this, it appears that our men who go to London and Paris are immediately subjected to pressure to turn into Allied propaganda agents. Actually the English and French should feel only profound gratitude toward *Life* and *Time*. We have tended to give them the break wherever reasonable. That does not seem to be enough for the English in particular, one of whom charged Sondern with being in the pay of Germany because *Life* gave an English bomber's cruising speed as 180 m.p.h. as against a German 260 m.p.h. This is to be expected. But I would ask that our London people, instead of shying their garbled misinformation at us, would go to work really to dig out facts that American experts won't instantly shoot to pieces. Let them gently tell the British and French our New York office is pretty confident about its facts and that we cannot be shouted down.

Michie was doubtless exposed to this pressure and was trying to remedy what he had been convinced was a wrong. Evidently, he knows nothing about aviation and unfortunately did not write down the British criticisms accurately as he must have heard them. His military aviation criticisms of *Time*, which I do not take up, range from the controversial to the ridiculous. His memorandum, in short, gives us nothing of value and only wastes the time of our whole checking staff. Del Paine some weeks ago spoke up in the same vein. Could not all this valuable energy on the other side be put to some useful purpose?

We did not know the extent of the Wehrmacht's opposition to the "housecleaning" in the Government General of Poland of "Jews, intelligentsia, clergy, nobility" by Himmler's SS. One officer said that it was "especially annoying to the troops that young men instead of fighting at the front were testing their courage on defenseless people." For the German army, like all good armies, still prided itself

° Except for a few absurd boners, most of which we caught on the following Tuesday to our chagrin.

on its honor, and no honorable man could watch what the SS were doing in Poland. Generaloberst Johannes Blaskowitz (a Prussian with a Polish name), commander-in-chief, East, began to criticize SS policy to Berlin in December and kept on doing it. He was moved out in the spring and never again received an important command until the very end of the war, but evidently Hitler did not dare to cashier him, for he was a member of the Prussians' club. Though the *New York Times* reported Blaskowitz's objections, we did not understand the depth of feeling as expressed in one officer's letter to his wife: "This extermination of a whole race, including women and children, is possible only for subhumans, that no longer deserve the German name. It shames me to be a German!" This man, as reported by Telford Taylor, was later hanged by Hitler. Had we known some of this, we might have foreseen the Prussians' anti-Hitler plot.

The episode also says something about the need for an aristocracy in any society. The German proletariat were delighted with Hitler. The only protest, and ultimately the only revolt, came from the aristocracy. For any worthy aristocracy must be, in Thomas Jefferson's phrase, one of "virtue and talent." The proletariat will always be deficient in these two attributes. Nations that cannot recognize and honor the superior man will always slide into the egalitarian hoodlum's pit of Hitler's Germany, or the equivalent. Against the mob, as of the children in America today, the superior man cannot survive or function, and America too may be ready for the pit.

The number of pages went briefly to 108 (October 16, 1939). The lead was on a Pan-American meeting which asked the belligerents to stay roughly 300 miles outside the Western Hemisphere south of Canada. England objected. The editorial page said, "It was a kind of half-armistice. . . . The Versailles System, upon whose injustices [Hitler] rose to power, was in fact finished." Hitler asked, "Why should this war in the west be fought?" Bernard Shaw unbrilliantly said, "The war is over"; Lloyd George, responsible for the Versailles system, was not in favor of fighting for it. And now Russia moved in on Latvia (one a week). "Next in line appeared to be Lithuania . . . and Finland." A piece on the war against U-boats, which should ordinarily have been staff-written, is by Major Eliot, reinforcing my belief—now but not at the time—that Longwell felt his career depended on undercutting me and Underhill. Eliot should not otherwise have written this routine piece.

The point of the earlier editorial page became the lead (October 23, 1939)—"Peace?"—probably by Hubie Kay. "Everybody seemed to want peace. . . . And, as Chamberlain superfluously pointed out, nobody can believe Hitler's unsupported promise that peace now would mean anything more than a truce between wars." In another war, the lead went on, America must "see the peace through, as well as the war." Thus, "the idea of federal union. . . . Much of it was inspired by a book called *Union Now*, an American's proposal of a world union in which America would join."

The issue went on to say that behind all the world's excitements "lies the idea of the Sovereign Nation as one race and culture. So ancient and potent is that idea that most of the world has not noticed that the United States stands for something quite different. It was populated by peoples of different languages and cultures. It might well have split up the North American Continent into a bigger Europe of sovereign nations, as the South Americans later did. But the North Americans discovered the idea of union among conflicting interests and patriotisms, and made out of them one patriotism, and got along with one another very well. . . . It suddenly dawned on [Clarence Streit] that the stand-out fact in the world was that 15 democracies, the rich, creditor, trading nations, held the overwhelming power in the world and were not using it. The result was a plan which he calls 'Union Now.' "

My belief in Clarence Streit's version of American history, here first expressed, later became a factor in Time Inc. history.

The "Picture of the Week" was, from the rear, of Hitler and Ribbentrop walking beside a Polish railroad, the caption noting that Hitler was on the dry ground, Ribbentrop in the mud. On the editorial page, "Russia had sewed up the third of the Baltic states, Lithuania, in as many weeks and was now turning on Finland. . . . While the Finnish Army prepared to fight under Finland's great nation-builder, Baron Mannerheim," Sweden's king called a futile conference and Roosevelt asked Russia "for mercy towards little Finland."

This was supported by a picture story: "The Liberator of Finland Mobilizes against Russia," with a picture history of Mannerheim, and the Finns hardened in "obscure and desperate wars" between Sweden and Russia. Their "historic attitude toward the Russians may be summed up in the fundamental fact that the cleanly Finns do not think the Russians bathe enough." There was a bloody story of the assassination of the Rumanian premier and a revenge massacre of the Nazi Iron Guard, seven bodies being left on the street overnight. And another story of the Prussian officer corps at the funeral of Colonel-General von Fritsch, actually, as we did not know, in defiance of Himmler's *Schutz staffel* which had demanded his execution. The last days of Warsaw are shown. And here is Eliot again, saying nothing much about British targets for the German air force.

I can see now that Longwell saw the war only—or, rather, primarily—in terms of journalistic careers, the lucky ones who would catapult to fame and fortune, and whom he would control. But I was the wrong man. I had known him too long and too well, and he was aware that I did not respect him. Eliot was the right sort of man. But what was happening was the main event.

Finland became more urgent (October 30, 1939) with an essay: America "is confident that Finland is one nation in complex Europe that entirely deserves the moral support of fellow democracies. Almost as soon as Finland declared itself free of Bolshevik Russia in 1917, the city proletariat in Finland put on a parody of the Russian Revolution, on the theory that the enemy of the Finns was the same as the enemy of the Russians—the landlords of both. They were backed up by Soviet armies. They were defeated by a Finnish landlord, Baron Mannerheim, at the head of a White Army, with German help. . . . Communist terrorism by 1930 had grown so bad that bourgeois vigilante bands began counter-terrorizing the Communists. The Government, doggedly democratic, continued to maintain the Bill of Rights. . . . Two years later [the Rightists] revolted. . . .

Their revolts failed totally." Finland's lakes and vast swamps "in winter are frozen over, vulnerable to expert ski troops. . . . Every man (perhaps a million) would fight." Here there was no skepticism about the willingness to fight, as there had been the year before, concerning Czechoslovakia.

The Finnish experience might be carefully noted today, in America, including the Communist terrorism (the same thing in Germany had *invited* the Nazi gangs) and the government's "dogged" maintenance of the Bill of Rights.

The issue included "Baltic Power Play" by Major Eliot, a skein of "may . . . may . . . may . . . might . . . if . . . if . . ." If Eliot's function was to inject Longwell's sort of balderdash, he was welcome, so long as he signed his name and we could contradict him elsewhere.

Finally, there was the Billings specialty, a story about neurotic pigs.

The Finland story supported Roosevelt's position in asking Russia not to compromise Finland's sovereignty, a gesture that failed to change the course of history.

Luce introduced a handsome profit-sharing plan for all employees except thirty-one. These lucky few constituted the so-called Senior Group, who each year around Christmas were to share a percentage of the profits after taxes, half to be paid immediately, half held by the company for later distribution. In 1939, the bonus equaled 51 percent of the individual's salary. The reason for all this, apart from Luce's generosity and gratitude, was that the company's after-tax profits that year were $3,206,751, an increase of over $2 million.

An astonishing memorandum from Stillman to Luce is printed in the book *Time Inc.* This drew a sharp distinction between a "business man" and a "hired man." The former, he submitted, had a right to expect to save a million dollars from his job; anyone not a businessman—editors, writers, researchers, advertising men— "should be paid the market price for their services. . . . [They] should be spared as much as possible from the risks of the business which they are unable to appraise and whose policies they cannot influence much." Luce did not accept Stillman's distinction. When the Senior Group was formed, a number of the creative personnel, including myself, were included.

Stillman's point might have been valid for a company producing breakfast cereal or beer; it was shockingly not valid for a company in the business of communication, and exhibits a blind conceit of the numbers man, the man who thinks in quantities rather than qualities. In fact, it was Stillman who could not "influence the policies of the company much." Compared to the editors and writers, Stillman did not know what the company was all about. He would have noticed only the most vulgar consistencies of the magazines as published, but these would probably have been the magazines' defects, not their virtues. Noticing the railroad and pig stories would not equal an understanding of *Life* policy. Stillman could comprehend that ordinary people believed in *Life*, but not why. For, as should have become evident by this point, the process was fairly complex and sometimes paradoxical.

Stillman's memorandum and Time Inc.'s reproduction of it were shocking indiscretions. The superior rewarding of the "businessman" over the creator in a communications operation could not be presented as desirable or just, but as merely inevitable. For all Stillman thought about was money; I, for example, found the subject disgusting, and Stillman as well. Inevitably, Stillman, I am told, is rich, while I have no residue from my contributions to the operation. This fact has not made me a Communist, nor even a mild Socialist. Stillman got what he wanted; I did too and, in writing this account, I am getting more of it. As we move toward the grave, I suppose that I will be the winner, and Stillman's estate will go to somebody else.

But I would also suppose that as Luce went toward his grave he remembered Stillman with more respect and gratitude than he remembered me, if he remembered me at all. For he could never participate in the writers' subtle decisions about the news material as they faced their typewriters; but he was face-to-face with the so-called "businessmen" from day to day, and they became the primary human reality in the corporation, especially as *Life* first drained, then flooded, the company's profits. If in the end he was guilty of a sin, it was a natural, human, and thoroughly prepared sin.

For all his Christian religiosity, he did not anticipate that Beelzebub would take him by the elbow.

The magazine suffered from a sort of dullness. Major Eliot had a piece (November 6, 1939) on the significance of the Dardanelles, proved by 3,000 years of important events nearby. Looking like a *Life* story on pigs, a Spam advertisement occupied four pages.

The Letters column (November 13, 1939) was unanimous that Union Now was a "wonderful idea." There was a story that repeal of the arms embargo enabled the United States to deliver 900 warplanes to the Allies, and a long unsigned piece on the Prussian generals (by me) emphasizing their nonallegiance to Nazism.

A cover of the German raider *Deutschland* (November 20, 1939) introduced another Major Eliot piece on "German Sea Raiders," about which he necessarily knew nothing. But for Longwell—and, I presume also, Major Eliot—not knowing anything was no deterrent.

The lead was on the objections of American seamen to the Neutrality Act, which would compel transfer of American ships' registry to other flags. The editorial page noted that a bomb in a Munich beer hall had missed Hitler by eleven minutes. There was a short essay on geopolitics and Karl Haushofer, who was supplying Hitler's ideas and supposedly suggested the alliance with Russia. Haushofer was totally unscrupulous. (He was Hitler's friend, yet had a Jewish wife.) The essay was on the British navy (9 pages): "A career in the British Navy is not a job, it is a life. That is the Navy's strength, but also its weakness." Behind this was the conservatism of the "Dartmouth system," training boys from the age of thirteen on. The "admiral's walk" on the stern of the ship was cited as an anachronism inherited from Nelson's day. "On the average, a British warship will be inferior to anything it meets in any part of the world. But Britain's answer is always to have a lot more ships than the other fellow. . . . In all probability, the British Navy is as good as it needs to be for this war." (Proved shortly in action.)

Nothing much was going on (November 27, 1939): a German newsreel documented the paralysis on the Western front; and, in a brilliant piece of home front propaganda, came an essay (8 pages) on Germans in America: "most are loyal Americans" who "have woven

great and colorful strands inextricably into the pattern of America."
Americans of German descent were listed as Astor, Herbert Hoover,
Babe Ruth, William Borah, Pershing, Rockefeller, Clark Gable,
Chrysler. An imposing list of American generals could have been
added.

Simmering beneath the surface dullness of the news lay, as we
know now, Hitler's impatience for an immediate attack on France
"this autumn," and eleven German mobilizations between November
and April, all opposed by the generals. But Hitler expected a Russian
attack at any minute.

The Gestapo slaughter in Poland continued under a blanket of
silence. General von Blaskowitz's protest to Berlin had ended his
effective career, though the Prussians prevented Hitler from cash-
iering or shooting him. Hitler's empiric power within Germany
depended on Himmler's Gestapo.

To anticipate coming events, we would not suspect that Hitler
did not want to attack Norway but was egged into it by Churchill's
broadcasts and his seizing of the prison ship *Altmark* in Norwegian
waters. Hitler had overrated the ability of Vidkun Quisling to bring
Norway over politically, for Hitler always overrated the streak of
treachery in mankind. On the other hand, he was possessed by the
notion that he should and could make peace with England, for
Liddell Hart cites Hitler's "admiration of the British Empire, of the
necessity for its existence," on the word of the German generals.

For World War II remains a mystery. How the German people,
not the worst people in the world, could have fallen into the hands of
this strange little nobody; how an officer corps of great gentlemen
could have been overruled by him; how the democracies of Europe
could have collapsed before him—all this is a mystery that free men
should examine very closely before some Communist maniac does it
also. The nemesis of Hitler, in the ultimate analysis, was another
maniac, Churchill, who should in all reasonableness have accepted
Hitler's frantic offers of peace, but did not, and in his blood *could
not*. The chief hope of the democracies is that in the crunch they will
produce other maniacs, other glory men, to oppose the power men.

The next issue closed Saturday, November 25, 1939, still in the doldrums, and the editorial page said, "it looked as if there would be no attack before spring." That was merely good advice for on Thursday, November 30, two Russian air armies without warning bombed Helsinki, Viipuri, and Enso, when they should have bombed airfields, railroads, mobilization centers. The Russians had picked the worst Finnish winter in twenty years, with temperatures of $-50°$ F. ($-46°$ C.). The numerical strength of the Russian army exceeded that of the German army at the time, and the Finnish army was one third the size of the Polish army. But air superiority has little value where it is usually snowing and the Arctic day lasts three or four hours and night troop movements under forest cover are lit by the northern lights reflected by snow. The Finns could ski, the Russians could not (they did not unload truckloads of skis). At the Mannerheim line, across the Karelian Peninsula (an isthmus), the Russians threw in about 12 divisions and 1,000 tanks of the Seventh Army, generally inferior troops. The Eighth Army of about 7 divisions was to close in north of Lake Ladoga. Two were to be destroyed between December 12 and 23. The Russian Ninth Army, with 5 divisions, hoped to cut across the waist of Finland to the Gulf of Bothnia. Six Russian divisions completely perished, plus one tank brigade. The Russians refused to fight except against the Mannerheim line.

The war as reported is somewhat different. Eliot had a column on the Russian attack (December 11, 1939—112 pages) saying that the lack of Finnish air defense "appears to be a fatal handicap to Finnish resistance" and that in general Finland was worse off than Poland had been against Germany. (So Eliot could add and subtract.) On the editorial page, I said, "The anger of the stolid, stubborn men of Finland sent every able-bodied man to the front to find the nearest Russian soldier. As the days passed, it appeared that the little Finns were putting up such a heady, savage fight as the modern world has rarely seen." Once again, Eliot and Longwell had missed the point. Finland was not Poland, December in Finland was not September in Poland, the Russians were not the Germans.

Assuming, as I now must, close communication between Longwell and Eliot, though I never noticed any overt evidence of it, Longwell had conveyed his hysteria to the stupid doctrinaire military thinker. For Longwell collapsed morally under any challenge, unless it was a matter of office politics, at which he was a cool master. As of Finland, Longwell and Eliot were disgracefully wrong, Underhill and I were right.

But why did Billings, a good editor, print both versions? One is led inescapably to the only possible conclusion: that Luce had told Billings that anything Longwell wanted was an order. The basic irresponsibility of Luce toward the truth is revealed by this fact alone. For Longwell was a man without character. The fact that Billings liked pigs and railroads and disliked Indians is a sign of character of a certain kind. Since I have an open mind, perhaps I don't have character either. But I always had more composure than Longwell.

The "Picture of the Week" was the famous picture of the French *poilu* sitting on a kitchen chair in an orchard beside his machine gun, waiting for the war to start. The lead said that the Japanese had cut China's highway to Indo-China, not fatal. A story presented the Garand rifle as the "finest standard military rifle in the world," though I think Underhill changed his mind about this later.

Eliot (and Longwell?) was silent on Finland (December 18, 1939), while the editorial page rejoiced, "The spectacle of the freemen of little Finland outfighting the slave hordes of totalitarian Russia last week raised the hearts of the free peoples the world over. . . . In the long run, Russia can push in, mile by mile. . . . But the long run may be too long. Anything may now happen in Europe."

In the next issue (December 25, 1939) Eliot asks "whether the Red steam-roller is, after all, only a false alarm." Longwell had pulled himself together, and so we have the counterabsurdity, as foolish as the first one. There is no way that a reader, from these two Eliot assessments, can understand what was to happen in Finland. There was a small story in the victory of three British cruisers (as explained in the earlier story on the British navy) over the German raider *Admiral Graf Spee*, which outgunned them but was hounded into Montevideo, Uruguay. The rapacity of the British navy was beginning, even before Churchill was elevated, to display the dedication of the British character, the very morale on which Churchill later counted. For he was remembering the performance of the cruisers *Exeter, Ajax,* and *Achilles* off the coast of Uruguay. The issue had a coincidental Southern tone (only 60 pages) with a lead on the Atlanta premiere of *Gone with the Wind* and an essay on South Carolina plantations, in the area where both Luce and Billings had homes.

Probably, Busch wrote the essay (January 1, 1940) on "England at War," which included an entertaining signed piece by him: "Among the primitive customs of the English is the institution of classes. . . . One of the reasons why the upper class dislikes war is that it impedes pheasant shooting." The lead was the German scuttling of two ships, including the *Graf Spee.*

The possibility that sales of U.S. planes to the Allies (for cash) would be a decisive factor (January 8, 1940) was the lead. (The hope was not borne out by events.) An essay satirizing American political clichés, presumably by Kay, was an astonishing irregularity, an un-*Life*like ridicule of American democracy. The editorial page noted ominously that crack Russian troops had replaced the second-line divisions attacking the Mannerheim line.

Major Eliot, for all his errors, was again explaining the Finnish War (January 15, 1940) with maps for four columns. He announced facts that he could not possibly have known and was free with such jargon as "interior lines" but it all sounded "expert."

A letter from Roy Larsen brought tidings of 25 percent joy:

January 12, 1940

Dear Dave:

A semi-final report for you on the results of the Senior Group Plan for 1939:

The final bonus is to be based on the 1939 profits of the Company as computed by *Time* and as approved by *Time*'s independent auditor. The final figures will not be available until sometime in March but, based on present rough estimates, it is expected that, as against the estimate given at the Senior Group dinner in September of between 30% and 40%, it will be approximately 50% of your 1939 salary.

As you know, the plan provides that one-half the bonus for the year 1939 will be distributed before the end of March 1940, that the other half will be placed in trust by the same date. That means that, based on present estimates, your March cash bonus will be approximately 25% of your 1939 salary.

This, by the way, for your tax return purposes, is 1940—not 1939 income.

Sincerely,
Roy Larsen

In the following issue (January 22, 1940), Finland was the lead: "Finland in January, in fact, is no place to fight a war. Joseph Stalin's imperative demand for a war there is characteristic of the arrogant Czarist and Bolshevik practice of asking subnormal Russians to achieve superhuman feats on pain of death. The customary result is death. . . . Finnish regiments and divisions struck heavily at the junction points of the extended Russian forces, divided them, starved and froze them and then routed them." If the last four words are excised, this is a true account, as of today. The six Russian divisions were not "routed"; they perished. "It began to appear that the Russian Army, at first loath to fight the Finnish War, was beginning to get mad. . . . Presently the Russians will get their guns and ammunition supply in position on the southern fronts and start blowing the advancing Finns out of the ground." Tragically, this was what happened. Without reserves, the Finnish army in the Mannerheim line became physically and morally exhausted, for all their indomitable courage.

Once again we had the Eliot-Longwell versus the Underhill-Cort version of history, both published, both permitted by Luce.

On the editorial page, it was noted of the Netherlands Indies, "on which oil-hungry Japan bends envious eyes," that if this and Australia were "to be defended against any major attack, either the British fleet or the U.S. fleet must do it." This was backed by the essay (12 pages) on the Dutch East Indies, giving a scenario for a Japanese invasion.

The position is taken in this survey that *Fortune* was totally irrelevant to the public impact and power of Time Inc. It was too obviously the secret shrine for Luce's worship of Mammon—not just private enterprise as such, but The Big Mammon. *Fortune* expressed Luce's belief that Charlie Stillman was right in thinking that he was infinitely more "important" in God's plan than the writers. Thus, *Fortune* was of no interest to me. But an exception must be made for the issue of February 1940, based, as a note says, on the theories of R. Buckminster Fuller, now on the payroll.

In this, Mr. Fuller made the astounding point that even during "the so-called depression" American industrialization had moved into a new era where energy was paramount over tonnage, of "violent expansion in the use of certain new materials, in efficiency, in the consumption of energy, in the productivity per worker, and in the consumption of many products. . . . The important fact is not that an old era has passed, but that a new era has been born." The failure of business was a lack of confidence in the consumer. Here he put forth the now familiar theory that the new tools were extensions of the human animal, transformed into "a new kind of species, whose extensions raise each of its members far above the levels of the past."

Mr. Fuller gave me the map of the world on which white dots showed population and red dots showed the energy "slaves" per capita, and this was installed in a lighted table top. This was the tenth anniversary of *Fortune*, boasting 130,000 subscribers.

The photographer at the Finnish front, Carl Mydans, had an admirable eyewitness essay on the slaughter of Russians (January 29, 1940) with his pictures. This was matched against an airview drawing of the Kremlin, identifying every building.

In connection with a text piece on Mrs. Roosevelt by Geoffrey T. Hellman (February 5, 1940), there was a carefully charted U.S. map of her travels from 1933 to 1940. Later, the White House asked for the research on it.

After the lead on President Roosevelt's birthday party (February 12, 1940), the editorial page said that "when the snows melt and the spring sun shines warm over the continent, all Europe now believes, hell will break loose." This was no unique intuition; *Time* had it too. As for Japan, "The danger is that, by overplaying its hand, the U.S. might drive Japan to deeds of desperation." (The former prediction was timely, the latter premature.) The essay was on "Spain Rebuilding." My intention here had been to be placating, but after the story was printed the photographer, Metcalf, told us he hoped we had understood that his captions were the exact opposite of the truth. No, I had not understood. Still, I think the story was close to the truth: "It appears that Franco has no intention of handing Spain back to the grandees. . . . Executions are said to be down to 25 a month. . . . Everybody is going hungry together."

The paradoxical fact is that if the Loyalists had won Hitler would have overrun Spain and Gibraltar, partially closing the Mediterranean. Franco's victory was to keep Hitler out of Spain.

The lead (February 19, 1940) was on Robert A. Taft's presidential campaign, followed by the editorial note: "Hitler and his generals, convinced that a policy of sitting tight on their territorial gains will only bring slow starvation, are apparently agreed that an attack is the only hope." On the other side, Churchill advocated an offensive and aid to Finland.

Substantial Allied aid to Finland might have brought the war into Scandinavia and the Baltic, in a campaign unpredictable but potentially disastrous for the Allies. (This thought probably did not occur to me at the time.) It would have pitted the Allies against Russia, perhaps brought in Germany against Finland, made Norway and Sweden full-scale battlefields, with a possible Allied invasion at Murmansk, perhaps deferring the German attack in the West. But any such eventuality ran into the concrete block of Sweden. Probably it was just as well, though Sweden can hardly be loved. The essay was "Rumania Has Oil Trouble": "It is in the horrible position of owning the oil that may win or lose the war for Germany. It is, next to Russia, the biggest leak in the Allied blockade of Germany." The text piece was on King Carol, by another photographer, John Phillips, the only man I knew who admired the Rumanian royal family. (He also thought well of King Farouk of Egypt.)

A premonition of current events (February 26, 1940) was the lead describing an unmannerly Youth Congress in Washington, D.C., which *objected to aid to Finland.* The editorial page described a most significant event. Churchill illegally ordered British warships to enter Norwegian waters to seize the *Graf Spee*'s prison ship, slinking down the Norwegian coast with a load of Englishmen. The page, noting the utter fatigue of the Finns, also said that "correspondents in Finland belatedly revised upward their estimate of the Red Army. . . . Their morale is standing up in the face of an appalling slaughter."

The British seizure was shown (March 4, 1940) in a drawing of the event in the Norwegian fjord, as was the return of the British seamen who had conquered the *Graf Spee*. It was evidently insupportable to Churchill to have British prisoners paraded by the Nazis when the British had won the battle.

"The Last Agony" of Finland was the lead (March 11, 1940): "The dugouts he [Carl Mydans, the *Life* photographer] saw are now in Russian hands and most of the Finns he saw are dead. But first they had fought like white demons, to the last frayed nerve of resistance. . . . Moscow radio crooned to the Finns: 'The Red Army does not destroy. . . . That is why the workers in every country love the Red Army.' " This last has its only rival in the deep sympathy of the Walrus and the Carpenter for the oysters they were eating, but it surpasses Lewis Carroll's attempt at monstrosity without half trying. In my essay on the "French Front," I took the position that France boasted a better army than Germany, which had had less time to train officers and noncommissioned officers. (The officer corps had expanded from 3,700 to 150,000 in six years.) I also maintained that France had more and better tanks than the Germans. Events seemed to prove me wrong. Long after the war, it developed that France had indeed had more and better tanks, but had not known how to use them. In April 1940 Germany had 2,574 armored vehicles, less than 300 the new Mark IVs with 75-mm. guns, in 35 tank battalions, as modern research has shown, while France had about 3,500 tanks, generally more powerful than the Germans', forming 56 tank battalions. But the French tanks were dispersed through the army. The subsequent French defeat was even more disgraceful than it looked at the time.

And so now I say, "Some military experts are predicting that the waiting will be brief, that the Great Assault will come soon after the March thaw. . . . France has the largest and best-trained officer corps in the world. . . . As fighters the French are tops."

Wrong as I was, Major Eliot surpassed me: "This article is no attempt at prophecy. . . . If the blockade is not effective, the Germans are likely to seek to sit tight, to let the Allies do the attacking for the present. . . . It is in general to the advantage of the Germans to maintain their present position, ringed in by neutrals. . . . If the Germans are to pin their faith on an attack in the west, it must come in 1940. . . . Direct penetration [of the Maginot Line] seems certain, however, to result in enormous casualties. . . . There is the French Army, the best in Europe, which the under-officered German Army might well hesitate to meet in open battle."

On at least one point Eliot and I were at last in agreement, both wrong.

The magazine was again at 112 pages (March 18, 1940), the lead on the U.S. Census, with the familiar cry of "bureaucratic snooping." The editorial page, noting the Finnish peace feelers, based on the possibility of Allied aid to Finland, concluded, "Actually any peace that leaves Finland its sovereignty would be a benefit to the Finns." And again Eliot rambles on about "Finnish Line Breaks." Wendell Willkie makes his first appearance as "liberal, temperate and articulate," saying that the abuse of power had now shifted from Big Business to Big Government. Two wildly contrasting examples of Americana in this issue had either a snide and invidious political intent, or came together by artless accident. One showed the unshaven hillbilly kinfolk of the distinguished Democratic Secretary of State Cordell Hull—"the Hulls of Tennessee." The other showed the pompous ancestors of Republican Senator Robert A. Taft, in an illustrated text piece by Joseph Alsop and Robert Kintner. We have the clue that Luce always favored Taft's politics. But to prove Taft's snobbish superiority to Cordell Hull would have been politically pointless. I regretfully conclude that the satire was unintentional. And, given American values, it must have backfired, for Cordell Hull's noble face looks out on one, compared to the somewhat porcine face of Taft.

A wonderful discovery in 1939 had been Albert Z. Carr whose book *Juggernaut* (a study of dictators) I had read and whom I had contrived to meet.

The only record I have of his contribution is the following table analyzing dictators. I give it as I have it, without checking out its accuracy, for it is pocked with question marks.

	PROVINCIAL ORIGIN	HATED	FALSE START	SEX PECULIARITY
Alexander	Macedonia	father		homosexual
Ataturk	Albania?	caliphate		promiscuity
Akbar	Turkestan	Hindus		
Bolívar	Europe	Spaniards	playboy	promiscuity
Bismarck	East Prussia	Catholics	lawyer	
Catherine	Germany	mother?		nymphomania
Caesar		dictators		
Charlemagne	S. Germany	pagans		
Cromwell		Catholics	lawyer	
Frederick		father	writer	woman-hater
Goméz		everybody	cattleman	young girls
Hitler	Austria	father	painter	voyeurism
Genghis	Mongolia			
Lenin	Tartary?	Czar	lawyer	ascetic
Mussolini		rich	writer	promiscuity
Napoleon III	exile	father	republican	promiscuity
Richelieu		English	soldier	incest?
Salazar			priest	ascetic
Stalin	Georgia	bourgeoisie	seminarian	

Illnesses and durations of empires are also given but reveal nothing. (Napoleon I, from Corsica, might have been added.) Bob Carr was curious about power, and looked for some clue to it. He regarded it, correctly, as a disease. Neither *Life* nor anyone else made proper use of this excellent man, who is now dead, except for his books. I believe that any errors in the above table must be ascribed to me, not to Bob.

Charlie Tudor is dropped from the masthead (March 25, 1940), a layout chief who had the complete loyalty and admiration of everyone. He was a real man. His disappearance may have been an omen. The figure of Longwell comes to mind. The editorial page says, "By far the outstanding fact about Finland's peace with Russia was that Finland had escaped with its life." The war dead were given as 250,000 Russians, 30,000 Finns (a small war).

Pictures of new Russian weapons released by the Finns (April 1,

1940) brought the observations that the Red Army tries out new ideas, its weapons standardized and workable with the faults of brittle steel and poor worksmanship. "But the Red infantryman still has the gloomy, suicidal courage of his race, better suited to defense than to attack." In contrast, the lead showed the egregious English pacifist Bertrand Russell, luxuriating pacifically at the University of California in Los Angeles (not in England). In effect, a small ally of Hitler's as of the "decadent democracies," while dreaming large thoughts.

The journalistic problem was not to guess what Hitler *should* do, but what he *would* do. The best assumption was that the enemy would be brilliant. In any event, I did not guess what Hitler would do. There was silence for two weeks in April and, it would seem, though I have no recollection of it, that I began to promote a trip to Europe.

For here is a letter from C. D. Jackson, general manager, dated March 17, 1940, to the Irish consul general, asking for a visa for Mr. David Cort, "who is leaving for Europe on the *Conte di Savoia* May 25. . . . During his stay in Europe, Mr. Cort plans to proceed from Italy to France, from France to England, and from England to Ireland. As his employers we of course shall assume full financial responsibility for Mr. Cort during his stay in Ireland." The accompanying Thomas Cook & Sons registration also lists Spain and Portugal on the itinerary.

The choice of an Italian ship was intelligent, since it would have been spared by German submarines, and Italy did not declare war against the Allies until June 10. But since I had written that all hell was about to break loose in Europe in the spring, I could not recover the mood or intention with which I proposed this gallop into the inferno. Italy, France, and England would hardly have welcomed me; only Ireland would have been glad to see me. Needless to say, the *Conte di Savoia* sailed without me on May 25, and reached Genoa safely.

But, first, some wordiness within Time Inc. On February 10, 1940, Luce had sent a *New Republic* editorial to the *Time* editors with copies to "Billings, Cort, Davenport, Hodgins, Kay, Larsen,

Paine." This discussed good and evil to no perceptible purpose. Luce's memorandum follows:

Herewith a note of warning from the *New Republic* and, as Tom Matthews says, a really respectable one. I pass it on to you because it is well worth pondering and also because I should like to take this occasion to comment, very informally, on the subject of basic attitudes towards the world situation. Please read the *New Republic* piece (attached) before reading the following.

First, as to the Road to War, the *New Republic* says: "if we go to war it will be because a large enough number of good Americans want intensely enough to do so." This was equally true in 1917. And recognition of this simple truth about cause and effect will sweep away at last a lot of the "intellectual" nonsense which has been fashionable about how we got hornswoggled into the last war and consequently are likely to get hornswoggled into this one.

But, secondly, what will make good Americans want to get into this war? Feelings of Right & Wrong, says the *New Republic*—and I agree and the same was true in 1917.

And, thirdly, what creates these intense feelings about Right & Wrong? What creates them are the facts as understood by people whom the *New Republic* in all sincerity calls the best people.

Here is where we come in. Whether or not we are "the best people" in the *New Republic*'s opinion, which would be highly improbable, it is our function to present the facts. Now, what we must *not* do is to try to cook the facts so that they come out even or anywhere near even as to their moral implications as to the participants in this war. In my personal opinion the case is already closed. In my personal opinion the facts overwhelmingly convict Germany & Russia whether or not they absolve the Allies. I am perfectly convinced that the facts, when and if really felt and comprehended by the American people, will overwhelmingly convict Germany & Russia in their eyes. And if the facts will not so neatly absolve the Allies, neither will they absolve the United States. I am not so concerned that we should belabor the moral that arises from the facts. But I am deeply concerned that we should not draw any veil of darkness or confusion between the facts and the moral deductions from the facts.

Fourth, granted that Germany & Russia are overwhelmingly convicted, does it follow we should fight? There is, in my opinion, no one easy simple answer to this question. There are many answers to it. In its brief essay, the *New Republic* gives only one answer. Although it says its answer is based on the clear logic of experience, the *New Republic*'s answer is actually an answer derived from age-old philosophical speculations on the Problem of Evil.

There is, I am sure, a perfectly respectable philosophical answer to the *New Republic*'s respectable philosophical answer. The *New Republic*, for example, has on other occasions not hesitated to "fight" and to urge others to "fight" the "forces of evil" in the United States—and perhaps even in Spain.

I am not one to deride philosophy. But it seems to me that those of us who are neither full-time philosophers nor full-time saints had best acknowledge that we are doomed to fight in one way or another and then concentrate on choosing the best battlefield for the least bad kind of a fight for the best kind of a victory we can imagine.

This somewhat pathetic memorandum was instigated by T. S. Matthews, as it says, and by Luce's obsession with religion and good and evil, of which neither he nor the *New Republic* knew very much. If MacLeish were around, he would have been in on it. Davenport and Paine might have contributed some tortured nonsense of their own. I am sure that Billings, Cort, Kay, and Larsen had no comment. The very fact that such agonizing memoranda pass in the high-minded democracies puts them always at the mercy of the dictatorships, such as Moscow and Peking today. For here Luce is daring to raise the question of whether Hitler and Stalin may just possibly be evil. And the noble brains of a kind at Time Inc. object to any such "simplistic value judgment." Given such people, one must welcome outright Nazis and Communists, murderous enemies against whom one knows enough to defend oneself.

For here came a still more pathetic follow-up from Luce addressed to the same people, dated February 17, 1940:

Regarding the *New Republic* editorial I sent you a few days ago and my comments on it:

At least one of the recipients drew from my comments the deduction that I am "all for going to war." For thus making myself unclear, my apologies,—and this attempt to correct that impression with all speed.

I put my comments under four question marks. The fourth question was: "Fourth, granted that Germany & Russia are overwhelmingly convicted, does it follow we should fight?" That should be amended to "Fourth, *even if* Germany & Russia . . . etc."

And as to that I said, and I repeat as my opinion: "There is no easy simple answer to this question. There are many answers to it . . ."—meaning, in Tom's phrase, that there are several very respectable answers,—i.e. several answers each of which is worthy of respect.

I further said that the *New Republic* gave only one answer. I should have said that the *New Republic* dealt only with *one kind* of answer, and that it by no means implied that any part of the answer is easy. The kind of answer the *New Republic* dealt with had to do with the moral questions involved and more particularly with the problem of "combatting evil." The *New Republic* knows the answer is not easy and says "Those who still can choose whether or not to fight in physical terms should weigh carefully how the enmity to evil may be most effective." I agree entirely with that—and all I meant to say in conclusion was, and is, that "careful weighing" does not necessarily lead either philosophically or pragmatically to the answer that "evil" should not and cannot be combatted in physical terms.

The *New Republic*, I think, agrees that there are inescapable moral issues. The responsibility of news-editors is to see that America's news-reading public has a chance to feel the moral issues just as deeply as do the *New Republic* editors. The responsibility of news-editors, that is, is not to becloud the issues—with, *for example*, an excess of "a pox on both your houses" attitude.

To put myself as clearly as possible on the record and, with as full a disclosure as I can manage in a few sentences, my personal position is:

1. "If I had my way," the United States would most certainly not declare war on anybody tomorrow or under any circumstances which seem likely to me to arise in the near future.

2. But—"if I had my way"—the people would decide what influence they wish the United States to exert in the world of today and tomorrow and would proceed, enthusiastic, united, unambiguous and unafraid, to exert that influence. The people would make this decision with as little delay as possible and without "waiting for more to happen." The President, for example, has enunciated a doctrine of world-wide basic civil rights. Do we mean that? What are its implications? The United States (under two different administrations) has refused recognition of "conquest"—Manchuria, Czechoslovakia, Poland—and, coming perhaps, Finland. If Germany conquers England (note: the Gauleiter has been chosen!)—will we refuse to recognize the conquest of England? Or if England "conquers" Germany? Where is all this leading to? At the present time it leads nowhere except to befuddlement.

3. I think the United States people have something like a duty to make themselves clear—a duty no less to themselves than to all the peoples of the world—to Frenchmen and Germans, to Indians and Philippines, to Englishmen, Swedes, Italians, Portuguese, Argentines, etc. & etc. & etc.

4. I think the great duty of editors is to speed up this day of clarity. What, for example, about Guam? To fortify or not to fortify? Why? Why not? For what purpose?—Let the people decide, above all let them know why they are deciding what. Let's have an end to the stultifying ambiguity

of last fall's neutrality debate. . . . And why spend billions for armament when maybe by using only a fraction of the power we now have we could, almost overnight, lift the armament burden from off the backs of all men? And not merely the burden of taxes but more especially the burden of sudden death and brutality and strangled lives? Why? Why? Let the American people know why.

In contrast to these maunderings was the unfinished business of Major George Fielding Eliot, Longwell's puppet to break the monopoly that Underhill and I had clenched on war. Given Eliot's ridiculous record, a true organization man would have given up on him long before, but Longwell was, in the organization sense, a truly feminine long-range killer. He still hoped that Eliot could undercut Underhill and myself, in spite of all the evidence: the events following Eliot's benighted fantasies.

I had no idea that my report was "dangerous" to my career, but any attack on Longwell was nearly suicidal, for Luce had underwritten him, and even Billings was afraid of Longwell's line of authority from Luce. Of all this I was perfectly ignorant. My sole interest was in a correct reporting of developing events. I thought that Longwell was invariably hysterical and in error about great events, and disagreed with him. My boss was Billings, or so I thought.

On March 19, 1940, I had submitted to Billings, with copies to Longwell and Luce, the following carefully drawn memorandum:

Six months of the war make a record from which it is fair to judge the record of Major Eliot. His expertings in *Life* represent, I believe, an experiment for Time Inc. in printing the statements of an outsider whose sources are unknown to us and who is not subject to the customary checking. The attached summary of Eliot's predictions from Sept. 7 to date throws a great deal of light on how this works out. These quotations, now partly revealed by events as totally wrong, did not of course appear in this form in *Life*. A good deal of office energy went into modifying the Major's assertions.

On the other hand, Eliot's background pieces are often satisfactory and sometimes make their point well. It would seem that he can be useful to us in that department. But even allowing for some war hysteria, his record of thinking in a hurricane adds up to about that of the man-on-the-street.

Sept. 18 issue written Sept. 7: "The Poles have successfully evacuated the Corridor without undue loss. . . . Polish resistance is stiffening. One might conjecture that they have assembled a counter-attacking force, which might seriously endanger the German right rear. In any event a serious battle seems now to be developing. . . . Very much stiffer Polish resistance may now be anticipated, with counterattacks on the German forces which in some cases appear to have pushed on somewhat rashly. . . . Britain and France appear to be mounting an attack on the German western border. . . . Will the Germans stick to the Poles despite the French threat? If they do, will the French be able to carry their offensive far enough so that the Germans will have lost the war by waiting too long, no matter what happens in Poland? Will the Germans start shifting troops from East to West to meet the French and if so will the Poles then stage a comeback against the Germans in the east?" (At this point, the Polish army was entirely defeated.)

ADD written Sept. 9. "But the Polish Army, not the Polish capital, is the true German objective." (The fact was vice versa.) "The Polish Army is still intact and ready to act at the proper moment. Polish morale is still high, retreat orderly and careful, a counterstroke is now in course of preparation."

Sept. 24 issue written Sept. 15. More on Polish stiffening, etc. "Long distance raids . . . for propaganda purposes to make it appear to the world that Polish resistance is being broken and Poland's case hopeless. . . . The Polish army is fighting well, shows no signs of cracking morale and . . . they have as yet strong positions and a much shorter line than originally held. . . . It is raining there at least in some parts, which will turn the roads into mere bogholes; the extended German raids if they are to be backed up will absorb more and more of the dwindling German reserve. In short, the German need for liquidating the Polish war becomes more acute with every passing day. Hence the frantic endeavors of the Germans to picture their raids as captures, to claim the occupation of such places as Warsaw, Modlin, etc., to speak of the encirclement of Warsaw . . . etc." (He missed the whole plan of the war.) "To sum up, Poland's case as it stands is bad but by no means desperate. Her first great ally, General Mud, appears on the way. . . . Germans will not be in a good spot, especially if by that time (Winter) the French and British have broken through in the west and are flooding into the Rhineland. . . . Polish resistance seems to be infuriating them."

Oct. 9 issue. "There was never any question of a desperate stand on the frontier in the Polish plans." (Actually, that was the plan.) "The Polish army, fighting on the whole skilfully and certainly bravely. . . . It was the occupation by the Russians which delivered the final coup de grace to the Polish resistance. . . . I do not think that the comments of the final German official communique, as to the poor quality of Polish leadership, are altogether justified." (This last skepticism is a justification of his previous position, not a further search for facts. Too many of his pieces are a defense of earlier pieces.)

Nov. 20. "The three pocket battleships . . . can destroy any Allied cruiser with ease and can run away from any Allied capital ship except . . . only five available ships which can successfully bring them to action. (They) will present very serious problems to the French and British Admiralties. . . . Thus the time factor is increasingly against Britain in this matter."

Dec. 11. Finland. "The lack of an adequate defense against a tremendously superior air force appears to be a fatal handicap to Finnish resistance, which otherwise might cost the Russians dearly."

Dec. 25. Having had time to find he liked the Finns: "A series of blunders (by the Red Army) which taken altogether, are beginning to bring back memories of the World War." (Strong pressure by us modified somewhat his original intention to dismiss the Red Army as worthless.)

Jan. 15. "Finland is thus in all probability freed from any further anxiety in the north for the rest of this winter. . . . By the end of March this northern country begins to get soft, there will thereafter be no movement of troops or transport north of Lake Ladoga all the way up to the Arctic until June at the very earliest."

March 11. Strategy for spring. This time considerably influenced by office ideas.

March 18. Finland. Office-written from sketch notes by Eliot.

At the time it was not necessary to specify how far off Major Eliot's prognostications were, for we were living with the event.

And so we entered the suspense of April (April 8, 1940, an issue of 112 pages). The lead showed the new B-19 bomber and the fact that U.S. air transport had finished a full year without a fatal accident. The essay was essentially a hymn to Ataturk, the late dictator of Turkey—"As it approaches its coming-of-age, it finds itself the key neutral in the lower right-hand corner of a world at war." It is pro-British because "Britain may lose a battle but never a war, because she has money, a Navy and character." Despite my memorandum, Major Eliot had one of his typical pieces on "New Air Tactics."

After a lead on the election campaigns starring James Farley (April 15, 1940), the editorial page notes: "The stagnation of the war is getting on the nerves of the British"; Chamberlain's ill-timed blurt that Hitler "had missed the bus" and General Ironside's highly significant statement that "during the last fortnight we have turned the corner" (in rearmament). There were key stories on new U.S. guns, still in short supply, and on the iron ore traffic from Narvik down Norway's coastline to Germany. This latter was to trigger the first explosion in the West.

The explosion came (April 22, 1940) with Germany's invasion of Denmark and Norway. Now we know that this was a crucial Hitler mistake, because nearly the whole German navy was destroyed or temporarily disabled, rendering it nonexistent when Hitler had his only chance to make the crossing of the Channel to England a little over a month later. In those terrible days, the end of the civilized world was a matter of weeks, days, hours, and minutes. The lead emphasized the partisan point, raised by President Roosevelt, that the conquest of Denmark involved the conquest of Greenland, which geographers place technically in the Western Hemisphere; in other words, that the Americas had at last been attacked. This may have been a little too cute. Hopefully, it was pointed out that the British had to "occupy Narvik, isolated iron port in the North." There were drawings of the steps in the invasion of Norway, including some of the damage to the German navy, the importance of which I did not fully grasp at the time. Again, Eliot had a piece on "The Strategy of the Norse War." The text piece was on Tom Dewey by Noel Busch, who has continued to write about political figures without picking a winner. Tom Dewey, I would think, was a poor choice for so knowledgeable a man. More to the point was an admiring story on Wendell Willkie's performance on a radio show.

My memorandum on Eliot produced a text piece (April 29, 1940) by Captain B. H. Liddell Hart on "The Prospect in Norway," pointing out the critical injury to the German Navy. On the editorial page was a propaganda I now regret, based on stories of Norwegian traitors, that all nations were preparing for traitors, for this idea, once implanted, must destroy any human society. The news lead was "Germany and Britain Push a Desperate Race against Time into Norway." I was apparently beginning to sense the naval implications of the Battle of Norway, for the essay was "World Sea Power—The Plane Challenges the Reign of Ships." After a picture history of the rise of British and American sea power was a spread drawing of Europe's assembled navies. Finally, came the U.S. versus the Japanese navy: "the slow, ruthless logic of events has steered the U.S.

closer and closer to a naval war with Japan . . . either over the Netherlands Indies or the Philippines." Good prophecy, but loftily overlooking Hawaii.

An undated handwritten note from Luce now appears (addressed to "Mr. Cort," hence probably no later than 1940):

> I deeply regret not having got round to this unfinished symphony—which contains some superb thematic material.
> I am now (confidentially) off to England for 3 or 4 weeks.
> Take up with Billings or Busch—or Del Paine—or me on my return.
>
> HRL

The strange essay that probably provoked this note is offered below though it is obviously, as Luce noted, "unfinished." By now it may very well be obsolete.

> The general view is that peace was wonderful, war is terrible and Hitler is unmitigated disaster. The facts point in precisely the opposite direction.
> The world of 1939 was hopeless. The peace of 1918–1939 was disastrous, but most of the disaster was underneath the surface and so people felt contented enough.
> In political terms, Europe was jammed with meaningless countries with kings, presidents, premiers and parliaments, flags, national histories, armies and air forces, national vendettas and party politics. A system of alliances invented in hell made certain that no nation would ever do anything for the general, long-range good. A system of trade barriers had large groups of people living on starvation levels in Rumania, Poland, Hungary, Bulgaria. The masses of people had no voice whatever in the national policies, were getting no experience of world politics and constituted no working majority in any nation.
> The leaders, however, felt fine enough. They at least were familiar with the "glories" of the national history. They were big frogs in more or less little puddles. They had the thrill of playing a complex, though meaningless and impossible, game.
> Worse yet, these impotent little nations had been abandoned by the U.S., Britain and France and not yet been taken under the wing of the ideologically hungry nations, Germany, the U.S.S.R. and Italy.
> Still worse, the morality of all three of these latter was an ignorant attempt to produce the kind of State they thought they saw in the U.S., but without waste motion. This morality had not yet been tested in events. It was still implicit, like a pus in the blood trying to form an abscess. It was based, in its most vulgar simplicity, on the principle that man is vile, but it

endeavored to produce political marvels by controlling vile man in certain harsh ways.

Worse again, the politicians and businessmen of the free democracies had for the moment utterly lost contact with the world they lived in.

Put it this way. In the 20 years between 1920 and 1940, the number of truly scientific discoveries and primary technical inventions had been increased 700%. That is to say, in those two decades, men advanced their knowledge ten times as far as in all previously recorded history. Anybody living through those years knows that Industry handed on to the people an almost invisible percentage of all this progress. The fact was that American and world businessmen were fighting for their lives to preserve their old bookkeeping systems, their profit margins, their markets. They had no time to spare even to ask what all the new discoveries were, much less to produce and try to market them too. They had handed their businesses over to salesmen and bankers and lawyers, certainly the slickest but probably the worst informed sectors of the population. The same kind of men had also overrun the governments of the democracies. In business and in world politics, all these men operated on the ancient and generally sound principle of Security.

Security of the Defense against the military Offense. Security of the many, loosely confederated in a League of Nations, against the one outside. Security of capital investment against change in techniques. Security of real estate. Security of the old and tried, of seapower and fortifications and four percent and the umbrella and a comfortable and warm and familiar world. There rose to the top in the democracies a class of men who were wonderfully adept at getting along with their fellow-workers and who knew how to avoid irritating anybody. They knew their world was not perfect but they were very loath to tamper with the works.

Yet worse again, the people of the world had been trapped by false issues. For the first time in world history, the masses of people were informed about world events and had decided opinions. About 50% of the people of the U.S. were considerably smarter than were their leaders, on the evidence of their leaders' acts. For between 1920 and 1940, the proportion of young people going to high school had jumped to 65% and in some areas to 95%; of those entering college to 22%. The impact of this mass of intelligence was something unprecedented in world history.

But it was drained off in the fruitless debate of Fascism versus Communism, which became identical with Capital versus Labor, Republican versus Democrat, A. F. of L. versus C.I.O. These bitter arguments were the growing pains of democracy, the discharge of all the inherited prejudices of Europe. But they blinded the democracies to the real problems of their society and inclined them to follow the leadership of men who acted with pompous, neutral dispassion.

This was the world of 1939. Without Hitler, it was pregnant with woe and disaster. Hitler, however, precipitated the disaster. The society of the free men was sharply presented with the obligation to be efficient or to perish. True, it had been caught at a disadvantageous moment of transition, but it might quite well have merely degenerated into stagnation. Suddenly democracy had to show results.

While waiting for it to do so, Hitler conferred some preliminary blessings on mankind. He abolished a number of meaningless nations. He knocked down congested and antique slums in London and other English cities. He blasted the stagnant value of real estate and compelled the democracies to turn their attention to new and functional forms of housing. He took the airplane out of its rut of plaything and rich man's luxury transport and ushered in an era when the airplane will be of service to all men everywhere. For shortsighted military purposes, he guaranteed the long-range social benefit of mass air transport of freight and passengers. He forced all the governments and peoples to think of themselves as parts of a whole planet, not merely of nations and continents and hemispheres. He made caterpillar tractor production so vast that every farmer in the world will have one after the war. He substituted the Diesel for the gasoline engine. He shattered the economy of four percent, already seriously cracked, forever. He brought together in unity nearly all the people of the world, the conquered peoples of Europe, the British, Canadians, Australians, South Africans, Moslems, Hindus, Chinese, Russians, East Indians, South Americans and North Americans. He made inevitable and imminent a World Federation of free peoples. He brought to the world the very thing he hates worst: a vast international exchange and co-operation and cross-fertilization of all cultures (except the German). He hastened the final consolidation of the whole planet Earth by at least half a century. And he unleashed the profoundest energies of Science, for evil and for good. . . .

The first British entry into that peculiar air-land-sea style of warfare that was to persist for five years was noted (May 6, 1940) in the lead, "British Land in the Fjords." The British necessity was to recapture Trondheim from its amphibious German garrison. Small forces were landed north and south of Trondheim. Major Eliot had a parallel piece, "A Fight for Valleys." A story focused on Sweden "whose seven little neighbors all have lost all or some of their sovereignty in the last year to Germany or Soviet Russia. In the role of Bluebeard's eighth wife . . ." After American stories on a Presbyterian minister's ordination and birth control laws in the Carolinas, came an essay which seems now like a farewell to beautiful France, "The Land of France—For It, a Devoted People Gladly Die": "For the love of France the Frenchman has been fighting for centuries, is fighting again today. It is what gives the wars of the French their stubborn, bitter quality." The pictures were beautiful; the writing was also "beautiful," and Billings brought in Andrew Heiskell to tell me how "beautiful" it was. I wondered what difference Heiskell's approval could possibly have made to anybody, but he had been educated in France (born in Italy). There was evidently something about the organization that I did not understand. An incompetent writer, Heiskell had been made assistant general manager of *Life* in 1939. Of course, like Luce, he was an Auslander. The story was shockingly wrong, except as magnanimous elegy. In that sense it was magnificently right.

My view of French resolution might have been affected had I known that on April 9 at the Allied Supreme War Council in London, Premier Paul Reynaud had described the German aggression as a "consequence of the [British] laying of mines within Norwegian territorial waters"—exactly parroting what his supposed enemy, Adolf Hitler, was saying. The French *policy* was not to frustrate Hitler, when the sole function of the French *army* was to frustrate Hitler—but, as it turned out, not really.

Though war under censorship is impossible to report correctly, we were at least quick to see (May 13, 1940) that the German blitzkrieg in Norway had overpowered the Allies. The lead said, "What Nazi Germany knows and what the Allies do not yet seem to know is that war has undergone a great change since November 11, 1918. . . . British old-style warfare suitable for Pathans on the Northwest Frontier of India but not for Germans."

We showed German-released pictures of the crew of the British destroyer *Glowworm* being rescued by the German cruiser *Hipper*, without knowing that she had gallantly rammed the *Hipper*, ripping away 130 feet of her armor belt and putting her out of the Battle of Britain, as of the date of April 8. Her British captain got the posthumous Victoria Cross, but Churchill, First Lord of the Admiralty, failed to grasp the significance of his radio signal before he died. So it goes. As against these deadly events, fifty rich Pittsburghers offered a million-dollar reward for delivery of Adolf Hitler within the month. A more deadly satire on the contented American plutocrats could hardly be invented, no matter how savage the satirist. Another form of satire was a story on "The Men of Sweden—Are They Now Too Civilized to Fight for Their Country": "The fact is that the aristocrats, the officers, the businessmen of Sweden have in the past been strongly partial to Germany, Nazi or not, as being the most admirable and efficient nearby civilization. . . . Many are personal friends of Hermann Göring, whose first wife was a Swedish noblewoman." My distaste for Sweden as a society, while noting that it had once been the most warlike in all Europe, may perhaps have been unfair, but I think not. The text was on Wendell Willkie by Hubert Kay—"by far the ablest man the Republicans could nominate for President at Philadelphia next month" and "has practically no chance of getting the call." At about this moment, Russell Davenport, managing editor of *Fortune*, was resigning to become the hidden campaign manager for Willkie; and Luce, sailing to Italy on the *Rex*, was writing the significant letter to Roy Larsen: "Our great job from now on is not to create power but to use it. . . . I have very little sense of the power at whose switchboard we stand. . . . To no one else could I say with the same assurance of understanding: by God, what a job we've done." Luce kept cabling that the United States should supply France with planes. Knowing the time lapse of making any plane operable in combat, *Life* ignored this belated advice.

The explosion graduated into the holocaust (May 20, 1940): "Total War Starts," opening with a drawing of a Nazi hangar cave inside a hill with bombers emerging. "*Der Tag* had come once more, this time in earnest—May 10" (the Friday, one day before the issue closed, on a Saturday). "If Germany takes The Netherlands, it is in a fair way to beat England to its knees. It could bomb the docks and shipping of London into paralysis." A spread showed the operations of Nazi paratroopers. In noting the resignation of Prime Minister Chamberlain, we did not have, or report, the declaration of an old Tory friend in the Commons, echoing Oliver Cromwell, "Depart, I say, and let us have done with you. In the name of God, go!" On May

10 Winston Churchill became the king's First Minister, and the battle was joined. There was a text piece by Clare Boothe who was nearly bombed in the U.S. Embassy in Brussels. Completely off the mark was the essay telling of a French army in Syria, safely out of the battle, under General Weygand, who was on the cover, and the text on Weygand was by Major Eliot. My selling the Syria story may have made Billings unhappy.

The stories emphasized the overwhelming deployment of German paratroopers. Now we know that against Holland only 4,000 paratroopers were dropped, plus one airborne division of 12,000 men; against Belgium, primarily against two bridges and Fort Eben Emael, only 500 beautifully rehearsed airborne troops; but dummy parachutes were scattered all over the Low Countries, multiplying rumor and terror. This was probably Hitler at work, not the Great General Staff.

The German attack is now, not then, well understood. It was an attack on Holland and Belgium, drawing the scrupulously distant (until then) French and British into Belgium and Holland; and then the *schwerpunkt* behind their backs, through the Ardennes Forest and Sedan. The plan was Manstein's (born Lewinski), approved by Hitler, over the objections of the Old Guard. On this alone, Hitler must be elevated from a "nobody." Bock conducted the northern bait attack, Rundstedt the *schwerpunkt* with the mass of the armor. It was a beautiful battle, that could readily have been turned the other way, if France had had the brash Polish general or been a coherent society, but it had not and was not.

Dated sometime in May 1940, I sent a memorandum to Billings, with a copy to Luce, which did not appear in the magazine but, after some floundering, more or less forecast toward the end the future history of the world.

The facts of the war in Europe are certainly worse than the impression conveyed by the newspapers. The hitting power of the German Army is hard to exaggerate. Nevertheless, I have maintained and still maintain without change the novel attitude that all is not, as everyone would have us believe, lost. For the following reasons:

The prepared, totalitarian blow must always be overwhelming on its first impact. Not the least important part of its impact is the propaganda one, that of dismaying exactly the people who are now so dismayed.

The blitzkrieg has, however, certain military weaknesses. The Allies may not exploit them but they exist. Chief of these is that a resolute enemy will maintain self-sufficient strong points on the flanks of a break-through, allow the mechanized stuff through and then close the gap with artillery. Without lifting the barrage, he can then attack beyond the barrage, pitting infantry and artillery against mechanized troops. Infantry are still the decisive arm, as this war is proving once again, and I am still willing to match democrats against totalitarians in that department.

The basic story, however, is one of weapons. And all recent wars have shown the paramountcy of masses of sturdy, run-of-the-mill artillery, guns that can be served, serviced and replaced without trouble. The French Army, a beautifully trained outfit, has this stuff and has the artillerists in enormous quantities.

The tough weapon just now is the bomber. . . . There is every possibility that the bomber will be completely stopped by defensive weapons. The need now is to force bombers to break formation and open up to the fighters. Suppose a fast fighter drops a bomb with a time fuse on a formation of bombers. Suppose he drops wires in the path of a formation.

Against tanks, we have read of the use of planes with cannon. We have not read that gas is very useful against tanks. Already tested is the fact that an adequate supply of anti-tank guns and heavy tanks stops tanks. The Allies can make that stuff, given a little time, granted that they were incredibly stupid not to have gotten stocked up on it.

The German Army is strong on routine preparation. It has the weakness of always doing things the same way. It has a morale magnificent in victory and capable of the death-blow (unlike R. E. Lee) but less great in defeat and perhaps more susceptible than we think of collapse. The will of the German people has been completely abandoned by German foreign policy, whereas the politics of England and France have, at a great handicap, generally reflected the will of the people. Many may regret the point to which this has brought Allied strategy but it is now an asset.

As for a landing on England, it should be noted that the land fort is sovereign over the ship. Unless the British are being very stupid, the Channel forts should by now be also invulnerable to bombers. The Allies also have submarines and planes. A direct German crossing of the Channel is very unlikely. Ireland is another matter. It is the natural Achilles Heel of England and Hitler is bound to try it out. A landing in fog and night is possible. Air bases in Ireland or even Scotland are conceivable.

The Allies are already in great trouble but they are by no means doomed to certain defeat. They will almost certainly lose the Channel ports but they may possibly even win a battle soon. Battles do not win wars. We presently

have a war of punishment of bases, in which England will be hurt worse
than Germany but in which the English people can take it better than the
Germans.

It becomes quite possible that the Allied High Command may ask for an
armistice, may even get it. The situation has profoundly altered. It is now a
lesser evil whether or not Germany keeps Poland, Czechoslovakia, the
Lowlands, Norway. More important is the need for time to prepare against
the blitzkrieg, a weapon now revealed and known, and to get a U.S.
guarantee of participation in resuming hostilities. An Armistice would
actually favor the Allies, unless they stop the Germans in the next month. In
that case, they will win in another six months, with the U.S. probably in the
war beside them. . . .

It is here that the blitzkrieg has chiefly given the democracies pause. It is
dismaying how quickly individuals in a democracy abandon their belief in
democracy. For the fact is that nobody ever really thinks about democracy.
It is of course the belief that in the long run the people are right and wise
and know what is best for them. The people of England and France have
long sensed the menace of Fascism. It was the subtle and sophisticated
leaders who thought a compromise might be made and who took their good
time about rearming. The people were of course right and wise. The blow to
France and England is in no sense a blow to democracy, but a crushing blow
to leaderism and the inanities of parliamentarianism, which is not the same
thing as democracy. England is particularly cursed with incompetent
leaders, France with incompetent parliamentarians. Whether victory or
defeat, both, thank God, are doomed.

The democracies before this war were "getting along all right." They
were not perfect, but sufficiently contented. It was not then critical that
their industrial organization was not using the abilities of the people for the
people. Science had been left on the shelf. But in world history it is always
the most efficient society, not the wisest or happiest, that wins. And
efficiency in weapons takes precedence over everything else. The German
invasion has shown clearly enough that if Science is not used for the people,
it can very usefully be employed *against* them. Hitler may even turn out to
be a force for good. He is certainly destroying a lot of things that had
outlived their usefulness.

In any case the U.S., the shyest and noblest hangdog the world has ever
seen, will presently be forced to face the appalling prospect of ruling the
world. England and France will become quaint little anachronisms maintained as buffer states against Germany. The only remaining hope of
non-Soviet Europe is a federation. Germany will eventually knock itself out,
if history is any gauge.

It should be understood that from here on Germany has no friends,
though it may have toadies. The rise of a conqueror must be counted on to

raise hostile powers against it, for it conveys the idea of annihilation to friend and foe. Right now Fascist Spain may prefer the France of Weygand and Pétain to Nazi Germany, as may Italy, though I insist that Mussolini is an assassin. Russia may very well be brought into a coalition against Germany. Stafford Cripps is certainly a key figure.

Finally there is the recurring fact that the most important unsettled issue in the world is China. It can be democratic, but it can turn out to be Japanese or communist, in either case losing its essential greatness and considerably increasing the future headaches of the U.S. Let us not, in the excitement, turn our back on the Far East.

Any trace of long-range optimism in this memorandum was dispelled by the lead (May 27, 1940, closing Saturday, May 18): "The confident, prosperous, complacent democracies last week were confronted with the appalling possibility that perhaps their day is done. . . . Instead of worrying about its flanks, the German blitzkrieg roars through its openings, fanning out in the enemy's rear. It can be stopped somehow but just how the Allies were dangerously slow in discovering." There followed a detailed and illustrated description of the blitzkrieg's components and procedures. Major Eliot contributed his "If an Allied Defeat, What?"

Underhill and I gave a departing correspondent a code for signaling the ultimate disaster in England. The code was the quintessence of simplicity. The instructions ran: "I shall not use any of these items unless I am 100% certain. In using them I shall always refer to Underhill, and the first of the above code words to appear after his name will be the tip-off. The word may not appear immediately after his name, but any intervening words will not be among the abovementioned. Example: If I want to tip you off that No. 1 has happened, I shall place somewhere in a cable: 'Regarding Underhill's query, banks always open on Saturdays.' Or 'Tell Underhill he is always too slow on his queries.' The code word will always appear after Underhill's name."

Our thinking is indicated by the messages, with their key words.

1. British asking for armistice   always
2. Churchill going out   whether
3. German invasion within two days   is
4. German landing force making considerable headway   could

    5. Germans getting control of the air over England   would
    6. Major civilian riots against continuance of the war   can
    7. British fleet sailing for American bases   might
    8. Royal princesses leaving England   in
    9. British about to invade Eire   are
  10. England is effectually blockaded   will
  11. Italy asks for armistice   won't

I was now concerned only about the survival of the United States and could not gamble that destiny on any blind faith in the Europeans' ability to survive. Probably because Churchill was now the First Minister, I did not list the surrender of the British fleet as a possibility. A German invasion of Eire was allowed for. No. 11 now mystifies me, but there it is. Had the British discovered this code, our correspondent would have been in serious trouble. As it developed, no message was ever sent. And nobody but Underhill and myself knew about the code.

I would assume that the theme of the next issue "America and the World" (June 3, 1940) was a Luce conception. The issue aroused enormous reader enthusiasm but I don't know why.

It may be useful to indicate the preparation for this issue.

In early April the memorandum was issued:

EUROPEAN ISSUE

LEAD:	Pan American Flight to Lisbon
ESSAYS:	Sweden by Mydans (A Democracy)
	Italy by McAvoy and Mydans (A totalitarian state)
CLOSE-UP:	The English Dukes (Aristocracy)
COLOR:	Four Pages—Paris in Color
	Italian Art
SPEAKING OF PICTURES:	A catalog of American Prejudices against Europe

––––––––––

ALTERNATIVES:	
	Color: Major Eliot's map
	Old School Ties
	Essay: Portugal
	Yugoslavia

––––––––––

ACTS:
> *Assigned:*

>> Beautiful England
>> The German Rhine
>> Castles
>> The Simplon—from Belgrade to London
>> Our three European families today
>> Brighton Week-end
>> The English Gentleman
>> Portland and/or Devonshire Ducal Estates
>> Friday, Saturday & Sunday in a German Village
>> A Junker's Family
>> Beautiful Viennese Women
>> A Bavarian Peasant
>> German Industry
>> Luxembourg
>> German Science—Hans and Stassman—Uranium, Sulfanilimide
>> German Industry—Chemicals, Electrical Machinery
>> Paris Night Club
>> A Danish Store
>> Strange English Customs

> *To be decided and assigned:*

>> A French Inn
>> A Village Curate in France
>> A French Café
>> Sunday in the Bois
>> Feudal Peasant Hungary
>> Free Peasant Switzerland
>> Knole House
>> European Humor
>> European Cars
>> A Roundup of Beautiful Europe
>> England's Great Victorian Age
>> An International Hotel
>> London's The City—High Finance
>> Wealth of the World into Europe—English or Amsterdam's docks
>> Peasant Culture—Macedonia
>> Cheap Fun in Europe
>> A Frenchman's Sureté Card
>> Borders—a guarded frontier post

The point of giving this perhaps boring memorandum is to emphasize my belief that what *appeared* in the magazine was all that was important. The issue (June 3, 1940) began with the story of the Clipper plane's flight across the Atlantic in 23 hours. Unexpected was a letter from our Paris correspondent, Clare Boothe. The lead was "German Conquest Threatens the World": "The people of America stood aghast as the hand of history unrolled the most terrible, fateful week in the memory of living men. The German Army, rolling down on Paris, wheeled suddenly west across the plain of Flanders, caught a huge Allied army in the trap and swept on to the English Channel ["wheeled suddenly west" was wrong; it was always headed west].
. . . Out the window went decades of war theory as the thin motor columns cut through the enemy lines and, leaving their flanks unguarded, raced on to seize strategic objectives. . . . Even more amazing was the [German] Army's superb organization. . . . The old nations of Europe may fall before the conqueror but the young, strong giant of the West will meet any challenge that Adolf Hitler dares to make."

There followed 14 pages exhibiting the magnificent German army in operation. This was no time for pacifism; such a time had been at the Treaty of Versailles when the French had been magnificently warlike; now, it seemed, they were pacifists. My intent was to show the Americans what a modern army must be. Obviously, most of the subjects specified in the memoranda of early April had been displaced by this major phenomenon of "The World," the German army of 1940.

Following this, Luce contributed a manifesto, "America and Armageddon," saying, "We know now that, fundamentally, their struggle is our struggle." He emphasized the high cost of armaments and the sacrifices that everybody must make. The essay was on European civilization, concentrating on the castles of the medieval warriors, culminating in a picture history of World War I. Then came Paris, mostly in color. "Paris means a way of life. It has probably given more happiness to more people than any other single place that ever existed. . . . Whether Paris will survive the devastation of this war depends no longer on her proud history or her charm but on the clash of violent efficiencies and intolerances that she has always despised." A long section on England shows the hauteur of Noel Busch, stationed there for some time: "England's stubborn belief in things that no one else believes in may yet be its salvation. In order truly to conquer a nation, one must understand it. No one understands the English. . . . Examined over a long period of time, they are less inclined to genuine absurdity than the Germans. . . . Old but not threadbare, England, like its books, has grown old well." The text piece by Walter Lippmann attacked isolationism.

The issue reiterated that nothing—neither the power of England and France nor the British upper classes nor Paris—would ever be the same again.

A wan hope flickered up (June 10, 1940) with a Clare Boothe letter that Paris expected Weygand to defeat the Germans. This was probably based on the fact that Weygand had known Foch and was supposed to have given Pilsudski the magic way to win the battle of Warsaw. (He hadn't.) The lead was entitled "Americans Face Choice between Democracy and Dictatorship at Home," referring to "the last great democracy in the world." I suppose this lead had an anti-Roosevelt implication, but it was not made explicit in the text. My concern was whether England could be invaded. The editorial page said, "best guess" is that the Germans would send troops across the Channel "in fast motorboats at night and land them all up and down the British coast." While this was going on, the French army "would certainly seize the moment of Germany's maximum effort against England to attack on the Somme." There was also the open warning, so far unspoken, that the surrender of the British fleet might mean the conquest of the United States. The news story, "The Battle of Flanders," noted that "more than half the British Expeditionary Force escaped to live and fight another day." More drawings diagrammed the German attack techniques. The essay on the Royal Air Force estimated first-line planes as 4,500 against 8,000 Germans.

The fog of war closed us in. It can now be told what happened. In the battle of the West the German Army had 136 divisions, 10 armored, against 135 divisions—93 French, 10 British, 22 Belgian, and 10 Dutch. On the right flank von Bock had 30 divisions, 3 armored. The main attack, *schwerpunkt* (a word I had not yet even heard), was by von Rundstedt with 45 divisions, 7 armored. Twenty-six French divisions were immobilized in the Maginot line. There was no strategic reserve. The worst French army, Corap's Ninth, was at the point of the *schwerpunkt*—Sedan. The 7 German armored divisions broke through, crossed the Meuse, and headed for the coast. On May 15 Premier Reynaud phoned Churchill, waking him. "We are beaten. We have lost the battle."

Thirty-five Allied divisions were caught north of the trap. From the south no French attack on the breakthrough ever came to pass. A few British divisions did attack from the north at Arras May 21, met Rommel's Seventh Panzer Division, and fell back. The incredible luck came when Hitler ordered the German armor of Kleist and Hoth to stop on the Canal Line from Gravelines to La Bassée. The British used the grace of 40 hours to defend the flooded perimeter of Dunkirk or, as *Life* always called it, Dunkerque. The RAF used 16 squadrons of fighters to defend the air over Dunkerque. The British succeeded in evacuating 338,226 men—139,911 were French and Belgian. The end came on June 4. It was a field in British history to rank with Agincourt, only 42 miles away.

The Germans had no plan at this point to invade England. What they had was Fall Rot, or Case Red (always translated Plan Red), to strike south across the Somme-Aisne line with 143 divisions against 65 French divisions. Now the French fought better but were annihilated.

No such precision was on display in the current magazine. Of the escape at Dunkerque, the lead headline read, "Allies Wrest Glory from Flanders Defeat," but the numbers were left vague. It was asserted that the individual Briton and Frenchman had outfought the German. And Churchill's ringing boast was quoted: "We shall not flag or fail. We shall go on to the end. We shall fight in France and on the seas and oceans; we shall fight with growing confidence and growing strength in the air. We shall defend our island, whatever the cost may be; we shall fight on beaches, landing grounds, in fields, in streets and on the hills. We shall never surrender." The final day at Dunkerque was given as June 4. Another spate of terrible and technical war pictures hammered at the reader.

Then America asserted itself. The text piece was on Joe Louis by Earl Brown, a knowledgeable study emphasizing his calm. There were also state birds and their notated songs; cancer research and the National Guard: "If you want to help U.S. defense, this is one way." The editorial page, far back, took seriously Weygand's "defense in depth," but noted that the Germans had broken through in two places: "The Germans marshaled a far superior strength of men and steel." It was also noted that "a tidal wave of American feeling burst last week through the dikes of Isolationism and swept the U.S. far down the road of Intervention." Finally, there was a nearly panicky piece "Will U.S. Mobilize Its Industrial Might in Time?" describing Roosevelt's search for great businessmen to speed rearmament. A curious note was struck by a report from Richard de Rochemont, a Francophile, that the French were fighting with "morale unsurpassed" and that the king of the Belgians had committed "treason" by surrendering.

This did not stand up a week for (June 24, 1940) the story was "Germans Enter Paris": "With France fallen, it is almost beyond hope that England can stand off Germany very long. Only slim hope is that England might hold the Germans until effective help begins pouring in from America. [This was propaganda for precisely such help.] The Tragedy of France: two years late it asks for 'clouds of planes.' After 20 years it sadly remembered that it was the U.S. that had won the last war and paid for it." Since France's fall could be laid to its twenty-year-old belief that it had won World War I, this was more than pouring salt into a wound. But, as an incidental snub to France, this story was not the lead, which was "Willkie Boom Is Republican Sensation as Philadelphia Convention Nears": "Mass wave of spontaneous, volunteer, amateur enthusiasm." (This was straight Republican propaganda.) The essay was on Philadelphia, where the Republican convention was to be held June 24. The "Speaking of Pictures" confessed a strange nightmare that *Life* had had as early as February 1939. This was to ask military sources to

imagine that as of July 1941 Germany and Italy had defeated France
and England, the British fleet had been scuttled, the French fleet
captured, and the Axis should then attack the United States. How
would they do it? The answer was shown in drawings: bombing the
Panama Canal, landing in Brazil, defeating the U.S. fleet, and landing
in New Jersey to overrun the industrial Northeast. The purpose was
to frighten America into massive rearmament, to meet what we had
consistently described as the "magnificent" Nazi army and air force.
Elsewhere, Archibald MacLeish was quoted as having repudiated
those writers, including himself (and, in an atrocious bracketing,
Hemingway), who had built up "moral unpreparedness." *Life* quoted
Hemingway as ridiculing MacLeish, quite properly. For this was
more MacLeish narcissism, blind to everything Hemingway stood for.
The issue began praising "America and the World": "I have watched
Life grow from a first-class picture magazine to a marvelously
selective mirror that reflects the world vividly and with a rare
intelligence . . . the outstanding literary achievement of the year."
The issue ended with a list of ways to help the Allies. In between was
the statement that Mussolini's declaration of war "was, in the
practically unanimous opinion of the American people, the act of a
vulture, a jackal, or a maggot . . . the much-talked-of might of the
Italian people simply did not stir. In a mysterious state of paralysis, it
faintly twitched here and there." I was much praised for this
vituperation.

The fate of the loser was again accorded defeated France (July 1,
1940), as the lead went to the Mexican presidential campaign—Billings' anti-Indian prejudice being again abated for the obvious reason:
Mexican oil. Thus, "with less than 400 killings . . . the quietest in
decades." The only chance of revolution lay with a labor leader,
Lombardo Toledano, "no matter who wins. . . . The two basic rules
of Mexican politics are that all Presidential candidates are generals
and that all elections are dishonest. . . . Like city workers elsewhere,
Lombardo's union labor has hogged the benefits of the Mexican
Revolution, leaving the overwhelming majority of Mexican peasants
worse off than ever." This antiproletarian position, spontaneous with
myself, seems to have suited my superiors. France was noticed on the

editorial page: "During the week of the fall of France, Americans asked themselves some of the biggest questions and thought some of the longest and deepest thoughts in their national history. . . . Isolationists began to realize that . . . America had achieved real isolation. Except for hard-pressed Britain, the nation was now without a friend among the world's major powers." There was a story on France: "There was no glory in this defeat." In contrast, the "nervelessness" of the English was shown in various scenes, including the evacuation of children from the cities in expectation of bombing. The text piece was on "Cap" Rieber, chairman of the Texas Oil Company, by Joseph J. Thorndike, Jr., tying in with the Mexican story, and foreshadowing Thorndike's reasonable interest in Big Money, never to be fully satisfied, for, in spite of himself, he was an idea man of considerable competence.

During this period, I began to realize that journalism was suitable to the description of small events. But great events had a way of describing themselves, making talk superfluous. The tribe of journalists had shriveled to something like Kipling's Bandar-log, monkey-chatterers; my role seemed to have lost dignity. However, the journalist's remaining function was to draw a lesson from the great event. This we had done, the lesson being that America was suddenly in real peril, and that it had better master the tools and skills of war in a great hurry.

That America had something worth defending (July 8, 1940) was the theme of the lead "American Independence," celebrating July Fourth and Revolutionary battlefields. A story on the Republican convention was supported by the editorial page comment that Wendell Willkie's victory at the convention meant "the emergence of the first great American leader in eight years." It was noted that Russia had just taken Bessarabia and Bukovina from Rumania, to nobody's amazement. There was a story on conquered Paris and a Major Eliot piece saying that the United States needed bases for hemisphere defense. Letters of protest emerged from Lombardo Toledano (furious) and from Joe Louis' manager, objecting to Earl Brown's friendly story.

About this time I seem to have gone on vacation, and begun

working on my own personal lessons of the great European event. For the internal evidence in the next issue (July 15, 1940)—a line that "Britain needs them bad"—suggested that I did not write the foreign news. What surprises me is that the editorial page, quoting Secretary of the Interior Ickes, had anticipated and perhaps inspired my blast against the totalitarians, as follows: "When is the great, hard, angry, shouting, razzberry laugh of the American people going to yell down the west wind of this continent and out to sea and on out past the horizon?" As will be seen, my later remarks were not quite as original as I have always thought. The lead anticipated England's "Life-and-Death Fight." The plan for a German invasion of England was carefully blueprinted.

We did not know that, while England had no army, Germany had no navy. The Norwegian adventure had put nearly all of the German navy in dry dock. Amazingly, after the conquest of France, the German question was: *Was nun?* (what now?) Hitler first mentioned the invasion of England to Admiral Raeder on May 21; asked for invasion studies on June 25; on July 16 ordered plans completed by August 15. The name of the plan was Seelowe (Sea Lion). In June, England had 250 medium and light tanks and 786 field guns. From the United States arrived 500,000 .30-caliber rifles, with 50 cartridges apiece, and 900 75-mm. field guns, with 1,000 rounds apiece. Churchill held 13 divisions and 3 armored divisions in reserve while the Home Guard manned the coasts. The air attack on England was called Adler (Eagle).

The *Life* lead ended with a "Yes-No" question: "Should the U.S. Help Britain with Destroyers?" referring to 109 destroyers that had been quietly refitted and recommissioned, unknown even to many U.S. naval officers. Undoubtedly, this made it politically easier for Roosevelt to send destroyers to England (in exchange for bases), even as Luce was championing his opponent, Willkie. This genuine nonpartisan patriotism of Luce's must be acknowledged. The editorial page noted Churchill's seizure of as much of the French fleet as he could get and the Nazi screams, "Piracy . . . gangsters . . . cowards . . . stab in the back," heart-warming stuff for the free world. The text piece was on "Joe Grew, Ambassador to Japan," by

John Hersey, a shockingly sycophantic, appeasement-oriented, asinine performance, concluding that America would be wise to be nice to Japan. Love, love, love. Immediately after came the survival stories of two Britons torpedoed by a Nazi submarine. Hersey was not living in the same world as the two seamen.

Europe's lesson was developed in the essay (July 22, 1940) "The Defense of America: Billions for Guns, Planes and Tanks Are Wasted Without Men Trained to use Them." Thus, "Adolf Hitler . . . must indubitably anticipate that when America has spent billions on armaments it will some day choose to use its arms, probably against him, rather than suffer economic collapse. For him, it is obviously the part of wisdom to strike at America before it has organized its terrible potential full strength. Whether he will strike soon, perhaps this summer, seems now to depend mainly on the resistance. In any event, America has little time to lose." But the story went on to demand that men be provided to man the guns, by "universal registration and selective service." The following pages showed the esoteric skills of tank operation, requiring long training. The text piece was Walter Lippmann's superfluous lecture to Americans who said that America could do business as usual even if Hitler won. At that moment Eurasia, except for England, was dominated by Germany, Russia, and Japan. Elsewhere, the French surrender at Compiègne was shown. A picture story of the large Time Inc. staff's flight before the German army noted that they "ended the trip with an increased admiration and affection for one another." But each who told me about the adventure had a very poor opinion of the others' comportment. The exception was the photographer Carl Mydans who, I gather, behaved well, but he had been in far worse spots.

Sordid machination was pinned (July 29, 1940) on Roosevelt's third-term nomination in Chicago, with a picture of the man in the cellar who controlled the public address system and at the strategic moment overwhelmed the hall with the sound: "We Want Roosevelt." He happened to be the Chicago superintendent of sewers, and thus was coined the famous cliché, "voice from the sewers." The text agreed that many people wanted Roosevelt but concluded, "In a time of world democratic crisis, the greatest democracy treated the world to one of the shoddiest and most hypocritical spectacles in history." This last seems extreme. I suppose that Hubie Kay wrote it, half believing it, half knowing he had to write it. The editorial page said, "For one more week the Battle of Britain was postponed" (we know now that it was postponed until August 13). The results of a poll of U.S. opinion showed that 88% wanted to arm to the teeth in case of an Axis victory, and 7.6% would prefer to coexist unarmed and peacefully. But, should America seem to be in danger of defeat, 54% would choose to fight at all costs, 33.4% would prefer surrender, 22.6% were still opposed to the draft. The propaganda had not been 100% successful. In the crucible of a crisis, the American democracy did not show up brilliantly. Those minority votes were a little terrifying. They convey to me, today, that no democracy will ever survive unless it has the leadership of what Jefferson described as "an aristocracy of virtue and talent." For the deliberate repudiation of this element in society, the Spanish republic was extinguished. France had abdicated to the labor unions, the bureaucrats, and the mob, and died. England was saved in large part by leadership, primarily by an undaunted aristocrat. Germany was debauched by abdication of the aristocrats. "Virtue and talent," remember; even without family and money, these people are superior—without them, the mass cannot survive. The mob's resentment of superiority may express itself against family and money, but not against virtue and talent. But the appalling 33.4% preferring surrender to Nazi Germany in case of difficulties revealed one third of the proud American citizenry as cattle, knowing their fate in the slaughter pens. Given the current young people, I do not believe that the present figure, as against Soviet Russia, would be an improvement. They are another wave of cattle. My unhappy conclusion, then as now, was that a percentage of Americans do not deserve America.

An admirable piece by Mrs. Luce (Clare Boothe) must be noted, in which she, somewhat belatedly, quotes the U.S. military attaché in Paris, Colonel Horace Fuller, as telling her in April: "The English never know when they're licked. *They'll* always keep on fighting. That's the only hope." As for France, he said, "If some miracle doesn't happen, they've [the Germans] got the guns, and the tanks and the planes and the men, and a plan, and the initiative." Mrs. Luce seems to have burst into tears. This information might have been helpful to me three months earlier. It is clear that at the time the Luces did not believe the military attaché. I suspect that both Mr. and Mrs. Luce were dilettantes of the great event, for this confession appears in the July 29, 1940, issue. Here we see Luce close to a great event. I think that, like me, but more drastically, he was humbled, and recognized painfully that in the presence of a really great event the journalist became a peripheral, even ignominious figure. Perhaps his appraisal of his profession began to change, and he may have reacted personally, as a man, to his impotence, even as his enterprise was beginning to make real money and he was being invited to dinner by President Roosevelt.

The pause before the Battle of Britain, when Germany had its only real chance to invade Britain, was shown (August 5, 1940) in a roundup of pictures and events, as Hitler made a leisurely tour of Western Europe, but not of the British Isles. There was a story on the skirmishing of Britain and Italy in the Mediterranean and North Africa. The editorial page hammered at the theme that "50 of those [U.S.] destroyers sent to Britain might tip the balance against German invasion." The text piece was on "Little Lord Beaverbrook," England's minister of aircraft production, by Noel Busch. The point was that men who had always concentrated on making money were told to forget money and make war. "Company managers and executives were replaced by foremen and engineers recruited from the factories and responsible not to the stockholders but to the government in general and Beaverbrook in particular."

The continuing pause was reported in the lead (August 12, 1940) with a newsreel strip of a German bombing attack on a small convoy in the Channel. The two Republican candidates for president and vice president were inspected, as were the first moves toward American rearmament.

A personal note. That summer, separated from my wife, I was going to a house she had rented outside Danbury, Connecticut, from the mother-in-law of my old friend Tom Wenning. There I polished my answer, to be called "Democracy Unlimited," to the quiet smiles on the faces of my Communist and Fascist friends and acquaintances. Since it reflects many facets in my thinking, it is worth reproducing. The historical moment may perhaps be blamed for its truculent crudity. However, Noel Busch, back from England and text editor, snapped it up. Even then, many another editor would certainly have turned it down. It ended any patience that the Communists of Time Inc. felt toward me. Today, many liberals would heartily disapprove of it and it would draw only obscenities from "advanced" youth.

Nevertheless (August 19, 1940), here it is, under the headline, "Democracy Unlimited: Hitler Talks of His New Revolution but America Says It's Tyranny and to Hell with It":

Americans have a weakness for letting the other man talk himself out. For 20 years now they have let the Nazis and Fascists and Communists explain how, each in their way, they were the "revolution of the future." The American people have listened with tolerance, curiosity, even sympathy. The listening time is over. Now at last, at the end of tolerance, comes the horse laugh, the great American razzberry.

What idiot mouthing is this that Nazism and Fascism and Communism are "revolutions"? They have a new lingo but they are the oldest thing in the world, the perpetual counter-revolution, the rule of the many by the few for the supposed good of the masses. We have had that before. In fact that is all that most of the dead men lying thousands deep in the world's past ever knew. They knew the Russian czars, Alexander, Baibars the Panther, the Ottoman sultans, the Mogul rulers of India, the Mongol and Manchu emperors of China, the Spanish conquistadors, the Japanese shoguns, the Hohenstaufens and the Hohenzollerns, the Borgias, Richelieu, the Bourbons and Habsburgs, the Corsican bravura of Napoleon, the bark of Bismarck.

Most of these men were known among their friends for their high ideals. They were not villains to themselves. But nobody now even tries to remember what those ideals were. In the history books of Democracy we recite only the record of their acts.

So it is with Hitler and Stalin and Mussolini. A hundred years from today, if there are still free men, how many will read *Mein Kampf* or Hitler's "promises" or the long gutturals of what Hitler told the people he had in store for the world? Nobody. It is hardly more useful to read them today. There is some truth in them but only a dark fragment of the truth there is in his acts. Of his acts we now know enough.

In fact we were on the track of something else. What?

The true revolution. The perpetual, self-perpetuating revolution. Democracy.

Democracy is like health. It is nothing. It is the absence of pain and sickness. It only becomes something when pain comes and a man remembers how pleasant it was not to be in pain. In a word it is life itself. It is breathing and eating and being and becoming something. It is being alive instead of being part dead. It is a world where every man feels something like the way only one man felt in the world of Alexander the Great, who was just one bright-eyed little man who held his head somewhat on one side. Democracy is limited merely by the ultimate potentialities of all men in the world and all their descendants. It is the total sum of hopes, of faith and of charity. It is humble and omnipotent. Those who wish to get fancy about it may say that it is God.

Naturally it is harder to define Democracy at any one moment than to define such crude obvious programs as Nazism, Fascism or Communism. For these are as limited as the brain of one man. They have all been defined and explained. There is no future in them whatever except the murder of every other kind of brain.

The proponents of these programs generally do not like their fellow men for what they are. They feel with wonderful sincerity that they are able to decide what is best for other people and they are resolved to give it to them, whether the people like it or not. Notice that they do not especially think of giving it to themselves. They expect to be on the giving, not the taking, end. They may be right or they may be wrong but there is to be no judge. In a world where God will not speak they are willing to be God.

In the daylight of sanity these are sick people. They are unhappy in their personal lives. They want more power than they have. They feel the thrill of power tingling in their veins. But this pleasant neurotic tingle of overpowering ambition is a poor qualification for a position of power. It would be more nearly correct to say that men in power should be picked for their total lack of tingle. Hitler and Mussolini and Stalin are full of tingles, dark surges of power and ruthlessness.

These sick men sincerely want to see the world run right, just as Alexander and Genghis Khan and Napoleon did. Anybody who thinks they will run it right if they have the chance should review the history of mankind.

First, it must be remembered that most of the men who have ever lived have lived under a tyrant. That is the customary thing, not the unusual thing. These tyrants were sometimes overthrown by other tyrants but in general their tyranny worked if it was brutal enough. Only when it softened at the top was it overthrown by the people, as under the England of 1776, the France of 1789, the Russia of 1917. The history books do not mention the centuries of enslaved peoples who made no news, the massacred masses of Asia and European Russia and Africa and the Mexican or Peruvian or

American Indians and the Turkish Balkans and the people of India. Democracy had no chance among them. It was not even a dream.

Democracy is a shy growth. It occurs only where there is an absence of fear. It survives only where it is protected by an overwhelming power. It has had its great growth only since 1714, since England ruled the seas. The peculiar English even encouraged the revolt of the American colonies. It is not often remembered now that English members of Parliament said then in the House of Commons that the Americans were fighting for English liberties as well as for their own (against the crazy King George III) and they referred to Washington's armies as "our armies."

The revolution of the French would have had no chance of survival against the armies of Europe's monarchs but for the genius of Napoleon. Then Napoleon killed French Democracy from within.

The democracies of Scandinavia, Belgium, the Netherlands were allowed to survive only because it was British policy to keep Europe divided in small, impotent nations. To these add Switzerland, but the Swiss first earned their freedom because the Swiss phalanx was by far the most formidable fighting mass in Europe.

The South American republics, including those that can be called democracies, have survived under the protection of the powerful U.S. And the U.S. got its start behind the protection of a great ocean. It did not neglect seapower. But Americans have been misinformed by their history books. They are told that their growth into power and freedom was inevitable—manifest destiny. They are not told that they won freedom from the British Empire largely because Louis XVI gave them guns and money and troops, that they almost broke up under the Articles of Confederation, that Jefferson almost did not beat Burr for President, that the Confederacy should have won at Gettysburg, that the British Navy kept the world stable from 1815 to 1914.

Luck helped the American colossus past its difficult times. Luck let the American people have the time and room to develop their greatness. It was not luck that they knew what to do with their opportunities. It was Democracy, the rule of the crowd that kept leaders from strangling America with their fixed and limited personal ideals. America grew as a boy grows into a man, making mistakes, learning the poor way, the better way, learning self-reliance, its faults and its strengths, feeling its oats, getting bored and disillusioned, getting over-enthusiastic, falling on its face and getting up again without crying.

For mark it well, there have been democracies that died. Some men had Democracy in Athens, Rome, Florence, Venice, Ghent, Bruges. Those cities were prosperous and happy for a time because their men were free. Pride of one kind or another threw them down. They grew jealous and class-conscious and greedy. The living let Democracy vanish, for far longer than their own lifetimes, for a period that may be described as forever. Centuries have passed and Ghent and Bruges are little more than tourist backwaters. Athens and Venice and Florence and Rome have lost even the hope of Democracy. The men of those places have no reason to teach their children hope. The night has been too long. Democracy there is dead.

It did not pay those men of long ago to sell out Democracy. They sold it out for their own convenience, whatever the black despair they bequeathed to their descendants. The responsibility lay as heavily on the men who did nothing as on those who did something, good or ill.

For there comes a time when the living free men have no longer any time or grace to make mistakes. Such a time must always come, and perhaps often, for a great, rich powerful Democracy. It seems to have come at last for the U.S.

Democracy can be overthrown. A man can be swindled and end in the poorhouse or the river. God does not and never did guarantee heaven on earth to men. God takes it away quickly from fools and sluggards.

There are two self-evident facts about our democratic world. The first is that the welfare of all the people is the job of the central government and that all the people must choose the men they want to govern and help them. The second is that a business enterprise exists solely to produce something or do a specific job. In the latter the method cannot be democratic. It is the age-old lesson of life that any job is done best under a boss, from digging a ditch on up.

So mixed up did people get in recent years that some wanted to put a boss in Washington to do the job of government. And other people wanted to make every little business a democratic government, in which all the workers would have a vote in how that business should be run.

Neither of these errors actually succeeded. But public thinking was mixed up, people grew angry with one another and to make their opponents as mad as they were they took over the use of two European words, Fascist and Communist.

This was a hot argument but nothing fatal. The losers in 1932 and 1936, though they talked mighty hard against Roosevelt, were good enough losers. More big words and loose thinking passed in eight years than in the previous 150. But strangely nobody ever mentioned Democracy in the argument. Both sides had really forgotten it. They had both fallen into the marvelous European booby trap, the fake fight between Communism and Fascism. Both sides decided that half their fellow men were so wrong and wicked in their political ideas that they really did not deserve to live. The wonderful class war fastened itself tentatively on a nation that has only one class, the great American middle class. It made us feel so "European." The real sincerity of the Americans showed itself, their enthusiasm for crusades, but it led America in two opposite directions.

And finally the booby trap was sprung. The Communists and the Nazis in Europe made a power alliance. The European dictators enjoyed a side-splitting laugh at America's civil war of name-calling. And the Americans came to a grinding halt in the middle of their argument, looked at the hollow words still coming out of their mouths and felt sick.

Strange as it may seem, Nazi Germany is a development of what the Germans of the 1920's thought the U.S. was. Germans worshiped the America of the Coolidge-Hoover era. They idolatrized American movies, jazz, gangster slang. Their word for American industrial method was "rationalization." They rationalized everything, from bathrooms to cigaret packs. American money paid for German reparations which paid for the war debts which, in the end, were never paid. American money built German factories on the lines of Detroit and Pittsburgh. American engineers, salesmen, advertising experts advised the reformed German nation. A beaten underdog, Germany grasped at the new thing to save itself, because it could have none of the old comfortable things. Even Nazi street fighting took on romance from the American gangster movies of the 1920's. German businessmen used the same gigantic desks and multiple telephones they saw in American movies, though they did not need them.

Adolf Hitler decided that the American way of life was to inherit the earth. But he and his adopted Germans mistook for the American way of life merely its end point of efficient . . . management of business. He missed entirely the fact that these businessmen who looked so snappy and high-powered in their offices were in fact sons of the poor, the middle class, sometimes of immigrants, that they were little people whose energies had been released by Democracy. Hence, he missed the moral, sociological and psychological law that has made America great: the law that the best man is the one who has been allowed to make his own way.

Hitler's tyranny and Stalin's and Mussolini's were a little different from the oldtime tyrannies. They had a pseudoscientific basis. This "science" was concentrated not in the fairly simple seizure of sources of power and the use of production for the dictator's chosen ends but in the use of propaganda. Hitler never hoped to convince more than perhaps a third of the people but under a parliamentary system this was enough to get him where he wanted to be. From there he merely knew how to use parliamentary procedure better than his opponents, in order to abolish it and them. Hitler's propaganda is based on the same principle that a jailbird uses when he tells every visitor, "I am innocent. I was framed." For it is the nature of free men to believe that other people really are innocent.

The Nazi propaganda machine imposes brilliantly on the practice of the democratic press of printing all the news without fear or favor. American editors do not usually print a convicted perjurer's protests of innocence but they must obviously print every handout, official and unofficial, that comes from the official rulers of Greater Germany, for they are all news. The German High Command carefully calculates those rumors it allows to leak out, with a kind of crude subtlety, to confuse the enemy, for all people everywhere are the enemy. What American editors think of all this is one thing but what readers may think is another. The papers are proud of the fact that they do not select, editorialize, prejudge in their news columns. But some readers, reading these august lies from the Head of a Friendly State, are perhaps a little persuaded. It sounds kind of funny, they say, but maybe there's something on Hitler's side after all.

By a shrewd misuse of all the American techniques, Hitler has already conquered continental Europe and is closing in on what the Nazis call the "Jewish pluto-democratic American Colossus." Yet the conquest of Europe was not quite so big a job as it has been made out. The bitter truth is that Europe deserved its fate. It was overripe for a single-minded, multiple-faced conqueror. Europe's ripeness has reached Americans in the oversimplified phrase, "Europe stinks."

The ordinary people of Europe do not stink. But Europe's leaders, aristocratic and bureaucratic, came close to deserving the short hard word. It is enough to reflect quickly on the ruling castes of Poland, Hungary, Rumania, Yugoslavia, Spain; to ask why Belgium, half-French, half-Flemish, ever existed; what are these monstrosities called Rumania and Yugoslavia; or how did Latvia, Lithuania and Estonia ever enter the conversation. The fact that colored all the thinking of Europeans was that 550,000,000 people lived for 20 years in an area smaller than the U.S. under 36 national flags.

There are in fact far more than 36 racial, language, dialect, geographical and historical units in Europe. The 36 flags did not represent them. Furthermore fear lay over them like a tent. Fear of one another, a multiplied fear.

Nevertheless, this Europe of Versailles was an attempt, a first fumbling blunder in the direction of Democracy. From the beginning it was a failure, as nearly everything Democracy attempts is—*the first time*. The real trouble was that there was no chance for revision, for trial and error and retrial, for this new Europe was poured and frozen into the mold of 36 sovereign nations.

Had Europe been one great Union like the U.S. it might have had the magnanimity, before Hitler, to give free Germany a better break. Failing this it would have marched on Hitler from the Vistula and Dniester to the Rhine and Meuse the instant Hitler marched into the Rhineland. Or if not then, when he took Czechoslovakia or Poland. But it never marched all together. Paralyzed by fright for itself, each nation lay frozen until Hitler was ready to take it.

What is the basic issue of the quarrel between the U.S. and Germany-Italy-Russia? What are we defending? We are certainly not defending Capitalism. Nor the Jews nor the Aristocracy nor the Self-Determination of Peoples. The only thing we are defending is our own Democracy under which we can always change our mind. If we get Nazism or Fascism or Communism we can never change our mind again. We are stuck with it, we and our sons and our grandsons and all our seed. Probably the U.S. is fighting for the eternal right to change its mind about anything any time, on the basis of new facts.

Perhaps totalitarian slavery is not so bad. You will still get a bed (not so soft), food (not so much), work (not of your choosing), love (within your appointed class and race group), books (dull), friends (without pride), the love of your children (but will you deserve it?).

Under Democracy, however, your child is a Revolution far superior to that of Hitler or Stalin. He is a new beginning of wisdom. No law compels him to believe even in what you believe. No ward heeler can take him out of the fifth grade and assign him to lifelong farm labor. No stool pigeon can send him to concentration camp because he argues too much. No black-shirted officer of the elite who likes his girl can have him shot. Under Democracy the small boy who is now 2 or 5 or 10 has a chance to grow up to be something greater than his father. He will slowly change his world. And when he is 70 and ready to die, though he may not realize it, his world will more closely resemble the dream he had when he was 20.

This is the world we have now. With patience it will solve its problems of unemployment and security and production and consumption. It is not perfect by far. It is obviously due for changes in business, the family, the Church, the State, science, transportation, et al. But certainly we can think of better changes than Hitler has to offer. Our world is, of course, worth fighting for. It is infinitely more. It is the cause on which all history and the hope of this planet depend. The eternal soul of man waits on its outcome.

The Nazi war technique of propaganda is by now quite plain and quite simple. It is exactly the reverse of all previous human experience; hence, it is astonishingly effective at first.

All adults and many children have observed that no man who yells threats acts on them. The loud talker does not fight. But the Nazis yell bloody murder; they demoralize the weak; they excite the contempt of the strong; and then they strike, just as they said they would.

The basis for this technique is that Hitler is certain that people who lack strict controls are total, uncontrollable fools. He figures that they will either panic at the yelling or decide he will not strike. Those who do the first accuse the others of being fifth columnists and vice versa. The notion that they will both prepare calmly for the blow is supposed to be impossible under Hitler's psychological laws.

So long as he was dealing with Europeans he was right. For he was dealing with leaders who believed in security without risk. But Americans have a gift of action. They like the offensive. They like results. They like to do something just for the sake of seeing whether they are right or wrong.

The great soldiers have always emerged from societies that were at least more democratic than their neighbors. Sometimes they were nomadic herders, sometimes mountaineers, sometimes plainsmen. They were the swordsmen of Athens and Sparta, the Roman legions, the Egyptian mamelukes, the horsemen of Genghis Khan, the Swiss phalanx, the English yeomen, the free Swedes, the republicans of Napoleon, the Scots, the Afghans, the Americans on both sides in the Civil War, the Americans in the last world war.

Apart from sheer fighting qualities, how do we stack up against Nazi Germany? Let us take some of the pettiest points on which Hitler prides himself. His government gives full support, rich subsidies and the best brains to all war industries. The result?

1. One inch of the German tank armor can be pierced more easily than one-quarter inch of American armor plate.
2. The whole vast German attempt to produce synthetic rubber has been matched by at least three American concerns' research laboratories.
3. Germany has only been able to approach the efficiency of the American bombsight by, supposedly, stealing or copying it.
4. Germany has not been able to produce an equivalent of the Sperry gyropilot for automatic flying.

The point is that 130,000,000 Americans using their own heads can do better than a few thousand German or Russian or Italian big shots using theirs. This is anything but remarkable. Democracy is simply better psychology than Nazism. It works. It needs room and time and men, but overwhelmingly, magnificently, in the long run, it works.

The effect of this extraordinary propaganda is uncertain. It was aimed at actual Communists in the organization and at an avowed Fascist or two I knew socially and liked. It might have inspired a Patton and generally convinced the American military that they had a job to do. As for the mass of people, it was intended to terrorize them. Democracy is presented as a benefit that living people do not deserve until they do something to defend it, generation by generation, and this is still my conviction. Should a generation prefer slavery, it has my permission if it will permit me to die in freedom. The subsequent fight is up to my descendants.

The piece may have been simple irritability, for at that period both Communists and Fascists were smiling. (The identification of crypto-Communists became suddenly no problem. And it is certainly permitted to remember such revelations, as I did with a degree of ferocity, purely introspective.)

Dated July 24, 1940, is a laudatory note from Ruth Berrien, my checker, from which wonderful candid Ruth could not exclude some criticism with which the reader may agree:

"Everybody is crazy about this and I think it is marvelous. Hubie says they will probably run it next week.

"I still think the 'law that made America great: the law that the best man is the one who has made his own way' applies specifically to Hitler and that your unconscious condescension to the people of Europe is just the same as Hitler's own instinct of racial superiority.

"Also if you can't limit democracy, how can you limit it to government? Democrats won't be happy until they get it in business too. Your calling it 'lunacy' is just what Hitler says about democratic government [the last sentence handwritten].

"Do you really want us to hit Hitler first? That is the strong impression.

"It's because I think the piece is so very fine that I have the nerve to persist with these points. It is not only fine but strikingly beautiful writing—very eloquent."

She cannot explain to me exactly what she meant, for she is dead. I gather she would have liked some sort of drift toward socialism.

The lead in the issue showed two American towns drilling against invasion and said, "Some Americans may still call such behavior 'war hysteria.' Britons no longer do. Some Americans may find it funny. Adolf Hitler will not."

In the next issue (August 26, 1940), closing August 17, began "The Big One," possibly dwarfing (in terms of the gigantic stakes) all history's great battles, the decisive struggle of the free world to survive, and it was not fought by Americans. The lead headline said, "The Battle of Britain Opens with the Greatest Air Attack in History": "For this was the stupendous opening curtain of the greatest air battle of all time. [Was I back on the job? The style is violent.] On Thursday, August 8, the attack began rising in pitch, until on Thursday, August 15, with more than a thousand planes over Britain, it reached a point of frenzy. On that day alone the British claimed to have shot down 180 German planes while the Germans claimed to have destroyed 143 British planes." Later: "The question is merely whether the vast German Air Force (18,000 planes plus) can keep attacking long enough to wear down and out the Royal Air Force (5,000 planes plus). Last week the Germans were feeling out in a thousand ways how the British had planned their defenses." The specifics were given. On the editorial page it was added that "the incredible British faced their Hour of Trial with a calm that America, watching from the distant sidelines, could not match."

The facts of the Battle of Britain, which reached us only through a swirling fog of war, are today well known. Hitler had ordered the battle to open August 5, weather permitting. The actual preliminaries were: August 8, 400 planes against convoys; August 11, 850 against ports; August 12, 1,400 against advance airfields, Portsmouth, shipping and radar masts. But the official beginning was August 13, Adlertag or Eagle Day. (Plane losses will be given in parentheses: German first, British second.) August 13 (45–13). August 14, under 500 sorties (19–8). August 15, 1,786 sorties against airfields (75–34). August 16, 1,715 sorties (45–21). August 18, 750 sorties (71–27) against airfields and radar stations. Then five days of bad weather. August 24, 1,030 sorties (38–22) against airfields. August 25–29, average of 700 daily sorties (117–77). August 30, 1,345 sorties. August 31, 1,450 sorties, the worst loss of British fighters: 39. September 1–5, average of 700 daily sorties (113–99). At this point, the British started bombing Berlin regularly and Hitler swore, "We will eradicate their cities . . . so help us God."

Hidden were the facts that the Luftwaffe was run by amateurs, the RAF by professionals, that the German organization was complex and unwieldy, the British simple and effective, and that the British (like the U.S.) had opted in the mid-thirties for the long-range four-engine bomber and the long-range fighter, as well as the radar network. On numbers of effectives, *Life* was fairly wrong. In early August, according to Telford Taylor in *The Breaking Wave* (p. 97),

Luftflotten 2, 3 and 5 had a strength of between 2,400 and 2,600 planes. Of these about a thousand were bombers, 300 were Stukas (very vulnerable and soon withdrawn), and about 800 Messerschmitt 109 fighters. Also 250 of the disappointing Messerschmitt 110. Against these, the British had an operating strength of over 800 Hurricane and Spitfire fighters and about 500 medium bombers, the heavy planes to arrive in 1941. Furthermore, by the summer of 1940 British plane production was at 1,600 a month (500 fighters), while the German rate was at about 800 (230 fighters). The chief British deficiency was in pilots.

The true story can be quickly finished. On September 7 Göring shifted his objective to London: on that day the docks, with 300 bombers and over 600 fighters. The follow-up was on September 9, 11 (24–29), and 14 (14–14). The climactic day, a Sunday, the day of victory, the end of the Battle of Britain, was September 15. In the morning's battle, 23 British squadrons met the enemy; in the afternoon, 30 squadrons. The Germans made 1,300 sorties (52–26). On September 17 Hitler postponed Sealion "indefinitely." The last of the great day attacks fell on September 27 (50–28) and 30 (48–20). The Germans announced that they had destroyed 2,000 British fighters. The correct figure was 779 and Fighter Command still had 732 operational planes and 1,581 pilots. The British had destroyed 1,400 German planes, bringing the Luftwaffe to about the same strength as the RAF. The blitz ensued, almost entirely at night.

We could catch the broad trend of the battle, however (September 2, 1940, closing August 24), on the editorial page: "Jubilant over Britain's success in standing off the first mass onslaught of the German Air Force [Churchill] had boasted for the first time that Britain had finally stemmed the 'cataract of disaster' and was heading for victory." He also offered America Atlantic bases in exchange for destroyers. Again, it was noted that "the German Air Force gave England a five-day lull . . . [five days of bad weather]. At week's end another mass attack roared in over the Dover coast. . . . Once more Britain wondered if the 'all-out' air war had started." This last was the August 24 of 1,030 sorties (38–22). The lead was the story of Stalin's long-deferred achievement of Leon Trotsky's bloody murder in Mexico. There were also affectionate stories on Willkie's campaign and the Dionne quintuplets' growing up. The letters on "Democracy Unlimited" ranged from "brought tears to my eyes" to "ridiculous bit of balderdash" (this latter printed by Longwell, oddly).

We were still on the right track (September 9, 1940) in the lead: "With all fingers crossed, cautious military experts were at last beginning to say that Britain seemed to be holding Germany in the air over England. The chief credit for this went to Britain's Prime Minister Churchill and Ministers Bevin (Labor) and Beaverbrook (Aircraft Production), who have practically rearmed Britain in the three months since Dunkerque." However, we thought the attack was against London, whereas at this stage it was against airfields and radar stations, though we showed pictures of London burning. From previous experience, the Germans thought they could knock out British air resistance in only three or four days of such attacks as they were delivering. In the third week, the Luftwaffe was wasting away.

The essay was "Canada," with which Roosevelt had just agreed to set up a Permanent Joint Defense Board. "The fact that there is a Canada is the best guaranty the U.S. can get that Britain will not surrender its fleet to the Nazis. France had no Canada to retreat to. Thus the startling unpreparedness of the U.S. is saved by the British Navy and the Canadian Air Force."

The destroyers-for-bases deal was consummated (September 16, 1940). The lead, probably written by Hubie Kay, emphasized their use should a "German Armada try to ferry the German Army to England. On that day of thunderous, screaming, drowning, clawing death in the sky, on the water and under it, the 50 American destroyers may well turn the tide of battle and bury so many German boats, tanks, guns and soldiers that Hitler will call it quits." The opening read: "The idea of sending old U.S. destroyers to Britain was only a nascent whisper when in the issue of July 15 *Life* posed the question and listed its pros and cons." It is possible that the idea originated in the *Life* Foreign News department, perhaps with Underhill. On July 15 I think I was on vacation, but I had believed that Roosevelt would accept the idea, solving the political problem of seeming to get something in return. The idea of additional bases had been raised by Major Eliot. Both the lead and Wendell Willkie objected mildly to Roosevelt's doing it by executive fiat. On the editorial page was the statement that "British fighter squadrons have lost over half their first-line strength, are now filled with replacements. Pilot losses have been about 65% in proportion to planes destroyed. But German crew losses have been nearly 100%." The guess on British first-line strength was about correct, but it had been replaced in full. British pilot efficiency was deteriorating, but German efficiency was deteriorating even faster.

Pictures had arrived of a complementary benefit to the defense of the United States: the destruction by Churchill's navy of seven French warships: "The French navy, immobilized and discouraged by the defeat of the French Army, happened to hold the balance of power over the entire world. . . . The 'promise' of Hitler not to use the French Navy conveyed to sensible men that he would do the exact opposite. . . . 'A melancholy action,' said British Prime Minister Churchill. And so it was," the story concluded. "But after it democracies breathed easier."

Churchill had behaved brutally, but he was dealing with a ruthless assassin, for whom evil was the sublime virtue. The French fools did not realize they were to be the pawns of the evil but, when they found out, it would have been too late for the free world. Today the same rule applies to the free world's relations with the Communist world, with certain reservations. The Communists are less dedicated and efficient assassins than Hitler's crowd. But they too despise the human kind, and perhaps they are right.

We see a long report on the German Occupation by Sherry Mangan: The French "simply do not understand the strange American notion that the Vichy Government is just a German puppet. The de Gaulle 'government' in London is considered a bad joke. . . . They hate Hitler equally with Reynaud, Laval and de Gaulle, but so far their anger is only a subterranean rumble." This strange linkage may be taken as indicative of the state of mind of people who have elected to become slaves. I must regard it as a disgrace to France and its publication a disgrace to Time Inc.

Since on September 7 Göring had directed the Luftwaffe against

London, we forgot the real battle (September 23, 1940, closing September 14) and concentrated on the human tragedy of London, not knowing that the real battle was to end the day after the issue closed. But such is the eternal disability of journalism. The pathos was before us: "Men were doing their best to destroy the biggest city man has yet raised on this planet."

The lead said: "Slowly the German bombers had forced the abandonment, at least temporarily, of fighter-plane bases southeast of London, slowly worn out the strength of the overworked fighter pilots, slowly filled British front-line squadrons with replacements. The Germans have lost 4,000 plane crews. . . . The charge across the Channel by the Nazi armada seemed very close."

The Britons referred to were about a thousand young men of Group II of the RAF Fighter Command, most long since dead. The group had seven sector airfields, each with three squadrons of 16 planes each—each sector averaged 48 operational planes, with 12 usually held in reserve. The Luftwaffe had crippled most of the advance airfields of Group II, but the other groups of Fighter Command were still effective. I had failed to realize that if London was suddenly the objective, Group II was not. Göring, the amateur, believed he had destroyed Group II. His staff and intelligence work was worse than mine.

It is not yet understood that this battle, from August 13 to September 15, was *the* decisive battle, eclipsing D-Day and the eventual destruction of Hitler's Germany. This was the end of the "cataract of disaster," the vindication of the sense and courage of free men against the slave mob, and the inevitable signal that Hitler had lost the war, in an industrial world in which Europe could not survive by itself. England and the United States still held the seas, and Göring and Hitler had been denied the world by about a thousand young men in the air.

The editorial page recorded the final passage of the first peacetime conscription law in American history, and gigantic appropriations for rearmament. The pathetic essay was on the Vichy government of Pétain and Laval: "Laval would like England to lose and help France pay for this war." More astonishingly, the text piece by Frank Norris, a cold-blooded journalist, said: "Perhaps nine out of ten people on either side of the demarcation line want the English to win. . . . The Vichy Government, on the other hand, while no fonder of the Germans than the littlest Frenchman, believes the Germans will probably win the war. The quicker the war ends, the better it will be for France. After that it will be up to France's rulers to make the best possible deal with the Germans, possibly even one whereby France may become Germany's strongest economic partner in Europe."

I admire coldness in crisis but this, from the Princeton son of a railway president, was not so much coldness as nihilism or treason. Norris' staff and intelligence work was also worse than mine.

Apparently reacting to my "Democracy Unlimited," there now appears, undated, but probably at around this time, a strange handwritten note from Luce, superscribed "envelope to Mr. Cort."

Dear Dave:

Thanks for your comment on my piece which Dan sent on to me. As to "Church, Work & Vichy." For Church *and* Work, read Church *or* Work—although for certain reasons I'm keeping "and" in the text. You don't have to go to church, for you have other sources of inspiration for work and conscience in work—as indeed most (but not all) brainier men at all times had. "Church" has never been a universal source of inspiration and conscience and very often it has been quite the opposite. But it is probably a wider objective-subjective symbol of social motivations and disciplines in western civilization than any other—from Canossa to the free-thinking Lincoln. So I use it here.

As to Vichy,—if we do not wish these (?) disciplines imposed on us from above, we must exalt those disciplines which are not too greatly at variance with freedom. The Third Republic lacked non-totalitarian disciplines. Result: Vichy.

Someday I shd like to write a piece on the Problem of Discipline in a World of [I think the next word is "abundance"]. But you'll probably get it written first.

HRL

At the time I snubbed this attempt at communication. Seeing it now, at least thirty years later, I might almost weep, for the man is now dead. He was trying to get through to me and I am not too far from his point of view. But in those cruel times, I must have thought such talk was frivolity, bull-session stuff, and a distraction. Whittaker Chambers would have replied with a masterpiece. Still, I do not think I could ever have been a true friend to Luce, and I knew it then.

I have not been able to locate the "piece" being discussed. But, belatedly, I apologize for my hardheartedness—to whom? To ghosts.

It is incredible that only now (September 30, 1940) did my intelligence agency, John G. Underhill, Jr., arrive on the masthead, at the lowest level (editorial assistants). Also added were Mireille Gaulin, Lisbeth de Morinni, Joan Pifer, John Purcell, and Lillian Rixey, a very important lady who had probably just been transferred from another magazine. The superior editorial associates dropped Diane Cummings and added Sally Kenniston, David Scherman, William C. Shrout, Jr., and George Strock. (I remember only Dave Scherman.) On the associate editors, Richard de Rochemont was replaced by Edward K. Thompson.

The editorial page continued the theme that the Battle of Britain had been won, though we did not know it had ended: "Last week's prospect of a German charge across the narrow seas on England made the suicidal Charge of the Light Brigade seem safe and cautious in comparison. For such an overseas invasion, the indispensable preparation was to have been the destruction of the Royal Air Force, the smashing of railroads and roads, the wrecking of every port that the Royal Navy could use for counterattack. . . . Last week [the job] had hardly been begun." An American observer was quoted: "I should say, from my observations, that the Royal Air Force is better off now in materiel and trained personnel than ever before in the past." "Unlike the Low Countries, Poland and France, London was not on the run, probably because it still had faith in its defenses but also because it had simple stubborn guts. The revolutionary fact was that the people of England, divided by peace and prosperity, were being welded into one friendly, willing, hard-working, fighting whole." This followed a lead dramatizing the U.S. draft. It was followed by a story on the excellent English humor, including an Empire tea party where two seats were left vacant for Hitler and Mussolini, who had promised to be in London by then. Their "regrets" were read aloud. Japan, overlooked for some time, was lampooned with a story on Japan's Chinese puppets and lying propaganda. The irony ended with a story on the evacuation of Frenchmen from unoccupied France to Occupied France. "Their dread redoubles when they get close to home. For in its last days France put on a little imitation of the French Revolution. It now picks up the pieces of its brief spree of mutual hatred, vandalism, drunkenness and rowdyism. The sufferers are often the very people who looted another man's property somewhere else in France."

I had once been a Francophile, regarding France as the most enjoyable society in the world. The last trace of Francophilia was draining out of me, and the end was not yet.

The revealing thing in the essay on "The Willkie Campaign" was that Luce had qualified his anti-Roosevelt crusade with a recognition of power when he saw it. This was the more remarkable because his friend Russell Davenport had quit his job as managing editor of *Fortune* to become Willkie's full-time brain trust. (His picture, that of an extraordinarily handsome man, is included in the essay. Perhaps he should have been the nominee.) For Willkie did not seem to have the power. The polls showed that "in a month Roosevelt's electoral vote had risen from 247 to 453 while Willkie's was dropping from 284 to 78. . . . But all agreed that Willkie's skill and effectiveness were increasing from day to day. . . . 'A man who cannot save democracy in peace,' warned Willkie, 'cannot save it in crisis.' " The *New York Times'* support of Willkie was emphasized. The issue's cover was Willkie. The best issues and the best candidate the Republicans had were presented faithfully but without force. There is the possibility that Davenport's power, had Willkie won, might have cooled Luce.

In this period, *Time's* reporting of the Battle of Britain was often reasonably sane. It had reported plane losses (Germans first, British second) as follows: August 11, 66–26; August 12, 62–16; August 13, 78–25; August 14, 31–4; August 15, 180–34; August 16, 75–15; August 18, 144–16; August 19, 4–0. The Luftwaffe was given as 6,500 bombers, 6,000 fighters; the RAF as 3,000 bombers, 3,600 fighters. British correspondents were quoted as saying the fight was going well. But later (September 16, 1940) the apocalyptic voice of Whittaker Chambers can be detected. "Terrible fates lay hidden in the folds of all the earth's continents last week. . . . Centuries were obliterated, time whirled in the heads of victims." The bombing of London was a "catastrophe," whereas it was really a fight. The strong implication was that England was doomed, with Hitler the apocalypse. Such subversion, which may be called treason, was to be Chambers' contribution for years, under Luce's pardon.

In contrast, *Life* (October 7, 1940) said of the bombing of London: "Though 50,000,000 lb. of German bombs have dropped on England . . . the position is emphatically being held. London is still a huge, functioning city." The lead concerned the agreement of Germany, Italy, and Japan to fight together, obviously against the United States. It led to an appraisal of the U.S. Navy, linked with British bases around the world, such as Hongkong and Singapore. Major Eliot contributed his usual reasonable jargon on the war in Africa.

Wendell Willkie was given the lead (October 14, 1940) with a condensed version of a speech, "American Faith": "My administration will be composed of people who believe in the American people." It was not very stirring. On the editorial page, several Japanese leaders threatened the United States, "If the U.S. continues to demand the status quo in the Pacific . . . to the dictator nations this would mean that the U.S. had started the war. For the honest belief of the dictator nations' rulers is that Japan, Germany and Italy have a 'right' to do what they want, that anybody who objects is 'provoking war.' This disarming concept gives them all an unbroken record of peacefulness, marred only by the ill will of others." We had accepted the fact that the Battle of Britain was over and the interminable blitz was on. I am mystified that the Germans spent men and matériel to punish England for having won a battle. The rational reasons were to save Göring's face and to keep the Russians persuaded that Hitler's real objective was still England. The more probable mad reason was to continue with destruction, even when pointless.

A picture story showed the Nisei, the Japanese-Americans of

California, with some sympathy: "They pointed out that their slow old fishing boats had been locally built, were physically unable to carry the heavy air-compression machinery required to discharge torpedoes. They insisted they loved America and were ready to fight in its defense. But many Californians still wondered." A year later, the Nisei were put into concentration camps. Magnanimity is a luxury, available only to those who think they can afford it. It should not be a synonym for suicide. One Japanese-American patriot does not exactly counterbalance one Nisei saboteur.

Henry R. Luce himself wrote the foreword (October 21, 1940): "This Great Moment." It was a fine though fumbling effort. "I believe that the great majority of the readers of *Life* would not want me to 'come out' for one candidate or the other." Of the state of the world, "we Americans are just as much to blame for it as any people anywhere. . . . This is your one chance to behave as a citizen of all America" (by voting as a citizen for the defense of all America). The desideratum was given as "efficiency" in rearmament (for "efficiency," substitute "power"). Though Willkie was a sort of businessman, Luce did not feel he had "power." Roosevelt did. In the world of Hitler, Stalin, and Churchill, Willkie would have been a doubtfully "efficient" champion for America. And a champion, plainly, was required—as was a unanimous heroic effort of the whole American people. The foreword was in fact a sequel to my piece, "Democracy Unlimited," toned down and made palatable.

Highly relevant is a handwritten letter from Luce marked "Personal":

Dear Dave:

In Sept 1939 it was my conviction that U.S. did not go into any fight unless overwhelming majority of people really approved—and know why. It is my belief that Willkie can best unite an overwhelming majority to fight for what America ought to fight for. For example, the Solid South will follow Willkie just as eagerly as Roosevelt.

Roosevelt will realize that it is desirable for an Am Prex to seem to be pushed into war. Fact that R is rightly or wrongly widely suspected of overeagerness for war is a serious point against his ability to lead in this matter. This very fact is best alibi for his delay and dilatory tactics.

HRL

Then, along the margin,

If R is elected—a great mass of the electorate (including many who voted for him) will be highly suspicious of every war-move.

This would seem to contradict the interpretation of Luce's thinking given above. But its being marked "Personal" indicates that it was only a move in a private argument with me. Luce seems to have assumed that I wanted America in the war. My position was rather that America would and should decide the issue of the war, and ought to make itself capable of doing so. I thought I knew what Hitler and Stalin were capable of—anything.

The one presentable factor in U.S. defense, the U.S. Navy, was given a full issue (October 28, 1940). Thus, "The U.S. Navy is good. . . . It is 15% undermanned. . . . It is strictly a one-ocean navy. . . . *Life* invents a battle, a hypothetical battle, against a hypothetical enemy who has not as yet identified himself to the U.S." The last sentence has a tone of understated threat, which I admire. I did not write it.

Letters attacking Luce's refusal to pick a candidate appeared (November 4, 1940). The lead reported a popular shift toward Willkie and belated acceleration of the Roosevelt campaign. The issue was dominated by the election campaign, including a statement of principles by Willkie. I was detailed to write quotations from a spread of celebrities. Under a picture of Mrs. Luce, I imprudently put some of her remarks that were graceless. Needless to say, these were removed.

The masthead changes (November 11, 1940): Underhill's name is no longer present. Dropped from editorial associates are Frank Hall Fraysur, Sally Kenniston, and Alexander King. The lead showed the "unification" of Europe under Hitler so that Pierre Laval cried, "Democracy is dead all over the world." Of the conquerors, it concluded, "They talk behind drawn shades, look at the map a lot, call in generals, wear their best medals and generally feel full of themselves. They do not ignore culture. On Oct. 28 in Florence Hitler and Mussolini attended a concert of chamber music where they heard beautifully rendered Monteverdi's 'Let Me Die.'" The first pictures released by Russia of the Finnish invasion (omitting the

Russian disasters in the north) showed "The Red Army is no joke, these pictures prove. It does not match the German in staff work and weapons. It does not match the U.S. Army in organization and morale. But it knows how to fight and how to die."

The election results appeared and Roosevelt was on the cover (November 18, 1940). The lead said, "By the direst of times, the soul of Franklin Roosevelt was now to be tried as few men's had ever been before." A switch of less than 1% of the vote would have given Willkie the victory.

The essay by Raymond Clapper is a typical masterpiece of saying something when nothing can be said. For example, "In other respects, the defense program can serve as a solvent." The essay on the English town of Churchill (which I do not think I wrote) explores the reasons for the English sense of group courage, unconvincingly. Much better is the closeup of William Saroyan by Geoffrey T. Hellman though, granted, on a less desperate subject. The failure of a play about Saroyan (who had three produced plays in thirteen months) is taken as "proof of the theory that Saroyan is too Homeric a character to compress within a play." This took a haughty view of Saroyan (amusingly), as if in wild parody of the genuine snobbery of Busch, but in the style of The New Yorker, for which Hellman was then working.

On these philosophical notes ended the first phase of the recorded terrible drama, and began the bated pause.

Section V

POWER

SOME discussion of power is appropriate at this moment, as the German blitz pounded England and Roosevelt had won his third term. The waves of night bombers over England gave the impression of Hitler power, but they were futility incarnate, for all the death that screamed down and streamed up. Roosevelt, in winning the election, had correctly estimated the balance of dynamics in the American electorate and consolidated his control.

I had a sort of power merely by expressing the foreign policy of *Life* magazine, without contravention by my superiors. Certainly these expressions influenced the rest of the American press. But I was unaware that I was not acquiring or consolidating power. A small indication of this is given by listing in Marquis' *Who's Who in America*. In 1934, when I was nobody, I had been approaching *Who's Who*, by listing in something called *America's Young Men*, for which I listed under "clubs" the names of my speakeasy cards (a formidable roster). I do not think I wondered in 1940 or later why I had not reached *Who's Who* but, if I had been smart, this failure would have told me that I was not acquiring prestige or power. And yet, as a factor in the American destiny, I was in 1940 more powerful than most people in *Who's Who*, and this is a modest assertion.

In contrast, the Time Inc. people in that year's *Who's Who* included Luce, Larsen, Billings, Martin, Ingersoll, Eric Hodgins, Goldsborough, Russell Davenport, and Robert L. Johnson (Advertising). For outside efforts, Louis de Rochemont, Robert Cantwell (two books), MacLeish, and Charles J. V. Murphy. To my surprise, Longwell and Stillman are not listed.

Luce was using his real power in awarding modest lots of Time Inc. stock to 50 employees. And this, apart from my general indifference to finance, distracted me from concern for my personal career.

The nature of power has two contrasting interpretations. The Negroes, now reaching for real power in the American society, have realized that it does not derive from teaching and preaching, to which their early elites had devoted themselves, but from the control of finance, budget, and personnel. The Negroes are in earnest and they know what they are talking about. To me, finance, budget, and personnel are ignominious, but I am not fit for power. Luce and Charlie Stillman controlled them, and they *were* qualified for power. The smart Negroes want *their* jobs, not mine. And, in being generous with a few employees, Luce must have begun to sense the nature of power, exactly as any dog-lover senses that he earns his dog's idolatry by feeding the animal. For the sense of power must be visceral. One feels the possibility, relates it (if one is a fairly rare kind of person) to certain key actions on one's part, makes the moves and feels the visceral satisfaction, and naturally the desire for more of the same. For some, such as all the Charlie Stillmans, the acquisition of Time Inc. stock represented their modest level of power desire, whereas to me it was a gratifying but bothersome complication, having nothing to do with my career or aspirations.

Another more sophisticated concept of power was given by Henry Kissinger in *A World Restored*, where he distinguishes between the prophet who tries to extort truth from observed reality (me) and the statesman who tries to manipulate reality (Luce). In this sense, Luce was a better philosopher than I; he understood, as Kissinger and Metternich understood, that this is a tragic world in which power has to be taken by somebody, and why not by the somebody who knows that much? To such as Hitler and Churchill and Luce, to fail to grasp the power is unforgivable. Of all this, I was perfectly innocent at the time. I did not know what was going on and did not care, so long as I could go on looking at reality and interpreting it. This desire, too, was visceral.

Another view of the power of *Life* in 1940 would be the ability of the physical magazine to survive through the years. The Charlie Stillman ilk were buying the paper. I have the 1940 issues before me, and they are falling apart. My floor is littered with the brown fragments as I handle them. In a few years my imperishable *Life* thoughts will be chaff. I can only hope that this recollection will be printed on a more lasting material.

For all Hitler's bombing of England and the counterstrokes of the British bombers, a pause had entered the war, as Hitler (and I) contemplated the map, including the English Channel. His power was stopped by the English people's simple fortitude and liking for one another and their way of life. These people were willing to pay for democracy, man by man, and this fact was shattering to Hitler; it was theoretically impossible, for he had already decided how decadent the democracies were. The idea that a resolution as stubborn as his own could form in the heads of millions of individuals was unacceptable. And so the futile Battle of Britain went on. But this is hindsight. And a magazine cannot admit that there is a pause in the news. First, the editors cannot be sure that it is a pause. Second, they must sell the current issue, whatever the news may be. The editors are only the echo of the event but, never forget, for profit.

The sea war was the lead (November 25, 1940), showing the gallant defense of a convoy by the merchant cruiser *Jervis Bay*, ships sunk and the Mediterranean mastery of the Italian navy by the British. The editorial page noticed that the Italian invasion of Greece was getting nowhere. A map of naval bases over the world was supported by an Eliot piece. It would have been premature to say that Hitler, lacking the sea, had lost the war. The absurd charge, then fomented by the distracted French, that Leopold, king of the Belgians, had betrayed France by surrendering, was thoroughly scotched by U.S. Ambassador to Belgium John Cudahy and by Herbert Hoover. An unsigned account of "The True Story of the Battle of Flanders" is another retrospection, roughly correct but not the "true story," as now known.

Labor's division over national defense between John L. Lewis (against) and Sidney Hillman (for) was the lead (December 2, 1940), Lewis having Communist support. A spread shows the Mussolini boast versus the Italian fiasco in Greece. William L. White contributes an admirable story of crossing the Atlantic on one of the destroyers given to Britain and the rescue of a raftful of British fliers. It is quietly very moving. An intimation of the future came in an essay on machine tools (talking about machine tools was then the mark of knowledgeability) and a story on our army's "six foremost generals," which did not include Eisenhower, Bradley, MacArthur, Patton, or Mark Clark.

A strange discordant note appears (December 9, 1940): "But many an American who believes that the U.S. should consider aid to Britain strictly in terms of U.S. defense has grown heartily sick of U.S. Anglophiles who assert that America is 'shirking its duty' to save the land of Shakespeare and Shelley." I don't know who wrote it, but Billings passed it. An insane "secret" speech by a Nazi lunatic is printed. (This issue's paper was better; it did not crumble in my hands, don't ask me why.)

As a matter of duty, I reproduce a memorandum from Ralph D. Paine to "Dave Cort." I don't understand it. He was in the Washington office but not yet concerned with censorship. It is remarkable as addressed to the man who had just published "Democracy, Unlimited." I take it as an expression of visceral hostility, revealed much earlier, still inexplicable to me. (If he is alive, he is probably still on the Time Inc. payroll—one of those.)

I'm told on highest authority that you don't believe in democracy anymore. Because if you do believe in Democracy, you must believe in the functions of a free press in a democracy. At the moment the U.S. Press has a unique opportunity. The British press had the same opportunity and muffed it.

One example: On the day the Germans invaded Norway, I saw

Robertson of the *Daily Express* at lunch. The *Express* began that very day to thump the tub of Hitler-missed-the-bus and it's-all-a-great-trap. I asked Robertson what he thought. Said he simply: "It is a catastrophe for England."

Why didn't the *Express* tell the people the blunt truth—as it did last week in Frank Owen's signed editorial? Because there was a false propaganda assumption; namely, that in a democracy you must kid the people to keep up their morale. So Britain slumbered through the first eight months. The Press could have ousted Chamberlain easily in November—had it had the guts and the wisdom. So—let's not kid the people. Let's try a new propaganda technique. Let's tell them the truth, I think they will react the right way.

The suspense underlying the military moment was suggested (December 23, 1940) in a story on the bombing of Coventry with emphasis that the firemen had concentrated on saving the aircraft and machine tool factories (not the citizens' homes), most still in business the next day. And on the editorial page the U.S. production chief, William S. Knudsen, is quoted: "Production is far from satisfactory. . . . We all seem to be worrying about how we are going to divide the profits. . . . The first half of 1941 is crucial." He deplored the shutdown from Friday to Monday. An Eliot piece drew some satisfaction from Italian defeats in Greece, North Africa, and at sea. The debate was begun on whether the United States should feed Hitler's starving victims "under strict neutral supervision," a fairly laughable idea. The essay was on army morale. These were unintentional indications that the real war had paused, that nobody had any power at the moment.

And so the lead (December 30, 1940) said, in contrast to the quotation a little earlier: "Only one question: what can any and all of us do, to speed up America's tragically bogged-down defense production, to get arms to Britain and to arm ourselves before it is too late?" Roosevelt was quoted as suggesting that we "forget all our old ideas about finance and the silly-fool dollar sign. . . . He proposed that henceforward British arms orders be considered a part of production for U.S. defense." This was followed by a description of the bureaucratic mess of defense and the suggestion that a superchief be named. Ninety defense faces were printed on one spread to underline the point. Then came a spread of some "prime production shortages." Undoubtedly, Underhill supplied these last data, a terrifying indictment, and I suppose that Hubie Kay wrote the story. The editorial page noted German preparations to invade England, and Lord Beaverbrook's prediction of an invasion attempt before spring. When Rumania's Premier Antonescu came to Berlin, I won much applause with the fanciful caption: "Americans familiar with gangster movies will recognize the situation at a glance. It is the moment when the deserter from the rival gang is brought into the back room to meet the boys and convince them that he is really one of them now. The faces of the highest officials in Nazi Germany would not be miscast in such parts. . . . Recognizable to American audiences are the confidence man, the strong-arm man, the squat bad-tempered bully, the dull lieutenant, the clever brain, the educated gangster and the most ruthless of them all, the prissy sadist. It is a great cast, assembled from the sorrows and treacheries of pre-War Germany." A long review of the war in 1940 reached the conclusion, more perspicacious than I would have credited myself with: "But the British Navy, wrapping the slow strangulation of seapower around continental Europe, still held the seas. Europe was in fact isolated, a huge hungry, groaning land whose factories worked only for the German Army."

The quarrel about giving aid to Britain without entering the war occupied the editorial page (January 6, 1941) together with a gigantic miscalculation: that Hitler "will not wait until U.S. arms production hits its stride before he makes a gigantic effort to knock Britain out. . . . A large majority in the country stands for (1) full aid to Britain; (2) every effort to keep out of war." Something Stalin might have noticed was the rumored movement of German troops into the Balkans. The essay was on Ernest Hemingway's marriage to Martha Gellhorn (later displaced by Time Inc.'s Mary Welsh, his ultimate widow). A picture in the story suggests that it was written by Paul Peters. (I do not recognize the other man with Hemingway.) A picture replay of *For Whom the Bell Tolls* had been patched together. A defense of the French defeat by André Maurois was pathetic. "Was France more guilty than other nations? I do not think so. . . .

The Allies were beaten in this war for lack of planes and lack of tanks." (France was superior in tanks, in both numbers and power.)

A "fantastic" story is told (January 13, 1941) of an eleven-year plot by German endive farmers to tunnel under Belgium's Fort Eben Emael to blow it up during the German attack. I have not seen any reference to this beautiful tale in recent accounts of the war; some historian ought to look into it. The lead showed General Motors production of Allison airplane engines, scheduled for 35 a day, and the editorial page quoted President Roosevelt as accepting the risk of war as the price for helping England, as 60% of polled Americans now wanted. This must have reflected Luce's total approval of Roosevelt at this point. An item titled "No News" said: "The situation was much the same as just before the German assault on Western Europe in May, when neutral strategists could only draw maps showing half a dozen possible moves by Germany. Germany last week was fostering every rumor." This was a touching confession of the journalist's ultimate impotence. The retirement of an old congressman named Luce is shown. And the Japanese are seen slavishly mimicking Nazi Germany, even to a Tokyo show *Heil Hitler*, in which the girls sing a Japanese version of the Nazi "Horst Wessel" song. An elementary piece on the art of camouflage reminds me that during the war Ed Thompson became an expert in it, editing an army magazine. An essay, "Democracy in U.S. Schools," says that the boys and girls "have in the best tradition of democracy, learned to show a healthy respect for the rules that they themselves set up." What modern students would make of this I do not know. As seen above, it is especially when there is "no news" that there is variety.

Luce's attitude may appear again (January 20, 1941) in an answer to a letter protesting *Life*'s treatment of Roosevelt as "Mr. Big": "All the hard work and effort can amount to nothing if it is not properly led. In England . . . Churchill. . . . In the U.S., the President is even more powerful than the Prime Minister of England. . . . It is Mr. Roosevelt's responsibility to provide such leadership." This makes nonsense of Luce's "personal" letter to me. My own appraisal of Roosevelt was echoed on the editorial page (I don't think I wrote it): "When President Roosevelt feels he is too far ahead of public opinion, his strategy is to sit tight, waiting until public opinion piles up behind him and begins to chafe at his inaction." (Maybe I did write it, for it expressed my theory of how *Life* could move Roosevelt to the position he wanted to assume.)

Joseph Kennedy speaks out (January 27, 1941): "Just as I regard it impossible for a foreign power to invade this country, so do I regard it impossible for us to invade Europe." The Kennedy patriarch was wrong both ways. There is a picture biography of Winston Churchill, climaxed by an inspired poetical paean to him by Dorothy Thompson.

Life was unaware that the two men who had won the decisive Battle of Britain, Dowding and Park, heroes for all time, had been ignominiously replaced by their critics. Even victory had not earned them power.

An awareness that history was in abeyance (February 3, 1941) may have been reflected in an unorthodox almost satirical edge to the editorial page, commenting on Italian failures, Rumanian massacres, British trivialities, and Nazi nonsense. This is offset by a long low-key piece by William Shirer on the "normality" of life in Germany, despite the mild British bombings. The people rather admired the British, assumed the war had been won, but, remembering 1917, were terrified of America's entering it.

A key hypothesis of mine, which remained basic policy, was documented (February 10, 1941) by before-and-after pictures of a bombed seven-track British railway and its complete repair four hours later, with a train running: "It means that the military effectiveness of bombing has been wildly over-rated. For these tracks are also defended by British fighter planes, anti-aircraft guns and British courage."

Another installment by Shirer focused on German shortages, due to the blockade, and Hitler's absolute ascendancy. In general, Shirer confirms the basic decency of the German people, leaving us with the inscrutable mystery of how they could have accepted the horrendous caricature or travesty of the German dream by Hitler. At this time the Jews were being persecuted but not exterminated. Shirer notes the rise of Himmler and the decline of Goebbels and Streicher.

Note must be taken (February 17, 1941) of Luce's famous essay, "The American Century," a title that strikes me as sound journalism —at least so far. (America became the leading industrial nation in the world in about 1890—a fact not generally known.) The essay is undoubtedly Luce's greatest expression. It says that America was already *in* the war, that Hitler knew it, that the American people didn't know it, that isolationism was insane, that Roosevelt had been an isolationist for seven years, that America fumbled world leadership in 1919, that war may "even be fatal" to man (a mystic prognosis), that America must be the Good Samaritan of the world and the powerhouse of the ideals of Justice, Truth, and Charity.

This essay has been much attacked, probably for the explicit boast, but I suggest that critics read it. There is hardly a sentence in it I could quibble with. The fact of American power in 1941 was simply a fact (before the atom bomb). The German people knew it. The Japanese leaders did not. In France, Blum and Reynaud knew it. This essay was Luce's finest hour, though I do not think I even read it at the time, since my contempt for Luce's understanding was by then nearly total.

A short piece (February 24, 1941) translates the book *Delilah*, by an old friend, Marcus Aurelius Goodrich, into a general rhapsody on destroyers—Goodrich had been an ensign on one in World War I. Goodrich had been writing this book for uncounted years; later, he married one of the De Havilland girls and astonished Hollywood by wearing a morning coat. A disgusting piece by Jan Valtin on Communist intrigue and murder need not be noticed, yet it helped explain the fall of France and the disgust Communists have so faithfully earned.

The transfer of my early hero, John S. Martin, to Cairo is noticed (March 3, 1941) by a letter, not in the style but in the mood of Hemingway, not really doing a job. Martin in Cairo disgraced Time Inc. by interviewing the commanding general drunk and unshaven and various other Hemingwayesque exploits. When Allan Michie went out to relieve him and mend fences, he found him stalking around naked entertaining guests. This was virtually the end of Martin's career. That he has done nothing of importance since, astonishing to those who knew his bravura and audacity, was perhaps foreshadowed by the cursoriness of this letter. In the upshot, Martin was not serious about himself. This may have crystallized Luce's ultimate disdain of the productive man. For Martin in Egypt savaged the image.

A prescient prediction occupies the lead on the new ambassador to Britain, John Gilbert Winant: "His friends include many of the British New Dealers, notably Minister of Labor Ernest Bevin, whom U.S. New Dealers expect to see take over Britain's Government either during or after the war." A New Dealer myself, I did not expect any such thing—but in a way it happened. For whatever reason, Winant eventually committed suicide. It is mentioned in the piece that Winant wore shirts with frayed collars and cuffs. This may have been a rebuke to me (I have been known to wear shirts with frayed collars when I could afford new shirts), but I have not committed suicide.

"The American Century" attracted total reader adoration, to which the entire Letters section was given (March 10, 1941).

Everybody has doubtless forgotten the "tiny war" between French Indo-China and Thailand which the lead said (March 17, 1941) was the most dangerous for the United States. Peace was imposed by Japan. It was added that, with Japan and the United States both having 14 battleships, Japan was "afraid its opportunity for conquest may pass with 1941. . . . This is the kind of situation that spawns wars." Here, quietly, the destiny was drawn. I would assume that Roosevelt noticed it, and wish that the U.S. Navy had too. Almost inadvertently, the date of the "day in infamy" was fixed, and the prime objective of the Japanese, the 14 battleships, defined. Perhaps Tokyo was reading me more attentively than Washington. For trivia, the issue had a German pilot's story of the bombing of England, ending, "There is no salvation for London." Ha, ha.

The readers' Letters were as nauseated as I by Jan Valtin (March 24, 1941). The lead was on the very serious matter that German raiders, submarines, and bombers had sunk some 3 million tons of the 20 million tons of British shipping, and that the rate was exceeding the rate of British replacement. But the American Lease-Lend Bill (never referred to as "Lend-Lease") had just been passed and Roosevelt had the power to correct this by various dispositions. The editorial page noticed the approach of one of the few truly heroic moments of the war. For the Germans, in occupying Bulgaria, had surrounded Yugoslavia on three sides. The Yugoslavs—or, specifically, the Serbs—are very tough fighters.

The British went on a small offensive against Norway's Lofoten Islands, shown in the lead (March 31, 1941), blowing up factories and taking away Norwegian volunteers. The Germans took savage reprisals against the remaining Norwegians. On the editorial page, it was lamented that labor was damaging the defense effort with numerous strikes. One of the most heroic (and unappreciated) episodes of the war was mounting, the mobilization of the Yugoslav army against Germany, even as the premier signed a Hitler pact with reservations.

The Yugoslav thing had come to a head a week later (April 7, 1941) as the Serbs of the air force took over the government, ousted the regent, Prince Paul, and installed the young King Peter, in defiance of Hitler. Unreported was the fact, later reported by a correspondent named Brock, that the Communists of Tito (a Croat) had paraded in Belgrade with the slogans, "Up the Pact, Down the Imperialist War!" the imperialism referred to being England's attempt to defend itself. The coup d'état was an inspiration to every decent European, Tito's declaration an eternal hubris against all morality. The Yugoslav situation was, and is, very complex, involving two kinds of Catholics, two alphabets, earlier domination by Vienna and Moscow, mountain and plains peoples, levels of education, and fighting spirit. For me, Tito was the black hat, but much later Churchill decided otherwise. The decision may have been historically pragmatic, but it was not moral. The fact is that Yugoslavia (the Serbs) was the only European nation to defy Hitler in those terrible times. (England and France declared a motionless war, after the invasion of Poland, and then sat still.) Brave men took the risks in Yugoslavia, but they did not reap the power; Tito did. This little episode may have decided the ultimate course of the war. Such small heroics often have such consequences. If heroism is indeed dead, the remaining heroes have that much more power.

It was in 1971 reported by some idiot Englishman that the Serbs, led by the army officer Mikhailovich, "collaborated" with the Germans, and that for this reason Churchill sided with Tito. A politician and public relations man, Tito understood the power equation; Mikhailovich was a soldier, patriot, and glory man who did not. Churchill was a power man who, when Stalin's armies were fighting in his cause, dishonorably opted for the Communist and against the heroic patriot. "Collaboration" is a word about as precise as the word "love." I "collaborated" with Hitler by eating sausage and criticizing the Versailles treaties. At worst, Mikhailovich was smarter than Chiang Kai-shek; he knew he was in a civil war that ranked at least even with the foreign war. The astounding fact, confirmed by the German generals and Liddell Hart, is that the resistance of such Serbs as Mikhailovich (while Tito was collaborating—without punctuation marks—with the Nazis) so delayed the attack on Communist Russia that it stalled before Moscow in the Russian winter. For this great contribution to the history of the world, Tito ultimately executed Mikhailovich. So it goes.

History has atrocious ironies. Just as Franco's victory in Spain saved Gibraltar from Hitler, Tito's victory produced the first anti-Russian Communist state. Yet the anti-Nazi patriot was Mikhailovich; the traitor was Tito; now the jovial tyrant is Tito. This statement will be deplored by all responsible U.S. diplomats; its sole virtue is that it is the actual history. The dishonor resides primarily with Winston Churchill, whom I admire, but who regarded himself as a thug dealing with thugs (Hitler, Mussolini, Stalin) and accepted the dishonor as a requisite for victory. I suspect that the British people subconsciously (never consciously) sensed this, thus repudiating him when the necessary age of thugdom had passed.

World War II was a madman's war and requires an understanding of dictatorship. If I want to be dictator, I need only invent policies relating to the hidden madnesses of the people, and (as in Haiti) the crazier the better. This understanding is now widely

shared, as with the leaders of the youth, the liberated women, the
Negroes, the homosexuals, and the mystics. The sanity of the white,
adult, heterosexual male, who makes the free world work, is almost in
disrepute.

Minor news the next week (April 14, 1941) was that the U.S.
committed its first warlike act in seizing German, Italian, and Danish
ships in U.S. ports. The major news was on the editorial page: that
Germany had invaded Yugoslavia and Greece, while the Croat
Communists no doubt sabotaged the Serb defiance, though the Croat
leader, who was Matchek, not Tito, joined the defiant government. A
detailed story, allowing for censorship, was given of the British
victory over the Italian navy off Cape Matapan. Since the same text
piece is appearing in 1972, it is amusing that the text piece by Niven
Busch was "Darryl Zanuck: Last of the Wonder Boys." Concern was
expressed for labor strikes against defense, suspected of Communist
instigation, in a faint reverberation of what went wrong in France,
but devoid of the universal French defeatism—that is, hatred of
other people in the society. This is still true of France and is
beginning to be true of the United States. For lack of it, England
survived the German attack. Yugoslavia did not fare so well.

The lead on the German invasion of Yugoslavia (April 21, 1941)
must be quoted: "Just as the main German blow in Western Europe
last spring was at the junction line between Belgium and France, so
in Southeastern Europe this spring the main blow was at the pivot
between Yugoslavia and Greece. Like the Allies in Belgium, the
Yugoslavs had either to fight their way out across the backs of the
whole German Army, take to the sea or surrender. . . . The superb
German assault teams simply rolled up the opposition for the first
week. By that time they were ready to make contact with the British
forces and the real battle for the Balkans seemed about to be joined."

The editorial page provides a reasonable rejection of American
censorship of damaged British warships arriving in American ports.
Soon after came the commissioning of the great battleship *North
Carolina*. Censorship was to become crucial to the character of *Life*,
in an unexpected way.

We know now that in this battle Yugoslavia lost more men (about

400,000) than the United States, Poland, and France in World War II (in descending order). The Yugoslavs who fought were almost entirely Serbs, not Croats, who now rule Yugoslavia under the Croat, Tito. Here, again, we get a comment on power. Croatia chose this moment to secede.

A glance at *Time* shows that Britain was about to lose the war, based on the defeats in Yugoslavia, Greece, Libya and at sea, and a feeling that Hitler would successfully invade England. In describing the Nazi attack on Yugoslavia, *Time* begins the sentences "As usual . . . As usual," a device borrowed from *Life*'s stories, for *Time* editors had two days to look at the *Life* copy.

The *Time* masthead reads: Managing Editors: Gottfried, Norris, and Matthews; Associate Editors: Roy Alexander, Carleton Balliett, Jr., Robert Cantwell, Whittaker Chambers, Laird S. Goldsborough, Walter Graebner, John Hersey, David W. Hulburd, Jr., Eliot Janeway, John K. Jessup, John Stuart Martin, Sidney Olson, John Osborne, Ralph D. Paine, Fanny Saul, Walter Stockly, Leon Svirsky, Dana Tasker, and Charles Wertenbaker. Oddly, the name of James Agee does not appear, though his history says that he was there.

Of this group, at least Balliett, Chambers, Goldsborough, and Wertenbaker killed themselves.

Still, *Life* did not dismiss the possibility of German invasion, for here is a thrilling drawing of a German tank coming up an English lane, toward a barricade with an antitank gun, and an ordinary Englishman with his own rifle, illustrating an article by William C. Bullitt, alarmist (rather, defeatist), wrong in saying that the Germans were "producing greater numbers of warplanes each month than Great Britain and the United States combined." But he made the same point as Luce and I: that if Americans did not wish to defend democracy, they would lose it.

The editorial page (April 28, 1941) said, "In the case of a war boom . . . thus setting the stage for inflation."

Apparently, this economic fact passed me by, for I thought of the war as a desperate survival struggle, from which nobody could profit. This latter perspective was expressed: "Last week was one of the most violent seven-day stretches in the history of the human race."

The battles listed were the same as *Time*'s, and a Russo-Japanese treaty opened "the way to a Japanese invasion of the Netherlands Indies." The lead showed the battle in Libya, where two British lieutenant generals were captured, and the aftermath in Yugoslavia, where "the Serbs had a great reputation as fighters. . . . But the Serbs' reputation availed them nothing against the Germans. . . . Yugoslavia's brave fight was by no means wasted. It will certainly be remembered at the peace table in case of an Allied victory, just as Hungary, Rumania and Bulgaria will not." Word reports on the fire-bombing of London April 16 were contributed by the London Staff; Bill Bayles, Walter Graebner, Mary Welsh, and William Vandivert. A new Chrysler factory that would produce M-3 medium tanks by July was shown. Bill Bayles has an excellent text piece on life in Lisbon, "The Bottleneck of Freedom": "The general attitude of the foreigners in Lisbon can be summed up as one of stark pessimism and conviction that powerful forces are just being released in Europe. They regard Hitler and his gang as temporary upstarts who will have little to do with the solution of the whole problem. . . . Europeans laugh at the idea that Hitler will win the war. But on the other hand they don't think that England will win a victory in the sense that we can all chalk up one for the Empire." Bayles recognized that this opinion was unrealistic and spooky, since the speakers in Lisbon were generally aristocrats. The essay was on Hitler's probable goals in the Middle East, running from Egypt and Suez to the oil fields at the border of India. Hitler might have won the war this way.

In spite of these great doings, the predominantly *American* effect of the magazine must be underscored. The next cover (May 5, 1941) was of a Harvard freshman under the statue of John Harvard, as the Eastern Hemisphere blazed and simmered. A cable from John S. Martin in Cairo was surprisingly irrelevant and casual—this from my hero. The lead was entitled "The American Decision": according to the Secretary of the Navy, "We are in the fight to stay." The alarums over Britain were strident while Germany, without telling Time Inc., was beginning to transfer its air force to the Russian border. Another story noted the Russo-Japanese nonaggression pact "which left Japan free to fight the U.S. if necessary, and Russia to fight Germany if absolutely necessary."

The executives were busy in a minuet of power-manipulation. Pierrie Prentice became publisher of *Time*, displacing Stillman who spread himself over finance, production, procurement, and planning. Because *Fortune* suddenly had too many bosses, Del Paine made the "perhaps presumptuous suggestion" that he become managing editor, Eric Hodgins publisher, Russell Davenport editorial writer. Stillman invested a million in a paper company, another million in oil, and also invested in research into inks and other printing developments. Mr. and Mrs. Luce went the wrong way, to China, to interview Chiang Kai-shek. But luckily we sent Margaret Bourke-White the right way, to Russia. I do not claim any marvelous intuition here for anybody, but it was fortunate.

The Luces' trip produced several inspiring pieces and speeches on the theme that China was the most important fact in the world and Chiang the premier hero. My copy never went this far, but it endorsed Chiang and helped to bury the true story of Chiang's China, of which I was unaware. I was only slightly more interested in China than in India, on which I had an essay (May 12, 1941), taking the position that India was a perpetual disaster and the British small help.

For all the dreadful clangor, the next decisive stages of the battle were still cloaked, among them Roosevelt's decision. As usual, I felt he wanted to be pushed, as I think Hubie Kay felt too—I am not so sure of Billings or Luce. The lead (May 19, 1941) said boldly that Roosevelt was "holding back" from "the swelling clamor for more aid to Britain, for convoys, for action." This was a signal to readers, but more particularly to Roosevelt.

Another nudge was given Roosevelt on the editorial page (May 26, 1941) in that "the defense effort was still in a juvenile stage." Interestingly, the British officially dated the great decisive Battle of Britain as running from August 8 to October 31, while giving September 15, the date of its finish, as its "greatest day." The British, of course, did not have the German records, but that is the history they want to believe in. It was their battle; so be it.

The editorial page (June 2, 1941) noted the novel invasion of Crete by German paratroopers (a brilliant feat that led to nothing) and the sinking of H.M.S. *Hood* by the incredible battleship *Bismarck*, two serious British defeats. Somewhat baffling to me now are the "rumors of peace," Rudolf Hess having parachuted into Britain to everyone's bewilderment, since Hitler's present purpose was to pretend that he meant to destroy Britain, not Russia. Time Inc. got a little way into events by having the photographer David Scherman and the writer Charles Murphy on the *Zamzam*, sunk by the Germans. The story was very discreetly told. The masthead was changed, Walter Graebner being added to the associate editors, Don Burke being moved up to the editorial associates, and Bernard Clayton, Jr., M. E. Crockett, David Ritchie, and Mary Welsh being added to the editorial assistants. There was an official British protest on my India essay as "simple malice."

Roosevelt responded, as the lead (June 9, 1941) announced that Roosevelt had at last proclaimed a state of unlimited national emergency, but the need for more pushing was indicated by his refusal to order convoys. A cherished interview with Hitler was contributed by John Cudahy, former U.S. Ambassador to Belgium, followed by a riposte "Roosevelt on Hitler." The sinking of the *Bismarck* by the British was noted.

The shortage of aluminum, blamed on both government and the Aluminum Corporation, and the defense plant strikes (June 16, 1941) were accused of crippling the American rearmament effort.

In the next issue (June 23, 1941) "Roosevelt Breaks Red Strike" told how Roosevelt had at last been moved to act against defense strikes, probably inspired by pro-Nazi Communists, and this in the week that Communists would forever become fanatical for the war against Hitler. With such a faith, a man must begin to feel like a puppet on a string.

Life went to press on Saturday, June 23, and so had only an editorial page notice of Hitler's invasion of Russia (June 30, 1941), not written by me. I heard the news at a cocktail party in Southampton, Long Island, and was delighted.

But this titanic turn in history was subordinated to a long-scheduled Defense Issue of *Life* on "U.S. Arms" (July 7, 1941), on the occasion of the Fourth of July. The lead on rearmament read: "Things could be worse but they should be a whole lot better. . . . When Germany turned on Russia, the U.S. was given more time in which to prepare—weeks, months, no one knows how much more." The lead ran for 21 pages: $30 billion for defense, an army of 1,441,500—not good, not bad. Only then came "War in Russia" which "temporarily increased the defenses of the U.S. by the whole Red Army." I was for it. It was noted that in these zones "the rampaging hordes of Scythians, Avars, Goths, Huns, Slavs, Bulgars, Magyars crawled endlessly up one another's backs."

Earlier, I had been assigned to do a piece on West Point, whose commandant, Brigadier General Eichelberger, was a kinsman of Larsen's. I was detained by the PR officer at West Point, enraging Eichelberger who evidently wanted as much time as possible to indoctrinate me. I think I went to chapel with him; he took me to his bedroom while he changed uniforms. I was assigned to an editor cadet. I had been skeptical of the propaganda that West Pointers never lie. But I asked the young man why he entered West Point in 1937 when he could not have known that America had any prospect of going to war. His reply was not that he wanted to die for his country but merely that he wanted security. I believed that West Pointers tell the unvarnished truth and wrote an admiring piece.

My policy on the Russian war was developed in the next (July 14, 1941) lead: "The huge mastodon of All the Russias was as close to total destruction as it has ever been. Its death struggle has a colossal majesty and terror not matched even by the fall of France." But, as of the border of prewar Russia, "the Nazi advance was a meager 100 miles after a full two weeks." Maps purported to show the strategy of the various battles; but then we did not even know that von Rundstedt was in charge of the southern armies, von Bock of the central, and von Leeb of the northern—the first to be the most successful, nearly reaching the Caucasus before he was recalled, the second fatally less so, the third not at all. As usual, we did not know what was happening. For example, we showed a picture of a Ukrainian "Heil Hitler" sign, indicating that it was planted by the

Germans. But now we know that, after twenty-four years of exclusive Communist propaganda, not only the Ukrainians but also the Crimean, Kalmyk, Chechen-Ingush, Volga-German (unremarkably), and Kabardino-Balkar republics went over en masse to the Nazis. No more authoritative comment on Russian communism has ever been, or can ever be, made. When these areas were reconquered, their people were transported in the same way (en masse) to Siberia in cattle cars, with much death, and all notice of these republics was excised from Soviet histories until 1957, when five were restored to existence. But in 1941 I saw no occasion to disguise the character of the Russian Communists. In a spread of nine "Men Around Stalin," I made the point that they would be acceptable at an American corporation board meeting and added: "The nine would make a fairly good impression but there is almost nobody alive who could count on making a good impression on them. They are a suspicious and dangerous crew. . . . Their chief pleasure is pure power." Listed among the coming men is (misspelled) "Kruschev." A piece by Kerensky, a friend of Noel Busch, predicts a Nazi victory.

Some pluses for the free nations were shown (July 21, 1941): the surrender in Syria of the Vichy French to the Free French and British; the U.S. occupation of Iceland (nearly an act of war); the return of Haile Selassie to his reconquered capital of Addis Ababa; and an essay on Singapore, indicated as threatened by the Japanese.

"The German Army Heads for Moscow" was the lead (July 28, 1941): "A fourth week of the biggest battle in history. . . . Germany was last week decisively beating Soviet Russia. . . . But it was equally plain that the Russians had fought a battle that was strategically and tactically sound. Given their equipment and transport problems, they had made few if any mistakes. Weeks after the experts considered them broken and doomed, they were still fighting stubbornly and cagily with great masses." The pictures were largely German.

The Russian side was covered by a short piece by Bourke-White's husband, Erskine Caldwell. A spread showed the sudden relaxation of the British; another showed the slaughter of Chinese in Chungking, heaps of women and children, babies strewn like garbage, all stripped of clothing. Here truly was the terrifying refuse of war. The prosperous Japanese, martyred at Hiroshima, might take a moment to contemplate these frightful pictures. And the journalist, advancing his career with this "news," might also reflect. Nor do I think that the American readers lingered on these pictures and reflected. The "Picture of the Week" visualized that "V for Victory" (the Morse code dot, dot, dot, dash opening of Beethoven's Fifth Symphony) had become Europe's symbol of defiance of the conqueror—another, but better, way to die.

Time, whose June 30 issue closed the Monday after the Sunday, June 22, of the attack, got off to a better start. The preceding week it had quoted the London Daily Mail: "Germans Mass Against Stalin." Now it was prepared to scrap its cover and replace it with one of Russian Marshal Timoshenko. It was rather faintly on the right track: "Now the U.S. had gained at least a few precious days or weeks to push its arming." It estimated the forces engaged at 130 German divisions, 175 Russian. Next week it quoted Herbert Hoover to the effect that aid to Stalin "makes the whole argument of our joining the war to bring the four freedoms to mankind a Gargantuan jest." It looked like "a speedy Hitler victory. . . . Communist propagandists know how weak Russia is." This premature scuttling of Russia was modified toward the end of July, as Time noted slower going for the Germans and their admission of "severe" counterattacks by the Russians. Once again, Time and Life were talking about the same war. The reporting in Time is reasonable; I cannot detect the Old Testament tone of Whittaker Chambers anywhere; whether his counsels influenced "the speedy Hitler victory" I do not know. If I read his copious subsequent writings aright, Chambers believed—not explicitly advocated, but totally believed—in the ultimate destruction of the democratic capitalist world of free men of good will. Aid to Russia was therefore American suicide. I need hardly say that this was not my view. Which of us was more naïve I leave to the reader.

Unaccountably, the Time estimates of the battle were not bad. The German strength was 121 divisions, the Russian 155 divisions in the West, while others remained in Siberia. Rundstedt attacking in the South had 600 tanks against 2,400 Russian tanks, and yet he succeeded. For the fault of the Russian leaders, stemming from Stalin, was overconfidence at the start. The German generals found in the Russian troops "a soulless indifference—something more than fatalism." At the beginning, the Germans had superiority in quality of strategy and tactics, but the Russians slowly learned, given vast areas to retreat into, and later the supplies from Britain and America, and some indoctrination in communications, in which Russians are historically backward.

It is said that the proper attack on Russia would have concentrated on Leningrad, opening sea communications, later sweeping down from Leningrad on Moscow. But Hitler wanted to gobble all at once, and no one was permitted to contradict him. The generals report that he kept sweeping his arms over the map, rasping, "Push here; push there," while the manhood of Germany was being exterminated as a Hitlerian abstraction. Surely a whole nation of real people has never been exploited so inhumanly, and with their consent—but not that of the aristocrats, who knew their armies would not march against Hitler. It would seem the enemy for free people to fear is not the Establishment, but the man they believe, the demagogue, the guru, the magician who is really only the apprentice, whose magic falters at the critical moment. For the true magician will never arrive unless the Christ decides on a Second Coming, an event I would be inclined to discount.

To a letter questioning the defense issue, the editors replied (August 4, 1941) that the American 37-mm. antitank gun would be ineffective against German medium and heavy tanks, as the similar French gun had proved in 1940. "Unfortunately a panzer division puts medium and heavy tanks up front in its attacks . . . to clear out anti-tank nests." Another letter was from a draftee unhappy about incompetent army training. The lead agreed with him. A rehearsal of an amphibious marine landing was criticized. On the editorial page, it was noted that Roosevelt had frozen all Japanese assets in the United States. Thus, "Japan probably cannot survive as a going industrial or military concern much longer than six months . . . the immediate future was death or glory." These lines make the later prediction of Pearl Harbor seem much less magical. Clever German camouflage of vital bombing objectives was exposed; but *Life* was never given enough of these pictures. A small story, with the only (German) pictures available, illustrated the point of "the suicidal determination of great masses of 'trapped' Russian armies still fighting desperately on the German supply lines. . . . The great German drives ground slowly to a halt. . . . At week's end, it was the Russians who were attacking with troops that according to the experts could not possibly exist." It became apparent that the German rulers were slightly less willing than the Russian rulers to send their men to certain death. The meat-grinder character of the Russian battle made it the nearest thing in World War II to the awful attrition of World War I on all fronts. The general picture of the whole war is described by Hanson Baldwin in a text piece which is entirely wrong, not only in prediction, but in current facts—for example, German and British monthly production of planes. "The world can anticipate in Russia another quick, and decisive German victory." Baldwin was propagandizing for a greater effort to defend Britain. But "Japan [is not] the real enemy." The piece is superficially sensible, but today reads like blithering nonsense. Granting its good intentions, it is very funny, reaching a peak in a confirmation of my own belief (wrong) that "total war means total sacrifice." Baldwin, an "expert," demonstrated that he had no glimmering of what was going to happen, or how. Later, I lunched with him in the Rainbow Room and got the same impression (as he told me how wrong I was). God knows I was often wrong but on the implacable record (in print) I was far closer to the mark than he. And I was an amateur (with, however, my secret weapon, Underhill).

The benefits of Bourke-White's arrival in Moscow began to surface (August 11, 1941) with an 11-page lead on Moscow just before the invasion. In the next issue the editorial page (August 18, 1941) said that a happy ending to the war was now possible, while the lead reported the Senate's extension of one-year military training by 18 months. A defense shortage of steel by 11 million tons in 1941 was the next lead (August 25, 1941), as the meeting of Roosevelt and Churchill in the Atlantic was recorded. The claim was authoritatively made that "secret" maps of the Russian battle were accurate. I do not recall the credentials of these maps but they correctly placed von Rundstedt, von Bock, and von Leeb, from south to north. The lead was again Bourke-White on war in Moscow and on a collective farm (September 1, 1941): "Moscow . . . Prepares for a Long War." Bourke-White had the lead again (September 8, 1941) with pictures of Harry Hopkins meeting Stalin, and her written impression of Stalin as exhausted and thinned. (The story is that she browbeat Stalin into holding her flash-platform; she was no respecter of dignities.) Aid to Russia was going forward. The fact that the Russians had blown up their cherished Dnieper Dam was recorded. The seizure of Iran to accommodate aid to Russia was also noted, as was the shooting of Laval by a rightist Frenchman. On the subject of China there was a baffling literary "dialogue" by Mrs. Luce which by any other name could not possibly have gotten into the magazine. I suppose it said that China is a nation of peasants, with Chiang its only salvation, but I am not sure.

The aid to Russia deserves a footnote. Some day an objective satirist should do a book on this. The Russians kept asking for preposterous things, such as enough of a particular commodity to last them for the next decade, stripping the United States of it. These were routinely refused, with one exception. Some Russian had been told that the best American oil was Wesson oil, the salad and cooking oil. The Russians, not understanding that the English word "oil" covers about 300 kinds of vegetable and animal oils and fats, as well as petroleum derivatives, requested that one tanker be filled with it and sent to Vladivostok. The assigned bureaucrat refused it. The request went to Roosevelt, with the bureaucrat's reasons for refusing it. With an inscrutable motive, possibly humorous, Roosevelt ordered that the Wesson oil be delivered. A tanker at Seattle was loaded with about 10,000 gallons and dispatched to Vladivostok. The Russians emptied all vehicles of engine oil and poured in the Wesson oil. Within the hour everything ground to a stop. So it goes.

A crucial aid to the Russians, as Gary Underhill told me, was some multiple of millions of miles of telephone wire. Russian communications were so bad that, when the Germans attacked, it took days for the rest of the army to find out about it and react properly. With the telephone wire the Red Army became a proper modern army.

Much of this was unknown to Time Inc., but I did not put even the latter into print, though I knew it. While giving the appearance of a perfect entente with Russia, I distrusted everything about them except their willingness to die in defense of their land.

A recurrent event was the "Time Out" party, held in 1940 and 1941 at the Longshore Country Club in Westport, Connecticut. A picture report on the September 9, 1941, affair was published. One is captioned as of croquet: "Life Foreign News Editor Dave Cort takes an unorthodox one-arm whack at the ball as M.O.T.'s Dick De Rochemont stands by with nothing but skepticism written on his face." Babe Paxton is shown using "perfect form." A spelling bee was scheduled between teams headed by Luce and Larsen. Considering myself an impeccable speller, I volunteered for the team of Roy Larsen, whom I liked, and Roy accepted me. A picture is captioned "At left: Life's Dave Cort, who missed two words out of three." I remember that I spelled "Philippine" correctly. If only life could give me another try.

I think I behaved reasonably at this party. At a later one, I conceived the idea of overturning a trestle table, running at it at speed and launching myself, feet first, against it. The idea caught on. I cannot suppose that this exercise was regarded favorably by the executives, and may have contributed to correct evaluation of D. Cort as concealing a streak of hoodlum, which might burst forth at any moment. But it is a truly cheering thing to look at all these happy faces, very few knowing what it was all about, I, swinging a croquet mallet, least of all.

Amazingly, some Japanese voices were raised against the Axis and in favor of the Allies, according to the editorial page (September 15, 1941). These may be interpreted as reserving an option in case of German failure in Russia and of disarming U.S. alarm. The high-speed pictures of curve-ball pitches by Gjon Mili "proved" that curve balls do not curve. This iconoclasm seems to have been forgotten.

Roosevelt became more truculent about German ship-sinkings and Japan still more soft-voiced toward the United States (September

22, 1941). The full arrival of the B-17 long-range bomber, for delivery to England, was shown, and the totally burned-out (by the Russians) city of Minsk.

The American defense effort was denigrated with the lead (September 29, 1941) describing aid to Britain as so far a "trickle."

When something really big was happening, the journalistic performance was not as interesting as before the start of World War II. In the fog of war, one can only guess at the event. For example, the cover (October 13, 1941) was Lana Turner and Clark Gable, and the lead was the revival of New York City over the Yankee-Dodger World Series, the Louis-Nova prizefight, nightlife, and a shopping boom. The Louisiana army maneuvers were described by John Field and Edward Thompson. Well back was an analysis of the enormous Russian battle; the crucial point was to defend Moscow and maintain north-south communications. But the brilliant journalistic solution was the Bourke-White essay on "Religion in Russia: Red Godlessness Fails to Empty Its Churches." Bourke-White never did a more timely job. Her research was excellent: 4,225 Orthodox churches, 37 monasteries, 5,665 priests, a rival Communist church organization which converted only atheists, encouragement of Protestant sects, and finally 60 million adults and 60 million children who worshiped God. The final spread was on the Russian propaganda to discredit God. Ruth Berrien called on Monsignor Fulton Sheen, described in the final story as a "famous professor," to get, explicitly, research on the Communist antireligion propaganda, and I incorporated this in the final text. Even before *Life* appeared on the stands, Sheen appeared in the Catholic magazine *America* with a story that *Life* had reneged on a promise to print an article of his. Miss Berrien was a model of integrity. Fulton Sheen was not. The episode still makes me wonder.

The lead (October 20, 1941) showed the belated British bombing of selected German targets. The editorial page detailed a gigantic German drive to take Moscow, and the first hallucinatory screams of Moscow for an immediate British invasion of Europe. One page was given to the Russian battle, with the only available (German) pictures: "These are clever, tough, experienced troops. But they were up against an adversary in Russia nearly as tough and clever as themselves. The Russians were using the artillery the French neglected. They were remaining disappointingly unterrified when 'surrounded.' " Probably by Gerry Piel was an essay on science: "The search for total release of the astronomical energies locked in the atomic nucleus. . . . Here again volume will count on the side of free science, with 35 U.S. cyclotrons and high voltage generators against Germany's five atom smashers and the estimated six it has captured in conquered countries." This was a valuable story, but I can hardly believe many readers absorbed it. The current theory (supported by events) that Chiang's China was a fake is solidly undercut by Carl Mydans' pictures of Chiang's army.

With Russian pictures, at last, the lead (October 27, 1941) was on the desperate defense of Moscow: "The destruction of great cities, the vanishing of ancient nations, the massive death struggles of armies, corpses by the millions had become such an old story to many Americans that this week's peril of Moscow seemed hardly real. It was another town on a timetable: Vienna, Prague, Warsaw, Copenhagen, Oslo, Rotterdam, Brussels, Sedan, Paris, Belgrade, Athens, Brest-Litovsk, Minsk, Vitebsk, Smolensk, Kiev. And now, perhaps, Moscow. And tomorrow, no one knew what. The tragedy was incomprehensible because it was vast and multiplied." Further pictures of Bourke-White were introduced, ending, "But Americans were confronted by the nightmare fact that, if Moscow falls and Stalin decides that bloody Russia deserves peace, the U.S.A. will find itself alone in the world, with only Britain as ally." Snow fell on Moscow September 27.

It was generally understood in the organization that I owned the war. Roy Larsen asked me whether the Russians would surrender if Moscow fell. I remember telling him that they would fight behind the Urals. Apparently, he accepted this prognosis as solid gold. On the editorial page was the statement, "Americans did not realize how dangerously close they themselves were to war," but I think this was written by Hubie Kay.

Partly due to *Life*'s efforts, the American people were beginning to understand their situation in the world. As the editorial page said

(November 3, 1941), "Even the frozen isolationism of the Midwest was beginning to melt." Noted were stalling of the German drive on Moscow, the Yugoslav (mostly Serb) guerrilla war, and cries for a British invasion of the continent; the lead showed the previous summer's U.S. occupation of Iceland. The taking of Kiev, mined and torched by the Russians, was shown in German pictures, including a superb airview. The scarred placidity of London ("London Stands") was seen in color; in effect, the war for the free world was in abeyance. Mrs. Luce has a colorful essay on a trip to the Philippines: "Will the Japanese thrust to Singapore, the Dutch East Indies, by-pass the Philippines? . . . Give us another six months." It was in every sense a fashionable piece, while quite un-*Life*like. Yet it throbbed with life, in a dilettante way. Now it would be called jet set journalism, but of the best quality.

Life had helped entice Roosevelt toward the boldness of his speech, quoted on the editorial page (November 10, 1941): "History has recorded who fired the first shot. In the long run, all that matters is who fires the last shot . . . we . . . have taken our battle stations." Later, the page said, "Last week's biggest news [in Russia] was the weather. It was terrible." The lead explains that, though the United States was taking losses from Nazi submarines, the total silence on destruction of the submarines has proved an "insidious corrosive of enemy morale." John L. Lewis outraged the country by calling a coal strike, shutting down defense plants. In contrast, the essay on "American Heritage" (a title later taken over by Joe Thorndike for his firm) evoked America's great past: Patrick Henry, Minutemen, Valley Forge, John Brown.

The masthead (November 17, 1941) marks an atrocity that left me with a sense of outrage for several years. Hubert Kay was gone, and I was now first. Billings had fired Hubie for proposing a type of general picture essay ("background of the news") which the magazine later adopted. And Hubie was Billings' alter ego. He had once told Kay that if he were ever moved "upstairs" he would resign. (We will see how valid was this boast.) Much later, Billings walked out of the Time-Life Building without a word and would not reply to Luce's letters. Kay had written Billings that if his idea was adopted, he would insist on being an executive editor, so as not to be subordinate to Dan Longwell. Billings told him, "This is a very dangerous letter. I'll tear it up." Dangerous! The power of Longwell passeth understanding. His wife, Mary Fraser, said, "Dan's ideas are 95 percent screwy and 5 percent wonderful."

Hubie went to *Time* as editor of the back of the book, encountering the lunatic behavior of Whittaker Chambers, whom he still likes in retrospect. At the tea party T. S. Matthews gave (incredible to me), Chambers stared full face at Kay throughout. When Kay left *Time*, years later, Chambers (who normally drank hardly at all) slugged the liquor down and then put on a weeping, cursing, howling soliloquy in the next room, ranting in German. The homosexual and histrionic intimations are unavoidable.

Lincoln Barnett was added to the associate editors, but put ahead of Walter Graebner, in another extraordinary move. I will not deny that I was pleased to have become the No. 1 associate editor. But this pleasure cannot be correlated with ambition. Longwell said to me, "Dave, we want to groom you for a managing editor job." My instinctive compulsive reply was, "Forget it, Danny. I'm a writer, and that's that." I guess I wasn't interested in real power. And I don't believe a real Time Inc. man, as I was, could have been.

As Kay departed, the lead was another dividend from Bourke-White's presence in Russia: "Russian Mud and Blood Stall German Army." The featureless empty battlefield of Yelnya, ten days after the dead had been buried and the smell blown away, fills a haunting spread. The dugout graveyards are shown, as well as correspondents banqueting on "chicken, beef, black bread, cucumbers, raw fish, Hunters vodka, white vodka, champagne, port" three miles from the German lines, and in wartime! A Russian soldier presented Bourke-White with an armful of poppies (in November?) on behalf of "the entire Red Army." (This must have been an earlier memory.) The editorial page notes that Japan's Ambassador Kurusu was flying to America as "a pinch-hitter rushed in to break up a tie ball game," and that Goebbels was considering the possibility of German defeat.

A wonderful picture story cribbed from *Vogue*, "of which *Life* is admittedly envious," showed a Mrs. Cornelius Vanderbilt dinner.

"This is the '400' about which Emily Post writes, but note elbows on the table, some eating while others are foodless, J. Norman de Rapelje Whitehouse using bread as a pusher." The lady is quoted: "I feel deeply for poor, dear Marie Antoinette, for if the Revolution came to America, I should be the first to go." "This statement was no appeal for sympathy. Mrs. Vanderbilt was demanding precedence. . . . Her only mistake was the failure to notice that the Revolution . . . is already here." Who wrote this I do not know but the *Vogue* story was written by my old friend Frank Crowninshield, whose social life had long since narrowed down to evenings of bridge with Mrs. Vanderbilt. He once dined me at the Knickerbocker Club to grill me on the old days at *Vanity Fair*, but instead filled me with the most delightful scandal about the members who passed by. I did not remind him that in those days he had told Corey Ford, Gene Wright, and myself that a fall on his head as a baby would have left him an idiot, had he landed a certain way, and I replied, "Let's end the suspense. Did you or didn't you?" Crownie was patient with all such nonsense. Corey once mistook Conde Nast's butler for Nast and tried to shake hands.

A splendid report out of Yugoslavia (November 24, 1941) revealed the full-scale war being waged by the Serbs, and the reply of Colonel Mikhailovich to German officers sent to negotiate: "It is true that the Yugoslav Army capitulated. But it was the Yugoslav Army, not the Serbian Army." This magnificent defiance was ignored by Churchill, and so we have Tito and the corpse of Mikhailovich. A revealing spread shows Mussolini and Hitler, both maxiskirted, gloating over Russian ruins. The posturings of power, less evident in Hitler, are naïvely exposed. The editorial page recorded Congress' permission to U.S. ships to enter belligerent ports. The essay was "A Chinese Town," pictures by Mydans, leading to a scholarly analysis of the Kuomintang's infiltration of the ancient Chinese family structuring of society. A story on Admiral King by Joe Thorndike is pedestrian, not sycophantic, but the admiral's service was almost immediately disgraced by events, in an infamy that must never be forgotten.

The lead (December 1, 1941) was on John L. Lewis' coal strike:

"Here at last, the nation knew, was the showdown which friend and foe of labor had long awaited. Three times Lewis had rejected President Roosevelt's pleas to subordinate his own ends to national defense. He had responded impudently, arrogantly. It was evident, even to Lewis' own followers, that he had come to believe himself bigger than the Government." Roosevelt had been incredibly patient, but the strike was ended. A story on the Japanese envoys to America said: "Worst of all, from Kurusu's standpoint, Americans do not even seem worried by the prospect of war with Japan, whereas the Japanese are worried stiff by the fear of war with America. The defenses of Manila and Hawaii are stronger than ever." (This last assumed that our officers were at least as intelligent as the *Life* Foreign News Department, without any knowledge of the facts.)

Life's spectacular ability to make a point was shown in the next issue (December 8, 1941). Under the headline "The Ancient Imperial Power of Japan Comes to a Showdown with America" and a picture of the Emperor's brother and his bride, the lead said: "The stage was set for war, a distant, dangerous, hard, amphibious war for which the American nation was not yet fully prepared." The editorial page was headlined "U.S. Cheerfully Faces War with Japan" and opened: "For a nation poised on the precipice of two-ocean war, the U.S. was extraordinarily complacent last week. Washington cocked tense ears for the first sounds of shooting on the wide Pacific." Surely this was strong enough, and it had reached the houseboys of Kimmel and Short at Pearl Harbor by Friday, December 5.

The mendacious book *Time Inc.* presents the above as an echo of *Time*'s warning at the same time (but closing two days later than *Life*). And, even after reading *Life*'s terrible prediction, the *Time* editors flinched back. "A bare chance of peace remains. . . . Very few men who were in a position to know thought much of this chance. . . . And every day that passes means that China is stronger, that the Dutch, the British, U.S. possessions are more nearly impregnable. . . . The U.S. and Japan were nearer war than at any moment in their history. . . . In Manila the air force was standing by."

This latter was a cautious fudged mishmash, taking no risk,

whereas I had assumed a reckless risk, which *Time* had had two or three days to worry at. But in this corrupt history, *Time Inc.*, the courageous prediction is given as *Time*'s weasel.

In the next issue (December 15, 1941), *Time* exposes what I suppose to be the extraordinary style of Whittaker Chambers, which for some reason was indulged by the editors: "Hundreds of hundreds of Americans had died bomb-quick, or were dying, bed-slow." It also noted, "A military spokesman in Berlin announced that the German Army does not expect to capture Moscow this year."

Toward the back of the *Life* issue were maps of a possible Japanese invasion of the Philippines (which did not predict all the actual routes in plan) and a text piece on General Douglas MacArthur by Mrs. Luce. It is forgotten that in 1935 Roosevelt lent MacArthur to the Philippines as field marshal of the Philippine army and then on July 26, 1941, took him back as commander of all U.S. armed forces in the Far East, or USAFFE, starting to send him the weapons a little too late. The piece was admiring and not oversanguine. The preposterous notion that the Japanese would attack Pearl Harbor was not brought up. At least *Life* had done everything possible to prepare the American people (as well as MacArthur, Kimmel, and Short) for the most massive turn in world history since Tsushima and the consequent, if delayed, fall of the czar. The Russians did it with bottomless pain, the Americans with contemptuous ease (in terms of comparative casualties). In this context, one must read again Mussolini's exquisite aphorism, "Blood gives glory its imperial color." Blood is not an artist's coloring matter. History was about to drown such artists as Mussolini in his favorite coloring matter.

On the following Sunday, Babe Paxton took me to the first and last professional football game I have ever seen, between the Giants and the Dodgers at the Polo Grounds, Dodgers 21–7 with Pug Manders and Ace Parker running wild. The Japanese attack on Pearl Harbor took place shortly after the game began. The entrepreneurs running this show thought it best not to divulge this fact. They did ask on the loudspeaker that Colonel Donovan call operator so-and-so in Washington. When we came out of the stadium, Paxton's brother-in-law turned on his car radio and the news came over that the Japanese had bombed Pearl Harbor. Assured that my society knew how to defend itself, I cried out, "Thank God!"

At the moment, I thought my job at Time Inc. was finished, in the sense of producing a result in history, not that of earning a living. I went home and had a drink. After a while the telephone rang. Babe Paxton said that everybody was in the *Life* office recomposing the magazine, and Billings wanted to know where the hell was I. Thereupon, I crossed town and wrote a few captions.

I have two copies of that December 15, 1941, issue. In one, the lead was "The U.S. Army Takes Over a New Farthest-South Base in Dutch Guiana." The story said: "It had planted a small but efficient A.E.F. smack next to French Guiana, South America's most malodorous nest of Gallic criminals and Nazi spies. It had notified Japan of America's determination to support the Netherlands Government-in-Exile—if in Surinam, then perhaps in the Netherlands Indies too." The editorial page gave a column and a half to the Japanese attack. I did not write it but it said essentially, "Thank God." Later came a story on the American 57-ton heavy tank with a three-inch gun, theoretically superior to the best German tank, as well as airplane production of 2,000 a month, merchant ships at one a day, prospects of 2,000 tanks a month by next summer. Another story revealed the flight of U.S. bombers to Libya from the Brazilian base of Natal, where German and Italian airlines were also based.

The other version, rewritten that Sunday afternoon when I thought my job was finished, opens with the three enormous letters, "WAR." The text earlier given to the editorial page is here the lead (the editorial page is eliminated). There are stock pictures of Hawaii. The text is ignorant of what happened at Pearl Harbor. I might as well have stayed home drinking.

A *Life* correspondent got on the last plane out of Hawaii and was brought into Billings' office by Wilson Hicks on Tuesday, December 9. The top echelon were called in and he gave us the real story: the *Arizona* sunk, the rest of the battle line disabled, the American navy suddenly nonexistent in the Pacific. I looked at my fellow executives, thought my thought, and said, "This is very dangerous information. I suggest that none of us take it out of this room, not even to our wives." Roy Larsen immediately said, "Dave's right." I had a total contempt for the good sense and even the patriotism of the executives, at least matching the contempt that the executives felt for the writers. Those present were Luce, Larsen, Billings, Hicks, and perhaps one or two more. My "Thank God!" was seeming less felicitous to me.

The next issue (December 22, 1941) was an extraordinary compilation, revealing some of Life's peculiar strengths. First, in large type over two pages, was "The Day of Wrath" by Henry R. Luce, editor of Life and Time: "We have come to the end, now, of as pusillanimous an epoch as there ever was in the history of a great people: the twenty years of American history between 1921 and 1941. . . . We demand victory, but the price of it, in risk, hardship, pain, adventure, is not yet clear to us. . . . For this hour, America was made." The key sentence of the lead, "America Goes to War," was: "Ideologically the nation was united as it had never been at any other military crisis in all its history." For this consummation, my strategies across the years could claim some credit, in ways of which neither Luce nor Billings was fully aware. The copy obscured the fact that the United States did not declare war on Germany or Italy until after they had declared war on the United States. The fact of censorship was now conceded, an end being announced to public casualty lists. The first hero was Colin Kelly, credited with sinking the Japanese battleship *Haruna* and then dying. However, the *Haruna* reappeared. Less fictitious were the sinkings of the British battleships *Repulse* and *Prince of Wales*. The United States seized the *Normandie* and thirteen other Vichy French ships. *Life* leaped in with a detailed proposal of how to rebuild the *Normandie* as a combination aircraft carrier and troopship. Self-censorship was applied to Carl Mydans' brilliantly opportune pictures of Philippine defenses, including Shelley Mydans marching with Filipino infantry from church to barracks. In case of air raids, a recognition chart of Japanese war planes was provided. It was emphasized that MacArthur had been rearming in frantic haste. The essay had the subject, so vast as to be presumptuous, of the whole Pacific Ocean—"oldest, deepest, bluest"—and made a plausible stab at it. It was noted that Russia had not yet offered the United States the use of its Vladivostok air base, 610 miles from Tokyo. "The Story of Christ in Chinese Art" (Christmas was imminent) brought home the Luce theme of how nice and civilized the Chinese were. Undoubtedly the idea of Dan Longwell (and a good one) was an excerpt from Hector Bywater's 1925 book, *The Great Pacific War*, in which a sneak Japanese surprise is followed by U.S. victory. (About this time the *Saturday Evening Post* ran a piece saying that the Japanese ships were topheavy and the Japanese eyesight hopelessly astigmatic.) Because of mistaken American assaults on Chinese, a helpful story showed "How to Tell Japs from the Chinese." The implication was: assault unmistakable Japs, although they were being whisked into concentration camps.

An unofficial committee consisting of Underhill, Buckminster Fuller (on his way from *Fortune* to the Board of Economic Warfare in Washington, D.C.), Babe Paxton, Hubie Kay, and myself had set about discussing how the United States should win the war. Underhill decided that the existing U.S. Army was underarmed, and should only be used within the year to invade North Africa (as did take place). What happened to it wouldn't matter. He proposed a detailed chart for multiplying divisional fire power. This new army, we concluded, should eventually land at Murmansk and fight on the right flank of the Red armies, with its right flank on the Gulf of Finland and the Baltic. How to sell this plan to Joseph Stalin was beyond our competence, but could safely be left to Roosevelt.

Underhill showed me the army's infantry manual, and I found it incomprehensible. On my own time, I set about rewriting it in line with Time Inc. communication techniques. It was hard work. Underhill showed a sample to somebody in Washington; that was the last heard of it.

Laughable as these efforts seem, at least we were trying.

But perhaps we were not laughable. Buckminster Fuller's contribution was that the new army should get to northern Russia by flying over the Arctic. The freight was to be carried by huge towed gliders, which he designed. At the front, these could be converted into logistical warehouses and, as the front moved forward, towed ahead to new positions. Paxton had artists visualize these concepts. The problem was how to present this fantasy to the readers. The idea of presenting it as a secret Nazi speculation on how America could win the war, if it had the brains, was vetoed by me, Fuller now says. The drawings were put away but did not die. Indeed, later they emerged to play a significant part in the unfolding plot.

The next issue (December 29, 1941) develops the point that when something big is going on the journalism collapses. The lead, "Attack on Hawaii," could not tell or show the truth about the damage. The dreadful information given us in Billings' office was elliptically hinted at. In Hawaii, Admiral Kimmel and General Short were relieved. The view of Roosevelt had changed: "As the President of a country at war and leader of the democratic world, Franklin Roosevelt was rapidly taking on a stature which awed even his close associates." (Well, well.) Background stories on the Marines and on the anatomy of bombs evade the issue. The text piece by Oliver Jensen was on the Annapolis regimental commander, "the man most likely in the Navy's opinion to become an Admiral of the Fleet," George Thackray Weems, who died as a lieutenant commander by crashing his seaplane into the Delaware River on January 17, 1951. Incidentally, at this point Time Inc. stock on the Over-the-Counter market was selling at around $110.

A brave show of American naval strength was presented (January 5, 1942) plus Winston Churchill's arrival and rallying of the U.S. Congress. An analysis of the Pacific war hammered futilely at the importance of defending Manila and Singapore while admitting they were probably indefensible. The most relevant piece was a picture essay on Japan. Though "an industrial pipsqueak," it "can throw down all its industrial production on the fighting line. . . . Japan does not have much, but what it has is quite enough to fight the kind of limited war it thinks necessary. . . . The Army of Japan has one enormous advantage over the U.S. Army. It is an army of veterans, hardened and blooded." This was followed by a surprising portfolio of "Lincoln in Wartime," and a report on the frenzy in Washington, D.C.

Some of the first pictures from Russia permitted a shift to that front (January 12, 1942): "To help digest this cold news (the fall of Manila) came great good tidings from the other side of the world." A typo turned the fact (not really sound) that the German army was down to 125 divisions to "25 divisions." A Russian cavalry charge with waving sabers, a tank advance, a battle analyzed by the air-photographed tank tracks and trenches, captured German maté-riel, were shown. MacArthur was falling back on Bataan Peninsula, and in America the auto industry was ordered to stop building new cars for civilians. The hysterical arming of the U.S. Pacific coast is described. A text piece by Henry J. Taylor confirmed my belief that Hitler had elected to fight a war he could not win because he had given up on the "interocean war" (which he had never grasped).

A deterioration of the thinking was evident with the departure of Hubie Kay (January 19, 1942). Hubie's departure is traced to Luce, furious when he realized he had not been told of Kay's requirement of $100,000 for research. The idea of a writer (the true source of his power) demanding so much power touched him on some unconscious nerve. He was not even aware that the credibility of the National Affairs voice of *Life* had been compromised. The new voice, whoever he was, did not have the authority of Kay and, believe me, the reader quickly realized it. The true power of *Life* was thus diminished, while the false power of Luce was demonstrated. For Luce held control of those true elements of power, "budget, finance, and personnel," as the Negroes recognized belatedly. But this is merely kitchen power.

The lead gave Roosevelt's call for "60,000 planes, 45,000 tanks, 20,000 anti-aircraft guns, 8,000,000 new tons of shipping in 1942," as a mere warmup for 1943. A page of close-packed dots visualized the number 60,000. The editorial page balanced the bad news from the Philippines and Malaya with good news from Russia and China, adding, "If wars could be won with money alone, the U.S. last week won the war." The loss of Malayan rubber ended sales of new tires, but not of a few retreads. A text piece on desert tank fighting showed British Matildas with a 40-mm. gun against the German 75-mm.

The Letters column (January 26, 1942) opened with part of a letter from *Life* publisher Roy Larsen to subscribers promising continued reporting on the war with, however, "barriers in our path: necessary military censorship, possible breakdown of international communications, material shortages. . . . Editorial and production expenses will increase; advertising revenue will probably drop. . . . *Life*'s staff has doubled since 1939 [not true as far as I could see]—and I have the utmost trust and pride in every member of it." (My trust and pride were more selective.) The new admiration for Roosevelt was expressed in early pictures of him. The lead on British commando raids defined their small merit in depressing the morale of all isolated German garrisons. The pictures were excellent. A story on the elevation of Donald Wilson to chairman of the War Production Board, "world's biggest single job," examined his assistants. A text piece described the meeting of British and Russian troops taking over Iran. The interest in real power surfaced in an interesting "close-up" by Noel Busch of Eugene Grace, head of Bethlehem Steel, "the largest U.S. specialist in ordnance and armor plate."

The emphasis shifted to the German submarine war on U.S. coastal shipping (February 2, 1942). The editorial page reported that Kimmel and Short at Pearl Harbor had been judged guilty of appalling "dereliction" by Supreme Court Justice Roberts' commission. Short had ordered the aircraft warning system shut down at 7:00 A.M. but a more patriotic soldier at 7.02 A.M. reported the approach of a large flight of planes, to the complete disinterest of a lieutenant. A report of the sinking of a small submarine was received at 7.12 A.M. The attack came at 7.55 A.M. The ruins of Cyrene in Africa, a great ancient city which had been unable to defend itself, were pointedly shown behind the advancing British army, but it was noted that German General Rommel had sprung out of El Agheila and was reversing the course of African battle. As Winston Churchill, losing in Singapore and Libya, flew back to England, a picture was captioned, "one of the most remarkable portraits ever taken of this humane and violent man." Both adjectives were apt. Stalin did not deserve the first, Roosevelt the second, to the world's discomfort.

The essay was "U.S. War Planes," beautifully illustrated. I accepted the fact that I no longer owned the whole war; the American part of it was given, as I recall, to John Field and Dick

Wilcox. From time to time I got back the whole war, but I was always slightly unsophisticated about the American military history or establishment. I still had the Philippines, but I believe I did not have Guadalcanal, except now and then. Quite inconsequentially, a story that is pure Longwell, who came from Missouri, is on the mule. Somewhat more thrilling is a sequence of Vereshchagin's famous paintings of Napoleon's victory and disaster in Russia, inevitably compared to Hitler's less successful endeavor as of the first few months. It makes one's heart go out to the Imperial Guard of France and the persisting French dream of *La Gloire*. But the French legions died in the same way as the six Russian divisions and tank brigade in Finland; such death is an even-handed friend, always waiting to somnambulize the bold. This story may be ascribed to the credit of Longwell.

The old dying Time Inc. spirit was evidenced (February 9, 1942) by printing a series of letters criticizing the page of 60,000 dots—as 61,225; 59,999; 80,347; 17,150—without an answer. After a lead on a Pan-American Conference, of ephemeral significance, the editorial page noted the nearly insane objection of Irish Premier Eamon de Valera to a landing of American troops in Northern Ireland. Evidently, he wanted America to give him weapons to defend Ireland against Americans, this from a man born on the site of New York's Chrysler Building. In contrast to cosy petulant Eamon, details were given of the winter clothing of the Russians, which they had copied from the Finns just over a year earlier. The eternal American absurdity was recorded that General MacArthur (besieged on Bataan) had not paid his income tax installment, while the Congress· authorized money for lepers on Guam, currently under Japanese rule.

Maps showed the harried Japanese fleet advance down Makassar Strait toward the Dutch Indies and the battle of Bataan, lamely embroidered by a *Life* correspondent on Corregidor. Mydans' pictures of the Philippines' PT boats (then called Q-boats) illustrated heroic raids on Japanese ships by Lieutenant Bulkley and Ensign George Cox, a friend of my childhood in the Thousand Islands and an instinctive boatman. Unmentioned was another PT man, John Fitzgerald Kennedy. A casual interview with Yugoslavia's King Peter

at Cambridge University was transcribed by Lael Laird who later
married Charles Wertenbaker. The theme of the essay pictures on
Australia was that they were not of similar parts of the United States.
The Australian, the text said, "does not like to be tied down . . . is
amazingly impervious to fear—to fear of penniless old age, to fear of
his superiors, to fear of the next world, to fear of the risks of being
alive generally . . . likes to know the facts and then acts on them.
. . . All this could as well be a picture of the average American and
of nobody else on earth." (My own theory about the American.) The
words of the song "Waltzing Matilda" were given. An anonymous
report by an "agent" detailed general Italian sabotage and dislike of
the war.

A story on New York night clubs reminds me of a personal
idiosyncrasy that colored my nights and reputation. I was a constant
patron of the night clubs across the board, with a bias toward Latin
music and the rumba and samba. This erased the tensions of my job
but annoyed my wife (who did not like night clubs). In fact, she
threatened to divorce me about once a month. Neither this nor my
hangovers were a serious handicap to my nervous system or my work.
This was the life I enjoyed and could prosecute, I thought, as long as
I liked. What anybody else thought of it did not matter. As of now, I
think it may have reached the executive types as an indication of
recklessness, unreliability, and potential insubordination—that is,
individuality.

The masthead changed again (February 16, 1942). Peter Piening
was dropped as Art Editor, leaving Worthen Paxton. As of associate
editors, Paul Peters was dropped and Dorothy Hoover was promoted.
As of editorial associates, Al Butterfield was dropped (brother of
Roger) and Ray Mackland added. As of editorial assistants, the bad
news was that Ruth Berrien, my assistant, had left, probably to get
married, and John Allen and Elaine Brown Keiffer also left, to be
supplanted by John Thorne, Eleanor Welch, and Richard Wilcox.

The lead showed the incredible (to Europe) conversion of Detroit
to the mass production of planes and tanks in overwhelming
numbers. Navy-released pictures showed a partial revelation of Pearl
Harbor: the destruction of the *Arizona*, of three destroyers, and of

the target battleship *Utah*, as well as the capsized *Oklahoma*, reported salvaged. Most of the battle line was towed to the west coast, repaired with frantic haste, and sent back to action. The implication was that most of the fleet had steamed out of the harbor in time. The eight highest U.S. military decorations were shown, with pictures of the eighteen men who had won them. The Medal of Honor can be remembered as white stars on a blue field. Luce had an essay "America's War and America's Peace." His view of Roosevelt was now "one of the most remarkable men in history." His theme, with which I would agree, is that the many wars of the time boiled down for the United States to "one war" against "the cleavage of mankind into Right and Left which, tearing Europe asunder, made Hitler's victories possible." (This echoes "Democracy Unlimited.") A splendid line is "Because it is America's war, no American need expect that this war will be explained to him by foreigners." It is a splendid piece.

But it collapses on his three "key" concepts. The second is "complete, unswerving partnership between America and China." Look at that one.

The third is that the war must be "mostly American-fought and mostly American-won." But, in fact, it was mostly Russian-fought and Russian-won, thank God.

It is easy to see that these great *conceptions* were great *deceptions*, but they are above criticism. Brilliantly, he continued: "This is the dawn of world history—the meeting up of all the peoples of the earth . . . the inevitable idea of our time—it is, quite evidently, the coming together of all peoples, within nations and between nations, in ever closer and more complex relationships, in short, the unity of mankind."

The liberal reader will agree with this. But, like all liberalism, it is really working on the level of power, like "finance, budget and personnel." I did not believe in it; in fact, I do not remember that I read it; it sounds unfamiliar. I knew too much foreign news ever to believe in "the unity of mankind." I had long thought Luce a fool about the world and its destiny. Still, I think this was an honorable piece, well worth reading today.

Concerning George Cox, a letter was printed (February 23, 1942) saying that he had been a hero during the Battle of France as a member of the American Volunteer Ambulance Corps, winning the Croix de Guerre. All this is a surprise to me, and I must compare it to the rattled deportment of the Time Inc. staff on the same occasion (by no means suggesting I would have done any better). The "Speaking of Pictures" was of two other heroic friends, Carl and Shelley Mydans, who had been captured and interned in the Philippines. All three heroes survived the war. The lead opened: "Men all over the world, white, yellow, black and brown, watched with awe the massive turning of history. With the fall of Singapore an era of empire ended. White men had taken their most catastrophic defeat at the hands of yellow men since the days of Genghis Khan." This was followed by a diatribe against the elite British colony in Singapore. "The Asiatic peoples had won equality in the only way that has ever counted, by force of arms. . . . From here out it was painfully plain that U.S. troops would have to fight by the millions and die by the hundreds of thousands (a close enough forecast) to achieve their own victory." Maps explained the strategic magnitude of the disaster. The editorial page described the week as "one of the blackest in American history." (I kept all copies of the *New York Times* for this period, and preserved them for thirty years.) With the escape of the battleships *Gneisenau* and *Scharnhorst*, Germany had a combined fleet of 3 battleships, 2 pocket battleships, 6 or 7 cruisers, 1 or 2 aircraft carriers—bad news. The page drew a very black picture which, it was hoped, would "shake [America's] very soul." The only good news was Vice Admiral William F. Halsey, Jr.'s, raid on the Japanese-held Gilbert and Marshall Islands, with full effect. The "nightmare" of German (actually S.S.) killing of Russians, Jews, and Poles appeared in a spread of grisly pictures. One's heart tightens on a picture of American troops marching in Northern Ireland under the American flag—big, jaunty, and tough-looking, an intimation of future power.

In my view, the free world was caught in a terrible squeeze that must drain its people of self-interest and profit. But I had misunderstood. I did not really know what was going on, sophisticated as I was at my specialized job, and deluded into believing that I knew it all. I suspect that such delusions are common at the upper levels of intellectualism. Not only at the moment, but for nearly thirty years later, I rejected any such ridiculous possibility.

The hypothesis that the United States might be conquered was presented in the lead (March 2, 1942): "The best enemy to attack is the one whose fall will tumble down all the rest . . . [and] is also at the moment the weakest in weapons. . . . If the U.S. is conquered in 1942, when it is still assembling its great war machine, its fall automatically means that England and Russia are fighting without hope of further supply from the Arsenal of Democracy." To complete the picture, *Life* called on an ex-friend of mine, Philip G. Wylie, who generously provided not one but six ways of invading America. These were, respectively, by way of the Aleutians, Pearl Harbor, the Panama Canal, Natal and Trinidad, Canary Islands and Bermuda, Greenland and the St. Lawrence River, each accompanied by feints and fifth-column uprisings. This masterpiece was an exercise in geopolitics, presupposing that "the enemy has nothing but good luck and the Allies nothing but bad luck." (I don't believe I wrote this.)

To take this seriously would have required Hitler to give America first priority and to stalemate the campaigns against Russia and Britain. This would have been a bold decision but the only right one. It would have meant taking on the "interocean war" indispensable to conquest of the world but apparently repellent to Hitler. In the doctrinaire faith that the democracies must be decadent, Hitler never took America seriously enough. Nor was he particularly anxious to help Japan. *Life*'s technique of writing novels in drawings was used to visualize hypothetical invasions by Japanese and Germans and make everybody mad. This fantasy was followed by more pictures of Halsey's effective raid in the far Pacific. Two bloody combatants debating military strategy were shown on the pavement outside a New York saloon. "The issue of military strategy was still unsettled." Two spreads showed drawings of all the heavy warships of the United States and Britain and the Axis. "After looking at this Allied line-up, quickly turn the page and see the Axis heavy ships. A feeling of discomfort should follow." Ships already sunk were crossed out in red. Luce's press agentry of Chiang Kai-shek as the answer to all China's problems was abetted by Theodore H. White, whose talent for plausible sycophancy is fully paraded. He does convince me that Chiang had more or less united China, for subsequent transfer to Mao's Communists.

After a trivial lead on a Jap shelling of the Pacific coast (March 9, 1942), the editorial page laid down the basic position: "It is idle to talk wishfully of Russia and Germany fighting each other to two pulps. . . . German victory would be a disaster for the U.S. Russian victory involves dangers and embarrassments which might or might not come true." There is a lunatic piece by Stafford Cripps, British ambassador to Russia: "The Soviet government has no intention, and of this I am certain, to demand anything more in the way of territorial acquisition; it will ask for future security and not territorial aggrandizement."

If this intelligent man could disseminate such treasonable lunacy, how can one criticize little people for believing that the Soviet czars of Russia are the last great hope of the world? I submit Stafford Cripps to Dante, as to which layer of hell he could best be accommodated in. It would be crowded.

There reached the Senior Group, dated March 17, 1942, a long legalistic document, the relevant part of which is that a Participant (me) "will be paid the credit balance, in his trust account . . . (1) in annual instalments . . . (2) in one or more other instalments as the Trustees shall determine. . . . Payment of the first instalment shall be made within ninety (90) days after the effective date of the employment of such Participant, and the remaining instalments, if any, shall be paid, respectively, within thirty (30) days after each succeeding anniversary of such effective date. If, upon the termination of such employment, there shall be in the Trust fund any insurance, endowment, or annuity policy or policies on the life of such Participant the Trustees, at such time or times and in such manner as they shall determine, with the approval of the Board of Directors of *Time*, shall (a) distribute to such Participant such policy or policies or (b) convert such policy or policies into one or more other such policies and distribute the same to each Participant or (c) surrender such policy or policies for cash and pay the proceeds thereof to such Participant."

In the sequel, nothing of this largesse was "distributed" to me. Given the verbiage above, the omission must have been legal; I trust that the reader understands that it was immoral. I think I have just read this document for the first time. I threw it in a drawer in 1942; I had work to do. I am sure that numerous legal escapes are embedded in it freeing Time Inc. from any obligation. In essence, Charlie Stillman won that round. He could always win in his own park; this book is in another park.

A ghoulish episode occurred, instigated by that plausible Cagliostro on *Time* magazine, Whittaker Chambers. His totally unnecessary routine of working his foreign department through every Saturday night on black coffee reduced one willing colleague, Calvin Fixx, to a heart attack. Naturally, Whittaker (who, like Cagliostro, was not using his real name) had to purge himself by feigning his own heart attack. (He is supposed to have died of the real thing, an impostor to the end, but in fact killed himself.) This called for executive action. All key writers were asked to report to a Dr. Edward Watt Saunders at 10 East 90th Street for a physical examination. It might be added that Calvin Fixx later died in earnest. My report is appended:

October 29, 1943

The following is the report on:
Mr. David Cort.
CHIEF COMPLAINT: 1. Athletes hand. Some on feet. 2. Gingivitis. Receeding [*sic*] of gums. Loosening of teeth.
PAST HISTORY. Usual childhood diseases. No rheumatic fever, scarlet fever, typhoid, or pneumonia. Catarrhal Jaundice aged 16. Slight recurrence 1935. No operations.
Head: Few headaches. Eyes: left 20/20, right 20/40.
Ears: No symptoms. Deviated septum. Slight sinusitis.
Chest: Slight cough. Some expectoration.
Heart: Exercise without symptoms. Abdomen: Appetite poor. No distress after meals. Bowels normal. Weight same, always around 135. Genitalia: Cystitis once. No symptoms.
Extremities: No symptoms. Back: Sacro-iliac strain.
FAMILY HISTORY: Father 70, living and well. Mother died 60. Four brothers, living and well. One brother has T.B.C.

Marital: Married. Divorced. One child aged 5.

PHYSICAL EXAMINATION: Age 39.

Head: Eyes: right 20/20. left 20/20. Ears: right 20/20. left 20/20. Nose and throat and sinuses normal. Neck: No glandular enlargement. No thyroid enlargement. Chest: Lungs clear through out. Heart Sound: Normal. No murmurs. Blood Pressure 110/80. Pulse 60.

Fluoroscopy of Chest: Lung fields clear. Apices clear. Bronchial markings not exaggerated. Diaphragm excursion normal. Heart and aorta normal size. Abdomen: Liver and spleen not palpated. No masses. No tenderness. No herniae.

Genitalia: Normal. Extremities and reflexes normal.

Diagnosis: Normal health.

Advice: Treatments for ezema [sic] of hands.

Mr. David Cort   October 29, 1943

Hemoglobin	85%
Erythrocytes	4,000,000
Leucocytes	5,400
Differential	Normal
Smear	Normal

Urinalysis: Specific gravity   1020
               Sugar   Negative
               Albumin   Negative
               Microscopic   Few W.B.C.

Wassermann reaction: Negative.
Electrocardiograph: No significant findings.
X-Ray of Chest: No significant findings.

I had athlete's foot while I was working for Time Inc. Hubert Kay and Noel Busch also had it in advanced stages. I can only report that since I left Time Inc. I have never had athlete's foot. The infection vanished, I know not why, and has never returned. I suspect, however, that athlete's foot was the mark of the real Time Inc. people; I doubt whether it afflicted Gerard Piel or Dick Wilcox and certainly not Dan Longwell or Henry R. Luce or Charlie Stillman. It occurs to me that athlete's foot may be the central truth of Time Inc. during this period.

A British bombing of Paris factories working faithfully for the

German army outraged Vichy France. The lead (March 16, 1942) quoted Pétain: "Cowardly slaughter." As for French-American relations, "The U.S. is polite because Vichy owns some very strategic colonies and a vital fleet. Vichy is polite because the U.S. may win the war and Vichy may lose the rest of her empire." The crimes of Vichy are listed. "The trouble was always that Vichy France is not a sovereign state. However energetically it makes a face like one, it remains the pawn of Germany. . . . In Washington, M. Henry-Haye goes on giving his select little dinners of lobster, strawberries Melba and 1929 champagne. For what his countrymen are eating in the sad land of Vichy, turn the page." And there: "This is Vichy France, the rump end of a great nation. . . . It is not black death, as in Russia and Poland and Serbia. It is something worse: ignominy and hunger and fear, petty theft and scavenging and compromises. . . . These pictures have the pathos of a man who has nothing to do and for whom nothing is solved, who sits and waits day after day. . . . Civilization has left him and he moves as in a dream through the husk of a world." Amid scenes of Nazi pomp, Goebbels is quoted with rare acumen: "I do not know whether Mr. Roosevelt will catch up with the war or not. . . . But Germany now faces its greatest but also its last chance." For such grim truth, Goebbels should have been shot. The editorial page takes seriously the threat of a vast Japanese fifth column on the west coast and in Hawaii. "Lease-Lend" cargoes for Russia and Britain are shown on their way in time for the spring's action. A big crack in the war effort was revealed by a Detroit race riot over new housing. A young Negro said bitterly: "I would as leave fight for democracy right here. Here we are fighting for our own selfs." A Nazi execution of Russian civilians is explained: "Perhaps the most vicious piece of Nazi double-talk is their pretense that, though modern war is total war against all the people of their enemies, the enemy is forbidden, by something the Nazis sometimes call 'international law,' to fight back 'totally.' " The Russians took their hanging coolly. The picture essay was the usual beautiful and sordid display of India: "India itself, the legendary treasure house, the ancient heart of the world, the tiara of the British Empire, was last week in peril. . . . British paternalism has filled India with far more rage than gratitude. . . . . There has never been, in fact, a single India any more than there has ever been a single Europe."

The key name of Port Moresby on New Guinea was raised in the lead (March 23, 1942) as the Japanese closed in on Australia and American troops and planes arrived. For this was to be another minor decisive battle. The Australian premier announced: "Every human being in Australia is now, whether he likes it or not, at the service of the Government to work in the defense of his country. . . . No longer will the Government appeal. I will order and direct." With a map of Australia went this legend: "To attack or to defend Australia is a peculiar problem. Even after the enemy has taken the tropical northern strip, the arid center and the great sandy beaches of the west, he is nowhere. . . . But certain it is that the fall of Australia to the Japs would cause such a pang of heartbreak through all the white man's world as was never caused by the fall of Singapore, Manila, Hong Kong, the Indies. The Australians deserve better of the white race." The writer is obviously a Caucasoid who feels solidarity with his race and is not apologetic about it, whatever the passing fashion. (I trust members of the other great races feel solidarity with theirs and defend them.) The editorial page echoed the Australian's position that in wartime civilians were part of the war effort. The misuse of American talent and energy was detailed, and the labor demand of war industries would move from 5 million to 15 million by the end of 1942. A National Manpower Mobilization Board was proposed.

This last innocent suggestion led to a significant sequel. When the board was formed, Luce got himself named to its magazine division. It ruled, in line with his interests, to give labor priorities to such news magazines as *Time* and *Life*. As a result, magazines such as *The New Yorker* lost their best writers and artists to the draft, while I was fenced off as "an indispensable man," invulnerable. But not so invulnerable. For any dispensable man who was drafted had his wife and children pensioned by Time Inc., whereas had I enlisted, my family would have received nothing. Thus, I was imprisoned for the duration. Furthermore, my salary was frozen as long as I held the same job. The scope of my job did change from time to time during the war, but I never had the financial wit to submit that I was therefore eligible for a raise, nor did my superiors, cleverer than I in such matters, volunteer the thought.

In the corresponding *Time* issue dated March 23, the news was given that Roosevelt had ordered MacArthur to leave Corregidor February 22 and take command in threatened Australia. In *Life*, the all-Negro 99th Pursuit Squadron was shown admiringly.

While these awesome events were reported, there was a sort of creature existing in a totally detached world. Who should this be but the Time Inc. executive? The document produced by this creature is something I did not read at the time. Its subsidiary meaning is that Time Inc. made me magnificent, if hedged, promises, which it did not keep, counting on my demonstrated indifference to money. It was a declaration for executives, not for writers, even as it assumed that I too was a "businessman," as I was not. Luce was an unusually generous employer, and this document meant well, until it reached the hands of the lawyers.

This marvelous admission to "The Time Employees' Senior Group Trust," dated March 17, 1942, runs to 31 pages, not to develop the generosity of the benefits, but to hedge them. It reads as if the lawyers were satirizing themselves. Notice this sentence (Article Third, Section One), competing with Marcel Proust. "The Trustees shall as of the end of each calendar year, and at such other times as they shall see fit, adjust the credit balance of the Trust account of each Participating Employee to an amount determined (a) by multiplying the net assets of the Trust, excluding the value of all insurance, endowment and annuity policies which shall at that time be held by the Trustees as part of the trust fund and any contribution or payment from Time or any of its wholly-owned subsidiaries which may be accrued but unpaid, as of the date of such adjustment, by a fraction, the numerator of which shall be an amount equal to the credit balance, excluding any payment or contribution from *Time* or any of its wholly-owned subsidiaries which may be accrued but unpaid, of the Trust account of such Participating Employee on the books of the Trust immediately preceding such adjustment, and the denominator of which shall be an amount equal to the total of the credit balances, excluding any contribution or payment from *Time* or any of its wholly-owned subsidiaries which may be accrued but unpaid, of the Trust accounts and Insurance accounts of all Participating Employees on the books of the Trust immediately preceding such adjustment, and (b) by adding to the result of the multiplication described in (a) above, the amount of any contribution or payment from *Time* or any of its wholly-owned subsidiaries for the account of such Participating Employee which may be accrued but unpaid." This masterpiece is larded with the phrase "Anything in this Agreement contained to the contrary notwithstanding." And it turns out that the directors of *Time* can be superseded at whim by the Executive Committee of *Time. This* is power.

Suffice it to say, the contribution to my present net worth of this largesse can be represented by a fraction, with numerator and denominator of zero. The lawyers' thirty-one pages were necessary to protect Time Inc. against the Participating Employee (me). Whether or not it needed so much protection, it made sure it had it.

Meanwhile, the really serious business of the war went on.

The destruction of about 300 Japanese planes over Burma by Colonel Claire Chennault's "Flying Tigers" (American Volunteer Group) made a cheering lead (March 30, 1942). For each kill the flier got a bonus of $500. Of the American war effort the editorial page said, "At some time—say 1944 or 1945—it is geared to produce a great army, on the field of battle, ready to fight. America's enemies know all this and they are not waiting." Archibald MacLeish of the Office of Facts and Figures (which also produced Philip Wylie) is quoted against "the idle women whose dinner hours have been altered and who call their country's struggle 'this wretched war.' " Overlooking the unnecessary tactlessness of this, *Life* said, "It seems to be Mr. MacLeish's view that Axis propaganda aims to undermine confidence in President Roosevelt; hence all criticism of Franklin Roosevelt is Axis propaganda. This is an extreme view but Mr. MacLeish is right in thinking that a certain section of American opinion is still unreconciled to the war policy. If American arms fare well abroad, this . . . may in time dissolve." The comment seems face-saving for MacLeish, but not to him. Pictures showed American troops arriving in Australia and MacArthur's arrival was announced, the first air unit reaching there in late December. This explained the gradual stalling of the Japanese sweep. Tojo, Japan's premier, war minister, and home minister (Hitler's opposite number), was the subject of a text piece by Ernest O. Hauser. An annoyance soon stopped was what seemed an editorial *Life* picture story but turned out to be an advertisement for Johnson's Wax. The very nadir of executive ignominy, in the person of Howard Black, is figured here. He had given an experimental tug on a chain that could have flushed the whole Time Inc. concept down the drain. The effort in various forms was to be repeated.

That agonizing over the west coast Japanese-Americans had ended was the lead (April 6, 1942), showing their arrival at Manzanar in Owens Valley. The internees would have their own "democratic government, stores, workshops, beauty parlors, barbershops and canteens" and would be paid a minimal wage. One said that he came "without bitterness or rancour—wanting to show our loyalty in deeds, not words." The marvelous food arriving in "unoccupied" France from French North Africa is shown, virtually all on its way to Germany.

Incredibly, 11 pages of Carl Mydans' and Melville Jacoby's pictures of the last hours of the Philippines reached *Life* for the lead (April 13, 1942), brought out by correspondent Melville Jacoby: "It was theoretically possible that Americans might have proved themselves unfit for this war, as did Frenchmen. But in their first impact with the enemy, as seen in these pictures, Americans showed themselves to be fighters, cleverer, tougher and more resolute than their enemies. Above all, their faces and bearing show here that they were enjoying the war, that the cooperative job of war was simply more fun than any singlehanded job of peace they had ever known." After a definition of their special difficulties, "in the Far East, the only men who did not fail were Americans, whose stake in the Far East was new and small." This must sound outrageous today to a generation that plans to live without risk or loyalty. Later, "History will record that the Filipinos proved themselves for all time in the defense of their islands against the Japs; . . . The loyalty of Filipinos to the U.S., which had long since promised them freedom, was in marked contrast to the disloyalty to Britain of the Malayans and Burmese. . . . The more [the Filipino] saw of the Jap, the surer he was that he could lick him. . . . The Filipino has caught something of what it means to be an American. . . . When the world crumbled, at one place at one time one man and his army stood up."

On the editorial page was notice of a Pacific War Council which did not include Russia, not at war with Japan. The secret *Life* plan for an American army on the Russian right flank was curiously abetted by a Russian statement: "The decisive place is the front of the U.S.S.R." We commented: "This was an open invitation to the Allies to send their military forces to Russia," as a possible nudge to Roosevelt to adopt our plan. The page ended on the note: "The war would be longer than most people dared to imagine." A report quoted voices that seem suitable to the present era. "The Japanese have a right to Hawaii. . . . I would rather be on the side of Germany than on the side of the British. . . . I believe this war is going to destroy America." Such talk was tolerated for nearly four months. It crested to "Young man, your lowest aim in life is to be a good soldier," "MacArthur and his men are not heroes but fools," until Earl Warren at last ordered them arrested. More came: "This is a Jewish War." Unhappily, Colonel McCormick's *Chicago Tribune* was part of this slime. Our long-term propaganda had not produced unanimous unity. I could not finish the very long report, though I tried, getting sicker. But it might well be read by the current crop of frivolous American traitors: these others were not frivolous. Any society—and this includes wolves, redwinged blackbirds, and oysters —would prefer to survive, and every member would prefer to survive and breed; therefore, members of the society are impelled to defend it against extinction. An infinity of cute little (or big) thoughts are conceivable and acceptable, but they should be somewhat over-shadowed by the possibility, to any open mind, of extinction. In 1942 extinction was a very present possibility.

Archibald MacLeish submits a letter (April 20, 1942) which primarily gives a further airing to his original remarks and secondarily makes the rather subtle point (which I like) that in America treason is not against the government but against the whole people. His writing the letter at all appears to express an insensate impulse toward bedlam, often true of MacLeish.

"England Falls in Love with Russia" made the lead showing the unveiling of a plaque to Lenin on the bombed house where he had lived in 1902–1903: "[The Englishman] knows too that his own house is much safer from German bombers so long as the German Luftwaffe is busy on the other side of Europe. And he knows that Russia has saved his home at terrible cost to itself, by appalling sacrifice and ferocious will. The physical signs of this profound respect and sympathy . . . are as unimpressive as all outward signs. For an inward sign, the new Archbishop of Canterbury wrote a new prayer: 'Almighty God, King of all nations, we pray Thee to send Thy blessing upon the peoples of Great Britain and Russia.' . . . Actually, though 'Socialism' is now a word heard very often in England, the English people want socialism and Government control less than they want more democracy and more efficiency." But Fortnum and Mason was selling hammer-and-sickle scarves. The editorial page said flatly that "the U.S.S.R. then proposed that Britain send its armies and planes into Russia to fight alongside the Soviet Army." One of the great problems of Bataan was revealed: "The soil of Bataan, like that of France in World War I, is rich in the anaerobic bacteria that cause gangrene in wounds. . . . Under the threat of losing a whole army from gangrene, Lt. Col. Frank Adamo, a reserve doctor from Florida, tried slicing the wound wide open, excavating all infected tissue, swabbing with peroxide and letting oxygen get in to kill the bacteria. This technique was not the least of the miracles of Bataan." In America the parades of the packed battalions of men were shown. Even the advertisements in this issue were patriotic: planes would "outfly and outfight our enemies' " because they had Ethyl gasoline; Parke, Davis drugs saved the workers' time producing "a bomber that doctors built"; Westinghouse built the aiming apparatus for "bad medicine for big bombers" and had nine products for "the common defense"; Royal Typewriter announced that it was shifting production to ordnance "for the defense of democracy"; Revere Copper and Brass had a natural; American Locomotive was for

"America in Motion"; Union Pacific country was "worth fighting for"; Bendix said sensibly of an airman, "He can't fly a rousing cheer"; Haig and Haig "helped Britain celebrate 100 naval victories"; Paris had "Victory" suspenders. These ads were not ridiculous; they were trying to get in step with a social solidarity for survival, however clumsily. I strongly suspect, however, that Howard Black had spurred his salesmen to solicit such advertising. More high-level executive thinking: patriotism might be turned into cash benefits.

The meeting of Chiang Kai-shek and Mohandas Gandhi (April 27, 1942) makes the lead: "Gandhi looks like an Asiatic but he is really a Hindu lawyer from South Africa. Like all India's Hindu leaders, he is loaded to the eyebrows with the patter (read cant) of English university education. His idea of being foxy today is to wait to see whether or not this war abolishes the British Empire. He was therefore opposed to coming to any agreement whatsoever with an Empire that may possibly be on the skids. To Chiang Kai-shek, the short-spoken man of action, this brand of thinking was blankly mysterious, but he was exceedingly polite." The negotiations with the Hindu leaders were described with utter contempt, and it was added: "Actually India ceased being productively important about a century ago. . . . In electric energy . . . India is about on a par with the State of South Carolina. . . . Only about 1% of this population is really represented by the Hindu leaders. Most of the rest of India do not know the name of Nehru, perhaps not even the name of Gandhi. These are the people who will presently meet the Jap, unless . . . Gandhi has decided to leave India the football of destiny. Chiang long ago decided that China would and could make its own destiny." The pictures were taken "in the house of India's greatest capitalist, Gandhi's chief backer, a man willing to do business with anybody," named Birla. Increasingly, both Gandhi and Nehru must become revealed as marvelously plausible and sanctimonious hypocrites such as only Dickens could invent, and are otherwise unknown in the West. To the hypocrisy must be added arrogance. In all reason, they were waiting to become part of a Japanese empire. The good news, apart from these two praying mantises, was that American planes were arriving at the battle lines. Japanese bases in the Philippines (now theirs), Timor, and Japan itself were bombed by American planes. Fortunately for Nehru and Gandhi, Chinese, British, and American military power was opposing the Japanese advance across the parallel mountain ranges of Burma toward India. In France, however, Laval had taken over for Hitler. A carefully mapped story explained how to burn out Tokyo.

Noel Busch does a piece on Nelson Aldrich Rockefeller, who has not diminished in interest. Trivial as this subject was, I must quote Busch: first, he describes the "soporific effect" of Washington's horizontal buildings like "skyscrapers lying down" and the corridors like "a nightmare-sized art gallery," resulting in "logorrhea of the aorta which currently impedes the U.S. war effort." The politicians "sized him up as a naïve boy from the big city." What they "failed to see was that Nelson, while obviously an amateur in politics, was a past master at coordination. . . . The Office of the Coordinator of Inter-American Affairs is practically unique in Washington in that members of its staff . . . rarely yawn in conversations and do their work as though they thought it was important." Finally, "in view of the undeniable success attained by his agency, it seems likely to outlast the war and go on to bigger things. Its founder is a good bet to do so also." Busch had read the young Rockefeller correctly. He is also the cover of this issue, looking as caddish as he does now, with the same false grin I have lately adopted, with no hope that it will open the same doors.

The formidable appearance of the first Americans, including conspicuously Negroes, in Australia, becomes the lead (May 4, 1942): " 'Certainly Americans and Australians disagree,' said an Australian officer. 'They disagree over who can fight best.' As the Australian autumn drew in, . . . the Americans turned north to find out who could fight best." The editorial page is beautifully written, but I have the feeling for the first time that I did none of it. The theme was the "surge to war," thoroughly documented: "Clearly the people were all set to fight the one kind of war that Adolf Hitler cannot win—a people's war. . . . This uprising was the greatest news of the war. Adolf Hitler, waiting moodily for the mud to dry in Russia, must have felt it on the back of his neck like a dark wind." And so on. This is not my style; it is that of a better propagandist than I. On investigation, I discover that it was Russell ("Mitch") Davenport, a delightful man with a few aberrations. He continued to do the editorial page until sometime in 1944 when, sensing that he would soon have to write pro-Dewey editorials, he refused to do so. The job was then given to John Knox ("Jack") Jessup, another delightful man. This new use of the editorial page transferred it from Billings' staff to Luce's staff as a further instrument of power ("responsibility"). I was happy to get rid of the editorial page.

The unexpected defense of Malta is given a text piece. It began with four mediocre Gladiator planes in a warehouse. They were wheeled out, found pilots, and defended Malta for three months, one being shot down. The island was given the George Medal by the king of England.

The problem of controls over an inflationary wartime economy occupied both lead and editorial page (May 11, 1942). Rationing was visualized in pictures, in terms of the sweetened cups of coffee and desserts one could have in a week. "Farmers must not expect more than parity. . . . On the other hand, it is downright unpatriotic for labor to argue that wages must fluctuate (always upward) with prices." Cartoons ridiculing the Godlike militarism of the *Chicago Tribune*'s Colonel McCormick as Colonel M'Cosmic were reproduced. Thoroughly interpreted pictures showed the German bombing of the Russian base at Kronstadt and a British raid on the U-boat haven at Saint-Nazaire. A portrait memorialized the death in a plane accident of correspondent Melville Jacoby. An amphibious landing by a Japanese invasion fleet is diagrammed, with text piece by Cecil Brown. "The Japs have proved excellent in attack but it is the generally held belief of military men that Japan will prove weak in defense and withdrawals." There was a report that on Bataan a routed Jap force threw themselves over a 150-foot cliff. A later observation might be that the Japanese were excellent at dying, not so good at not dying. Also, they had been indoctrinated in an overcompensating overconfidence versus white men, buttressed by the Russo-Japanese War.

The shares of Time Inc. stock that we had been allowed to buy had done so well that they had been split, perhaps at four for one. In this period we were buying out of salary the new shares at $25. The war had dealt them a blow: on April 9 the bid was 17⅝ and the asked 19⅛. Roy Larsen sent out a memorandum advising that anyone who wanted to terminate this contract could do so.

This brought about a curious confrontation. Theoretically, I was the one who understood the war, and I was committed by my own writings to the belief that it would be a long hard war and thus, in my naïveté, that Time Inc. stock would continue to drop. Therefore, I called on Roy and told him I was not interested in paying $25 for something worth $17 and bound to be worth even less, and that I elected to end the contract. Roy accepted this without demur. But as an executive he knew that inflation was under way and that the stock would rise again. (By August it was back to 25, and rising.) What was his obligation to me?

As a businessman, he had none, but I regarded him as a friend. I liked him, and one is inclined to imagine that anyone one likes returns the feeling in the same kind and degree. Therefore, I *knew* that Larsen was my friend. As such, he *did* have an obligation to save me from making a financial fool of myself. I must admit that this reflection did not occur to me until twenty-five years later.

The war had put me in an eschatological mood, and I had decided I was tired of having my wife climax every quarrel with a hollow threat of divorce. And so the next time she said it, I replied, "That's right, you are about to divorce me, and you'd better get to Reno as fast as you can." Afterward, she told people that I had asked for a divorce. I moved out, first to the Gotham and then to the Royalton, until she and my son left for Reno. But my original allowance for expenses did not satisfy her and so, to send her in luxury, I sold my Time Inc. stock at 17, probably its absolute nadir. The advancing spring was lightened by her very funny letters about Reno life, which I read aloud at poker parties. And my life was lightened of a bundle of Time Inc. stock.

I must read into the episode not only my own indifference and incompetence about money but also Larsen's contempt for the writer, like Charlie Stillman's earlier preference for the "businessman." They were in dead earnest about their net worth, while I was in dead earnest about the magazine, the reader, and the truth. Neither could understand the other and my side lost—as it usually does.

The Japanese advance over the parallel mountain ranges of Burma (not successful; it had never been in history) is described in a first-hand report by Jack Belden (May 18, 1942). It was a weird battle, at a whole series of hinges where Chinese and British troops met, but it was not decisive. The editorial page was again a single hurrah for sacrifice. A story on the Japanese chess-type game of Go demonstrates the game in terms of the war in Southeast Asia, but that game did not follow the rules of Go.

An "approximate" picturing of the battle of Coral Sea was the lead (May 25, 1942), using the "amazing technique of ship models, props and lighting" developed by Norman Bel Geddes, former partner of Worthen Paxton. Visually, the battle is nearly incomprehensible to me today, but it is a good try. In a chastening text piece, Colonel Herman Beukema sketched the spotty military record of the United States and the cowardice of its half-trained militias. He advised against a premature offensive, as advocated by a current best-seller, *Defense Will Not Win the War*. American troops at maneuvers with a wooden artillery piece made the point. "It is entirely possible that the end of the war will find the U.S. the most powerful single nation in the world. The longer the war, the greater the possibility."

The miraculous perspicacity of the new electron microscope, revolutionizing science (June 1, 1942), makes the "Speaking of Pictures." The lead was on springtime bombing. British bombing of Germany had inflamed Hitler into trying a new way not to win the war: the so-called "Baedeker raids" on England's historic sites, such as Bath, not a military objective. Doolittle's amazing air raid on Japan April 18 was also memorialized. The editorial page noted the popular belief in quick victory (defying Colonel Beukema) and the stock market boom, mocking my financial doings. The whole page tries to undercut this "gee whiz" mood.

Life had earlier pointed out that Goebbels' release (outside

Germany) of bad news was designed to drown the American war effort in overconfidence. It was working. In this period, when huge deeds and decisions were in course, the journalism was petering out, doing background jobs, as on the North Atlantic patrol and the spring planting. The darkening effect of censorship had set in. All *Life*'s copy on anything remotely related to the war was teletyped to Washington and censored, often with inane bureaucratic stupidity. Because of its nature, *Life* had to be more abject than *Time*, for all the military had to do was withdraw permission from *Life*'s photographers to get to the fronts, ships, and bases, and *Life* would vanish, like a Cheshire cat. Thus, there was no nonsense about defying the censors. In fact, the government's refusal to release bad news contributed to the unjustified "gee whiz" mood of unruffled optimism.

American production of two ships a day was celebrated in the lead (June 8, 1942) on the occasion of National Maritime Day when 21 merchant ships and 6 other craft were launched. But "night after night the U-boat packs struck down their quarry in forays that ever less frequently reached the columns of the press." (More censorship, more euphoria.) *Life* had covered all 21 launchings. The editorial page is gradually transiting to the true editorializing that Davenport maintained in the coming years, abandoning Billings' concept of "The Newsfronts of the World." Here he compares the real war which the enemy was winning and "the Hollywood war" which the United States was winning. But all was not lost for "the U.S. has always been bigger than its Government." This balancing of the black cloud against its fortuitous silver lining was the genius of Davenport. Pictures of the last days of Rangoon when the crazy Burmese ran riot arrived from photographer George Rodger. The day after the British avowed "every confidence" of holding Rangoon, the Japanese entered the city. The increased firepower of the P-40 fighter, six .50-caliber guns, is photographed. An example of the journalism of trivia was a story on the simple wartime pleasures of picnicking, three-legged races, blindman's buff, progressive community dinners, quilting parties, first aid practice, musical chairs, spin the bottle, the string trick, and the chair trick. A text study of the

Australian people by Cecil Brown is affectionate but mixed. It makes them sound appallingly lazy: they took eight weeks to do an eight-day job of unloading a ship of crucial supplies; they took all day to unload two Kittyhawk fighter planes, refused to let the Americans do the unloading, were defied, and the whole load was on the dock in ten hours. A gate blocked the exit from the dock. The foreman promised to get it down in four days, including one holiday. The Americans rammed a jeep into it and had it down in two minutes. And the Japanese were bombing northern Australia. Finally, the sixteenth birthday party of England's Princess Elizabeth is the party "*Life* Goes to."

The British bombing of Cologne ("gone forever") was the lead (June 15, 1942), using stock pictures plus maps and a fanciful drawing of the burning city, with the High Gothic cathedral untouched: 3,000 tons of bombs were delivered by 1,250 planes. The editorial page compared Japan's raid on the Aleutians to Columbus' discovery of America, making the point that America's insularity was also gone forever; in contrast, the muddling of politicians was attacked. The new editorial page was being translated into power. The essay was also powerful on "Negroes at War": "It is perfectly true that U.S. Negroes have never had a square deal from the U.S. white majority, but they know their lot would be far worse under the racial fanatics of the Axis. Now, when their country needs them, they are glad to work and fight and die alongside their white fellow-citizens. That is the spirit which will some day wipe every trace of racial bigotry off the map of America." Further, "Negro soldiers have fought under all the great generals, in all the great wars and in most of the famous battles of U.S. history. And they have fought well." Some heroic details of Negro performance followed. The story demanded "more negroes in war plants," perhaps 2 million.

The formal alliance of Russia with Great Britain and the United States occupied the lead (June 22, 1942), the British pact being for mutual assistance and against "territorial aggrandizement," the American only for Lease-Lend. "Russia had suggested to Great Britain that after the war she be allowed to keep the three Baltic States and some of Finland, Poland and Rumania. The U.S. objected and Russia cheerfully dropped that clause" (but not in the closet). Finally, referring to a picture of a Russian soldier in action: "In the last showdown, the verbiage of the diplomats is backed up by the man at lower right." The editorial page continued its fretting over the ineptness of the American war effort. I would think that Luce was directing the slant of these editorials. The news stories were the end of the great carrier *Lexington* in the battle of Coral Sea; another Bel Geddes model, this time of the air attack from Midway on the Japanese fleet; and Britain's seizure of Vichy's island of Madagascar, a partial key to the Indian Ocean. The war did not seem to be moving so slowly. The essay was on military logistics: first, the equipping of one fighting man, then the equipment of one whole task force, always tailor-made to do a specific job. The complexity of the operation is detailed.

It appeared that my attempt to rewrite the army field manuals had inspired some executive, probably Longwell. For in the "Speaking of Pictures" (June 29, 1942) are illustrations by a *Life* artist for Field Manual 21–45, with the text still written by the army. *Life* gets full credit for helping the war effort, while the army still mangles the art of communication and the recruits are still bewildered. It was a sad little defeat. The lead crowned the aircraft carrier as the new queen of sea battles, dethroning the battleship which could no longer get close enough to anything to shoot at it. More cheers were accorded Vice Admiral William F. Halsey, Jr., in command of carriers in the Pacific. The editorial, probably inspired by Luce, urged more aid to China and her full inclusion as an equal in the councils of the United Nations. An anecdote that probably never saw print concerned the Roosevelts' opinions of Madame Chiang Kai-shek. Mrs. Roosevelt thought Madame was just another humanitarian democrat; Roosevelt disagreed. At a White House dinner, Madame criticized Roosevelt for his handling of John L. Lewis. "What would you do in China with such a man?" Madame passed the edge of her hand across her throat and made a gagging noise. Roosevelt looked down the table at Mrs. Roosevelt and smiled. The text piece by Gerry Piel was on Henry J. Kaiser who since April 15, 1941, had launched 82 ships and reduced building time to 46 days.

The letters divided on the "Negroes at War" story. Most were admiring but one from Covington, Kentucky, said, "You excuse the degraded actions of Lincoln in sending Negro troops against the homes of those people who had raised them. Why remind the Southern people of an injustice as foul as any Hitler conceived?" (July 6, 1942). Nevertheless, the Fourth of July lead celebrated 66 men from Harrodsburg, Kentucky, reported "missing in action" on Bataan, all members of Company D, 192nd Tank Battalion (36,853 U.S. and Filipino troops were captured when Bataan fell). A well-researched job was done on Harrodsburg, before and after the boys left. The editorial tries to be as pessimistic as possible about the war effort without collapsing into total dismay: "The dawn will come as soon as every man, woman and child in the United States begins to fight." The bad news was on the following spreads with the success of the U-boat war on Allied shipping in the western Atlantic; and the great battle for Sevastopol in the Crimea, the key port of the Black Sea: "America's war was being fought heroically last week by foreigners on many a foreign field." Finally, came the American casualties from a Japanese bombing raid on Dutch Harbor in the Aleutians. A happy development was the transport of American and British supplies on a renovated Persian railroad and several highways to the Caspian Sea, where they could be transshipped to Russia. An amazing 15-page tribute to the fighting spirit of the American South: "The South has known, as no other U.S. section knows, that war does settle things. It knows too that men may die by fighting, but that nations die only by surrendering." The history of southern valor is documented. In contrast to this, a text piece by Noel Busch followed on hardheaded Donald Nelson, director of the War Production Board. Nelson's quiet, imperturbable, as if perfectly routine, success at the biggest job in the world leads Busch to write: "It is precisely because other nations cannot produce such characters or even understand the means of doing so that the U.S. is periodically put to the nuisance of pinning Europe's ears back in a war." Otherwise, Busch ridicules the literati's contempt for the American businessman very tellingly. It is Busch at his most typical. He did not share the editorial writer's awe of the problem of "pinning Europe's ears back."

The war seemed to have fallen into a lull as the next issue (July 13, 1942) showed an Oklahoma primary election, painted legs (for want of silk), the Tennessee Valley Authority, a canoe trip, and Clare Boothe on "the battle for Egypt" while the editorial scolded the farm bloc, labor, and everybody else except the young men. But the war exploded all over the next issue (July 20, 1942). The lead showed Rommel's Afrika Korps in Egypt against the British "cavalry officers who liked to think of the tank as a very heavy horse. . . . They had failed to understand that the mobile gun on tractor or tank had taken mastery over armor. . . . Everything in the Afrika Korps has a purpose; nothing is there because it is customary. . . . There is a common-sense simplicity about every move that is in marked contrast to complicated British military methods. . . . The so-called 'methods' of the blitzkrieg had been long since dropped by the Germans, just as the British caught on to them. . . . At this neck between the [Qattara] Depression and El Alamein, British General Auchinleck massed 'a forest of guns' and held Rommel with guns rather than tanks." Finally, a map of Eurasia was captioned: "The most tragic map ever seen by living men is that shown above." The text said: "The British and the Americans are fighting out on the edges but the men in the grim center of this deadly melee are two great fighting peoples, the Russians and the Chinese. . . . If the United Nations had a plan, any plan, it was being beautifully concealed." The last sentence was meant to be ironic, but it almost gave away a great military secret. For the United States was using Ascension Island in the South Atlantic as a refueling stop for planes, often carrying tanks, on their way to reinforce the army in Egypt. Rommel was unaware of this reinforcement. El Alamein was yet to become one of the decisive battles of the world. The editorial was gloomier than ever, quoting a hick but powerful congressman as prophesying the end of the war almost any minute, making sacrifices unnecessary. Japanese pictures of the American surrender in the Philippines and also their pictures of Pearl Harbor added to the gloom. Titled "The Horrors" was a display of bombed English cities, partly cleaned up. The good news was the birth of the American jeep. Finally, "The Russian Battle-front" was described by C. L. Sulzberger, then quite young. He estimated that the Axis had suffered 4 million casualties in Russia, the Russians at least that many. He suggested that the Russians did not take prisoners (he had seen four) and tells a hygienic version of the transfer of Soviet populations to Siberia. Unmentioned were the quiet efforts of Donald Nelson, underlying the sinews of the Allied cause.

Suddenly the masthead was pocked with asterisks (July 27, 1942) indicating "With the armed forces." These included Thompson, Bach, Maitland Edey, Oliver Jensen, George Caturani, and Richard Pollard. A dagger indicated "Prisoner of War," designating Carl Mydans and his wife, Shelley Smith. The lead spotlighted for the first time Dwight David Eisenhower, commander of U.S. forces in Europe. The title was "Second Front?": American troops in Ireland, England (these Negroes), New Guinea, notably Port Moresby, another decisive battleground. The editorial tried to prove that labor's demands for higher wages were insane and would ruin the workingman. The idea of a desperate fight here proposed was why I had stopped buying Time stock, but in money terms, for the executives, it was a ridiculous fantasy. I do not know whether even Davenport believed it. I did. The proof came in the next story, "Main Front: Russia," with two pictures of front-fighters. The possibility that they were posed was hinted at in the caption, "Machine gunners enact an assault." The naval battle of Midway is shown and mapped, presumably with the censor's permission. The next story describes the mess of censorship, especially on the navy side. Here the versatile Noel Busch contributes a piece on circus seals, uncensored by the navy. Then came a rather pedestrian essay on the Atlantic convoys, notable for the line "A convoy is 99% boredom and 1% being scared to death." I did not write this. My monopoly on the war had long since ended.

One of the others probably wrote the lead (August 3, 1942) on a Nazi attack from Norway on an American convoy approaching Murmansk. Only one German torpedo plane drove in resolutely; the others veered off. The convoy delivered a huge mass of war matériel to the Russians. The editorial complained that Washington found everything worth doing "impossible" to do, comparing it to the original George who did not admit that it was impossible to cross the Delaware Christmas night 1776. A chart gave the American losses in men so far and the record of ship sinkings on the east coast. A story of two open American Fascists sentenced to prison was a quick sequel to the *Life* story, "Voices of Defeat," April 13, 1942. It was added that 26 other subjects of the story were being indicted for sedition. A feature on transport planes was designed to back up Henry Kaiser's ignored proposal ("impossible!") to solve transport with planes.

De Gaulle with ornate French cap was shown meeting Eisenhower with plain American cap in the lead (August 10, 1942). Talk about an immediate second front (I disapproved) was acknowledged. Some pictures of the desolation of Paris followed. The editorial urged a second front, though it admitted that the real task was to "save her [Russia] in the end." The editorial, which brings in the various cradles of civilization and Armageddon, seems too flamboyant, even for Davenport. Further support for Henry Kaiser's proposal of massive building of air transport was supplied by his own explanation of the plan, and its nonimpossibility. The Japanese bombing of Dutch Harbor in the Aleutians and Stilwell's flight from Burma, both pathetic, somewhat contradicted the brave talk of the editorial.

The prospect that the United States would go the pitiable way of France looked like a possibility in Detroit, as the lead (August 17, 1942) told how workers were quitting because they weren't allowed to smoke on the job, sympathized with other strikes, didn't feel like working. One punched holes in a bomber's gas line because he had been drafted. "Detroit can either blow up Hitler or it can blow up the U.S." "Fabulous" was used on successive pages to characterize tennis-playing Jinx Falkenburg and wounded General Freyberg in Egypt. The lamentable case of Gandhi and his disobedience campaign is explored in a text piece. At an opposite extreme, guerrilla fighting techniques are dramatized. A story on the U.S. Command School explains the differences among G-1, G-2, G-3, and G-4 (G-2 is Intelligence). Roger Butterfield writes a delightful text piece, "Is It True What They Say about Congress?" The answer was well, partly, but really no. Butterfield listed twelve isolationists who should be defeated.

"This First American Offensive in World War II" engages the lead (August 24, 1942) and the magic name Guadalcanal appears, but buried in the omnibus name Solomons, specifying respectively Tulagi, Guadalcanal, Florida, and Malaita. The Solomons, the northeastern flank of Australia, were the first of the stepping-stones for land-based air attack. The marines were doing the job. Maps showed the situation, but the emphasis was on Tulagi. The main Japanese base of Truk was about 1,000 miles northwest. The editorial compared the marines in the Solomons to the civilians not *thinking war,* concluding that the United States was the fifth or sixth war nation in the world—behind Germany, Russia, Japan, China, and probably Great Britain. The heroism of the National Maritime Union, unlike Detroit, earns an essay. The madness of the French Underground was not confirmed by a text piece by my friend Richard de Rochemont in which the "black list" included Mistinguett, Georges Carpentier, René Fonck, Celine, Derain, René de Chambrun, Weygand, Sacha Guitry, and Maurice Chevalier. No Frenchman had a right to call another a traitor; they were all in it together, and I could hardly blame those who spoke civilly to the Germans, after the whole nation had fallen on its back like a woman. Since a small segment of America has done the same thing today, Dick's piece deserves analysis. The "daring exploits" of the Underground were largely futile, though the men were risking their lives. "The rebellious French spirit" is cited, and this must make one laugh. The piece is full of little practical jokes, proving nothing, and adds up only to a private megalomania of "Revolt!" No doubt a small explosion happened inside their heads. Hurrah!

At this point I sent a key memorandum to C. D. Jackson highlighting the stupidity of Time Inc. It follows:

First, congratulations on your new job.

Secondly, my data on the strange case of Gary Underhill who is, I understand, in grave danger of disappearing into the armed forces.

Underhill has done a lot of work for me. Nobody else has seen anything but the end result of that work. My testimony is that his help was indispensable and unduplicatable.

If Underhill goes, I would be in the spot of either having to adopt a completely yes-man approach to our war effort or of running the risk of being incorrect, naïve and half-cocked in any realistic account of war events. I believe the same thing applies to everybody else who writes about the war for *Life*.

Any notion that our Washington office can get equivalent information out of the armed forces is absurd. They never have, perhaps because nobody in Washington has it. In fact, the Army and Navy frequently approach Underhill for identifications of enemy weapons. With Underhill, we are all set. Without him, we gradually and imperceptibly lose 50% of our authority in war news, perhaps more.

I do not believe there is any job in the armed forces where Underhill could do for the U.S. what he is now doing, on *Life*. Our most valuable contribution in this political war is to give the armed forces expert needling now and then. As things stand, however, I do not believe we will have Underhill another two months.

This memorandum hides a sense of desperation about the functioning of *Life*. Realistically, C. D. Jackson showed it to Longwell who, sensing the desperation, saw that this was the way to cut me down and win his little intramural war, which was his specialty. A degree of cynicism about his patriotic obligation is inevitably implied. In any case, Underhill was thrown to the armed forces. Yes, we had traitors, and they were not all Communists. These are, of course, very belated thoughts.

Allied allocations of strength began to surface as the burgeoning battle around El Alamein was given a long 11-page lead.

The earlier story on Detroit malingering inspired a wave of mail and the editorial (September 7, 1942) raised the point of "Democracy Unlimited" that freedom must be earned, perhaps generation by generation. The story had convinced some Princeton students that it was useless to fight. The kind of story, impossible without Underhill, was a judgment on all U.S. fighter planes, to answer confused press critics who did not understand that each plane is designed for a single purpose. Another Bel Geddes model (he got $3,000 for each three-day job of pushing sand into heaps) purported to show the Russian Caucasus which the Nazis were approaching. This story ended: "Actually, the main battle for the Caucasus was being fought last week not on its slopes, but 400 miles north around Stalingrad.

For the steps in the battle, turn the page." The German choice of a 1942 drive in southern Russia was explained: "Here at last they are driving the Russians not back into the cold and endless wastes, but up against seas and mountains" (in an area where winters are mild). The names of the great Allied battlefields were beginning to creep into the story.

This misinterpreted the situation. Stalingrad had not been a primary objective of the German attack, but merely a secondary flank operation to protect the drive on the Caucasus and the oil. It could have been taken in July virtually without a fight. The name of the city enraged Hitler, and he demanded its capture. Thus it became the grave of Paulus' army. The subsequent retreat of Kleist's army which had reached the Caucasus was one of the masterpieces of the war.

To the American people, as to Hitler, the real battle was Stalingrad. The name has become a legend, but it was an irrelevancy in any military sense. It was merely a passion of Hitler's, and wars are won by men without passion, who kill in great masses without feeling anything at all. Stalin had this necessary quality, whereas the Russians usually do not. The German generals had it, but they were overruled by the passionate man whom the mob loved, and so, all together, they fell into the pit.

The matter of Gary Underhill, whom I devoutly mourn, may as well be concluded. The army took him. Soon anybody interrogated by G-2 in Washington was faced by six colonels, with a sergeant at the end of the table. A colonel would ask a stupid question. The subject would fumble with the answer. Then the sergeant would inject, "What the colonel wants to know is . . ." and a searching question would be asked. Who else should this be but Gary Underhill? Gary memorized all the army rules and, if challenged by anybody up to a general, could cite the particular regulation justifying his position. But he was no longer available to answer *my* questions.

A man was hired to replace Underhill, at least as an interviewer of military men. This turned out to be Henry James of a doctor's family who spent their summers in Southampton, Long Island, where

I was often a guest of the John and Magda Tarletons. Henry tried hard, but his chief contribution to this story came from the accident that Southampton had a distinguished colony of Irish Catholics, to which the Kennedy family gravitated. At some point, Henry informed me that the young PT boat pilot, John Fitzgerald Kennedy, had expressed an interest in meeting me. Though I had an ironic view of his father's function as our ambassador to Great Britain, I agreed. The dinner was set up for Henry's club in Manhattan, the Yale Club. My testimony on John F. Kennedy is that I have no recollection whatever of John F. Kennedy. None. Of course he was then quite young, but I was only thirty-eight or so. No generation gap. I can remember the table, with my right shoulder to a partition, but I cannot remember the man opposite me. There was much I could have told him, as can be gathered from the foregoing pages, and I knew his more talented colleague in the PT squadron, George Cox, but the evening is a blank.

The other witness to this nonevent, Henry James, when cross-examined, says that he had been extremely nervous about my expressing my candid opinion of Jack Kennedy's father's job as ambassador to the Court of St. James, but that I was discreetly critical of Joseph Kennedy, and that Jack may have agreed. He remembers that I referred to George Cox, and that Kennedy downgraded Cox (now dead). James even thinks that the meeting may have taken place in Southampton, but I am sure it was at the Yale Club. It is hardly historic. My nonrecollection of John F. Kennedy may, however, be significant. Later, I voted for him. I would assume that he was not personally impressed by me.

There were two small but significant changes in the masthead. Richard Lauterbach, whom most knowledgeable people identify as a Communist at a later date, was moved up to the editorial associates. And Dennis Flanagan was added to the editorial assistants, probably as an assistant to Gerry Piel on Science. Flanagan, a handsome and genial man, was a true oddity: with that name, he had been brought up in the Jewish faith. Time Inc. seemed to attract oddities, starting with myself.

U.S. prisoners, as presented in Japanese propaganda magazines, jolly and purportedly happy to be out of the war, occupied the lead (September 14, 1942). The editorial continued criticism of the war effort, specifying Donald Nelson and the scrap collection campaign. The word "victory" was used with captured Japanese equipment in the Solomons. American B-17s at last joined the British in bombing Europe. Gypsy Rose Lee was seen marrying an acquaintance of mine, William Alexander Kirkland. The essay on Turkey was interesting: "The world is divided into three parts: the Axis world, the United Nations world and the only neutral country lying between the two—Turkey. . . . The Turks are the least impressionable people in the world. . . . They also like to fight. . . . And the Turks have maintained a neutrality of irreproachable aplomb." Of interned U.S. fliers: "The Americans declined to give their word that they would not escape, so the Turks have put a very lenient guard on them." Today we can imagine that a partial reason for the Germans not to have attacked Turkey was to maintain in business the very productive spy, coded Cicero, in the British Embassy.

My old line was revived in *Life*'s answer to letters protesting pictures of the wounded in North Africa (September 21, 1942): "Dead men have indeed died in vain if live men refuse to look at them," quoting the issue of January 24, 1938. By then it should have worked its way into Bartlett's *Familiar Quotations*. The lead was on inflation; the editorial betrayed a little optimism, mostly because Bernard Baruch had gone to work; and the essay was on one of Billings' two favorite subjects, railroads (at war). No pigs, however. Another lull was in course, but not at the fronts.

Censorship reduced to absurdity was pilloried in a "Speaking of Pictures" story (September 28, 1942) of British blanking out of features of a castle occupied by a U.S. general: "The finished product is guaranteed not to reveal anything to anybody—German, British or American." The lead was given to Wendell Willkie's buoyant tour of all friendly capitals to tell everybody that the United States was producing 5,000 planes a month and had hardly started. The editorial said, "Think war." The carrier *Yorktown* was seen sinking, hit by Japanese planes. The Aleutian Islands are shown brilliantly in a Bel Geddes model, the outermost islands, Attu, Agattu, and Kiska being in Japanese possession, this followed by pictures of U.S. planes bombing the port of Kiska.

The war roared back with the lead (October 5, 1942) on the Russian front. Young Germans were shown: "A million such men were last week in a rage because they had not been able to overrun Stalingrad on the Volga." Reluctantly, I reported, "There was even ugly talk that Stalin might make a peace with Hitler." More constructively, Red tanks of 25, 42, and 52 tons were shown and the Russians "take to swamps like muskrats, to forests like bears, to desert steppes like coyotes, to snow like ptarmigan. . . . The 1942 campaign in Russia looks suspiciously as though the Russians had planned it that way," attacking the German upper flank to swing the drive southward. Willkie wrote on his interview with Stalin, giving a favorable view of Stalin but withholding everything discussed. A drawing of Stalingrad, with a tank factory still in operation, is captioned: "The battle of Stalingrad exceeds in violence anything before seen in this war." The Russian soldier was regarded as more determined than the German. He at least was not contemplating "a peace with Hitler," a fact that made the rumors ridiculous. The editorial came up with the surprising idea that Hitler might try to divide the Allies by offering to quit his job. (That's what it says.) A story on the Solomons campaign pointed out that it put the Americans on the flank of any Japanese attack on Port Moresby in New Guinea. On Guadalcanal the marines "waited and watched. The people at home waited too." Another lull? Joe Kastner contributes a piece on the new P-47, the powerful Thunderbolt. Whoever thought up the editorial's cute idea had evidently sold the executives on it, for a *Life* advertisement takes it up: "Suppose Hitler asked for an Armistice November 11th?" Of course Luce would have looked incredibly powerful if *Life* had ended the war singlehanded. Somebody was taking hashish. In sober contrast was an essay by me, "Armies That Win," illustrated by a flow chart of the winning weapons through the ages. This is appended, as a useful elementary introduction to war, together with Gerry Piel's somewhat invidious activity concerning it. Since I had grown up with Gerry, this surprises me.

War is now deciding the future of America. That decision will come, as always, on the battlefield and nowhere else. Everything but the military blows that hit the enemy at a vital spot is secondary, if not irrelevant. The happiness of the home folks, the profits of business, the hours and conditions of workers, the postwar plans are beneath consideration in the final victory or defeat. Half measures and hot talk do not win wars and lost wars mean oblivion to the children of the defeated.

To a people like the Americans, who have been devoting their energy to other things, the art of war seems strange and mysterious. War is as old as human life but it has developed erratically, in bursts of violent efficiency. The decisive weapons have changed as the times changed, making it difficult to see the connection between the longbow of medieval England and the airplane of today. Yet in all times war follows certain principles, neither very mysterious nor very complicated. On the American battlefield of tomorrow, those principles will pay off just as they have paid off for the last 3,000 years.

It will be seen that three basic kinds of war constantly struggle with one another from age to age. First is the solid body of infantry, highly equipped both to defend itself and to push the enemy off his ground. Second is the cavalry, less able to defend itself but equipped to travel far and fast and hit the enemy with a great shock when and where he least expects it. Third is the artillery, which stands out of reach of the enemy and throws destructive weapons into his midst. The infantry tends to dominate in the highest periods of civilization, usually in conjunction with artillery. The cavalry sweeps the world when civilization is at a low ebb. In this war, tanks and planes have already been used as both cavalry and artillery, to prepare the way for the kill by the infantry.

The victorious general is the one who chooses the correct weapons and tactics for his age and his problems. He may have learned the art of war, but what really counts is his ability to think straight and act decisively in the heat and confusion and doubt of battle. He must know that war is human. Soldiers must be trained to stand together and fight. They must try to hit all together. They must have room to fight, but they must not disperse too thinly. They must have and use the best weapons. Above all, they must feel themselves a great army or regiment or squad to win.

After a brief history of warfare, I concluded:

War was now ready to go to town.

First exploding irresistibly in 1914 to test the arsenal scientific men had given it, it took five great steps.

First was artillery which in great concentrations smashed all enemy infantry by parabolic or lobbing fire over obstructions, aiming by trigonometry.

Second was deep trenches which concealed infantry during bombard-ment behind resilient earth, in the stalemate that began in 1914, after the first Battle of the Marne.

Its third was the rapid-fire machine gun, which enabled one man favorably placed behind barbed wire to mow down a company or a regiment of the most courageous men ever born.

Its fourth was the strengthing of gun barrels by the British out of a neglected German invention of chrome-nickel steel. This led to much more powerful charges, longer life of guns and the modern rise of steel alloys.

Its fifth was the tank which first appeared en masse at Cambrai Nov. 20, 1917, protected the charging men from the machine guns and could more or less dodge through the artillery fire. The development of the tank inevitably called for the production in enormous quantities of antitank guns with tremendous muzzle velocity and extreme mobility. These began to become general after the lessons of the Spanish Civil War in 1936.

Meanwhile, in the sky overhead, the plane went through various useful phases between 1903 and 1942. First it was merely the ideal scout that spied out the doings of the enemy. Then it became a raiding scout that surprised and machine-gunned troops, that bombed cities, railways, munition depots for some future general benefit. Then it became an immediate combat artillery, that bombed enemy troop and tank concentrations and pillboxes, to help the actual assault. Always it retained its first use, that of the eyes of the army, making blind the army without it.

The airplane on the attack has been stopped by three things: the defensive fighter plane, the radio direction finder and the old-fashioned tree. The last of these made the plane almost entirely useless in the fighting in Bataan, in Malaya and in the forested areas of Russia, for planes simply could not find the ground troops. Perhaps the greatest function of the plane is yet to come: to pick up an entire army, put it down deep in the enemy's rear and then supply it.

The plane is of all weapons going through the most violent evolution. A new fighter plane catches an old bomber, a new bomber flies above the range of the biggest anti-aircraft guns and the old fighter, a new fighter goes up four or five miles to catch the old bomber with new detecting devices even against night bombers. Engines move from 600 hp to 1,200 to 1,500 to 1,800 to 2,500, giving fabulous ranges and load capacities and speeds. Eight guns fire streams of armor-piercing bullets or shells at one touch of a trigger. Bombsights and calculating machinery calling on the most abstract and visionary mathematics became standard issue.

To nonsoldiers all this seems strange and confusing—a long way from the "simple" wars of the past. The plain fact is that only "abstract" scientists, engineers and production men today know what war is all about in detail. Yet there is a comprehensible pattern for laymen behind these scientific complexities. War, after diddling along with inefficient weapons for several thousand years, suddenly began to find its problems solved in about 1900. National armies came to number 5,000,000 men. Since then, the speed of invention has not slackened, but fabulously increased. The weapons and tactics of war at this period are in a violent state of flux.

Many things are possible. For example, there may be better ways to fire a shell than by gunpowder. A fast airplane that could stand nearly still in the air, land in a small space, hover and fly among the trees, would revolutionize troop command from the air. No weapon is above change. Any way to enable a tank to fire accurately while moving, any design to deflect striking shells, to increase a tank's speed and maneuverability, would be useful. Any device that will take troops safely up close to the enemy, that reduces casualties during attack, is useful. Some inventor may achieve destruction of enemy men and machines by the use of atomic-energy control. Every army would like to have a bomb that explodes just before contact, some feet above the ground. Such a bomb could also be used by planes to bomb other planes in air. And so on.

The Germans have been so far the most brilliant exponents of this modern war. When they had a fantastic superiority in weapons, as in Poland, Flanders and France, superiority in tactics and strategy was unnecessary. They could have marched in backward. When their weapons found an equal in Russia, superior tactics won them a way across a thousand miles. But the Russians evolved a countertactic. Part of their system was to fight from forts. The fort this time was a forest, in which the surrounded Russians vanished. They expected to be driven out of their fort, but at great loss to the Germans in men and matériel and time. They made punishing sallies out of their fort and sometimes fought their way through the German rear to their own lines.

In the historic cycle of warfare, today's conflict is in the high-mobility stage of heavy infantry. Its tactics are suggested by Alexander, Caesar and Gustavus Adolphus. It is not in the light-cavalry stage, as some experts deduced from a misinformed study of the Battle of France and as the British briefly thought in North Africa. Surprise and maneuver are all-important, but they must be backed up by heavy and superior firepower. As in all highly developed periods, war is now a coordination of all arms, all tricks and devices, based on heavy infantry and artillery. And in such a warfare, where the very complexity of the army renders it vulnerable, the army that moves fastest and strikes with surprise has every advantage, if it has real firepower. So far the democracies have been slowest to learn the technique of coordination of all arms. Only when the American army has the best weapons, the best mastery of tactics and the best coordination of all arms will it be safe to add the U.S. to the victors of history.

As early as March 4, 1942, Piel had had a comment on the piece from Colonel T. D. Stamps, West Point's professor of military art "on the subject of Cort, whose piece I sent him." There is a tone of puppy impudence in this that I find distasteful, and what in hell was he doing with my piece at all? Billings, who probably felt the same way, passed the thing on to me with the note "You keep this" and, as can be seen, *Life* printed the piece in due course. As for the West Point professor, he is too provincial to understand that true history cannot be written at all, the past is far beyond recall even in an individual life, and he has missed the point of tank warfare (the mobile gun) as specified in *Life*. For a West Point professor, this is bad. Also, in the tradition of military professors, he overrates the usefulness of telling cadets just how Napoleon did it. The present crop of generals is sufficient proof of that—no Napoleons, alas. But all the poor professor knew about war was what Jomini and Clausewitz had told him. He might have been reading *Life* as of 1942. As for his praise for my writing, I have received these same laurels from people who merely do not know how to think.

But here is his letter, smugly passed on to Billings with what motivation I would prefer not to know:

Dear Mr. Piel:

The copy of Mr. Cort's article reached me while I was somewhat snowed under with a multitude of things, and it is only now that I am able to make a few rambling remarks. These are as follows:

Page 1. While the statement is true as regards wars of ancient times and even those of the middle ages, I do not believe that it is correct to say that modern wars are badly reported, even though it is true that they are reported rather late. There are very voluminous records of the American Civil War, which tell us exactly what happened. For the First World War, we have the official histories of the British, French, and Germans. The records of the American Army's participation are, unfortunately, not yet available, although much work has been done on them. Enough has been published on the last World War to enable us to know what really happened.

Page 2. The idea is good that the principles are simple, but the execution most difficult.

Page 9. He makes reference to heavy cavalry and might like to bring out that tanks are the heavy cavalry of today.

Page E. He does well to emphasize the human factor. However, if its understanding were beyond "ordinary military technicians," we should indeed have a very poor army. Even the platoon commander must understand his men.

Page AA. The one serious fault in the article is that he does not properly evaluate Napoleon and his contribution to military art. No one disputes the fact that he was the greatest master of the art of war that the world has known. One has only to study his campaigns to see that. Mr. Cort says that he did little to revolutionize it. He was the first who really applied the principles that have guided the great generals since his time. All that Jomini did was to tell us of the principles illustrated by Napoleon's campaigns. It was not the revolutionary fanaticism of the French soldier that was primarily responsible for Napoleon's victories. It was his genius as a leader and strategist. He was not outstanding in tactics, but was the only one over a long period of years who made war with his head.

Page CCa. I am not in on the War Department's secrets, but have airplane engines moved up to 3500 H.P.? Aren't the most powerful only about 2,500 H.P.?

Some good missionary work can be done in educating the American people to the fact that war cannot be won by tanks and airplanes alone, but that there must be a huge mass of infantry. This was proved by the German campaign in Belgium and France in 1940. However, I am not one to minimize armored forces and air power. This quotation from one of our pamphlets may be of interest:

"In each of the months of March, April, and May, 1918, the Germans achieved a break-through on the Western Front, but after creating a deep salient their attack was stopped owing to (1) lack of a mobile force to exploit the success before Allied reserve divisions arrived to close the gap, (2) inability of the supporting artillery to keep up, and (3) difficulties with supply. The present German Army has overcome the obstacles to success encountered in the spring of 1918. The armored force exploits the break-through before the enemy reserves can be brought up; the airplane, in addition to its attacks against communications, is used to supplement the support given by artillery, and to take its place if the guns cannot keep up; the infantry has heavier supporting weapons of its own; the modern motor-truck train is used to lessen the difficulties of supply."

Mr. Cort indeed writes in a most interesting manner and I believe that, when published, the article will create a great deal of interest. I wish that I could write like that.

With kindest regards,

Sincerely,
T. D. Stamps,
Colonel, U.S. Army,
Professor.

The failure of the military professor to understand the war is not very surprising. Gerry Piel's effort to ambush me seems now, so much later, discouraging. But there it is. As with Larsen, it is another failure of friendship, which at the time I hardly noticed.

Under the guidance of Underhill, I concluded that the professor's point about planes as artillery was seriously in error. We had too much evidence that bombed factories in England and Germany were back in full operation a few days after being heavily bombed. (Of course, the atom bomb is something else.) This applies only to land objectives. A ship has three grave disabilities: (1) it is loaded with combustible fuel and ammunition; (2) if seriously damaged, it sinks to the bottom, something a factory cannot do; and (3) it is vulnerable to torpedoes, as a factory is not. Factory operation was most seriously hurt by fire-bombing workers' homes, so that they had to spend valuable days and nights finding new lodgings for their families and were exhausted on coming back to the job. The comparative futility of conventional land bombing was seen again in Vietnam.

The real perils of censorship to *Life* were highlighted in the lead (October 12, 1942) because Roosevelt had restricted picture coverage of his two-week tour of the country to two navy still photographers. *Life* printed 39 of the pictures, pointing out how terrible they were and the threat of excluding civilian (professional) photographers from military news. This would have cut *Life* down to a stump. The editorial, addressed "To the People of England," advised that England might have to lose its empire to win the war. This impudent howler is still remembered in many quarters. A different opinion was expressed in my story on the revolt of Gandhi's Congress party: "All this gave great aid and comfort to the enemies of the United Nations." The captions ridiculed Gandhi. A Hitler speech is quoted: "But if one has before him military idiots, in such a case one cannot even guess where they will attack." In a nod to Longwell, who came from Missouri, the picture essay was on Missouri and its history, including Jesse James and Tom Sawyer. Longwell also admired Missouri mules. The picture essay complimented Southern California on its war effort, especially in plane production. Presumably, this stimulated the rest of the country, including Missouri.

In this terrible year, there is only one statement by Luce, in the book *The Ideas of Henry Luce*, collated and with a brilliant Introduction by John K. Jessup, at that point in charge of the postwar plans department, a singularly futile arena for big thinking, typical of Luce. The one was on the postwar dreams of China, meaning Chiang Kai-shek. Luce thought, not surprisingly, that the Chinese wanted "the material welfare of this age of science and technology." Chiang was in Chungking, far from the populous centers of China, while the Communists were far nearer those centers, hoarded in guerrilla enclaves. Thus, when the Japanese surrenders came in 1945 to *representatives* of Chiang, his troops could not take immediate control of the territories, and the Communists seized the moment to move in. Chiang could never recover the lost ground, and a year later the Communist leaders wore confident smiles. They too wanted "material welfare," in their own way. They also wanted to kill the China of Chiang and Confucius. The U.S. government, fingering its atom bomb, was unaware of the real situation until far too late. "Postwar dreams," indeed!

This matter of what happened in China will be resumed later, but on the premise that it is not understood and will not be understood until some people talk who have no intention of talking. The current books on the subject are crippled.

The success of daylight "precision" bombing of the continent by U.S. Flying Fortresses with the Norden bombsight was the lead (October 19, 1942), written by Wilcox or Field. Bourke-White had posed an ex-*Time* writer, Lieutenant James Parton, with the pointer showing General Ira Eaker something on a wall map of Europe. Later he became a colonel, I believe, and criticized me to another air force colonel, Corey Ford, who confided in me, though Corey was congenitally averse to gossip. In the editorial, Davenport found quotes from the British *Manchester Guardian* and from his good friend Wendell Willkie to support his previous suggestion that the United States was fighting not to maintain the empire, but for universal self-government. A picture story showed the United States landing on the Aleutian Adreanofs, leading a month later to the Japanese retirement from Attu and Agattu. The essay was a beautiful set of color pictures of steel production at Birmingham, Alabama. The conversion of a merchantman to an escort carrier with complement of a squadron of planes is seen. Another essay which caused a lot of trouble was on French Canada: "It is more foreign to Americans than is France, for it is essentially foreign also to the 20th Century. . . . Now its youth admires the France of Pétain. . . . The French Canadians are among the nicest people in the world, sweet-tempered and amiable, virtuous, frugal, industrious and honest, very sociable and hospitable." But it is pointed out that the Catholic Church runs Quebec, and Rome is part of the Axis. The Cardinal speaks of "the wild, lying, atheistic democracy which reigns today in almost all the countries of the world" but opposes Hitler, whereas the lower clergy oppose the war.

The above is a fair prototype of my journalism, whose "secret" (which eluded Luce) is scandalously obvious. It is simply to tell the truth, discarding any doctrine, such as that all fifth columns (or all empires) are evil. The test is that, on the given facts, the subject's behavior is natural and, by his lights, virtuous. On the facts, Quebec had to oppose the war. The *Canadiens* were a nice, charming, sweet-tempered, virtuous, hospitable fifth column, but fifth column they were. Today America has fifth columns with less justification and they may even be as sweet-tempered and virtuous as the *Canadiens* in 1942. Such facts are the real stuff of life. Instead, Luce floundered around with principles, incessantly trying to define them more sharply, and convincing some people, including Jack Jessup, that he was principled. I am more inclined to confuse any doctrinaire whosoever with the devil. My journalism was calculated not to accumulate power but to lose it; the innocent readers believed in it.

My piece "Armies That Win" gets a letter (October 26, 1942) from an army instructor who gives it as a reader's reference "for the first three lectures on military tactics," which was just about its scope. The English M.P. and news analyst Vernon Bartlett submits an answer to "*Life*'s Open Letter to the English People" with a sound point: "Ours is the only country among the United Nations that has taken up arms without being first attacked." The editor (Luce) replied: "The paramount task . . . is to evolve a greater world-states-manship." The present state of the world may be ascribed to an application of this "greater world-statesmanship," whatever was meant. The lead reported lowering the draft age to 18, a flood of young volunteers, and the vital statistics on manpower allocations, including 9 million for the armed forces by the end of 1943. The editorial is bent chiefly on placating the English and goading the Americans. The Japanese counterattack on Guadalcanal, driving off U.S. ships and sinking three cruisers, was reported. A story about a crime wave among children, especially in the 10–13 age group, was headed: "Experience Shows That Punishment Doesn't Pay." It sounds very contemporary. The Germans had produced pictures of the convoy route to Murmansk, where not one ship was in the harbor. In accord with a point made earlier in *Life*, the United States was shown specializing in "tank destroyers." Luce's admiration for Roosevelt's power was expressed in "The Roosevelt Party," a portfolio of 42 of its members. And the expression "They Were Expendable" is coined by William L. White in an excerpt from his book on the MTB squadrons (better known as PT boats) in the Philippines. The success of the book was based on America's desperate need for heroes. The excerpt said that Lieutenant John Bulkeley, squadron commander, was "a national hero for his part in bringing MacArthur out of Bataan." This story is due for a little correction. Admiral Hart had ruled that officers could not have two positions; thus Bulkeley as commander could not command a PT boat. The boat he chose to ride in was Ensign George Cox's No. 41, because Cox always had it in working condition. Thus it was Cox, not Bulkeley, who took out Philippine President Manuel Quezon to a submarine, and took out MacArthur and his family (but, contrary to the shameful story, no wicker furniture of MacArthur's) to Mindanao, whence MacArthur flew out the PT officers. MacArthur, not a naval man, is credited with building up the PT squadrons before the Japanese attack. The plot of "They Were Expendable" is based on a rumor that a great American offensive was imminent in that spring of 1942. A betrayal is heavily implied. The book is pure nonsense. But the expression magically lingers on. Unanimously, the PT men believed that John F. Kennedy's supposed heroic exploit later on should have won him a court martial instead of beatification. These would include Bulkeley, Kelley, Akers, and Cox, in private, but with no attribution. Not many have survived, whether or not they were "expendable."

Somewhat supporting my position, the mail poured in (November 2, 1942) ridiculing the "principles" of the "Open Letter to the English People." Said one, "Matter of fact, what's the matter with the British Empire?" The matter was that the famished people of India, still famished under their own rulers, made their well-fed British rulers look wicked by too close juxtaposition. In wanting to govern, Gandhi and Nehru made themselves identical with the British, with the plus that they were of the same race as the governed, and the minus that they had not shown they could govern. Gandhi had the great virtue of looking as if he had malnutrition but, remember, he was a South African lawyer for the Hindu community. Davenport and Luce, in short, were bulling into something they did not understand, and we have seen the sequel. The lead examined the approaching elections as slightly favoring the Republicans. The editorial is given over to a magnificent speech to the House of Commons by South Africa's Prime Minister Jan Smuts: "The people of this island are the real heroes of this epic, worldwide drama." Another set of heroes was celebrated in a spread on the battle for Stalingrad, mostly in German pictures, with a good airview of the city. A short piece gives the origins of the songs "Praise the Lord, and Pass the Ammunition" and "Der Führer's Face." John Hersey contributes a straightforward record of the agony of nine airmen in a liferaft in the South Pacific for seven days. The launching of one of the new immense American battleships was shown. An interesting ridicule of governmental "principles" is provided by Gerald Johnson's text piece that only the American people (not Roosevelt or Luce) can win the war or resolve the peace. Speaking of the past, "What we did not know, or chose to ignore, is that power is never acquired without the simultaneous acquirement of a commensurate responsibility." He points out that Wilson merely wanted to make the world "safe" for democracy, not subservient to it, a highly sensible and conservative desire. He was as skeptical as I about turning India over to Gandhi. As for postwar use of power, much of present American policy is justified by this excellent piece, which is far from Luce's kind of thinking.

This latter deserves a word. Loyal employees were expected to say that nobody understood Luce, or that not even Luce understood Luce. Why? For the idea is ridiculous. It has a simple explanation. Luce's two favorite subjects were business and religion, with the former in the lead—that is, he obeyed both Caesar and God, in that order. All his worrying of principle was intended to deceive himself on this score, to keep his father's legacy of idealism nominally intact. He wanted power on highminded terms, and Davenport's editorials were a perfect cover for this design. Luce's poor grasp of current history is understandable if we realize that he was torn by an inner conflict which had nothing to do with it. Neither pull in his strange conflict had any status with me.

The Letters section (November 9, 1942) includes two letters protesting the French Quebec story and one from a *Canadien*, calling it the "most understanding, accurate and true report I have ever read." The lead was the renewed battle for the Solomons, featured by an impressive Bel Geddes model of Guadalcanal and environs. John Hersey has a perceptive description of the U.S. marines doing the fighting. The editorial suggests that American boys at the front are at last teaching America what war is. What war isn't was illustrated by the "Picture of the Week" where one horse, Whirlaway, ran out the course of the Pimlico Special alone because the other horses had withdrawn. There is a story on mountain troops, which Underhill had always emphasized as a great asset of the German army. Pierre Laval was shown sending French workers to Germany in exchange for French prisoners (3 for 1). The French did not like it. Estimated number of non-German workers in Germany: 6 million. The text piece is on "Ike" Eisenhower, first raising the question of whether he was born in Kansas or Texas. All the brothers were once called Ike. Lincoln Barnett rates the ultimate Ike as very intelligent, sociable, and amiable—a fair appraisal.

In this issue is an instance of the fog of war as it affects the contemporary journalist. Of the fighting in Egypt we said, " 'Destroy Rommel and his army,' Montgomery had told his officers," and American planes "wreck Rommel's long supply lines." What we, and perhaps even Montgomery, did not know was that Rommel was not there. He had gone home with a case of jaundice. Thoma was in command. Nor was the proper name, El Alamein, given to this historic battle. Thoma was soon captured, and Rommel was back.

The next Letters section (November 16, 1942) corrected *Life* on misnaming in "They Were Expendable" a picture of George Cox. I don't think I mentioned that I knew George, but now that was not my part of the war. The lead proclaimed, "The USA Goes Republican," though not to the extent of getting majorities in either House, but at least of putting Clare Luce into the Congress from Connecticut, with a charming picture. The editorial agreed that this was a good thing for democracy and the war effort; Luce's euphoria can be detected. The great gamble of the invasion of North Africa, in the teeth of the ambivalent Frenchmen on hand, is first mentioned in a story using pictures of Montgomery's war in the desert, and bracketed with the marines' fight on Guadalcanal, illustrated by the returned wounded. But what could a picture magazine without pictures do? The relevant essay is on the techniques of amphibious war and another story, perhaps in parallel, tells how Mrs. Roosevelt sweeps through England. John Field, not a literary artist, describes the death of the carrier *Yorktown* in a way more moving than John Hersey's account of the airmen.

The invasion of North Africa had fallen on November 8, just barely in time to get mentioned in *Life*. But a week later it was the full-dress lead (November 23, 1942) with radio pictures, maps, a Bel Geddes model, and a cast of personalities. Some French officers had fought the Americans; Darlan had surrendered as Vichy vice premier; Mark Clark was Eisenhower's field commander; Patton landed in Rabat and honored Marshal Lyautey's statue on Armistice Day. "What this does to control of the Mediterranean," I wrote jubilantly, "is as cheerful as a sunrise. . . . (1) it enormously simplifies the war for the United Nations; and (2) it enormously complicates it for Hitler. The complications for Hitler come thick and fast. He had to occupy France with more troops. His Italian ally grew shaky. His Spanish half-ally grew cold. . . . Watchful Turkey grew colder. The food resources of Africa were lost to Europe. . . . The United Nations divisions, holding the Mediterranean, could concentrate, and their supply lines were cut to one-third. Hitler's air power was thrust back and the United Nations got air bases closer to Axis Europe." However, Eisenhower was quoted, "I do not regard this as any great victory. . . . The Argonne and Chateau-Thierry of World War II are yet to come." It must have been a problem to separate the "American" war from the "foreign" war. I did not write it all. The Bel Geddes model of the terrain was wildly erroneous cartography. For example, Mount Etna was omitted but *Life* consultant Richard Harrison reinstalled it before the photograph was taken.

The issue starts with letters applauding Gerald Johnson's piece, and a "Speaking of Pictures" unconsciously satirized the current American emotion with pictures of Hollywood Axis villains, deploring the shortage of Japanese actors and the reluctance of Chinese to play Japanese. The editorial wrestles manfully with overoptimism, but obviously Davenport felt fine. The less spectacular war by Australians in New Guinea was seen in movie stills. A long essay, partly in color, on "The Puritan Spirit" correlated God, work, and power, as Luce must have asked. John Hersey contributes an eyewitness story of an action on Guadalcanal which proves mainly that real war is not his métier.

A wonderful letter opens the next (November 30, 1942) issue: "I have a lot to atone for; my generation and your generation has a lot to be ashamed of. It is through our stupidity, selfishness and greed that we have this worldwide mess . . . and we are asking the younger generation to go out and die by the millions for our stupidity. This to me is unendurable. As if this responsibility were not enough, many of the people with whom I come in contact are more concerned with how much money they are going to make." He quotes some shameful fellow Americans. Though a successful businessman past forty, he had enlisted. The lead bracketed three American victories: the naval battle in the Solomons (with Bel Geddes models, based on guesswork), New Guinea land fighting, and the amphibious invasion of North Africa. The editorial spoke up for the political war and peace and echoed Gerald Johnson's piece. An unexpected dividend of the North African invasion was the relief of Malta from bombing (one last time). The essay on air transport oddly lifts, without credit, Bucky Fuller's ideas of transpolar transport with towed gliders, proposed in our post–Pearl Harbor seminar on how to win the war. The story keeps repeating that none of this is new (symptom of a guilty conscience). Even Fuller's idea of using the fuselages as workshops is plagiarized. The drawings used had been made for Paxton at the time of the first conference. I am told that the acting managing editor for this issue was not Billings, an honorable man, but Joe Thorndike, as an interim editor. This exhibits a clawing for success that does more than border on dishonor. Later, Fuller asked me for a letter confirming that the ideas in the story were his.

Dear Bucky:

I have just seen the issue of the German magazine *Wehrmacht* that reprints in full *Life*'s Nov. 30, 1942, story on "Air Transport."

I very nearly wrote you when the story first came out to tell you how completely it was based on your ideas and suggestions, specific and general. I am writing now belatedly to do so. I think it was in October 1941 that you met at my house with Paxton and Underhill of our force and outlined in detail the reinforcement of Russia by air routes over Alaska and Greenland, the use of vastly bigger freight planes drawing four plastic plywood gliders each. You proposed that these gliders could be mass-produced cylindrically, taken one way and re-used as shelter units in the U.S.S.R. You also suggested that the wings would make roof trusses for the assembly plants at the delivery end.

At that time we were thinking of a *Life* story on all this, but then came Pearl Harbor and the security factor came in, or so we thought. However, so sympathetic have we all been toward your ideas that when the story finally ran, I was disturbed to notice that we had not even used your name. My guess is that you were only delighted to get these sound ideas into the stream of national thinking. You may be sure, however, that we all know where our ideas came from.

Actually, I think most of these ideas are up to 15 years old in your writings: "Nine Chains to the Moon," etc. You must chortle as you see these "visionary" notions one by one turn into perfectly orthodox thinking!

My best regards to you and your family.

Yours, DAVID CORT

I never disliked Thorndike, but his cold calm obsessed devotion to self-interest amused me since it was so patent. Through him, however, Time Inc. had resorted to naked visible dishonor, and I find the fact significant for the inner dynamic of the organization. Something was happening, and it is interesting that the immediate agent was Joe Thorndike. I should have noticed (but did not) that Joe was another of the power boys. The evidence was plain enough. I got only as far as amusement and concern for Buckminster Fuller. What the hell! I still had a war to win. Ha-ha. Joe Thorndike was not my problem. He had been a colleague of my youngest brother at Harvard. Another brother had been an associate of Nelson Rockefeller at Dartmouth, another of Winthrop Rockefeller at Loomis and Yale (and rather liked him), and another at Princeton of various celebrities. My family does not exploit its connections. We have no understanding of power.

To return to the November 30, 1942, issue, an admirable piece on "Old Blood and Guts" George Patton is contributed by John Field. Patton's first reason for fighting, before patriotism, was "desire for glory." "You can defend a position with patriots," said Patton, "but you can't take a position with them. I am not interested in defense." Field's career was not to be in writing but one would not have known it from this splendid piece.

My letter to Bucky Fuller may indicate that I did not feel an unthinking loyalty to everybody at Time Inc. This was evidenced in a more flagrant way around this time. I was in the night clubs most evenings and formed some friendships, among them Mario Tossati, manager of several Latin night clubs. Finally Mario, backed by George Raft, got financing for his own night club and asked me for a South Seas–type name. I came up with several, including The Hurricane, which he adopted. What about decorations? I asked *Life*'s picture department to ask the services for all illustrations of South Pacific scenery. I gave Mario a selection, which he had blown up for murals, and these were the decor of The Hurricane. I returned the pictures to the picture department without explanation. Mario got into· trouble with the government and I put in a word for him with the local U.S. attorney, my college classmate, with the result that the official, John Cahill, stopped speaking to me. He revised his attitude a decade or so later. By my code, however, it was taboo to use influence to get anybody into *Life*, and I never tried.

I must refer to George Patton's philosophy, noting that the desire for glory is the obverse of the desire for power. The one who wants glory is ready for any sacrifice, even death; the one who wants power knows he must remain alive. Glory is given to the producer, power to the businessman. A few maniacs have wanted both—Alexander, Napoleon, Hitler, Mussolini, not Washington, not perhaps Lenin or Stalin—and in a way Luce, not a maniac, did. At an upper echelon, mankind can be divided in this way; for at the lower level most men have no option on power, while nearly everybody has the option on glory, even if only to live decently. Glory may thus be defined as, in Jefferson's expression, the aristocracy of virtue and talent; power is the desire to subvert virtue and talent to one's own ends. This book is a case history of glory versus power. Patton's slapping of the self-pitying soldier was an expression of a fixation on glory. The soldier was every abomination that destroys a society; his sobs were his power. A society that prefers the soldier to Patton is in trouble and the society, in the voice of Eisenhower, did. This choice is again before us today. The neurotic sobs arise on every side, and the society cowers before them. Even so, the virtue and talent submitted itself to Luce's desire for power, very plausibly masked as virtue. The soldier's virtue was equally plausible and false. The glory lay with Patton, the brave man, the producer of victory. Eisenhower was the ignominious executive, who intended to survive, and did. A hundred years from now Eisenhower will be remembered; a thousand years, Patton.

My letter to Fuller was belated, but my outrage was not. For I find a copy of a letter to *Life*'s Letters column at the time:

Sirs:

May I congratulate *Life* on going out whole-hog on the ideas of R. Buckminster Fuller, so long neglected. The story on "Air Transport" in the Nov. 30 issue is jam-packed with Fuller ideas, which *Life* presents as all quite new. Actually they are from 15 years old to one year old in Fuller's works.

The idea of transport planes flying across the Pole appeared in Fuller's 1927 book *Time-Lock*. The polar projection in *Life*, now becoming more and more popular, is an adaptation from his 1934 projection of the 'one-world island' used in his 1938 book, *Nine Chains to the Moon*.

The letter goes on to say much the same as I wrote Fuller a year later, concluding,

My further thought, however, is that you have here at last a perfect proof that abstract calculation can and does forecast the shape of things to come. *Life*'s championing of these good causes is most gratifying, but I feel that this is not the hour to overlook the name of the author.

David Cort

Life did not print this letter, but it may have wafted to Joe Thorndike a suspicion that I thought he was a skunk. No man likes his most precious secrets to leak out.

"The Allies were singing on their way to the fronts," sang the lead (December 7, 1942) on the Allies' "world offensive." Total German dead were estimated at 1,750,000. "Brigaded with 'blooded' British veterans of Dunkirk, the cream of the British Army, green American troops were now exposed to savage and expert bombing and a shrewd and nimble antagonist . . . [in North Africa]. . . . The 100-day battle of Stalingrad will take its place in history beside the battles of Zama, Tours, Waterloo and Gettysburg." The editorial took this up with the theme that in the year since Pearl Harbor the United States had become "almost like a different country." The terrible fire at the Cocoanut Grove night club in Boston provided some grim pictures of the 492 dead. Anne White tells me that she had accepted a job to sing in the lounge there just before the fire, but at the last minute went to work instead for the Club 18 in New York. She knew Alpert, the Grove's bandleader, who escaped out the window behind the band shell. Rather insensitively, the issue also showed the beautiful girls at the Copacabana, a New York night club I often patronized. Torpedo bombers were presented (correctly) as the deadliest weapon against ships.

A short piece on the complete crackup of Italian fascism opened the issue (December 14, 1942). At last, the appalling pictures of Pearl Harbor are released for the lead. Since all the battleships except the *Arizona* had been towed to the west coast and repaired, it was possible to reveal that the *Oklahoma, California, Nevada,* and *West Virginia* had been put out of commission. Black smoke dominates most of the pictures. The editorial, after a glowing tribute to the Russians, asks the open-eyed question: "Whose peace table will it be?" The fifth of six sea-air battles in the Solomons was shown as a drawing. An essay is given to the U.S. Coast Guard and its volunteer auxiliaries. The mysterious subject of "Jap Pacific Bases" is investigated. A picture of a peak is captioned "God knows which this is." An artist's drawings are used to show how to destroy enemy tanks; the set was presented to the army for instructional use.

Conceivably a reaction to *Life*'s manpower story, Roosevelt put all U.S. manpower under Paul McNutt of the War Manpower Commission. This was the lead (December 21, 1942). Another Bel Geddes model introduced the fact that the Germans were beating the Allies in Tunisia, to the shock of the American public. The new Pentagon is shown for the first time with Secretary of War Stimson's palatial suite. The essay, "The Aftermath of War," exposes the debris, including the cemeteries of North Africa, with the comment, "Victorious armies do not leave many graves. Defeated armies fill the subsoil and the prison camps." Joe Thorndike contributes a text piece on "Geopolitics." A map is included, "based on an orthographic projection by Richard Edes Harrison which will appear in the January issue of *Fortune.*" It strikes me as geographically unsophisticated but makes some beautiful points: "The U.S. has been a super-state, by geopolitical standards, for many generations. Russia, which has long had the space for a superstate, is just now organizing its inheritance. China looms up as the dominant power of Asia. . . . True disciples of Mackinder (the English inventor of geopolitics) will wonder whether, over the years, the Heartland powers—Russia and China—will not rival Anglo-America." Only a man devoid of feelings could have arrived at these correct predictions of the future. (At this time, China was virtually supine.) His primary source on geopolitics was one Eric Archdeacon, described incorrectly as an English banker. This was a highly dubious character who advised Thorndike to ignore a book on geopolitics, *Generals and Geographers*, by Hans W. Weigert, on the grounds that Weigert was "under suspicion," because his wife was the daughter of the official Nazi publisher in Nürnberg. Naïvely or not, he was wrong two ways. First, he was talking about another Hans Weigert, in the U.S. State Department. Second, this latter one's wife was indeed the daughter of a Nazi publisher, but she herself was anti-Nazi. Finally, Archdeacon was not exactly "an English banker." He had fought in the German navy at Jutland. When he applied for British citizenship after the First War, he was snubbed. He tried the United States instead, married a solvent wife, and got U.S. citizenship. He worked in the Berlin office of a U.S. bank.

The details are given to indicate Thorndike's incompetence at picking good sources, for he sold this one to Luce, and Archdeacon was one of three speakers at a Luce dinner for opinion makers in 1946.

In that period any "Englishman" in America had to be examined narrowly. I fell in socially with a set of intelligence people, including an Australian, an Englishman married to an American I had long disliked, and several caddish Americans. I puzzled over their interest in me and disgustedly dropped them. Their prize was the violinist Nathan Millstein.

The lead (December 28, 1942) is a piece by South Africa's Prime Minister and Field Marshal Jan Christiaan Smuts, saying that "the emancipation of India without internal disruption is today perhaps the greatest prize in the world." (The disruption is a terrible fact of modern history.) The editorial developed the idea that "there are no atheists in foxholes." Naturally, the essay consisted of pictures celebrating Jesus Christ's birth (a poor display, in my opinion). Incredibly, John Foster Dulles has a think-piece. This was a godly effort, saying that England, France, and the United States dominated the world not by wealth but because they "radiated great faiths." The world wars, he thought, "may go down in history as a series of rear-guard actions by disillusioned peoples who, equipped only with the material products of past greatness, sought valiantly but vainly to resist the penetration of alien faiths" (meaning communism). This is a dedicated Christian sermon and undoubtedly influenced Eisenhower later. A first-hand account is given of the preinvasion meeting of General Mark Clark with the North African French, making Clark look something like John Hersey, as in fact he did, but a terrible thing to do to a fighting man. These liberal officers might have destroyed America, except for the fortunate arrival of the Halseys and the Pattons, in numbers, who felt no humane benevolence at all, who did not feel that this was the time to "love thine enemy." Mark Clark was a fool, and what America did not need was a high-minded liberal fool. It needed assassins.

That these existed in Russia was the burden of the lead (January 4, 1943) on the Russian front. On the battle of Stalingrad, a Russian general was quoted, "I honestly have never seen anything comparable to that. I would not have believed such an inferno could open up on earth. Men died but they did not retreat." The editorial keened that the half-rationed home front was not worthy of the fighting men. The text piece was on high-casualty fighting in New Guinea, from trenches and pillboxes. A useful story showed dangerous tropical creatures such as scorpions and snakes. The closeup was on Jimmy Byrnes who had quit the Supreme Court to become Roosevelt's "assistant president" in complete charge of the home front.

A second war ration book covering canned goods took the lead (January 11, 1943). The editorial used an army corporal's letter to predict that foreign policy must take precedence over domestic policy after the war. Another story is given to Gibraltar, a *Life* obsession. A few precepts on how to behave with Moslems in North Africa are given. Walter Graebner contributes an admiring report on the Russians—very perceptive, worth rereading today.

The meeting of the new (78th) Congress made the lead (January 18, 1943). The editorial tore apart a State Department White Paper trying to justify American policy since 1931—"a tale of horrors"—as in fact it was. A very tentative story on the Tunisian war surprisingly says that "the courage of the ill-armed French amazed both British and Americans." An interesting historical note is provided by a story that a Chinese military mission had been snubbed for nine months in Washington: "The theory behind ignoring Hsiung has been that this is an Anglo-American war for the present. Since Russia does not want to sit in on Anglo-American strategy now because of its neutrality toward Japan, it is not considered polite to Russia to let China sit in either. This is obviously nonsense."

The adventure of Eddie Rickenbacker, on a raft in the Pacific for 21 days, made the lead (January 25, 1943), with two more installments to come. The editorial noted a new American spirit of sober confidence, supported by public acceptance of the government's ban on all pleasure driving. (I can't remember being faintly inconvenienced by this supposedly enormous sacrifice.) A few pictures of air war in the South Pacific are released. *Life*'s intermittent Roll of Honor now included General Robert Eichelberger, Roy Larsen's kinsman whom I had met at West Point. A spread of night club soothsayers includes the Copacabana palmist who had given the identical reading to four different ladies I had brought. I think this story was written by George Frazier, though he is not in the masthead. I told Billings the palmist was a fake. (Another soothsayer predicted Hitler's suicide.) The journalism was in another lull, if the war was not.

General Giraud, high commissioner of French North Africa, opens the next issue (February 1, 1943) by accusing France of a fatal decadence between wars. The grim soldiers on Guadalcanal (relieving the marines) are seen attacking a Japanese-held hill, in the impressive pictures of Ralph Morse. The editorial, however, thought the key to victory was the battle of the North Atlantic, and criticized the navy's miscalculation of it. A U.S. propaganda movie, *Hitler's Children*, is synopsized. The essay is on the Aberdeen, Maryland, Ordnance Proving Ground. The nightly dimout of New York City makes an eerie display, and of this too I have no recollection, though I was out on the town nearly every night.

Illustrations from a book on the Battle of Britain made the "Speaking of Pictures" (February 8, 1943) showing September 7, 1940, when there were "nine 'conflagrations' (the technical name for a fire area so large that several hundred pumps are required to bring it under control), nineteen 30-pump fires, forty ten-pump fires and a thousand other fires." The lead opens with the incredible, now forgotten sight of President Roosevelt in a jeep outside Casablanca, the first American president to leave America in wartime and the first to use an airplane to do so. Roosevelt, shown with Churchill in conference, saw to it that Giraud and de Gaulle shook hands—no kissing. The faces of all the high command at Casablanca were shown: 24 in all. The editorial noted that Stalin had declined an invitation to Casablanca and that even in America the war had arrived at "the mood of total and unforgiving war" or "grim death." We were facing death squarely in the Time-Life Building. I should have been terrified, but I did not read this bravado. Submarine pictures of Japanese ship sinkings are shown. Montgomery is seen taking the surrender of Tripoli, the last of the Italian Empire, after a three-month advance using mostly American trucks. The story is told of American airplane spotters, awaiting Nazi raids that never came.

General Eichelberger appears again in the lead (February 15, 1943), commanding troops in New Guinea; the photographer is George Strock. The story notes "three brave Japs who preferred death to escape or surrender" and are shown dead. Instead of an editorial, there was an extended piece on how America could "lose" (in quotes) the war, based mostly on a Russo-German armistice.

The readers interpreted General Giraud's indictment of France (with which I substantially agreed) as an outright confession of fascism (February 22, 1943), but two took it as a timely warning to America, whose decadence was to be delayed another thirty years. The navy's best war shots, some magnificent, most already used by *Life*, make the "Speaking of Pictures." The lead showed the Washington antagonists in eleven conflicts in the war effort. The editorial, hymning the American dead on New Guinea, pleads that Americans be permitted to look at their pictures. The surrender at Stalingrad of five Axis generals and 230,000 troops is shown: "The face of the German Army in Russia now appears frozen, dazed, exhausted of will or pride." Roosevelt congratulated Stalin on the "epic battle for the city which has forever honored your name." A splendid airview shows the Japanese-held base of Rabaul under attack by American bombers. The essay shows the Japanese booty captured at Buna.

The masthead was revolutionized (March 1, 1943) demoting me from the leadoff associate editor spot by listing senior editors alphabetically, thus: Noel F. Busch, Roger Butterfield, David Cort, Joseph Kastner, Joseph J. Thorndike. This had dropped Maria Sermolino, Edward K. Thompson (who was in the armed services), Dorothy Hoover, Walter Graebner. The chief editorial writer is at last identified as Russell Davenport. The people in the service were dropped (but Mr. and Mrs. Mydans in prison camp were listed) and all photographers grouped under "Staff Photographers": Bart Sheridan and John Morris (assistant picture editors), Myron Davis, Alfred Eisenstaedt, Eliot Elisofon, J. R. Eyerman, Marie Hansen, Bernard Hoffman, Robert Landry, Thomas McAvoy, Hansel Mieth, Ralph Morse, Carl Mydans, John Phillips, Hart Preston, George Rodger, David Scherman, Frank Scherschel, William Shrout, Peter Stackpole, George Strock, William Vandivert, and Hans Wild. Associate Editors (new): Lincoln Barnett, Don Burke (promoted), John Field (promoted), Richard Lauterbach (promoted), Gerard Piel (promoted), Maria Sermolino, Margit Varga (promoted), and Richard Wilcox (promoted). Assistant Associate Editors: Peter S. Cardozo, George Frazier, Lisbeth de Morinni, Dennis Flanagan, John Purcell, Jean Speiser, Philip Wootton, Jr.; Rachel Albertson (who was Walter Lippmann's ex-sister-in-law and drank) seems to have disappeared. Senior Researchers: Bernice Shrifte (chief), Margaret Bassett, Mireille Gaulin, Suzanne Hammond, Elizabeth Kelly, Elaine Keiffer, Dorothy Larson, Helen Morgan, Lilian Rixey, Shelley Smith, Marion Stevens, and Lura Street. Helen Robinson has disappeared (she married a friend of mine, Horace Coon). Researchers: Ruth Adams, Marion Bradley (Billings' secretary), Earl Brown (the brilliant Negro consultant), M. E. Crockett (London), Kay Doering, Gertrude Epstein, Shirley Herzig, Caroline Iverson, Jacque Lansdale, Jeanne Perkins, Katharine Scherman, Dorothy Sterling, and A. B. C. Whipple (Chicago). The Picture Bureau is listed: Dorothy Hoover (chief), Mary Carr, Alice Crocker, O. A. Graubner, Natalie Kosek, John C. Manthorp, Maude Milar, Gladys Shramek, Margaret Smith.

(My favorites were Hoover, Carr, Kosek.) The layout department was noticed with only Charlie Tudor and Mike Phillips. Disappearances were Diane Cummings, Michael Drury (later a distinguished writer), John Thorne, Mary Welsh. Some others had gone into the listed News Bureaus, including Helen Robinson. The total editorial staff came to just 100. The policy was to break in new researchers by assigning them to me. I remember as such Gaulin, Street, Doering (who went into the army), and Perkins. Incredibly, the great Bourke-White is nowhere in the masthead, and so the lead in this very issue is "*Life*'s Bourke-White Goes Bombing," with fine airviews. However, the writer seems to have misread the map. A Bel Geddes model of Tunisia illustrated the first mention of the battle later known as Kasserine Pass, where Rommel threw back and first blooded the Americans. The editorial was another tribute to Madame Chiang, quoting her address to the U.S. House of Representatives. A Nehru greeting to the Chiangs is quoted with the comment: "Nehru is as untypical of India as are other leaders of the Congress Party. He is of a Brahmin family and was educated at Harrow and Cambridge. More sincere than Gandhi, he is intellectual, quick to tears, unostentatious and lonely." The arrival of the French battleship *Richelieu* at the Brooklyn Navy Yard is seen. And here comes the climax of a long campaign by Paxton and myself to get Billings to use Buckminster Fuller's "dymaxion map"—a map that could be folded by the reader into a fourteen-faced globe. The Americans on Guadalcanal are shown shaved, bathed, and grinning after the last Japanese have left the island. Some of Richard Tregaskis' *Guadalcanal Diary* is excerpted.

The twentieth anniversary of Time Inc. was approaching and a huge dinner at the Waldorf-Astoria for nearly 1,000 employees as of March 11, 1943, was planned. A booklet shows the first editorial staff: Gottfried, John Martin, T. J. C. Martyn, Niven Busch, Hadden, not Luce. A page of drawings is included of 158 supposedly key personnel in 1943. The table seating at the dinner is mysterious. I was at a table with five ladies and two gentlemen I had never met. The power-sensitive might figure I had no prestige. But Dan Longwell was at table 104, on the balcony. Hubie Kay was at table 9, it is true, but with uneminent companions. Billings and Goldsborough were not present at all. I feel now, though I did not then, that my monopoly on the war was eroded by the fact that, for Americans, it had in part ceased to be "foreign news." Guadalcanal was only 50 percent "foreign news," but for Americans not foreign news at all. I think there was another journalistic, not fighting, lull in the war. The action was to be piecemeal, in Sicily and Italy, and in the South Pacific, until the massive climax of D-Day, while the Russians wallowed in slaughter, screaming for the second front which the Americans were mounting "with all deliberate speed." I was content with development of the war and felt sure that neither Germany nor Japan could win. Earlier, I had told my colleagues that if one German panzer division could be landed on the American continent, we were defeated. This was true, but that day had long since passed. The oceans had given us the time to save ourselves. As for atomic warfare, today, the oceans are no longer there. But this too is a false prophecy: the infantry is still the queen of battles. Man with his weapons will always be superior to the weapons alone. Men will decide the sequel even of atomic war.

Ironically, at this dinner Luce made a speech. "We insist upon . . . seemingly irreconcilable virtues. . . . We require . . . many people who are more or less temperamental. . . . But then at the same time we need an awful lot of just plain sanity—efficient, methodical and reliable people—fortunately we have more of them than of the temperamentalists. But the point is that we absolutely need both—and both these kinds of people need to work in close harness with each other." He then compared Time Inc. to the university in that "we seek to serve Truth" and to a business organization where there is "strict accountability." He thus defined the gap between the producers and the executives, between the seekers of glory and the seekers of power. Since his bent and talent were for the latter, he was deciding that he did not need the former, with all their insurrections and unpredictabilities. He was beginning to think he did not need the people who really spoke to the people, who were believed because they were not interested in Luce's doctrines but who were helplessly honest and wrote only what they felt to be true. Luce did not understand that the corporation's real asset was not his executives' efficiency but his writers' credibility. The great structure rested on that needle point, and he hadn't the wit to know it. Instead, he spoke of "temperament," misreading his own people. I, for example, was not remotely temperamental in my work—nor were the others, such as Busch and Kay. My self-discipline was far more rigid and continuous at work than Charlie Stillman's, except that I probably had more hangovers. What Luce was really saying was that we were occasionally a personnel problem, and that Stillman was not, and he was sliding toward the conviction that he could do without such problems. In this quite common delusion of the executive lay the ultimate destruction of Time Inc. and of many other institutions of the industrial world. Unfortunately, Luce died before there appeared on the wall, "Mene, mene, tekel, upharsin," but in this cheerful slaphappy speech he ordained that day. The slow implementing of the speech will be described in due course. The needle point did not break, it slowly bent and flattened. Luce counted, counted, weighed, and I and others will do the dividing. And Charlie Stillman, if he is alive, will go on counting and weighing, as he sinks out of our ken.

I blame Luce's sense of acquiring power partly on Davenport's editorial page, for Roosevelt had to accept Davenport as probably the voice of Wendell Willkie, a potential political threat, and he was right. Thus, Luce's apparent power was adventitious, based on Davenport's honesty and connections. Luce did not recognize the insubstantiality of this sort of power. Executives never do.

The ensuing period will require a more cursory analysis of *Life*. The editorial (March 8, 1943) called an 11-million-man military establishment not enough, the lead identified Puerto Rico's problem as the "unlimited fertility of the people," and the essay was on Sunday in America. The editorial (March 15, 1943) asked whether the home front people were "pigmies" or "giants," the lead criticized American tactics in North Africa (prompted by the army), the French fleet at Toulon was seen scuttled, and Noel Busch makes deadpan fun of a South African witch doctor. The editorial (March 22, 1943) says, "Everybody in the government has a foreign policy—his own."

The one important move was the Special Issue on the U.S.S.R. (March 29, 1943). For some reason, incomprehensible to me, the Russians had deferred cooperation because of some previous *Life* captions. The lead said that Lend-Lease aid to Russia had cost $1,825,600,000, showing some of it. The editorial brought out postwar dangers of Russia's playing a lone hand in the name of security (which came to pass). Next came "Peoples of the U.S.S.R."— 16 union republics assembled by "the race of Great Russians, a prolific, gregarious, talkative, aggressive and friendly mass of blond Slavs. . . . They will go anywhere and try anything. They were one hell of a people long before the revolution." Of the 175 peoples, 18 types were pictured. There is a life of Lenin, short summaries of the Red leaders, and a piece by Ambassador Joseph E. Davies which can be overlooked. The story of Russia's astronomical resources said that "here is the 20th Century's New World." Looking at it objectively, this century may prove to be the Russian, not the American, century, given the decadence of the new American avant-garde. A little known history of Russia says that "service to the state [as the] first duty of all men" was the rule first of the early grand dukes, reinstated by the Communists. Generally, the attitude was to forgive the Russians for whatever they were, without ignoring it.

The next issue relapsed into celebration (April 5, 1943) of a supposed food crisis, Gandhi (ending a fast), the death of the carrier *Wasp* (painted by *Life*'s "Artist War Correspondent" Tom Lea), Darryl F. Zanuck (involved in the Tunis campaign), Henry J. Kaiser (whose non-Hohenzollern "Empire" included ships, planes, engines, steel and magnesium and cement), and Irving Berlin (closeup by the egregious George Frazier).

The so-called "Spring Offensives" were the lead (April 12, 1943), meaning mostly bombings. A "greatest battle photo" was analyzed, pointing out its faked elements but not (since it was an official picture) saying so.

Oddly, *Life* publishes a purely humorous piece by Noel Busch (April 19, 1943) on the two Egyptians he had watched from his Cairo hotel window trying to pull down an old dead tree. The lead was on Fascist Spain which will "probably not be overthrown by the United

Nations after the war" (correct). The editorial pondered the mixed reaction to the Russian issue, including the Russians' (not the people's). The official Communist horror of truth was discreetly exposed, as was also the anti-Communist dogma, less discreetly. The editorial was essentially an apologia. It was Davenport, at his best and worst, sweeping up after Luce's ideological clutter. But I had been in no ideological confusion about the Russians: they "were one hell of a people long before the revolution." They had proved it again, man by man, in fighting the Germans. Russians had died only for Mother Russia. How much more vital for the human race for somebody to defend democracy, generation by generation! But the generations are decaying. Life, not to speak of death, is too much for the most recent. For to have a reason for living is requisite for having a reason for dying. And the Russians, but not the recent American youth, had it. Death of itself is not glorious (as by drugs, suicide, syphilis, brawling, crime) but death for an end may be glorious if the end is so.

The lessons of Tunisia and Rommel were the lead (April 26, 1943): "Of courage and brains and fighting rage, the Americans had all they needed. But it took action to get the trade of war out of the manuals and into their blood."

One letter writer (May 3, 1943) conveyed that he was smarter than *Life* because by that time the dubious "battle photo" had been confirmed as a training center picture. The lead showed Roosevelt touring the South which resented "the growing sharpness of the race equality issue which Southerners blame principally on Eleanor Roosevelt." The editorial correctly appraised the significance of the first of the international conferences on the postwar world held in America, but bungled several ways. A sound picture technique was used in an airview of a small Iowa town, labeling the homes of the families of boys "missing in action" at Kasserine Pass (23 of them). The essay told the truth about South Africa, which had at one time "teemed with spies and fifth columnists," until El Alamein told them the way things were going. But, under loyal Prime Minister Jan Smuts, "since then the fifth column has faded fast. . . . Toward natives the Boers have an ancient hostility and an iron policy of white supremacy. . . . These Boers were big, humorless, hospitable, stubborn, icy-eyed Calvinists, great fighters, hunters and arguers. . . . South Africa . . . is quite probably on the verge of its greatest era." But South Africa, like Quebec and Moscow, could not take the even-handed truth. Our South African correspondent, John Barkham, evidently under government pressure, wrote that the story was in error. This irritated me into the effort of compiling a detailed rebuttal. Most of the piece had derived from Barkham's own cables, the rest from a current book. This went only to Barkham, not to the South African government. He was under the gun. People who take a moral position on South Africa today might be reminded that South Africa and Israel are identical: they are outposts of Western civilization in backward societies. The black majority in the one is comparable to the Arab majority in the other, with any comparison rather favoring the Arabs over the blacks. Furthermore, when the Boers took over the territory, it had been denuded of human life by the Zulus under Chaka and Dingaans. The Zulu had "conquered" it to make it a vacuum. Historically, the Zulu has a poor moral case. And the Boers are "icy-eyed Calvinists."

Busch's playful piece on the two Egyptians brought letters (May 10, 1943), pointing out that all four accompanying pictures showed the shadows at the same angle, hence not spread over a whole day. Busch may have wanted to explain that photography is the easiest way to lie. For the most important person in the picture is not seen, and it is hoped that the reader will not realize he is there. It is the photographer who is not invisible to the subjects of the picture. Truth is not produced by any equation in which one factor is hidden. The lead told the grim story of John L. Lewis' coal strike in the middle of a war, and the U.S. government's takeover of the mines. Current exposures tell us that John L. Lewis was a Hitler agent. Maybe. But I am reluctant to accept such a story even about a Welsh maniac so fortunate as to be an American. The editorial told of more trouble: the Russian-Polish dispute over who killed the 10,000 Polish officers in the Katyn forest: a truly grim and undying mystery. On the joke level was Ambassador Davies' movie, *Mission to Moscow*, dismissed as a silly capitalist whitewash of Russia.

The coming surrender of the Germans in Tunisia was the lead (May 17, 1943), as the Americans, having proved themselves, began to relax. The editorial declared that America "has not yet begun to fight as a nation." The text piece explained "why an airplane flies," the answer being its shape and air action.

From the South African legation came a letter (May 23, 1943) protesting that despite "the great goodwill which one senses in this essay," South African blacks ("natives") led a life that "compares very favorably with that of the peasant class of many of the older European countries." The letter dramatizes the fact that I, as the writer, took a total risk of my power, and even my job, with every issue. But this was essential, in loyalty to the reader, who seemed to me more important than Billings or Luce. The lead was on "the battle of rubber," the editorial on inflation, the news the Tunisian surrender of 17 generals and 150,000 men, and the text another piece by Noel Busch, "The Fall of Tunis," told with splendid disdain which sounds almost real. Unlike his cousin John Martin, he seemed to regard war as a minor nuisance which had not attracted his attention. If only this remarkable family had continued to control Time Inc., the story would have been marvelously, unpredictably different. Perhaps not for the better.

The Japanese are reported (May 31, 1943) taking atrocious revenge on the Chinese who harbored Doolittle's bombers of Tokyo. A letter came in (June 7, 1943) corroborating my story of the brutal treatment given South African "natives," contradicting the South African legation and John Barkham. The stupid Nazi war on Russian civilians was shown in drawings. (Underhill had told me that if we ever invaded Russia, we would go in throwing candy and cigarettes to the people.) An oblique pro-British propaganda was the essay on "Literary England," undoubtedly fomented by Longwell—King Arthur's birthplace, Gray's churchyard, the lad's Shropshire, and so on.

A map of possible invasion routes (June 21, 1943) used 27 arrows, the smallest of which indicated the actual point of invasion a year later. A story on "Special Devices" (June 28, 1943) introduced Longwell's friend, now Commander Luis de Flores, who had

innovated various ingenious ways of training navy fliers. I began to
see that my doctrinaire rejection of de Flores may have been wrong.
A short piece on war souvenirs reminds me that I received one from a
former researcher, Kay Doering, from Italy. This was a red Nazi
armband with a swastika. I took my small son to what was then my
favorite restaurant (another sign of poor judgment) and gave the
armband to my son, who slid it up his arm. Another customer came
over to object; imperially, I ordered him away; the restaurant owner
took her son, sitting with us, away from the table. The threat was that
the cops were coming. My son asked me whether that was so. I said,
"Certainly not." "Daddy, here come the cops," said my son. One cop
took me into the washroom where I explained who I was, who had
sent me the "war souvenir," that my brother was an air force
lieutenant in Persia, my uncle a U.S. brigadier general in the Pacific,
and that only the winning side had "war souvenirs," such as swastika
armbands. Sometime later, however, a detective came to my office at
Life to investigate how I had obtained the swastika, since Mayor La
Guardia had some hysterical ideas about a swastika factory in New
York. In the restaurant, I do not think I lost face with my son. The
proprietors, with whom I spent $35,000 in seven years, later earned
my total contempt and disastrously influenced my opinion of my
fellow man, when a dollar is at terrible stake. But before that
happened, Time Inc. showed itself equally ungrateful and this should
have prepared me for the treachery. To lose faith in one's fellow
man, with reason, is an injury that can never be forgiven and is better
not forgotten. These would be great sins, neither of which I have
committed. I am obliged to report that disaster pursued the
restaurant proprietors and Time Inc., but for very different reasons.

Luce frequently said, "We get credit with that story." This
reveals that a strange perversion had taken hold in him. His father
had brought him up to do good; nominally, he still believed in this.
But he had discovered, perhaps through the alchemy of pictures, that
it was more profitable to *look* good than to *do* good. The virile
concept of Hadden to tell the truth as quickly as possible had been
slowly perverted by Luce, transvested perhaps, into the feminine
concept of the image, though Luce was entirely masculine, except for

his interest in power. The hard virile concept of Hadden was dying, without my noticing the fact, and Longwell's image mania was taking over.

The victory of the image over reality has taken over the United States in the intervening period. We elect presidents as images rather than as realities. Dewey was a most capable man (I voted against him) but he had a poor image. Willkie was a capable man (I voted against him). The young today are trying to be images with long hair, face hair, picturesque costume, and a life style conceived as theatre rather than function—they are not trying to *be*, they are trying to *seem*. The best way to seem is in a mob, and this is also the worst way to be.

Luce's striving for a huge circulation was that same lust for the mob.

I did not understand that any such process was going on. The truth and the reader were all I cared about. I did not care whether we offended some people—as in the stories on Quebec, Russia, and South Africa, and many more. I suspect that I set the tone for the writers, who would in any case have preferred the way of the truth. There were exceptions, mostly late-comers, such as George Frazier. For Time Inc. had been—and was still for a little while longer—an Eden for honest men. One such, I believe, was John Billings. As long as a great war was going on, the final corruption of Time Inc. could not take place.

The 12,987 Americans so far killed in action were listed (July 5, 1943). The invasion of Sicily (July 26, 1943) was noted, with Patton "jumping into the surf and leading his troops to victory." The rivalry of Patton and Montgomery was not even suggested. Mediocrity was beginning to appear. The heroic defense of the beachhead (August 2, 1943) by the First Division and the Rangers against German tank counterattacks earned such prose as "situation . . . well in hand," "stiff resistance," "an almost perfect air umbrella," "confounded the experts who had expected them to conduct a holding operation . . . the Americans pushed rapidly." The Homer of these heroics was probably Joe Kastner. To the editorial was left the announcement that Mussolini had been dislodged and that the Italians are "a lovable, laughing people . . . not warriors." A full picture history of Italy's last century (August 9, 1943) developed the point.

Pictures of the great Tokyo earthquake and fire of September 1, 1923, were used (August 16, 1943) to explain the strange Japanese habituation to horror and death. More Bel Geddes models "under the technical advice of Nicholas Corotneff, expert on Russian tactics," illustrated the Russian victory at Orel, expounding the theory of the Russian "islands of resistance" within the blitz area, relying mostly on guns rather than tanks. Corotneff was a delightful aging White Russian who had once, as a colonel in the civil wars, commanded a division because all superior officers had been killed. He told me that in the czarist *Almanach de Gotha* his family was listed not once but twice.

The genesis of John Hersey's *A Bell for Adano* appeared (August 23, 1943) in a piece on AMGOT (Allied Military Government of Occupied Territories), quoting the American character: "Democracy . . . the people in its government are no longer the masters of the people." This material suited his temperament, for here it turned out that war had a charming face. (Hersey's later book *Hiroshima* expressed his horror that war was not always charming.)

The meeting of Roosevelt and Churchill at Quebec made the lead (August 30, 1943), suggesting that the war was probably won. In the group picture, front row, there was an empty chair at the right end. The symbolism, and who conceived it, I do not know. Whom for? Stalin? de Gaulle? the Shah of Iran? Chiang Kai-shek? But there was the empty chair which, as a Roosevelt buff, I believe to have been his idea. The lead concluded the battle of Sicily, describing the new German troops as "raw, inexperienced and jumpy." The editorial, trying to say something when there was nothing to say (a fault of editorials), said that Americans were more "enlightened" than in September 1939. The feats of Victoria Cross winners were juxtaposed to a farm story with pigs.

A story on U.S. war production as "at the highest level in human history" but still not enough (September 6, 1943) should have brought immediate surrender from Hitler and the Japanese. Excise Hitler from the last sentence, for he was clearly suicidal and wished

Germany to die with him. The German elite knew it by this time. Roosevelt must have laughed at Russell Davenport's text piece on the rebirth of the Republican party.

The recapture of the last Japanese foothold in the Western Hemisphere was noted (September 13, 1943) at Kiska in the Aleutians, deserted except for the unburied dead.

Then came "The Surrender of Italy" (September 20, 1943) with pictures of the landings at Salerno and Taranto. A flashback to June 10, 1940, commented, "The Italians took the war on that day as a joke, a chance to assassinate without risk, as safe as snatching an old woman's purse in an alley." Then: "One great downhill skid to ignominious defeat."

A description of American troops at Salerno as green and overconfident (because of Italy's surrender) (September 27, 1943) was by Jack Belden whose credential was that he had been wounded at Salerno. Time Inc., however, was bad news with the troops for some time. The editorial maundered that what America needed in foreign affairs was a policy, not a plan. I am in awe of people who can think up this sort of thing. What America got at this point, happily, was the birth of the bazooka rocket gun.

The fact that two thirds of the world were undernourished was the theme (October 4, 1943) of Joseph J. Thorndike, Jr. This opened the doctrine that the American taxpayer is responsible for every misgoverned belly in the world. For all his conservatism, Luce encouraged this sort of fragrant liberalism. To feed India, for example, would require an honorable distribution system which does not exist and could only be invented by honorable men—a commodity in short supply.

Praise of Tito's Yugoslav Communist Partisans by Howard K. Smith (October 11, 1943) was preceded by a note that Mikhailovich's Patriots were an "older, more professional and possibly more formidable force." (The checker must have insisted on "possibly.") The picture essay was on Palestine: "The Jews of Palestine are a new people, bold, energetic, friendly, unconventional. . . . Jewish Palestine is not an experiment any longer. It is a fact."

The coming first conference of the Allied foreign ministers was discussed (October 18, 1943), the mystery being that the Russians were preparing two opposite policies, the Americans none—hence, the Americans were the more mysterious.

The Italian uprising in Naples against the Germans, but really against the war, was the lead (November 8, 1943): "The military value of this fighting was not great, the cost in Italian lives was very great, but it was not a time to weigh profit and loss." Of the German atrocities in Naples: "None of this is the job of a self-respecting army." (It was probably Gestapo work.) Noel Busch contributes the text piece on South Africa's Prime Minister Jan Christiaan Smuts, who made the Afrikaaner of that time respectable.

Probably Gerry Piel wrote the essay on mathematics, suggesting both the range of *Life*'s subject matter and its limitations. This says: "Mathematics is nothing more or less than reason—the process of thinking which leads to proof. . . . As such, mathematics has nothing whatever to do with arithmetic." This is a gem of pseudoscientific snobbery, which later propelled Gerry into publishing the *Scientific American*. The great Euler, however, would have laughed at this definition, and so would Einstein. However, it had the effect of snubbing the ordinary reader, a function I did not think was the purpose of Time Inc. Gerry is an odd character, somewhat inscrutable to me.

The beginning of the buildup of Dewey appeared in the lead (November 15, 1943) on the elections: "The U.S. is now a Republican country." The context made the strange statement reasonably reasonable. The editorial, on the other hand, built up Wendell Willkie as sponsoring the friendlier public view of Soviet Russia. It can be surmised that Russell Davenport was beginning to get leary of his job, if Dewey were to be the man he must champion. But I do not as yet detect the style of Jack Jessup in the editorial.

Since Time Inc. was founded on the healthy conflict between writer and checker, it is significant that at about this time the ascendancy was arbitrarily awarded the female checker. From here on, all arguments were decided in her favor. This was ruinous, for all life, as Buckminster Fuller says, must have two sides. The move probably came from Longwell but forwarded Luce's program of cutting down the grandee writer. I did not make an official protest, for I had it licked. Daily, I underlined the *New York Times* with facts I wanted to use. The checkers could never get those clips from the morgue, and I let them suffer. Finally, I pointed to my stack of the *New York Times* and told them where they could find what they wanted, *underlined*. This destroyed the morale of any checker. In the series of tyro checkers I got, I one day found on the girl's typewriter (I think from Shrifte) a note: "Don't worry about David the Cort. His bark is worse than his bite." I showed it to Billings. I don't know what he made of it.

We had begun a story on the Great German General Staff Corps (GSC) and Gary Underhill had produced G-2's booklet on the subject. Nothing would satisfy G-2 but that the foreign editor must come down to Washington to clear the story. There I was ushered in to a G-2 colonel, a backward type who ended the interview by putting his wastebasket in the safe. Having read in the booklet that von Paulus had been operations officer for the Stalingrad campaign in which he was captured, I asked him whether I could write this. He groped through his copy of the booklet which he should have known by heart (Underhill could have recited it backward) and finally told me I could. It went on like this, a mummery that brought back my days of gulling the Columbia administration. He bore out the impression that the brains required in the rest of the society are superfluous in the army, and this was G-2, "Intelligence." Even I had nearly memorized the booklet. I cared; he did not. I do not want idiots running my country's wars, and lately we have had numbers of them. No Patton, alas.

And so we come to the issue where the story appeared (November 22, 1943). The lead was on Secretary of State Hull's return from Moscow and the agreement with Russia, an ephemeral high point of our good relations. Then came the essay on the German GSC: "Its members are a mystery to the outside world because they wish to be mysterious. . . . This formidable body of men . . . is far more powerful than Hitler for it knows how to plan. It cannot be suppressed. . . . It is reborn as soon as two trained German officers meet in a ratskeller and talk war." Then came a history of the German army, featuring Gneisenau, Scharnhorst, and Clausewitz. "What the Army needed from Hitler was a 'mass base' of will-to-win in the German people." Under the headline "The Same Old Crowd Still Runs This War" was "Von Paulus designed the Stalingrad campaign, then commanded it and was captured at Stalingrad. . . . The G.S.C. has had clashes with Hitler [the casualties were listed but notably omitted Blaskowitz]. . . . Spiritually they cannot be defeated. For, no matter what happens to Germany, they believe that war will always remain." On this last I agree now. But I failed to foresee, given so much information, that the Prussians were still honorable, could not accept Hitler and Himmler, and must try to assassinate Hitler to save Germany and, more important, their honor. Once again I came up close to the truth and stalled. (But even if I had anticipated the plot against Hitler, would I have announced it? Certainly not. I doubt whether I would have even told G-2 about it.) But the parenthesis is no excuse. Understanding the GSC, as I did, I should have known that they could not coexist with the SS, and that atrocities I had ascribed to the German army were the work of the SS. This enormous schizophrenia in the German nation was the most important fact at the moment, and I missed it. Well, so did everybody else, but that is not an excuse that comforts me. I didn't think much of everybody else.

The return of Carl and Shelley Mydans from a Japanese concentration camp was celebrated by a piece (November 29, 1943). The lead was on "The World's No. 1 Army": "One fact overshadows all others in the world today and that is the unquestioned and overwhelming superiority of the Soviet Russian Army over all others." This statement was documented with pictures of its weapons and tactics.

Somehow I had gotten a team into my favorite unknown place, Sinkiang or the Takla-makan Desert, for this makes the lead (December 6, 1943), showing a very ancient graveyard of man's history. The editorial is an emotional story of the marines' taking of Tarawa, the landing boats grounding on the shoals offshore, a terrible challenge to marine courage, which was met. A text piece by Dorothy Thompson makes the sound point that the living Germans had never known a normal stable life since 1914 ("nothing . . . ever lasts") and hence that they should not be driven to yet wilder paranoia but taken into a European union.

The fantastic fight for the square mile of Tarawa—in which of under 5,000 marines, 1,026 were killed and 2,557 wounded in 76 hours—filled the lead (December 13, 1943) with bloodcurdling pictures. The story is well written (not by me). The editorial was not satisfied with the current Cairo Conference of Roosevelt, Churchill, and Chiang Kai-shek, with the Teheran Conference with Stalin coming up.

The Cairo and Teheran conferences made the lead (December 20, 1943) with Stalin saying, "Without U.S. machines we could never have won the war." The Teheran meeting, on Churchill's birthday, for which Stalin had neglected a gift, was a love-feast. I had two private opinions. One: How did they know the war was won? Two: I was, for the first time, growing leery of Roosevelt's dealings with Stalin. I had begun to suspect that we had lost the war. The editorial was not satisfied with the Teheran Conference, giving the statement "world family of democratic nations" a richly deserved ha-ha.

I was informed sometime in April 1944 that, as of December 31, 1943, my assurance of future solvency was fattening rapidly. I am not an accountant and refuse to try to be one. But here are the figures:

STATEMENT OF YOUR ACCOUNT
IN THE
RETIREMENT ANNUITY PLAN
at December 31, 1943

EMPLOYEE CONTRIBUTIONS	During the Year 1943	Since You Entered the Plan
You have contributed to the John Hancock Mutual Life Insurance Company for the purchase of a Future Service Retirement Annuity	$ 907.56	$1,815.12

COMPANY CONTRIBUTIONS	During the Year 1943	Since You Entered the Plan
Time Inc. has added to your contributions for the purpose of a Future Service Retirement Annuity ($1.00 for each $1.00 contributed by you up to $5.00 per month and $.50 for each $1.00 contributed by you in excess of $5.00 per month)	$ 483.78	$ 967.56
Time Inc. has contributed for the purchase of a Past Service Retirement Annuity	884.96	2,580.46
Total Company Contributions .	$1,368.74	$3,548.02

STATEMENT OF YOUR ACCOUNT

IN THE

NEW AND OLD SENIOR GROUP TRUSTS
at December 31, 1943

NEW SENIOR GROUP TRUST	During the Year 1943	Since You Entered the Trust
Time Inc. contributed to the Trust for your account	$1,350.00	$4,051.65
Your share of the Trust earnings amounted to	59.00	59.00
Total additions to your account .	$1,409.00	$4,110.65

OLD SENIOR GROUP TRUST	During the Year 1943	Since You Entered the Trust
Time Inc. contributed to the Trust for your account	—	$8,797.65
Your share of the Trust earnings amounted to	169.61	392.19
Total additions to your account .	$ 169.61	$9,189.84

A new attitude (not mine) toward war surfaced in the lead (January 3, 1944) in the quote that war seemed "like Alice in Wonderland played in a madhouse" (in a story on how rain had slowed the war in Italy). This is a valid view, as in *Catch-22*, if one does not believe in the integrity of societies, or that groups of people stand for anything beyond their own self-indulgence, dismissing their children and grandchildren as nothing. John Hersey was expressing this "humanistic" opinion of war. It has always struck me as inhuman. Only a humanist, in a paraphrase of Orwell, could have been so inhuman, as he later proved in his book on Hiroshima. The dead on the Tarawa beach nailed home the point. These boys had not petitioned Japan to be there. Humanism as "faith in the supreme value and self-perfectibility of human personality" is the basic evil in liberal societies, the charming bacterium that must destroy them, if they cannot learn. The book and movie *Catch-22* were delightful but omitted one trifling detail: Hitler. They made fun of the gigantic American industrial effort which rendered the German and Japanese efforts ignominious. But this awful juggernaut had the purpose of keeping free little people still free; it was not invoked out of sheer frivolity, as *Catch-22* assumes. In short, the warmaker wants real advantages; the counterwarmaker tries to deny him those real advantages. If anybody wishes to say that Germany and Japan should have gotten what they wanted, I am willing to listen. Even to John Hersey. For there are two evils in human society: the assassins and the assassin-forgivers. One is as evil as the other. My opinion of killing derives from the fact that I am perfectly capable of it, as I suspect most people are. Hence I cannot forgive killing. And Hersey, without knowing it, was forgiving Hitler's killing, as he built up to indicting the United States for the great and virtuously purposeful killing at Hiroshima.

The nonmadhouse opinion of war was indicated in the next lead (January 10, 1944) on the hazardous U.S. landings on New Britain, stressing the casualties (real dead men, not fantasies) as against MacArthur's bland communiqués. The editorial made the brilliant generalization that the war's star part had been played first by France (a flop), Britain (a smash), Russia (a smash), and that America was next. (The omission of Germany is striking.) A chart of the commanders of the projected invasion of Europe was given. There was also an analysis of the U.S. Army Service Forces which arm, feed, clothe, fuel, transport, heal, and bury the army. Its chief was not well thought of but it must have been doing something right. A chaplain analyzing German prisoners of war finds them relatively small, strong, mongrel, and musical, with an anti-Nazi minority. (I should have paid more attention to this last point.) The Nazi looting of European art ("The Louvre is empty") is described.

The arrests, a little late, of U.S. Fascists and Trotskyites occupied the lead (January 17, 1944). Dwight MacDonald was not among the latter. Simultaneously, the editorial excoriated U.S. labor strikes "for a lousy four cents an hour" and deplored "invective." Somehow the blame was transposed to Roosevelt. This was not the true measure of Jack Jessup; it must be traced to Luce. The "Picture of the Week" was of an heroic duck, Siwash, which landed on Tarawa with the First Battalion of the 10th Marines. (If you think this is Alice in Wonderland, tell it to the 10th Marines.)

Misery in Naples was the lead (January 24, 1944). The editorial gave good marks to Roosevelt's home front program—but does he mean it? The story is told of a great air battle by 700 U.S. daylight bombers. The essay on the Church of England develops Luce's favorite theme of solvent religion.

The lead on the war in Italy (January 31, 1944) noted that the Allied forces included French, English, Americans, Canadians, Scots, Moroccans, New Zealanders, Maoris, Punjabis, Gurkhas, Belgians, Poles, Italians, and American-born Japanese. There was satire in this. The editorial fretted over the "Moscow rumor" that Britain was negotiating for a separate peace, and settled on the idea that this was merely a typical Communist rebuke for British support of the Polish government-in-exile's demands for reasonable boundaries after the war. (Russia did not recognize the Polish government-in-exile, a blinding revelation of the Communist mentality, for Russia had helped send it into exile. Communism is never wrong. If you plan to be a Communist, never forget that.)

I wrote a memorandum on misreporting of the war by the press (including myself). It may have grown out of an exchange in which I contradicted something Billings related that General "Hap" Arnold had told him in Washington and he protested, "Are you saying that General Arnold lies?" and I answered, "General Arnold lies twenty times a day." This stopped Billings cold. My memorandum never saw the light. Instead, a "toned-down" or "smoothed-out" version was mimeographed and distributed as "Minority Report on the War." This latter is not worth the reader's time, but it might teach any journalist the stupidity of "toning down" a statement. I will give only the original statement; it would have jeopardized *Life*'s relationship with military censorship and could not be printed. I suppose the facts came from Gary Underhill, then in the army. I assume the reader understands that, though in wartime I was on the side of the military, I would never trust it to run this nation or make major decisions affecting it. No Frenchman assassinated Napoleon but millions of Americans would be glad to assassinate an American Napoleon. Or so I hope.

The American press, including *Life*, has been withholding from the public a body of facts about our conduct of the war. Heretofore, the reasons have been obvious. Our military security was involved. And there was some danger of affecting for the worse the fighting morale of our soldiers and sailors. Now, however, it is the men in uniform who are discussing these very facts and introducing them little by little, in private talk on leave, into the homes of America. It is the men who use the words, snafu (situation normal all foxed up) and fubar (foxed up beyond all recognition), who say, "There are always two ways of doing anything: the right way and the Army way." The gripe sessions go on far into the night at every camp in the land and beyond the seas.

However, there were important reasons for not publishing information that might reflect on our higher officers. It is agreed that the conduct of war differs from the conduct of peace and that the conduct of war must be put in the charge of military men. We will win or lose this war with the officers we have. And our officers, if they make mistakes and tend to cover them up, do so only because they share psychological traits in common with the rest of the American people. Officers in charge of a military outfit feel naturally that its business is at least as secret as that of any American industrial corporation and that its public relations have as good a right to be handled tactfully. The techniques of American promotional advertising have insensibly been taken over by our armed forces, for they have a great deal more at stake than any commercial enterprise. The American press has sympathized with this and tried generally to do a promotion job for the armed services.

There may be cogent grounds for moderating this policy. The U.S. has been mobilized for over three years and actively at war for more than two. It has about 100 divisions today, mostly half-trained, as against 60 Jap divisions, 65 British, 300 German and 600 Russian. Nobody has imposed on the nation a clear sense of what modern war is or on the army a clear sense of what an army is. At any rate, too many men in the armed forces do not appear to be satisfied with the way we are waging war. Some of the things they talk about can be told the civilian public.

All soldiers have to study the *Soldiers' Handbook* (FM 100–10). In the latest version of this work, there is no mention whatever of the chief hazard to personnel not directly under fire: booby traps. Nor is any note taken of anti-personnel mines. The manual is well-written and takes up all kinds of cover and camouflage and general security precautions, including anti-tank mines, but up until now, the officers in charge of publications have not thought it necessary to instruct the troops in the one menace they really must know about, or die.

Our infantrymen carry the 30-caliber Browning machine gun, whose tripod must usually be fixed by laying sandbags over the two front legs. It fires 500 rounds a minute. The Germans have had since 1934 the MG '34, now carried by one in 13 German infantrymen. This is superior to the American equivalent in that it fires 1100 rounds a minute, can be set up quickly by use of a bipod and a shoulder rest, and is so built that a hot barrel can be changed in ten seconds. The whole gun can be converted from a light machine gun to a heavy (fixed) gun in half a minute by substituting a tripod. This has a simple arrangement of hydraulic shock absorbers in the top of the mount, which keeps it fixed. On every count the old German gun, now improved in the MG '42, is superior to the Browning as a weapon. Americans in the field know and say that the Germans have the advantage in machine-gun fire, especially "searching" fire, and naturally they are not very pleased about it.

The Sherman Special tank with the long 76 mm. was not yet available even for the Back the Attack show in Washington in June, 1943. For that reason, captured examples of the German Mark IV Special with the long KWK 40, a 75 mm. gun, were not included in the Show, although they had been fighting in mass on the Russian front for over a year. The intention of course was to make American weapons look superior to the enemy's, whether they were or not.

The most conspicuous example of this policy appeared in the newspapers of Nov. 30. "FOE'S WEAPONS DETERIORATING" was the cheerful news. Unfortunately, at about the same time the terrible cost in lives of U.S. Marines who had to face the "third rate weapons" of the Japs on Tarawa was filling the papers. The headline, however, was not only ill-timed but utterly wrong and misleading. The Germans have huge supplies of captured Czech, Polish, Norwegian, Dutch, Belgian, French, Yugoslav, plus British, Russian and some American weapons. Much of this is on a fairly high level of quality. Furthermore, Germany's experimental weapons may be no further advanced than America's, but the German High Command is more likely to use them.

Similarly, a story headlined "U.S. Artillery Tougher Than Russian, Say Nazis," is always good. It is meaningless as military data.

It is easy to fool the home front. The American people were certainly given the impression that the battle at Salerno was an all-American job. All papers used the expression "The American Fifth Army," and there were numerous stories about how the American 45th Division "played major role in saving beachhead." True, if you looked closely, the newspaper stories said "Allies" every now and then and one correspondent reported, in a small voice, that the Fifth Army was "probably 40% British." The fact was that, of the two beachheads at Salerno, the British held one alone and half of the other.

Much more serious is the promotion campaign for our air might. An Air Forces Colonel was quoted in the newspapers as saying "strategic air power might be able to so wreck the German war potential . . . that an invasion might be more like an occupation. Fifteen of the key cities of Germany already have been knocked out as industrial factors in the war." The trouble with this is that, if a million American men get hurt trying to "occupy" this prostrate Germany, the air colonel will have a lot of big words to eat. Possibly air power is capable of doing such a job, but not the air power we are now supplying.

The headlines are considerably out of line with the facts. When the British first wanted the headline, "1,000 PLANES BOMB COLOGNE" on May 30, 1942 they did actually send out 1,250 planes. But they conscripted training units, coastal command planes and almost any old thing that could get to Cologne and back with a grenade, to deliver "the greatest mass air bombardment in history." The airmen knew what was happening and did not appreciate being used to make promotion headlines.

The recent "1,000-plane bombing" of Berlin and Ludwigshafen Nov. 18 was another of the same. For one reason and another, less than 400 planes reached Berlin. The release runs "The largest force of British and Canadian bombers ever sent against Germany—possibly 1,000—dropped an estimated 1,500 tons of the 2,500 total on Berlin and the rest on Ludwigshafen."

Piling it on, we read that the excellent British plywood bomber called the Mosquito reaches Berlin by day and adds to the utter devastation of Berlin. But the Mosquito cannot get to Berlin and back with a 500-lb. bombload. Nevertheless the stories go: "unsurpassed audacity, . . . of fastest bombers in the world capable of carrying four 500-pound bombs each" (not to Berlin). "One of the outstanding attacks of the war"; "AIR BLOWS MOUNT"; the great fiction builds up.

Giving this kind of false impression to civilians is perhaps merely self-protective. But when the infantry is given it and then goes in and has to take terrific casualties from an enemy supposedly "smashed" by air, as at Tarawa, the infantry grows irritable. The infantry grew very irritable indeed on Sicily, when "overwhelming Allied air power" seemed notably unable to bother the Germans much in the mountains. If anybody was going to bother them, it had to be the infantry. But the releases continued to give the air campaign credit for the Allied ground advance.

When we are deliberately misled, everyone knows that somebody somewhere is benefiting by giving us that misinformation. These stories fall under the usual head of American promotional advertising. The ability of officers at desks in Washington is the commodity we are being sold. After the war, they may be offered front-man jobs as board chairmen of substantial American corporations, to follow in the footsteps of General Harbord, General Robert Wood, General Thomas Hammond and even General Short and Admiral Kimmel of Pearl Harbor fame. Anyone who wants that kind of work is to be congratulated. But the work at hand is another matter.

There is a growing gap between the American forces at home and at the front. When American troops reach any fighting front, they are immediately retrained in new combat methods that Washington has refused to recognize, possibly because they are in conflict with the manuals on which the Washington officers' reputations rest.

The American people have been given the impression that the war is by now virtually won. Stalin's statement at Teheran that without American machines, "the war would not have been won," sounded as though even he thought it had already been won, but he was probably mistranslated. Actually, though, Russia's 600 divisions have received from us well over a billion dollars less in lend-lease than Britain's 65 divisions (3 and a quarter vs. four and a half billion).

The war has not been won. It has not really begun for the U.S. Secretary of War Stimson said Dec. 9: "Our fighting has been of a perimeter nature. The overwhelming part of the American Army is still inside the U.S., the only one of the Allies that has encountered the main German forces is Russia, and the U.S. Navy has not yet engaged the principal fleet of the Japanese. . . . Only in the air have we encountered the main forces of the enemy and the immense industrial power of Germany and her recuperative strength make it impossible to say that she may not again face us with a very powerful air force."

Certainly the Americans, soldier and civilian, are slowly getting the point. A correspondent cabled back from Tarawa: "our period of blind refusal to learn, which was so exasperating early in the war, has all but passed. . . . We know now the shortcomings of naval gunfire and aerial bombardment. . . . On Tarawa we learned what weapons were most effective on the atolls. Before the battle had ended, more of these weapons had been ordered and improvements were being made in them. Everything military is not inflexible, albeit in the U.S. the military has long connoted conservatism. We are learning and we are learning to learn faster."

This is great and cheering news. If true.

An American surgeon returned from Russia, Col. Elliott Cutler, described war as it should be waged. "Everyone is fighting the war. No building has been painted in Russia during the war. They are not taking time now to fill up bomb craters. I didn't see a dog in Russia. They have been killed and used for food. The Russians are very practical. When a soldier comes out of anaesthetic, they throw a machine gun in bed with him and he spends his time taking it apart and putting it together again. There are no Red Cross girls around to rub the backs of the wounded soldiers and no basket weaving. Within a few days those who were lightly wounded are getting up, fingering their rifles. Extreme devotion to the common private is one of the keynotes of the Russian treatment of troops. The best food and everything else including the most medals is reserved for the ordinary fighting men instead of the generals."

That is the kind of war the American men would like to be fighting too. But first some generals must take off their medals and face some facts.

Some persisting themes were raised by the editorial (February 14, 1944): "The Pope's neutrality has been too far 'above the battle,' " as Stalin had charged. In return, the egregious Monsignor Sheen had "accused [the Soviets] of anti-Semitism and of plotting a separate peace." These arguments have had more recent champions.

Two very different beachheads occupied the lead (February 21, 1944), one successful at Kwajalein in the Marshall Islands, the other in difficulty at Anzio in Italy. A report on the former was given by Dick Wilcox, who was there. The text piece was on Morris Ernst who knew literally everybody, even me. The privileges of success were exhibited in a box saying that all Time Inc. magazines were cutting down on paper (patriotically); hence, "obviously there cannot be enough copies for everyone"; thus, raising the value of the advertising.

Republican presidential maneuvering began (February 28, 1944), with Dewey leading in the polls and Willkie, under the Davenport bias, given preferential treatment. DDT (discovered in the nineteenth century) first appeared in the delousing of the people of Naples, threatened with a typhus epidemic. At that point it looked good. A collection of perspective maps by Richard Edes Harrison (text by Gerry Piel) gave, for example, a new grasp of what Europe is: a peninsula thrust out between the Black and Baltic seas from the Eurasian land mass.

Possibly to reassure the Russians rather than to alert the Germans, the lead (March 6, 1944) was on the mounting of the invasion of Europe from England. Except for the probability that German espionage would have known all about it, this was a questionable exercise of a free press in a democracy. However, the copy had been seen by U.S. military censorship. The pictures showed enormous numbers of Sherman tanks, half-track prime movers, tank cars, cranes, pontoons, antiaircraft, shells, Nissen huts, barbed wire, gliders, howitzers, Bofors guns. The editorial was a "last call for war aims": "Front-line reporters know that not many U.S. soldiers are fighting to extirpate Fascism, or to spread the Four Freedoms, or to win ribbons." Very sensible. The reluctant destruction of the Abbey of Monte Cassino, used militarily by the Germans, was shown. The colossal new American Pacific Fleet, most powerful in the world, began to make its mark. The Japanese too were beginning to lose the war. A mystery is an unsigned text piece, "Your War with Japan," quoting an imaginary Japanese admiral on the huge difficulties of defeating Japan. It begins as comic parody and ends with strategic sobriety. Whatever game was being played, and whoever was playing it, it was not sound Time Inc. material. It was not my policy to play games with the reader. Before a game is begun, the ground rules must be defined. I never play other people's undefined games.

Another terrible small Pacific battle, that for the key islands of the Eniwetok Atoll, was the lead (March 13, 1944). Photographer George Strock and correspondent Richard Wilcox probably went in with the marines. Strock's pictures and Wilcox's story are there to prove it. The nation had the right to send troops onto that beach; but did Time Inc. have a moral right to send Strock and Wilcox, both probably protected from the draft, into the possibility of being killed for a corporate wage? The answer is that the two young men doubtless agreed but here the courage, unlike that of the troops, is turned into corporate profit. The editorial echoed George Washington's cry in 1775, "Such a dearth of public spirit, and want of virtue, such stock-jobbing, and fertility in all the low arts to obtain advantage," and also the infinitely cruder cry of American officers at the front, "More bodies." The two points of view can easily be transposed to more power or more glory. There was a story on the electoral defeat of the marquess of Hartington, who was to marry a Kennedy girl and die with her in an airplane crash. A story on a great Hindu prayer for peace reads: "To die, the Hindus believe, is merely to begin living again; to be born is a disaster; both are small expressions of the One Absolute, Infinite, Impersonal, Self-Existent, Inexpressible 'It' that can be worshiped as one four-headed God, Brahma, or as many gods."

A German refugee writes (March 20, 1944) in appreciation of the U.S. Constitution: "We who have lived under the heel of dictatorship, who have suffered racial and political persecution, who were stripped of all our personal liberties, cherish more than anything else the rights the Constitution grants the citizens of this great country." A long lead on U.S. segregation camps for "disloyal" Japanese is essentially by the photographer Carl Mydans who had been repatriated from sixteen months in Japanese internment camps. To him, the American camps were sheer luxury. The problem was a cultural conflict.

The fretting continued (March 27, 1944) about "American foreign policy" (a book could be written about the difficulty of any "policy" toward "foreigners"). American war aims were to "maintain freedom in America" and, because of the new worldwide interdependence, to discourage "political tyranny wherever we find it. And . . . we shall act accordingly." Add the sequel: "The United States will maintain a powerful military establishment after the war—at least as strong as the military establishment of any other nation," and Jack Jessup had completely defined U.S. policy. Item: another story on the "destruction" of Berlin. John Hersey contributes another war story, this on the adventures of an LCI (Landing Craft Infantry), in the voice of a gentle fond uncle. William C. Bullitt, the perennial ambassador, retells the sordid story of Versailles, pinning the major villainy on Lloyd George rather than on Clemenceau and showing Wilson as a glory man who threw away immense power and ended in self-delusion and breakdown. (He also refers to an "atomic bomb.")

An attempt to describe "the biggest battle in human history" was the lead (April 3, 1944), using maps to show the ebb and flow of armies across Russia. The editorial is unhappy about the unspecific Atlantic Charter and prefers the previous week's editorial. Grisly pictures show that in the battle for Attu, after the last furious attack, the Japanese were swept by an orgy of suicide, usually by grenade. The essay explains America's need for 20,000 new oil wells in 1944 and how they will be found. The text piece is by John Chamberlain, fretting that the trouble with Wendell Willkie is that he is not a clear-cut caricature. (I'd have voted for him that year, on the strong suspicion that Roosevelt had given away a peace approximately as bad as Wilson's after World War I. Wilson's created inoperable nations; Roosevelt's peace produced a number of slave nations. I loved the man, but not blindly.)

Hard going for the Allies is documented in the lead (April 10, 1944) at both Monte Cassino in Italy and in Burma. There are more Japanese corpses. The editorial, analyzing American patriotism, inadequately quotes its basic elements as "a belief in individual liberty, in human progress, in the unique mission of the U.S. as a nation, and . . . a belief in the existence of moral law." One page brings up the sad fact of Vichy's jailing of Daladier, Blum, Gamelin, and others, soon to be removed to Germany.

The readers' letters (April 17, 1944) agree with Mr. Bullitt (and me) that another bad peace was about to follow Versailles. However, as of the 1970s, it is clear that the free world's peace was anything but vindictive, and only Communist Russia has sowed the wind of vengeance, for communism is conceived in vengeance. How the whirlwind will be reaped in the occupied territories, if ever, is beyond my clairvoyance. On the other hand, should the United States get into economic trouble, it must be remembered that there is no such emotion as international gratitude. The only magnanimous people who have ever existed are Americans, perhaps only because they could afford it. The lead is entitled "Tarawa Revisited"—the terrible battlefield having been converted to a "paradise," complete with cemeteries, airfields, topless native girls, and softball. The editorial pointed out that "many servicemen are getting so they hate civilians" and advised "building a bridge." Willkie's defeat in the Wisconsin primaries was shown, as well as Thomas Dewey's victory. A successful war in Indo-China—in this case, Burma—is seen run by General Joe Stilwell. Life's favorite volcano, Parícutin in Mexico, is seen spouting, partly in color. This leads to a study of the earth's 600 currently active volcanoes, concluding with reliable Vesuvius, once again in action. "America's World Purpose" was approached again by a Harvard philosopher, William Hocking. Basically, he urged America (whose goodwill he acknowledged) to lead in the formation of an effective international law, based on "interpenetration" (rather than collision) of national interests, policies that benefit everybody. Incredibly, he thinks the League of Nations had a chance of success, given more time. On the other hand, he points out that while a man may be typical, every nation is unique. This piece may have contributed to the ideological buildup leading to the dissolution of empires after the war, except for the Russian and Chinese.

The little war in Burma takes a bad turn in the lead (April 24, 1944), as the Japanese threaten the Allied supply line, while the Allies are trying to cut the Japanese supply line. The story included magnificent pictures of the Himalayas. The editorial is on "Negro Rights," quoting Gunnar Myrdal's discovery that southern whites feared, in order of magnitude, intermarriage, social equality, joint use of facilities, equal voting, equality in the courts, and equal economic opportunity. But the Negroes' priorities run from the bottom up.

Thus, the answer is to start at the bottom. "The other three quarters of the country cannot permit the South to disfranchise its Negroes forever." The first twelve Negroes commissioned as officers in the U.S. Navy are posed (with one warrant officer). All but one are light-skinned. It is noted that Princess Elizabeth of England is now 18, "has very little coquetry and not much sense of clothes." I am astonished by an essay on "Spring, 1944," beautifully written by I cannot guess whom, for this was to be an historic spring for America: "Spring had become a season that made the waiting generals anxious and impatient, that made men grow busier with death than with life. The time recalled the chapter of Ecclesiastes where the Preacher, summing up all joys and sorrows, says: 'To every thing there is a season . . . a time of war and a time of peace.' " Perhaps Roger Butterfield or John Hersey. The first notice of the great talents of Earl Warren of California appeared in a witty sympathetic text piece by Robert Coughlan.

The consecration of a new Protestant Episcopal bishop (more solvent religion) filled the lead (May 1, 1944), while the editorial tried to ameliorate the effect of a realistic description of Chiang Kai-shek's China by Teddy White. This latter explains Chiang's ultimate defeat by the Communists, White's villains being the blockade, inflation, corruption, inadequate U.S. aid, and the Chen brothers, in charge of education and censorship. (Any one would be enough.) The impression I get now is that Nationalist China underrated Western industrialism and overrated appearances ("face"), not that White says exactly that. The stalemated Anzio beachhead produces American dead under German shelling from the high ground, and a chillingly large American cemetery of crosses and Stars of David. The play was *The Searching Wind*, by Lillian Hellman, whom I had known while on *Vanity Fair*. She was described as "among the half-dozen ablest playwrights" in America. The movie was, in contrast to the lead, *Going My Way* with Bing Crosby (insolvent religion).

An inscrutable interview of a Russian general, Rogov, in Russia, opens the issue as a *Life* Report (May 8, 1944). It is by Dick Lauterbach, who may not yet have turned Communist. Rogov kept reverting to "the second front." In the masthead, John K. Jessup is assistant editor and Russell Davenport has disappeared. Senior editors are the same. To associate editors, Robert Coughlan has been added (and Don Burke dropped), as well as George Frazier and John Hersey. To assistant associate editors have been added Caroline Iverson and Lilian Rixey. The huge new American navy is shown. The editorial philosophizes about the picture of Montgomery Ward's president being carried bodily out of his office by two American soldiers. A story begins: "With unaccustomed Christian humility, the U.S. Army released a sobering newsreel of the Aug. 19, 1942 raid on Dieppe, as a reminder of the risk of invasion . . . an unmitigated disaster."

Military censorship had evidently passed the lead, "American Invaders Mass in England" (May 15, 1944), for probably everybody in Europe knew about it, and Eisenhower's facial gamut is shown. The commanding officers of the invasion are seen ("the faces the Germans would like to see") from the rear. A map of the west coast of Europe was displayed in the layout room, and people chose their invasion beaches. I think I took two—one Calais, the other Deauville. The editorial gave rules for civilian deportment toward wounded discharged soldiers. A story on southern primary voting shows Negroes being turned away from the polls: "This is a white primary." Some cute legal tricks by South Carolina to maintain "white supremacy" are described. Joe Thorndike contributes an admiring piece on Montgomery who had done well in North Africa (for reasons Thorndike did not understand) and was shortly to fail in Europe. There was a certain similarity between Thorndike and Montgomery, to neither's great credit. America's colossal war production made the essay. It was this monstrous avalanche of industrial metal that defeated both Germany and Japan, added to the fighting talent of the young American, and a few great officers, not including Eisenhower, I am sorry to say. A thousand American corporation men could have done Eisenhower's job; there was probably not another Patton. As usual, we were short of glory men and overloaded with conniving power men.

Even as the world's attention was on the European invasion, the lead (May 22, 1944) was on American successes in New Guinea, Noel Busch contributing a curiously dilettante piece that does not work. The starred officers, including Eichelberger, look much more desperate. The editorial wasted its power in demanding that the Republican candidate for President be, not Dewey, but a Midwesterner—Bricker, Burton, Stassen, Taft. The complex problems of the British Commonwealth were coalesced in a spread of a group portrait of their chief officers. An oddity is the printing in the front of four fairly crude sonnets on the invasion by Joseph Auslander, whose name is German for foreigner. The fourth takes the theme: "And with a loud voice Jesus cried exclaiming, 'It is finished!'" making things still odder. A hidden witness of the assassination of Reinhard Heydrich, No. 2 Gestapo man in Prague, tells his story two years after the event, including the Nazi terror that followed. The essay was on England's "Mother of Parliaments." Churchill had demanded the rebuilding of the bombed Commons with three features: (1) oblong, (2) too small for all its members, (3) no reserved seats. Of the Lords, "more good sense, as well as nonsense, is talked here than even in the Commons. For the Lords are responsible to nobody and say what they please." Provisions for checking swords are shown.

The renewed attack on Cassino (May 29, 1944) crumpled the German lines in Italy. Emphasis was given to the contribution of the Free French, thirsting for revenge, and Will Lang reports the arrival of "Le Grand Charles" (de Gaulle). The editorial predicts a permanent U.S. friendship with England. Rather sadly, Roosevelt is pictured to prove his perfect health. Rare pictures show the problems of the American fleet in the Pacific as the battle moves on from low-lying atolls to mountainous islands. A story on the Germans' Atlantic Wall notes that Rundstedt was commander-in-chief in the West, with Rommel and Blaskowitz (we were wrong) commanders in the field. John Hersey has a piece on the pictures of three airmen—Doolittle, Balchen, Chennault—with such writing as "to climb the pale ladders of the sky." Nor do I accept his psychoanalyses of the three men. How could Hersey understand such men? And so what should come now but a story on the solar system, presumably by Gerry Piel?

The desolation of the Italian front as German resistance began to crumble (June 5, 1944) is seen. The editorial groaned over a cynical Churchill speech revealing that "national power [is] the prime post-victory objective of British, Russian and American leaders in this war." Against this was set the conscience of La Follette's Progressives—"belief in universal freedom." Incidentally, the American Communist party had liquidated itself and become the Communist Political Association, supporting Roosevelt ("a minor headache" for the Democrats). A story on American airborne troops in England featured the towed gliders Bucky Fuller had proposed in 1941. As the continent waited, a German economic expert predicted the war would last "possibly until 1970." James Forrestal, who ultimately committed suicide, was seen taking the oath as Secretary of the Navy. Fillmore Calhoun writes the strange story of the Afrika Korps' favorite song, "Lili Marlene," taken over by the British as the spoils of war. The text piece by Charles Wertenbaker, trumpeting invasion soon, is on General Omar Bradley, whom he prefers to Patton, because Patton had slapped a crying soldier the year before.

The next issue (June 12, 1944) closed normally on June 3. However, plans for an invasion issue had long since been completed. A set of maps and drawings had been plated and sent to printers at Chicago and Philadelphia. The cover on the issue was labeled "Invasion by Air." And early on Tuesday, June 6, came word of the invasion. A telephone alert brought in about ten key people. Roy Larsen came into Billings' office, moaning, "What are we going to do?" Billings showed him the invasion dummy, asking, "Any changes you want?" Lacking was the writing, which had to wait on the information. The frontispiece, which I assume I wrote, said: "The great attack, advancing behind mine sweepers and smokescreens laid by planes, miraculously and mercifully won surprise. The Germans announced it half an hour later. Three hours later Commander in Chief Eisenhower confirmed it. . . . *Life* Photographer Frank Scherschel, flying over the beachhead, reported very few gun flashes on shore and generally a scene of great peacefulness." A drawing showed the Channel coast, with planes and ships crossing. More drawings showed various kinds of action, a typical German defense system, a possible landing in Holland. A vestige of the preinvasion lead, the fall of Rome, was inserted, and the editorial was evidently rewritten, springing from Eisenhower's statement June 6, "You are about to embark upon a great crusade." It made a good case for fighting Germany. Then came the story "Invasion by Air" which had occasioned the felicitous cover. By Billings' brilliant planning, a story on "The Invasion Plan" by Charles Wertenbaker could be inserted in back of the magazine, focused on the chief planner, General "Beedle" Smith. If it has not become plain, I must emphasize the continuous importance of Billings' planning, objectivity, balance, poise, good sense, and luck; the cover of this issue was another example of his qualities. All copy on the invasion lead went to Chicago and Philadelphia by teletype and the printer's make-ready was rushed through in twelve hours. Some copies were in circulation by Thursday, June 8—an incredible performance. (The original lead, before the invasion news came through, was "Airborne Raiders in Burma" but this had opened: "The unbelievable mistake of an English teletype operator shocked the U.S. with false news of invasion. . . . In baseball parks, games were halted and spectators offered silent prayers." The editorial is about a cancellation of a navy contract for Corsair fighters. The story that "The Invasion Plan" replaced was a manifesto by six eminent Italian expatriates.)

It would have been nice to know, as we now do, that in June 1944 the Germans had 59 divisions, 10 armored, in the West, but only 6 divisions along the Normandy coast, most substandard. The Germans, particularly von Rundstedt, had expected the main Allied attack at the Pas de Calais and, even after the Allied landings, kept considerable force there, supposing that the main blow under Patton would come at that point. Rommel had picked the correct invasion point, but only after Hitler had picked it first. Rommel and Kluge, who replaced Rundstedt in the West, were implicated in the assassination attempt against Hitler of July 20, 1944, and committed suicide, as did many others. In the early stages of the battle, the German generals, according to Liddell Hart, were distracted by waiting for the Gestapo to take them away and by the desire to surrender. The later Battle of the Bulge, for example, always described as the "Rundstedt offensive" (which was why Billings printed my piece on Rundstedt), was purely Hitler's offensive, which Rundstedt contemplated with disdain. The realities within the Prussian officer corps were unknown to me, though I had a very vague intuition, based only on my sense of what gentlemen would think of Hitler. The battle, grossly overestimated by the Allies, was conducted by two panzer generals, Sepp Dietrich and Monteuffel, but they had only 800 tanks, and quickly attracted an overwhelming counterforce. Since, some time before, most German generals had wanted to surrender, the "unconditional surrender" policy succeeded merely in uniting the German people and the lower echelons, and ultimately in allowing the Russians to overrun half of Europe and impose their will.

The story of the great battle, the turning point of the world, was still confused in the next issue (June 19, 1944), which closed on June 10. The weather was not good. Cherbourg had not been isolated. Caen was holding out. The pictures on the beach by Robert Capa were discouraging. Wertenbaker has a good text piece which was also confused, but he correctly reported that the Americans' eastern beach (Omaha) was in trouble. (We did not know that a German infantry division, purely by chance, had been holding maneuvers there.) Our map of the beachhead area is reasonably correct. The editorial, philosophizing on the fall of Rome, said, "Last week *Life* published a 'Manifesto' signed by six eminent Italian expatriates, condemning Allied policy toward Italy and demanding a rebirth of Italian freedom. While this article was on the press, the invasion of France began. We stopped the presses and remade 23 pages of *Life*, with the result that the Italian Manifesto appeared in only 900,000 of our 4,000,000 copies. (If your copy of last week's *Life* does not match your neighbor's, that is why.)" On D-Day, Eisenhower's son John received his commission as a second lieutenant at West Point; this is pictured. The use of incendiaries, flame-throwers, smoke screens, white phosphorus, and jellied oil is described as of the Chemical Warfare Service.

Letters congratulated *Life* on its invasion issue. The issue (June 25, 1944) gave 26 pages to "Our World-Wide War." One caption reported: "Familiar German tactic in Normandy has been to leave little harassing parties behind to slow allied advance." These accounted for the huge bag of German prisoners. The incredible panorama of the beachhead fills a spread. Bradley is seen ashore, and the German division on maneuvers is noted. Generals Marshall and Arnold are also ashore. Churchill and King George VI visited the front. Shrouded American dead are seen in their French graves. The fact that the German V-1 rockets had first appeared, fired from the Calais area, was noted. We did not know that Rommel, not Rundstedt, was the German commander; that toward the end of June Rommel was first injured, then invited to kill himself, and Rundstedt put in charge; that Rundstedt proposed a retreat to the line of the Seine and was dismissed by Hitler. Before this, Patton had brought his Third Army, with four armored divisions, ashore, and proceeded to cut the Cotentin Peninsula, isolating the Cherbourg garrison. The editorial groans over de Gaulle, who believed in the right to authority of the few, and our mistakes in handling him.

The queer contrast of Americans fighting and dying in France and General de Gaulle's open mouth, braying away, occupies the lead (July 3, 1944). The French people were not entirely delighted to see the British and Americans. Some German administrators had not been "too bad." The editorial was borrowed from Judge Learned Hand and would be rejected by many young people today: "And what is this liberty which must lie in the hearts of men and women? It is not the ruthless, the unbridled will. It is not freedom to do as one likes. . . . A society in which men recognize no check upon their freedom, soon becomes a society where freedom is the possession of only a savage few. . . . The spirit of liberty is the spirit which is not too sure that it is right."

The Republican National Convention that nominated Dewey and Bricker ("one of the dullest political conventions in history") was the lead (July 10, 1944). Clare Boothe was seen blaming the war on Roosevelt with a brilliant smile. Poor Jack Jessup has to run an editorial endorsing Dewey and is most ingenious: "In one sense Roosevelt has run against Hoover in all three of his elections. . . . Dewey's problem is to convince the mugwump that Hoover is no longer running." The fall of Cherbourg is shown. The German V-1 or robot bomb or buzzbomb is explained in some detail. Paintings illustrate Luce's favorite war, on the seventh day of the seventh month of the seventh year of the war in China, and Y. C. James Yen concludes that postwar China will be democratic. He manages to ignore the Communists. "Our War Against Japan" showed the fighting on Saipan, without adding that its capture was the key to Pacific strategy (possibly inhibited by censorship). There is fair coverage of the operations of Admirals Spruance and Mitscher, without adding that the great actions of June 19–20 were a victory called "fully as decisive as Midway." In part, nobody (except Japanese) at the time realized how badly the Japanese fleet had been hit. The B-29 Superforts that were to bomb the Japanese mainland are shown, with the boast that "U.S. officers are eager to prove with their new weapon that an enemy country can be crippled and killed by attacks from the air." I didn't think so until the atom bomb arrived, but bombing was effective against ships. Noel Busch's closeup of Admiral Chester Nimitz ascribes to him credit for the strategy of Saipan. (Elsewhere, it is given to Nimitz's superior, Admiral King.) The Pacific strategy is made understandable ("the plan is to shut the door between the Japanese and their new island empire"). Later, Busch became a great admirer of the Japanese and wrote several splendid books about them, possibly because the aristocratic code of Bushido dominated the society.

The lead (July 17, 1944) correctly evaluates the air battle west of Saipan June 19–20, in a thrilling story by Noel Busch: "As a naval victory, the Marianas fight seems to belong somewhere in a class with Jutland . . . the final score being 428 Japanese planes lost against 122 of ours, and two Japanese carriers, a destroyer and three tankers sunk against none of ours." (We did not know about two Japanese carriers sunk by submarines. American planes lost are given as 47.) Of the marines on Saipan, Robert Sherrod wrote: "This morning I saw a battalion of the 2nd Marine Division marching to the rear. . . . They were dirty and grimy but they marched briskly, even proudly. . . . One got the feeling that no men on earth could have stopped these Marines who did so much on Saipan." The editorial is about "those

Russians" and makes an obvious and brilliant point: "We are both great continental powers on opposite sides of the globe. Geopolitically, our enemies have always lain between us; we form a natural pincers against anybody who disturbs the world's peace." It expressed a pious hope that Communist Russia could be trusted. A tactic that began to raise my disgust was seen as Corsican men shear and strip collaborating Corsican women: "In all countries it is the same. Some women make the best of life with the conquerors. . . . Much the same thing has happened in Norway, Denmark, Yugoslavia and, lately, in Normandy." Billings did not allow me to express my utter contempt for these men.

The new blitz on London with the V-1 made the lead (July 24, 1944): "If the robot bomb had been developed earlier in the war, giving the Germans time to set up several thousand launching stages, it might well have become a more serious military weapon than even the Allies' bomber fleets." The editorial quotes Roosevelt: "For myself, I do not want to run. . . . Reluctantly, but, as a good soldier, I repeat that I will accept and serve in this office," and gives pro and anti reactions. (I voted for him again, but with misgivings.) Norman treason trials are shown, with the note that elsewhere "bad feeling and bloodshed among the French is more likely to occur." De Gaulle is in the United States beating his drum and has been given de facto recognition, without unfreezing French funds to him. A story showed damage to Italian art, which the Allies had tried to spare. Thomas Dewey, his family and farm are displayed. Sumner Welles offers postwar proposals: that Germany be partitioned and the General Staff abolished, with the prediction that Germany will turn Communist. He also proposed a Poland much like that created by Soviet Russia, and had some ideas for his own United Nations. In general, it opened the era of American naïveté as a world power, replacing the sophisticated British.

Under *Life*'s Reports (July 31, 1944), Jeanne Perkins quotes Roosevelt's doctor, Vice Admiral Ross McIntire, as saying, "The President's health is excellent." In the lead, on the nomination of Roosevelt for president, he looks terrible: drawn and winded. Fortunately, Truman replaced Wallace as vice president. The editorial, noting that the Democratic party is "inherently incapable of real unity," deplores the whole thing. As the assassination attempt against Hitler by the Prussians (according to Sumner Welles, the worst element in Germany) failed, a gallery of the victorious Russian generals was exhibited. A catalogue of new U.S. planes, climaxed by the B-29, is shown. The heroic Rangers, who had lost nine-tenths of their manpower, were shown.

A comment on the various stories on China is given by Sun Yat-sen's son, Sun Fo, in letters (August 7, 1944); it is as bland and merely verbal as Sun Yat-sen's philosophy. The lead was on the "Battle of the Hedgerows." Without mentioning Patton, it described massive bombardment on a narrow front, breakthrough with tanks and bulldozers (to get through the hedgerows), motorized infantry, the tanks and infantry fanning out behind the German lines. This was just west of St. Lo, while Montgomery was stalled around Caen. The editorial worries about the postwar peace and says: "[Stalin] doesn't want to communize all of Europe tomorrow. . . . In short, it means that Stalin doesn't want to run Europe," but that "Russia is to have it her way east of Germany," whatever America thinks. A story, "Explosion in Germany," trying to report the bomb plot against Hitler by the Prussian elite, was naturally full of errors, but seemed to contradict Sumner Welles' theory that the true evil in Germany was the Prussian military elite. On the contrary, it appeared as the only decent element. One error was the caption that Rommel had "quarreled with his superior, von Rundstedt, over tactics in Normandy. Last week a rumor had it that he had been killed in action." We were not omniscient. The movie *Wilson* lets *Life* retell the tragic story of Versailles, pinning the guilt on Clemenceau. Gerald W. Johnson, in a text closeup of Senator Harry Flood Byrd of Virginia, makes the point (highly relevant today) that in fact southern whites get along better with Negroes than do northern whites, because the Southerners feel some intimacy (which is what Negroes want) and the Northerners observe only respect (which no sub-Saharan black even understands and only fully Westernized blacks can tolerate). This choice for American Negroes, by no means presented in the piece, is between a thousand millennia of no written African history, no written literature, and unrecorded genocidal wars before the white man arrived, and some 4,000 years of white civilization in the Near East, Europe, and the Americas. If the black prefers the empty yawning horror, it is his to choose. But this is impossible; anyone must prefer sunlight to night.

Section VI

DECADENCE

BILLINGS had said earlier that he would quit if he were kicked upstairs, but now he is found at the top of the masthead as editorial director, under Larsen as president and Luce as editor-in-chief. The new managing editor is Longwell, the sole executive editor is Wilson Hicks, the "editorial chief" is Jack Jessup, and assistant managing editors are Thorndike and Paxton. The editors are now Busch, Butterfield, Fillmore Calhoun, Robert Coughlan, Cort, Field, Hersey, Kastner, and Gerard Piel. This should have told me that Luce no longer thought the war a serious matter, if he put Longwell in charge of reporting it. Luce was also cutting down Billings' tremendous power, as he set up a hierarchy of relative nonentities to do his job. I would date the degradation of Time Inc. as of this issue, August 7, 1944.

Responsible men are always looking ahead. My diminution in status is clearly signaled in this history, yet I was unaware of it or indifferent. Luce was preparing to get rid of me.

The Letters (August 14, 1944) point out that *Life*'s statement July 24 that Mount Vernon was Washington's birthplace was wildly wrong. I had written this, confirming Billings' belief that I was totally ignorant about America, but it had sailed through the whole checking and editing process. The lead, "Break-Through in France," without mentioning Patton, was describing his Third Army's sweep both westward toward Brest and Saint-Nazaire and eastward toward LeMans and Paris. One picture shows six knocked-out German tanks in a field, another shows over a score of Allied tanks (equipped with bulldozers) cutting through the hedgerows that seem to have baffled Montgomery. (Patton had the Second, Third, Fourth, and Sixth armored divisions.) The editorial worried over civil liberties, taken to include keeping the troops informed—not being done, due to Congress. A picture story is partial to Marshal Tito of Yugoslavia whose "relations with sulking Serb Leader Mikhailovich have, if anything, worsened." Tito is shown winning a game of chess from his chief of staff, Yovanovich. Former Ambassador William C. Bullitt contributes an able analysis of the politics of France, current and prospective, both dominated by de Gaulle. There is a fascinating line: "[The French] see developing not a united Europe but a Europe divided against itself: Finland, Estonia, Latvia, Lithuania, Poland, eastern Germany, Czechoslovakia, Rumania, Hungary, Austria, Bulgaria and Serbia being controlled from Moscow." (Note that only Austria entirely escaped.)

That revolution was brewing in Germany was the burden of a report from Sweden by John Scott (August 21, 1944). The lead showed the arrival of 983 tragic refugees from Europe to become temporary wards of the U.S. War Relocation Authority. The editorial accused labor leader Sidney Hillman of a foreign totalitarian import in his Communist-ridden American Labor party. (I am incompetent to judge this.) The Fascist façade of Juan Perón's Argentina paraded a foreign-built war machine on its Independence Day. A perspective drawing of central France showed Patton's drives (again without mentioning him) toward Paris. The ruins of St. Lo, "as thoroughly destroyed as any town in this war," were so bad they "might be left untouched. . . . The French had done this once before at Douaumont, near Verdun." The saga of an American navy man who had spent 31 months hiding on Japanese-held Guam is told by Robert Sherrod. The debatable expedient of showing the war, in this case a landing on New Britain, in paintings (by David Fredenthal) is tried again and makes an appallingly dilettante effect. Harry Truman suddenly surfaces in a good picture story: "Truman is a political accident. He is a country politician, intelligent and hard-working, suddenly become big-time." Probably Roger Butterfield wrote this. A story on the importance of ball bearings to "almost every piece of war equipment" brings up Speer's revelation to General Fred Anderson after the war that the Allies were within a week of ending the war by bombing the German ball-bearing plants sometime in 1943. Maybe so. In a text piece on John Foster Dulles, John Chamberlain figures him to be Dewey's Secretary of State (he had to wait eight more years) and gives his views on foreign policy. It is evident that everything that horrified me about the peace had been accepted and discounted by the power men, such as William Bullitt above. My emotional feeling is that Roosevelt had not accepted it, though he did everything to permit it.

Another thing we did not know was that around this time Omar Bradley, Patton's superior, began asking Eisenhower to give his armies the Red Ball express for gasoline and supplies. For he had every prospect of being inside Germany within a month or so, well ahead of the Russians. According to Ralph Ingersoll, Montgomery heard of it and on sheer competitive itch demanded the Red Ball for his army, which was barely moving. This conflict triggered the lifelong characteristic of Eisenhower that, in order to appear fair, he always sided against his friends. Thus, he gave the Red Ball to Montgomery who could do nothing much with it, and the Allied armies were all stalled at the German border, Patton by lack of supplies, Montgomery by sheer immobility. This was essentially what handed all central Europe over to communism. The quirks of two men, Montgomery and Eisenhower, plus the fact that Patton had once slapped a neurotic soldier, decided the fate of some hundreds of millions of central Europeans, who are still staring into the nightmare. (What happened to that accursed crybaby?) The glory men's chance of beating the power men was lost again.

A similar conflict within Time Inc. was brought on by the fact that Noel Busch had written a book on Roosevelt, and Luce had notified everybody that this was contrary to company rules.

After due thought, I dispatched a memorandum to Luce, as follows:

> Somewhat as I once protested against the Newspaper Guild's invasion of my personal rights in the demand for the Guild Shop, I would now like to turn on you. I am told that the company claims that Busch's book on Roosevelt belongs to the company. This is based partially on the belief that its publication may tend to reflect an opinion of the "company's"; partly on the belief that Busch's conditioning as a *Time*-writer made him competent to write the book, therefore another publisher should not enjoy the fruits; partly on the paternal belief that Busch should give all his energy to work for the company. All three of these contentions are false; but the third is the one I am interested in.
>
> I have so far published nothing, so far as I remember, since I joined the company. But I reserve the right to do so at the drop of a hat, after consultation with nobody. The company should indeed be pleased and admiring if I use up extra energy at night to investigate a subject not normally in the line of duty (either to acquire more facts or to reflect further on facts acquired on company time). As a natural writer I would only do that with a view to expressing some conclusions in print. I would not do it at all, if that were impossible. At the end of the operation, I will have acquired more knowledge, skill, capacity, and be a greater asset as a member of Time Inc. Writers acquire capacity by exercising it. The other way produces hollow hacks.
>
> The theorem advanced re Busch's book represents a true counter-revolution in the relations between writer and publisher. It has nothing to do with the relations between journalist and editor. I feel sure that it is only a tentative counter-revolution, which on further reflection will be abandoned.

The line on "hollow hacks" was specifically relevant for the immediate future. But in this memorandum I was not just talking. I was about to demonstrate in action just what the writer could do, and to paralyze for that interim the whole executive apparatus. Of course I did not win the local power struggle; I lost. But I won in the glory struggle, and such victories remain. I had told Luce clearly that I was not his man, and that my value resided precisely in that fact. As will appear, he did not want that kind of value, and for want of it his colossal enterprise sank into a creeping death. And I believe he never knew what he was doing or had done. And Luce was not stupid. But he felt that in the hunt for power, the only way was to assemble a collection of hacks who were, if possible, less talented than he. For he was not without talent, except that he still did not understand the secret of Briton Hadden's kind of attack on the news, liberally displayed in these pages, for I understood it as quite a simple thing, devoid of either business or religion, immune to either God or Caesar. Perhaps what annoyed Luce particularly in my memorandum is that I described myself as a "natural writer," which he was not, and that I had told Longwell when he invited me to become an editor that I was a writer and nothing else. This was not exactly true, but I did not propose to indoctrinate a crew of baboons in my secrets.

"The Coming Battle for Germany" was the lead (August 28, 1944): "German armies in western France were being battered against the Seine. . . . The Russians were already close to Germany in East Prussia . . . aimed at Krakow and German Silesia. And it was acknowledged 'Last week General George Patton Jr. set a new record for the distance between the doghouse and popular acclaim . . . a fire-and-brimstone fighter like General Patton was just what was needed.' " The editorial was on postwar reconversion, but to what? It cheered for the free market, threatened by both big government and big business. The first Big Four talks at Dumbarton Oaks have John Foster Dulles as Dewey's observer. Russia is seen holding a funeral ceremony for the Jews killed in the German "extermination camp" at Lublin. The importance of the Saipan battle is told by Robert Sherrod in the unusual form of long captions. Two text pieces, backed by a picture history of Poland, are very faintly optimistic about Poland's chances of surviving as a sovereign state.

A strange ambivalence infected the magazine (September 4, 1944) as the French welcomed the Americans and humiliated collaborators in the lead. A picture history of Paris' great moments is inserted. The editorial tries to remember past adoration of Paris, while noting that General Bradley had to send Leclerc's French troops into the city after the leader of the Free French of the Interior told him he had granted the Germans an armistice. The "Picture of the Week" shows the rejoicing in New York. There is a story of the tentative British landing in Greece. An unsigned piece (possibly by me) describes Korea's history and prospectively happy future. The essay predicted television would be a postwar "billion-dollar U.S. industry." William Bullitt gives another version of his views on the postwar world, as seen from Rome.

The lead (September 11, 1944) was "Paris Is Free Again!" The jubilation rings a little flat today and such lines as "Paris again is Paris" sound, in light of the great contest, silly and irrelevant. De Gaulle entered Paris and some atypical Parisians began shooting from the housetops. The serious business was given: "The U.S. Third Army rolled through Verdun and St. Mihiel." Teddy White contributes the story of "The Hump," the 525-mile air route between India and China. The essay is on the CIO's Political Action Committee, previously pinned down by a Jack Jessup editorial. Eric Johnston, president of the Chamber of Commerce, jubilant over a tour of Russia, concludes that Russia and the United States "have no insoluble economic or territorial conflicts." A huge increase in text pieces is noticeable.

We were roughly correct about Patton's Third Army having passed through Verdun, checked now by General Marshall's map as of September 15, 1944, in "Atlas of the World Battle Fronts in Semimonthly Phases." Patton was closer to Berlin, by a shade, than the Russians, and had he been given his head and the Red Ball, the dreadful postwar history of Central Europe would have changed for the better. So much for Eisenhower's kind of marvelous tact.

The writing is grammar school in the lead on Dewey's campaign (September 18, 1944): "The rails were lined with cops . . . [Roosevelt's] studied indifference . . . studied boredom." Polls gave Roosevelt 52.6%. "That was the figure Dewey was out to try to change by his campaign trip and the vigorous arguments he was setting forth." I attribute this to Joe Kastner whom the new regime was to make copy editor, as a master of English prose. However, Dewey, the power man, seemed to agree with the local power men that the war was no longer a serious matter. The naïve American people did not agree with him, in the event. The editorial was on the side of the power men, noting "the postwar psychology now sweeping America" and the hope of reduced taxes. A huge phalanx of American soldiers, with slung rifles, is seen coming down the Champs Élysées. The luck of the

U.S. First Army in trapping a German corps of five divisions is somewhat garbled by Jack Belden. A picture story on General George Marshall quoted him as advocating universal military training but no large peacetime army. The end of Chicago burlesque exhibited a bevy of pretty girls without navels (airbrushed out). An odd example of journalism was a color essay on beautiful Japan, certainly incomprehensible to Billings: "The Japanese are not actually inhuman. They behave with inhuman restraint or inhuman violence because they exist not as individuals but only as families, a nation, a race. . . . Of this eternal conflict the national symbol is the sleeping volcano Fujiyama, which is certainly beautiful but also very dangerous." It is quite possible that I wrote this. Longwell now, reflecting his start as a literary press agent, runs nine poems by Joseph Auslander, sobbing over *Life*'s pictures of the war. He contradicts the power men: "Is the war almost done? Like hell it's not!" Auslander, in fact, was closer to General Patton. Robert Coughlan tells an unhappy story of feuding on the War Production Board, and the hopes for "reconversion" (very long).

The readers swamped the magazine with letters (September 25, 1944) denouncing William C. Bullitt for "asking for World War III" between Russia and the English-speaking powers "in about 15 years." *Pravda* invective is also quoted. The lead is another Longwell gimmick, "A Letter from Home," expressly addressed to men in the service. It was an excuse to do an omnibus purview of the United States—from the Statue of Liberty to Boulder Dam. The editorial, contrasting it to earlier neglect of veterans, celebrated the new GI Bill of Rights. A text piece on veteran benefits is included. Surveys of farming, fishing, girls, food, baseball run around long excerpts from Dos Passos' *State of the Nation*, so that the "Letter from Home" is largely a letter from Dos Passos, who would be an oddity in most GIs' homes. This peculiar issue, which could have been credible only to the most credulous GI, must have expressed Longwell's guilt for not being under fire, a guilt that Billings and I never felt. Or it was simply sycophantic.

My recollection is that I was perfectly polite to Longwell in this period. I felt I still had work to do.

In fact, the allied armies were stalled on the Siegfried Line, historically because Patton had not been given supplies. Fletcher Pratt, the *Time* military "expert," writing in 1950 in *War for the World*, does not agree. He supplies Eisenhower with every sort of alibi: the rainy season, Allied straggling, the Siegfried Line, difficulties at the ports, War Department supply errors, the demolished railroads, the destruction of a British airborne division, the need to secure the Dutch polders, concluding with the jargon, "the position had stabilized."

We knew none of this, but were still fairly accurate in the lead (October 2, 1944), "First Battle of Germany Begins," noting the dropping of a British (and a Polish?) division on Arnhem. A prisoner was quoted as saying, "This is sheer madness." And it was added: "The madness extended to Berlin where a spokesman announced that the Nazi high command viewed the losses with 'sovereign calm.'" Jack Belden reports on the "Ziegfeld Line" and the troops' belief "that the war will end in a few days," as indeed it should have. A highly intelligent editorial makes a rational case against Roosevelt's fourth term (the Right had a writer). It concentrated on the government's "corruption of the spirit." A perspective drawing of the Southwest Pacific diagrams the rolling wave of bombings and landings, going north. The great war reporter Ernie Pyle was shown on a recuperative vacation after 29 months at the front. The sad execution of six Vichy militia by the Maquis is described by John Osborne who correctly expresses very mixed feelings. The essay was on Paris and it was pointed out, in the matter of collaboration: "In the most literal sense anybody living in France and tolerating the enemy had 'collaborated.' . . . The German occupation . . . had modified the traditional attitude of Paris, that anything in the world can be tolerated, laughed at and understood." Again, "The Parisians were never given to useless martyrdoms and a part of their spiritual campaign against the Germans was to remain conspicuously the same as ever." I know I wrote this story because it includes a tribute to the *Mona Lisa* and its neighbor, *The Madonna of the Rocks*. A glorification of U.S. General Lucian Truscott of the Sixth Corps of the Seventh Army was offered by Will Lang, with some ridicule of Patton. Oh well.

A dubious interview with Mussolini opens the next issue (October 9, 1944). For here is a lost man gibbering in a madhouse that is caving in on him. The lead was "Europe's Exiles Look Homeward" and showed the exiled governments, looking as dismal as politicians anywhere, except for the Poles who had the smallest hope of sovereignty, as stated. The editorial continues to dismember Roosevelt: "The Great Man thesis is not good enough." Gandhi praying is the picture of sanctimony for all time. The slam-bang presidential fight is reported, with my old college friend Elliot V. Bell, designated as advising Dewey, apparently badly. For the people, unlike the power men, did not believe the war was virtually over. Ordinary people generally believe in glory, not power. The magazine proceeded to a perspective drawing of the Western front, where a war was violently in progress, with Patton's Third Army through the Siegfried Line toward Koblenz. The lynching of one Italian Fascist (misspelled "Facist") and the execution of another were shown with the warning that the rest of Europe, as well as Italy, was a mess: "The U.S., breathy with goodwill but stumbling over its own political feet, was losing face and friends." "Wartime England," in paintings by Byron Thomas whom I think I once knew in Greenwich Village, is well done. I know I wrote the story, "The Land of the Franks," for it dwells on some of my favorite themes, the battle of Teutoburger Wald, Burgundy, Bruges, Gothic Europe, and Charlemagne. Elsa Maxwell gave a glamor-loaded party in Beverly Hills to celebrate the liberation of France. (Invitations had been sent out in midsummer, naming the date.) Roger Butterfield contributes a sober piece on Dewey, a very sober man.

"New Movie Find" is the picture on the cover (October 16, 1944)—Lauren Bacall. The letters Longwell expected answering "Letter from Home" duly appeared. The lead is "The Boom," noting that U.S. income had reached $150 billion. The editorial emphasizes that Dewey is a leader "not in the Messianic sense but in the parliamentary sense." A story on the funeral of the great Al Smith

398 □ THE SIN OF HENRY R. LUCE

ends on the postscript that Wendell Willkie had also just died. The essay is on William Penn, a supposed ancestor of my mother's, on his three hundredth birthday. A long story on the Negro vote shows considerable political activity. Undoubtedly, Earl Brown researched it (and perhaps wrote it). Credit for the planning that had put the German Luftwaffe out of effective action was given to Major General Frederick L. Anderson, Jr., deputy to General Spaatz, by Charles J. V. Murphy. Anderson admired the maxims of the ancient Chinese philosopher Sun Tzu, notably: "Cut off the head of the leading concubine and the rest will behave."

There is no mention of a peculiar problem that General Anderson had to deal with. When clearly marked American planes (usually fast P-38 reconnaissance planes) flew past the Germans and over Russian-held territory, they were fired on by the Russians, their allies. Anderson protested repeatedly to his Russian opposite number in England and scrupulously cooperated with the Russians by notifying them of any prospective sorties near their areas. The shooting continued.

We did not know of this.

There is a story extant of the sequel which removes Time Inc. from the area of history. As the story goes, General Anderson informed his Russian opposite number that the Americans were coming over, and quietly asked all other air forces to remain grounded on that day. He sent in the P-38 reconnaissance planes with fighter cover. The Russians attacked again.

According to the story, on that day, the Americans shot down 286 Russian planes. The Russians never again shot at American reconnaissance. At last, they had heard the one language they understood perfectly.

Again, according to the story, Stalin demanded that Roosevelt have General Anderson court-martialed and shot. (General Anderson died in bed March 2, 1969.)

The key fact of this story, that the Russians shot at American reconnaissance planes, is confirmed by Anderson's aide, Colonel Frank Lauro, who is alive. He professes ignorance of the sequel.

An inquiry to General Spaatz brings from the Historical Research

Branch of the air force a denial. A letter to the Secretary of State brings from the Historical Studies Division a report that there is "no confirmation" of the communication from Stalin to Roosevelt. The secretary for the estate of General Anderson reports that she has not yet found any such document. An event that possibly occurred has thus disappeared from history.

The question arises, Why should the Russians have committed such an unpardonable offense? The answer (which, again, we did not know) is that many American generals wanted to go right through the Red Army to Moscow, and the Russians knew it. The Americans would have had total air superiority, and many Soviet republics would have come over to the Americans as they had, incredibly, to the Nazis, before the Gestapo went to work. The glory men, such as Patton, were for the idea. The men who understood power, Roosevelt and Eisenhower, vetoed it. For, after one had taken Moscow, what would one do next? Glory men do not understand these things.

Another thing we did not know is the complex interweaving of personalities exposed in Liddell Hart's *The German Generals Talk*, which tells us among other things that Rommel was forced to commit suicide and that the German army was essentially pure. For an army needs honor if it is asked to die. The Gestapo did not need honor, for it killed primarily the defenseless.

The amiable American attitude, in contrast, was shown by a Russian scientist on the cover (October 23, 1944). A gallery of "Great Soviet Scientists" was the "Speaking of Pictures." They look much like American scientists. I suspect some Time Inc. people of becoming too naïvely sympathetic to Communist Russia, including Gerry Piel, who probably wrote this story, and Dick Lauterbach, who had the precious privilege of being sent to Russia. The lead was on the bombing by Halsey's Pacific fleet of Formosa, the Ryukyus, Mindanao, and Manila. The editorial eulogizing the late Al Smith and Wendell Willkie as "between them, they might have made the ideal president" may have been by Willkie's friend, Russell Davenport, but describes Willkie as "vain." It may still have been by Davenport. The ultimate structure of the United Nations is outlined at Dumbarton Oaks, with a chart. A magnificent essay on the Colorado River fails to

predict the ruin to be visited on it by the Corps of Engineers. In a
review of Roosevelt's record, John Chamberlain agrees that the war
is all but won, ridiculing Roosevelt's career: a pure power gambit. A
new department, "Life's Miscellany," is introduced by Longwell at
the tail of the magazine—and it is just that, or worse.

I was smart enough to sense that something was going wrong. My
loyalty to the organization could hardly be transferred to Longwell
and Thorndike. Clarence Streit, author of *Union Now*, asked me to
compose a paperback rewrite of his work for mass distribution. I did
not ask Longwell or Billings or Luce whether they would kindly give
me official permission. I said yes, and went to work. Later, I asked
the picture department, with whose people I was friendly, to ask the
picture services and the *Life* morgue for pictures to illustrate the
book. These were used and not paid for. After use in the book, they
were returned to the services and the files, without acknowledgment.

This was a defiance of Luce's ukase of how Time Inc. writers
should use their spare time, blitzing through the ukase as drastically
as Patton. Babe Paxton was to be the art editor of the book, but at
some point begged off. Strangely, nobody at any time ever reproached me for doing this "revolutionary" job. One factor was that
Mrs. Luce was an adherent of Federal Union. My book was called
The Great Union.

Thus, I presented myself to the executives quite frankly as an
independent hoodlum beyond their control. I never got any profit
from the Federal Union paperback, which I think sold for 25 cents.
Other outfits sprang up, such as the World Federalists and finally the
United Nations, which either missed or evaded Clarence Streit's
brilliant point.

Actually, a "blind" reference had been published by the Federal
Unionists in March 1944: "A very competent writer, whose name will
be announced later, has been selected for this important task after a
thorough search for the author best fitted to do it. He is high on the
staff of one of the country's most popular magazines. His ability to
write sound sense for the man in the street is attested not only by his
position but by those most familiar with his work. He is of course a

convinced Federal Unionist . . . magazine as a magazine having nothing to do with the project."

As if this enterprise were not enough to shake Luce, I find in my effects the following memorandum to Luce, dated September 8, 1944:

I like my present job, by and large. I would like any job where I can do the two things I like to do, to learn and to tell. Naturally, the present moment is a tentative one, of seeing what the present *Life* management wants of me. This letter would be an utter waste of paper if I did not say at once that Dan Longwell has conveyed to me his contempt for my opinions, my facts, my honesty. However, that is not an insoluble problem and a period of adjustment is now on.

I know what are the subjects I want to learn about and tell about in the postwar period. For the past ten years it was the coming war and the nature of war that we had to tell the people about, whether or not they wanted to hear about it. Today and for the future, it is politics, the nature of the various peoples and cultures all over the world and what those peoples think and want, that I believe we must tell the Americans about. Those peoples by no means think and want the things we expect and hope. Telling about them is a limitless assignment.

I have not been abroad since 1937. I should like to go abroad.

I have not been under any strain since mid-1942 and I am not tired, consciously or unconsciously.

Actually, I worry more about this organization than the foregoing page would indicate. Personnel is a large part of it. I wish the competition were a lot faster than it is. Too many people here are stupid or hypocritical or mere time-servers. They may be a menace or a hindrance politically, but not in any competitive sense. Routine has been worked out to such a wonderful point that nobody, editor, writer, researcher, feels any need to assume for the moment absolute responsibility before God or to try to exercise an absolute curiosity about his subject. Everybody just rows along with the boat, dipping the oar with the others. (This is purposely an exaggerated statement of it.) On *Life* at least, the notion has been dropped that every story is an attempt to cover the whole subject. Now we produce a little text as ornamentation for an episode in the life of one of our photographers. The point is never what actually happened, overall, but what fragment of it did *Life*'s Photographer, at great company expense, witness and how did he feel, and here are the pictures to prove it. This attitude and technic are of course superior promotion technic but not journalism, except as when a Stanley finds Livingstone. Sometimes, it is true, our photographers do find Livingstone and then the technic is justified. Otherwise, I believe, not.

What I am and how I work must by this time be known to you. I should like to ask you the direct question: is there ultimately room for me in this organization? Or is my kind of guy becoming extinct here? I will take any answer: Yes, No, or either with reservations.

I do not remember that Luce ever responded to this remarkable confession. It is obvious that the terrible power of Longwell had never gotten through to me, for I had known him too long and ignominiously. It is a testament to something that I continued to be "indispensable" for a year and a half after this blast at the man of whom any criticism, as Billings told Hubie Kay, was "very dangerous." Yet most of the capable people there despised Longwell and may have looked to me as some sort of counterstandard. This was silly, for I was not a power man. I had no interest in any hypothetical followers; I was there to do a job. But what was Luce to make of the memorandum? The question "Is my kind of guy becoming extinct here?" must have signaled to him that I knew (as I did not) the sin he was about to commit against the Holy Ghost. As of now, so long later, it is obvious. Because he was otherwise a decent man, I weep over his grave.

The lead on the coming elections (October 30, 1944) stressed that this was "a solemn, serious campaign" in which "the people knew this was no time for nonsense." It then exhibited the nonsense. Roosevelt spent four and a half hours in the rain with no overcoat. The editorial admits the Republicans have some powerful isolationists, but voters should be selectively Republican. The invasion of the Philippines by MacArthur's Sixth Army is mapped. (My uncle Brigadier General Hugh Cort has said that he planned the invasion of Leyte, which opened the campaign.) The great new battleship *Iowa* is shown (also on the cover) but the class is described as "still battleships in an aircraft carrier's war." Paintings by Aaron Bohrod of the bloody landing on Omaha Beach in Normandy are fairly effective. A text piece advises liberals to vote for Dewey. Longwell's cliché literary bias is applied to a beautiful picture essay, "The World of Washington Irving." Next to it, horribly, is a first-hand account of the German executions of Jews. Longwell was never more clearly not Billings. But this performance was satisfactory to Luce.

The magazine is losing the sense of mastery Billings had given it. The lead and editorial are for Dewey (November 6, 1944). There is a cursory story on the great Philippine Sea naval battle, and an irrelevant one on how nicely the Americans were treating Japanese civilians on Saipan. A sycophantic story ennobled Tito's Partisans again. In short closeups of the vice-presidential candidates, it was said of Truman: "There is abundant evidence that he never intended to get there and probably is still puzzled as to how it all came about."

The famous picture of MacArthur wading up the beach at Leyte in the Philippines opened the lead (November 13, 1944). (MacArthur had a man waiting on the beach with a pair of dry pants. The picture was of course staged, but the fact does not shame MacArthur.) Some details of the naval battle (sometimes called Leyte Gulf battle) are given: Japanese lose 2 battleships, 4 carriers, 3 small cruisers, 6 destroyers, and 34 other ships damaged. (The figures given by Pratt are all remaining Japanese carriers, 3 battleships, 8 heavy cruisers, 5 light cruisers, 9 destroyers: the end of the Japanese navy. He is somewhat critical of Admiral Halsey, another glory man.) The editorial notes the recall of General Stilwell from China, dramatizing American neglect of Chiang's war, which was understandable but may have led to the Communist victory.

In *Time*'s issue of November 20, 1944, is a little story on Clarence Streit's Federal Union of the democracies with the line, "They are currently concentrating on a sales campaign for *Life* Editor David Cort's newly published *The Great Union*, a brief, eloquent, brilliantly illustrated restatement of Streit's thesis."

I am sure that Billings edited the next issue (November 20, 1944) because I remember that his assigning me the story on Paris fashions outraged all the women. The lead on "The Election" said that everybody seemed pleased by the result. The editorial said that the election, win or lose, was a good thing. The sad story of the Chinese retreat from Kweilin and Liuchow was told. Eight families of war dead were interviewed and photographed. The loss of two U.S. escort carriers in the Leyte Gulf battle was admitted. The fashion story said: "Paris, however, proved with ease that it still has the most amusing and ingenious taste in the world, the subtlest feeling for materials and the way to put them on the bodies of women. . . . Paris is full of tricks." Half a dozen women came in to tell me they would never wear the fashions shown; six months later they were wearing them. New York harbor, portrayed in paintings, opened the way for superlatives such as "half again as much ocean shipping as all other U.S. ports combined." A strange feature was a series of quotes from the *New York Times* on such rusticana as orchards, root cellars, stone walls, watering troughs, and wheelbarrows, with photographs.

The lead on the German evacuation of Greece (November 27, 1944) illustrated the mass murder and starvation, the destruction of over 2,000 villages, and the insane Nazi demolition of a nation. The editorial on when the war would end reminded, "It should be remembered that all the Germans have not gone crazy." An inexplicable shortage of cigarettes in the United States is reported. The flooding of the war in Holland and around Metz is exhibited. The arrival of jet propulsion, based on the rocket, is pictured in the P-59. The essay is on cartoon books by Partch, Goldberg, Steig, Taylor, and Arno, with a tribute to *The New Yorker*'s cartoons. This is odd but odder still is a long poem of six columns, "My Country," by Russell Davenport. I am glad for Mitch Davenport but this is not Time Inc. journalism. Longwell was editing some imaginary magazine, not *Life*.

The CIO's Political Action Committee, which had become *Life*'s special *bête noire*, occasioned the lead (December 4, 1944), with Sidney Hillman given a fifteen-minute ovation. Labor's aims, however, worthily included "an end to racial discrimination." The editorial noted that a congressional committee, this early, recommended that Congress reform itself, specifically in its committee system. An old portrait of Hitler was captioned: "Rumor filled the world with stories that Hitler has paranoia, concussion, coronary thrombosis, paralysis of the right side, a throat tumor, ear inflammation, a broken arm, damaged vocal cords, that he is dead, mad, on a submarine headed for Japan or a remote island." "The Big Push" was illustrated by a perspective drawing of the Western front. In a story on the first meeting of the French Consultative Assembly—"the rebirth of France, not the first in its history"—Foreign Minister

Bidault was quoted: "The peace with Germany should not be one of vengeance; it must be just and humane." The essay, "The Rhine," was a tribute to the cultural glories and political impotence of the Rhineland.

The postwar world was heralded in the lead, "Communists Ride Europe's Wave" (December 11, 1944). My suspicions were indicated by the lines: "Nobody had asked the people to vote on anything. The most effective form of politics . . . was the big public demonstration." The fatheads on the staff, usually called leftists, could not forgive my failure to share their delusion that communism and democracy were synonyms. To them, and to many people today, a riot was democratic. The editorial took the replacement of Cordell Hull by Stettinius to speculate on Hull's "greatness" and decide that he was deficient in *Realpolitik*. Charles J. V. Murphy observes about the European battle: "Some generals think that if it had been possible to deliver another 8,000 to 10,000 tons of gasoline and ammunition . . . to General Patton's Third Army early in September . . . the German war would now be over . . . the German Army will never again be able to take the offensive." Another Longwell press agentry is a reproduction of 30 *Time* cover paintings, all war leaders, including one of Rommel who killed himself before it could be used. The essay is pure Longwell—"Teen-age Girls." Lacking Billings' seriousness, the point was: "Aren't they cute!"

We did not know of the German attack December 16, 1944, between Monschau and Echternach toward Bastogne. Two corps of Patton's Third Army struck up from Arlon to Bastogne. Liddell Hart points out that, in supporting this stroke, Hitler was in general "quicker to spot the value of new ideas, new weapons, and new talents," while also liquidating the nation he commanded. I cannot help feeling that this also describes Longwell. Luce, on the other hand, did not realize what was going on, or did not evaluate it, except as it affected his power.

Liddell Hart demonstrates that the failure of the June 20, 1944, assassination of Hitler resulted in a high percentage of suicides in the German high command, higher than even at Time Inc. Rommel, Kluge, and Stulpnagel committed suicide, the last failing and being hanged instead. Rommel had guessed where the Allied invasion would come. Kluge at one point had replaced Rundstedt on the Western front. Still, there is a certain correspondence between the Great German General Staff and Time Inc. Rundstedt did not die by his own hand, nor have I.

"The Battlefield of Germany" was the lead (December 18, 1944). The editorial fretted over the Surplus Property Act of 1944, the first step toward reconversion. Churchill defended his summary action against Greek Communist guerrillas: "Democracy is not a harlot that can be picked up in the street by any man with a Tommy gun." Teddy (*sic*) White sends in a report from "Inside Red China." Photographer George Silk, showing a battle in Holland, tells how he dove into a dugout where a soldier said quietly, "Don't shoot." Silk replied, "Don't worry, pal, I haven't got a gun." The other said, "Well, take mine. It's a Luger." He was a German officer.

I think Billings edited the next issue (December 25, 1944) because I had at last got my closeup on Rundstedt, "The Last Prussian," into the magazine, obviously through Billings. The lead was "Hospital on Leyte," the editorial on Christmas, endorsing faith. A portfolio of religious paintings by Miss Lauren Ford honored the date. Lionel Barrymore and cast are seen acting out *A Christmas Carol*. And the V-2 is explained in all its rather inefficient horror. Finally, comes "The Last Prussian." Of his class, it said, "The result has certainly been the ablest and certainly the most exclusive military caste that the world has lately seen, numbering perhaps 5,000 aristocrats. . . . They regard with disguised contempt the Nazis, most of the rest of Germany and civilians everywhere. But they know how to wage war." At the end it is said that, if you met him out of uniform, "he would look at you evenly, with the controlled face and the hooded eyes, and he would be thinking about the next war"—this in an issue whose cover is the "Madonna and Child," in a rather flat version by Miss Ford. At last, we understood the huge moral chasm between the Nazis and the officer corps.

The German counterattack in the Ardennes Forest, their favorite woodland, occupied the lead (January 1, 1945), launching into a plea for more war production, especially heavy artillery ammunition (the truth was that the Germans were running short of everything). The editorial complained about too much victory too soon, and that it was "the same old Europe" of power plays, as indeed it was. An anecdotal story of the battle of Huetgen Forest was offered by William Walton. I think I wrote the essay on the beauties of ancient Athens, built by Pericles and Phidias in thirty years in the fifth century B.C. Stalin as the supreme hero is presented by Richard Lauterbach in the closeup, "Stalin at 65." Today it is laughable.

The lead, unconventionally, is a long text piece (January 8, 1945) by, as he styled himself, Charles Christian Wertenbaker, on the Battle of the Bulge. However, he reports Patton's race to attack the southern flank of the German breakthrough. The editorial suggests that American soldiers' performance might inspire civilians to accept hardships. It adds that the power boys' worries about reconversion might well be pigeonholed. Dick de Rochemont puts the best possible face on the future of France. This ceremony had become Dick's career.

Moving photos of American men and tanks closing in on Bastogne (January 15, 1945) were by photographer Robert Capa. Creighton Abrams, later commander in Vietnam, is cited as a lieutenant colonel commanding one of Patton's tank battalions. The Americans broke the siege the day after Christmas. The editorial explained some Englishmen's irritability by their disappointment in America's failure to take on world responsibility. It was revealed that Hitler had held up an order for Swedish granite blocks for a monument to himself nearly a mile long and a thousand feet tall. Churchill is seen arriving in Athens on Christmas to settle the Greek civil war. John Hersey has a simple, effective, slightly humorous closeup of a Russian big businessman.

With a picture map of the Philippines, the battle for Luzon makes the lead (January 22, 1945), with a selection from a Japanese book of 1942 celebrating the Japanese victory then. There had been very few Filipino collaborators in the three years since. The editorial applauded Republican Senator Vandenberg's speech proposing an antiaggression treaty among the United States, Britain, France, Russia, and China. For America was not yet aware of the very probable dismemberment of Poland and Germany by Russia, and of Germany by France. The third Time Inc. correspondent killed in combat theatres, William Chickering, was memorialized. John Chamberlain has a text piece, "The Nine Young Men," saying that the "packed" Supreme Court is so badly packed it is unpredictable.

A long (11-page) picture story following a wounded American from the front in Lorraine back to the United States and recovery is the lead (January 29, 1945), showing that 96% of American wounded who reach the hospital survive. The editorial debated a draft of women, saying, "For of all the social revolutions abroad in the world, that of the women is the least dynamic, the least predictable, the most aimless and divided—in short, the most feminine." A factual story of a Siberian gold rush improbably ends with pictures of a French actress, Danielle Darrieux. Perhaps Longwell thought this clever. A magnificent feature was a series of Russian historical paintings, illustrating Stalin's new version of Russian history which rehabilitated most of the czarist heroes (but not Catherine the Great or Orlov). The war is fading out as "Battle of the West" is relegated to the back of the issue. A beautiful snowy valley is seen empty but for three cows, but it is lined with death hidden in the woods.

The factual integrity of Time Inc. still functions, but we can already detect in Longwell's editing that subdivision of power represented by instant glory, that is, evoking an instant response from some section of the public. Enough examples have been given. This device is employed by people who do not like themselves, and lust to prove their likeability. Thus Longwell. My solemn word is that this miserable characteristic was not typical of Time Inc. personnel. Longwell was almost universally despised by the old-timers, but I believe that I was the only one who was outspoken, largely because of my past collegiate acquaintance. I can now understand that Longwell, given his corporate skills, had decided to eliminate me, but I was not even conscious of such peril. The war was still on and I (almost) had a monopoly on it.

Snow blankets the lead (February 5, 1945) in pictures of the American destruction of the Ardennes salient, and the massacre by the Germans of American prisoners. Fifteen survived to tell the story.

A story on the Russian advance, "On to Berlin," includes a map roughly the same as General Marshall's authentic one. "The Forgotten Fronts" called attention to the Australian fighting on Bougainville, New Guinea, and New Britain, the various Chinese fronts, the combat in northern Norway, Crete, and the Dodecanese, and postscripted Ethiopia, India's northwest frontier, the border of Manchukuo, and Central American revolutionaries. The closeup is on Bill Mauldin, the GIs' cartoonist. The essay on "American Legends" told the semimyths of Mike Fink, Blackbeard, Davy Crockett, Paul Bunyan, John Henry, Johnny Appleseed, Joe Hill, and Judge Roy Bean. David Fredenthal contributes drawings of the Russians in Yugoslavia with Tito's Partisans. *Life*'s weekly party was Roosevelt's fourth inauguration.

The Russian approach to within forty miles of Berlin made the lead (February 12, 1945). The writing is curiously uncertain: the fall of Berlin "would be a great entering wedge for the idea of defeat in the German mind." Hitler's story is retold in pictures ending with Berchtesgaden: "Here, amid mountains, he laid his grandiose plans. Here he will see them all crumble." This is grammar school stuff. The editorial applauds a judge who ruled that Roosevelt's wartime power was not unlimited. A story on the new "Stilwell road" reinforcing Chiang Kai-shek mentions "jungle leaches." Pretty and brainy Shelley Smith Mydans has a good story on flight nurses bringing home the wounded. The essay is an attempt by the poet Robert P. Tristram Coffin "to capture the winter moods" of his native Maine. The pictures are nice, the poetry passable, but neither belonged in *Life*. More Longwell. The closeup is on Marshal Zhukov by Dick Lauterbach, the Russian "expert." Of such individually trivial things are decadence and dissolution made.

Robert Sherrod has a piece on Radio Tokyo's lunatic insistence that the war was going splendidly (February 19, 1945). The lead was on the joy of the Filipinos and on a story "My God! It's Carl Mydans" for Carl helped liberate the Japanese camp Santo Tomas where he and his wife had been for nine months in 1942. His story cannot possibly be condensed. A routine picture history of the Philippines since Magellan is included. The editorial says that in general our giving the Philippines independence was a splendid idea. A story on the new nine-year-old Dalai Lama concludes: "Most lamas die at 20, reportedly by poisoning." An excellent text piece by Francis Sill Wickware is on psychosomatic medicine. The essay, probably by me, is on Japan: "Japan may have an appearance of quaintness but it is about as quaint as Genghis Khan. . . . So intense is the Jap rage against the Americans that it has turned against all whites still visible in Tokyo, especially Germans. . . . They are in fact, according to themselves, the gods, descended from the gods and propagating more gods."

A side effect of Longwell journalism, in this case the story of the war casualty's return home, was a page (February 26, 1945) devoted to the flood of letters and gifts deluging the man in a Utica, New York, hospital. The lead was an essay by the Fascist leader Count Dino Grandi on what happened to Mussolini. The editorial thought the Yalta (Crimea) Conference's decisions (joint occupation of Germany, Russian dominance in Poland) good because they averted the calamity of an Allied breakup. In a spread of very poor pictures of the conference (*Life* was annoyed at not having a photographer there), Roosevelt looks terrible. A great fleet air raid on Tokyo is illustrated by a perspective drawing. Iwo Jima is noted for the first time. Carl Mydans tells a moving story of U.S. Rangers' rescue of dazed American prisoners in Manila. Another bunch of incoherent paintings purport to show the war in the Aegean.

Another Philippine rescue of American prisoners is the lead (March 5, 1945). The editorial rejected Henry Wallace's naïve hopes for full postwar employment. On a display of Roosevelt's visit to the Middle East is the caption, "By tradition and centuries of practice, the small and scrofulous states and would-be states which are cluttered around the Middle East's routes of empire are masters at snakepit politics." Nobody but I was arrogant enough to have written this. Incidentally, it is noted that Turkey has just declared war on Germany and Japan, both happily remote. The battle for Iwo Jima ("the toughest we've run across in 168 years") put 70,000 men fighting in an arena of eight volcanic square miles. Robert Sherrod verbalizes the story in "The First Three Days." Longwell's series of pieces on European nations by their citizens rotates one on Denmark. This was a move to outflank Time Inc. journalism (specifically me) and was unsuccessful. The movie *Fighting Lady*, about an American carrier, brings back the name of John S. Martin as writer of the commentary. A good example of proper *Life* journalism was the essay on the great Italian "House of Colonna": "They have a vague claim of descent from Julius Caesar, are said to have had seven medieval popes, and had, in fact, one great pope, Martin V. . . . Colonnas have a traditional feud with Orsinis and in Rome the two princes never sit at the same table. . . . No other noble family has maintained its unbroken power for so long—1,000 years—as the Colonnas." I wrote this. John Chamberlain has a text piece claiming that the only way to get to Roosevelt is currently through his daughter Anna. Briton Hadden's journalism continued to explode through Longwell's colored icing, but it was to be the losing side. I cannot say that I realized the nature and power of the creeping decadence. I was unaware of anybody's lust for power. I was merely doing a job, as Billings had done; Danny was carving a career, to what end it is useless to speculate, for it was not consummated; historically, he was nothing, a mere bacterium that ultimately infected the whole organization with the disease of trivial ostentation. For Luce used to say, "That's a story we get credit for." He was very strong on "credit." And all the letters to the wounded GI would have struck Luce as "credit." In fact, they had nothing to do with Time Inc.'s job. They had turned Time Inc. into a soap opera. Doubtless, Longwell claimed that he was a better managing editor than Billings, and Luce apparently believed him. One must read into this a basic contempt for the American people in both Longwell and Luce. I am not infatuated with any doctrinaire idea of the intelligence of the whole American people. But I insist on talking to them as if they are fully as intelligent as I, or even a little smarter.

The crossing of the little Roer River, masking failure to unleash Patton's Third Army, made the lead (March 12, 1945). The editorial boasted of America's "military might," especially in sea and air power and in "range," but the impression is of appalling waste. After a story on the bloody marines' exploit on Iwo comes Roosevelt's speech, "We shall have to take the responsibility for world collaboration or we shall have to bear the responsibility for another world conflict." This meant, to me, that he had bowed to Stalin's power plans for Central Europe. I understood the great gentleman's instinct to pretend that the gangster was also a gentleman, in the hope that he would become so. But I had no faith that it would work. For I am not a great gentleman, as Roosevelt was. After a piece by G. A. Borgese protesting the inevitable postwar arrangements came the fashionable littérateur John Dos Passos, as "special war correspondent for *Life*" (a farcical misnomer), describing his rambles over the Pacific atolls in a nice little diary.

These heresies horrified me and every true Time Inc. writer. For Longwell was violating the basic concept of Briton Hadden, that literary people were worthless, and that pure muscular factualism could short-circuit the communication to the reader. Oddly enough, the concept was particularly attractive to literary people (such as myself) who had stopped wanting to sound beautiful, and wanted to tell the truth. Longwell, I am sorry to say, didn't care about the truth. I am saying here that only the great literary masters, such as Proust, tell the truth; typically, the others tell their favorite lies, and this intuition is what inspired Briton Hadden. He had dreamed of a journalistic operation that would produce the (current) journalistic truth. This fanatical crusade was not even understood by Longwell, nor, I would assume, by Luce, but it was understood very well by a number of us.

Longwell understood the fact, and its reverse side, that the literary world was infuriated by Time Inc. Therefore, Longwell's strategy was to try to placate the literary world, by way of its celebrities such as Dos Passos. Of course it did not work, and only compromised the Time Inc. crusade. At the time I did not realize what Longwell was doing, or why; I was only disgusted. Dos Passos in *Life* was travesty.

Reader revulsion against Dino Grandi's apologia fills the next Letters section (March 19, 1945). A German account of the American character brought out such items as: "They believe everything they see in print," "They grin all day long," and "All of them bluff." The lead showed the German crumbling in the West, as the Americans crossed an unblown Rhine bridge at Remagen. The editorial called a Pan-American Conference in Mexico a success, giving credit to "Assistant Secretary Nelson Rockefeller whose four years of good-willing in Latin America are bearing fruit." Perón's Argentina, however, had been excluded from the conference. This early, it is noted, the New York Legislature passed a law banning employment discrimination based on race, creed, or color. A high in triviality was a bewildering piece by Annalee Jacoby on the practice of standing eggs on end in Chungking one hour before and after the coming of spring, or 1:00 P.M., February 4, 1945 [sic], but the spell carried on through February. Here Longwell had leaked into Time Inc. *The New Yorker* clique's fascination with the pointless.

The facts of the famous Iwo Jima flag-raising picture are given (March 26, 1945). That was staged and taken in the afternoon by Associated Press photographer Joe Rosenthal. The real picture was taken at 10:30 A.M., February 23, 1945, by S/Sgt. Louis R. Lowery. Other flags raised that day were that of the Confederacy and Lone Star Texas. The lead showed in sequence the capture of Paris black marketeers (mostly U.S. Army deserters and blacks). The deserters were executed. The editorial on the Un-American Activities Committee considered the definition of the adjective and decided it meant concealment of motive. Airviews illustrated the bombing of Tokyo by 300 B-29s (vast conflagrations), of Nagoya two days later, of Osaka two days later, and of Kobe three days later—with a loss of four planes, all from Mariana air bases. The destruction rivaled the later Hiroshima and Nagasaki, but I added, "Airmen . . . knew how much pounding a modern industrial nation could take and still fight a full-scale war." In parallel, the destruction of Cologne is shown, captioned with a snatch of poetry by Coleridge who must have had a bias against the city. (This evidence of Longwell's education is excusable, at worst.) A comparison of the Stalin, Royal Tiger (Nazi), and Sherman tanks gives the Stalin the laurels as the most powerful with the lowest silhouette. It was noted that the Russian system of weapon production was civilian and individualistic, while the Western system was military-bureaucratic—that is, so to speak,

Communist, and inferior. This could have been written only by me, for it reeks of Gary Underhill. A long passage is given to the anecdotal homespun book, *Carrier War*, by Lieutenant Oliver Jensen, who later helped start *American Heritage* with Joseph Thorndike. They were shaping their careers, sensibly.

Longwell found one reader's letter adulating Dos Passos' piece, and a number praising Borgese (his prewar book on fascism, *Goliath*, is worth reading, if only for its low rating of Dante Alighieri), getting his idea that the seeds of the third world war were being planted by Soviet Russia (April 2, 1945). The lead described the Allies' crossing of the Rhine en masse, noting that German civilians were "neither arrogant nor fawning . . . surprised that the Americans were cold, unfriendly. The Germans seemed to have forgotten the war." The editorial was on Easter and religion, a sop to Luce. Another city, Manila, is seen destroyed, as MacArthur "returns." Lincoln Barnett is very perceptive in a closeup of the great war correspondent Ernie Pyle.

Here, at the approach of an immense historical climax, the journalism of Time Inc. is trivial and playful. The triviality reached me personally in an invitation from the air force to accept free transportation to Brazil and thence to Ascension Island in the South Atlantic to witness the air force's miraculous breakthrough in growing fresh vegetables on desert islands by means of hydroponics. Earlier, I had asked the company to send me to Yugoslavia, and been refused. Since in my Napoleonic hallucination I had won the war, I gladly accepted. I even took a camera and photographed Ascension but Billings, as I remember, did not choose to put my pictures in the magazine. I recall that soldiers bathing on Ascension's fine beaches sometimes vanished without warning in the huge breakers piling up from the Antarctic. It was indeed a desert island except for a green mountain where the British governor lived, and the airstrip was a ravine dug between sand cliffs. I did not learn its key relevance to the battle of El Alamein.

A multitude of readers, including my friend Clarence Streit, write that eggs stand on end almost anywhere (April 9, 1945). Belated army pictures of the Yalta Conference show Churchill gorging caviar, wearing a Persian lamb hat bought for him by *Life* photographer John Phillips, and trying out his Russian (a disaster). John Hersey reports on another great ruin, Warsaw, on which the Germans had expended disproportionate destructive energy. They seem increasingly mad. The lead was on "The Last Round" in Germany, a quote from Field Marshal Montgomery—11 pages. The text described a fantasy of 100 German divisions hedgehogging around Berchtesgaden—"some estimates put the length of possible Nazi resistance in the mountains in years." It was suggested that Hitler's hostages would include the kings of Belgium and Denmark, Stalin's son, Daladier, Blum, Herriot, and Viscount Lascelles, and that the Emperor Charlemagne was also waiting nearby. This must have been the mad dream of Longwell with a complaisant writer. It sounds like Whittaker Chambers, but of course was not. At this great historic point *Time*, under T. S. Matthews, was timid, pedestrian, wordy, and boring. True, it labeled a map with "Hitler's Inner Fortress" around Berchtesgaden, but without explanation. In the issue of April 9, it has Patton 152 miles from Berlin. A "Salute to the Armies" was a grandiloquent tribute, chiefly to Marshall, and to Hodges' First Army. Patton's Third Army was called "the cockiest," but a German officer is quoted as naming Patton the most important U.S. general. The dissolution of Germany is recorded. Thus Goebbels: "History is a hard taskmaster." After a review of the New York theatre season, a story on Iwo Jima says: "For a month Iwo was one of the most densely populated eight square miles in the world, with 10,000 men to the square mile. It then became one of the most densely populated cemeteries in the world." If I did not write this, somebody had learned something.

The lead was "The Backwash of Battle" (April 16, 1945), turning to the millions of refugees on the roads of Germany, and noting that Patton was 125 miles west of Berlin, while the Russians were 30 miles east of it. This compared fairly closely to General Marshall's map of the date. If we remember that the *Life* of April 16 closed on April 8, Patton's Third could still have reached Berlin before the Russians. The editorial compensated for "Salute to the Armies" with "Salute to the Fleets"—"the greatest navy the world has ever known"—and mentioned the invasion of Okinawa. The supremacy of American power, never cashed in on, is the paramount impression at this point. Charles Wertenbaker makes a garbled story of "The Victory of the Rhine" and Noel Busch does better with Good Queen Wilhelmina's return to Holland. A fairly pointless story on the American Fifth Army in Italy lists its components: the Negro 92nd Division, English, Canadians, New Zealanders, Indians, Poles, Brazilians, Italians, and Palestine Jews. One Wilfred Fleischer presumed to define "What to Do with Japan" as punishment, agriculture, light industry. He didn't know what he was talking about.

The next cover (April 23, 1945) is a shocker for it is "President Truman." I cannot remember where I was when I heard of Roosevelt's death, dated 3:35 P.M. April 12, a Thursday, timed just right for *Life*'s publication schedule. Of interest to me is that my mother died on the same day and at about the same hour in 1936, when the day was Easter Sunday—she of pneumonia, Roosevelt of a massive cerebral hemorrhage. I felt worse when Roosevelt died than when Jack Kennedy was murdered, and properly, for Roosevelt was not permitted to finish his war, whereas Kennedy had not yet entered on his so much less prideful war. The lead gave Roosevelt 13 pages—"this gallant, fearless man"—and quoted the *New York Times*: "Men will thank God on their knees a hundred years from now, that Franklin D. Roosevelt was in the White House . . . in that dark hour when a powerful and ruthless barbarism threatened to overrun . . . civilization." (A very reasonable prediction, I think.) The editorial was a somewhat hedged tribute—"there was something finally elusive about Roosevelt's character, the elusiveness that suggests magic and breeds myths" (I would agree)—and considered the sequel with Truman, who did not really want to be president (I agree again, happily, remembering Aaron Burr). The closeup is of Lieutenant Colonel Creighton Abrams (more recently in Vietnam), commander of the "cutting edge" 37th Tank Battalion of the leadoff Fourth Armored Division of Patton's Third Army—in other words, an officer totally indoctrinated in and dedicated to the offensive strike. This completely convinces me that our generals in Vietnam were not responsible for not taking Hanoi and Haiphong in 60 days and ending that war, but were under the orders of politicians, who must accept final responsibility for the futile killing of 50,000 Americans in the name of politics. The story is by Will Lang. He includes (apocryphally) a Nazi legend that every soldier in the Fourth Division was required to prove (1) he had killed his mother, (2) he had been born out of wedlock. The Nazis certainly applied this test to Creighton Abrams. The essay is a collection of portraits of "Roosevelt's Men." Willi Schlamm, an Austrian refugee, contributes a persuasive piece on Roosevelt's chief antagonist, Hitler, who also had a finally elusive character, as I follow his conduct of World War II. His suicide confirms his insane faith in himself, as magic and myth, as he makes a claim to being one with Charlemagne and Barbarossa (at least in being dead).

Truman's first week occupied the lead (April 30, 1945): "The country . . . applauded again when he quickly turned down Russia's demand that the [Communist] Lublin Polish government be invited to attend the [San Francisco] Conference." Mrs. Roosevelt dismissed a reporter with the statement, "The story is over." The United Nations organization, practically as it exists today, was outlined, and the conference and San Francisco surveyed. The editorial pointed out the flaws in the plan, notably the veto power of the Big Five and the absence of an international bill of rights (a horror to Communist states). A Hitler hideout in the Hessian Mountains was shown after it had been bombed and overrun. A huge portfolio of war scenes painted by "*Life* artists," a pet project of Longwell's, leads to the notation at last that Ascension Island had been "a decisive factor in winning the North African campaign." I suppose I wrote all this. It is also revealed that Trinidad's queen of the Carib Indians had declared war on Germany and Japan and that American troops hung a brown paper bag at the door and declared as white anybody lighter than the bag (a certain frivolity in the writing is noticeable). For example, the famous women dancers of Manipur in India, who had grown rich during the war, were on strike in protest against the income tax. And the English "will always be grateful to the Manipuri for having taught them the game of polo." Eliot Janeway attributes to Roosevelt a tortuous and tricky politics beyond the imagination of anyone save Janeway.

Along with various rumors (Göring suicide, Hitler cerebral hemorrhage), the lead (May 7, 1945) reports the final drumbeats of the war in Europe, and the meeting of the American and Russian armies on the Elbe near Torgau. (The Elbe ran down about the center of what was to be Communist East Germany, an invention that might bring on World War III.) The editorial brooded on the peace, allowing that it would be a good idea to help the Europeans get back on their feet. The discovery of the concentration camps reminded Americans of the massive Nazi atrocities against mankind. The grisly pictures were shown with the old refrain, "Dead men have indeed died in vain if live men refuse to look at them." Fillmore Calhoun had a piece saying that the Russians were making a bad impression on everybody at San Francisco. A text piece on the German people was so unsatisfactory to me that I began writing such a piece in my spare time (cut out of a later book). The picture essay was on France in the spring. This was a typical example of Longwell playing his peculiar sharps and flats on the magnificent compliant Time Inc. instrument. I would imagine that Luce did not understand Time Inc. sensitively enough to know what was going on. But the personnel knew. The contempt for Longwell's journalism was repeatedly conveyed to me. When a great creation starts to die, somebody notices.

Theoretically, the war in Europe ended early in the morning of Monday, May 7, disastrous for *Life*'s publication schedule which concludes on the Saturday, but perfect for Time, closing Monday night. The event was not that cleancut, however. The Germans had been trying to surrender to the Anglo-Americans (but not to the Russians) since Friday, May 4, but Eisenhower had steadily refused this offer. The whole staff, especially the correspondents, were therefore trying hard. The final issue dated May 14, 1945, was bound in hard covers with a pasted-in letter:

All the weeks and months of preparation, the last days and nights of anxious work to be ready when the great day came; all the devotion and brilliance and inspiration of a great editorial team are reflected for me in this memorable issue of *Life*.

You can justly be proud of it.

Roy Larsen

The cover is "Victorious Yank," and the lead is "The War Ends in Europe." A radiophoto shows the backs of the German delegation, Admiral von Friedeburg, Colonel General Jodl, and Major General Oxenius at the surrender table. The best sentence was "Germany gave no evidence of knowing it was sick until it was dead. Hitler and Goebbels were rumored suicides, Himmler and Borman had disappeared, and a wave of suicides was supposed to have swept Germany." Sidney Olson reported the scene in Germany, dominated by displaced persons. The bodies of executed Mussolini and his mistress, Clara Petacci, are seen in Milan's Piazza Loreto. They had been caught by the disgraceful Partisans in Dongo. We were beginning to see Hitler's image reflected in his conquerors, or the beneficiaries of the conquerors. For the evils of Nazism and communism were to give a nightmare example to the world population for the next quarter of a century, dissolve morality, and perhaps qualify mankind for justifiable destruction, but the victors did not realize what was happening to them. Clare Boothe Luce expresses her disgust with everything she sees in Italy. The editorial had qualms about the destruction called victory. A Longwell touch is an illustration of a book, *Phantom Victory*, about a preposterous postwar history, essentially based on my stories about the Great German General Staff. Stories on a theatrical press agent and the new archbishop of Canterbury precede an admission that men are still being killed on Okinawa.

In the following issue the Longwell preference for small jokes becomes spectacular, remembering the historical moment. The "Speaking of Pictures" item is a room built for the fifteenth-century Duke of Urbino in which all the furnishings are convincing optical illusions, now transferred to the New York Metropolitan Museum. Following this is an ironical piece by Noel Busch on his attempt to inject competitive discord into five Yugoslav shoeshiners who pooled their income. The lead (May 21, 1945) had to acknowledge the history, "The Germans Sign the Surrender": "As the Nazi Reich sank into a history that nobody will ever enjoy reading, the Allies ended it without even a grimace." The Russians signed May 8 in Berlin, and Stalin declared May 9 the Soviet V-E Day. The editorial turned to the war in the Pacific, solely an American war without collaborators, for "a principle: non-aggression, the territorial integrity of all nations, equal rights for all." And for "the emergence from the war of a strong, free, modern Chinese nation, America's No. 1 friend in the Orient. . . . If ever American power and ideals had a chance to influence world history, here is the place." This is literally the history and the intent of American policy toward China, and with Mao Tse-tung we see the horrid travesty of it. Only great satirists can afford to laugh. The "Picture of the Week" showed that President Truman sent an honor guard and flowers on V-E Day to Roosevelt's grave, an event that must bring tears to anyone's eyes, but perhaps does not to the young. As of the San Francisco Conference, pictures of 30 national spokesmen introduced the proper sense of bedlam. France is noted having quiet elections, 25% Communist. Dos Passos has more nonsense on "The American Marianas." John Davenport begins a story on the lives of Winston Churchill. The story presents Churchill's dazzling credentials as a war man, and wonders whether he will be allowed to make the peace. (Of course, he was not.)

The Allied manhunt for the Nazi criminals occupied the lead (May 28, 1945). It already had an impressive list "but there was still a possibility that they might indict from four to six million Germans." Such talk made me very suspicious of war crimes trials. The inclusion of the brave Serb, Mikhailovich, exposed the uses to which the theory could be put. He had been promised "a fair trial" before being shot. ⁎A happier list were those who had just found freedom. But, of these, King Leopold of the Belgians and General Weygand were in trouble. The editorial examines war crimes. The Communists had been executing "war criminals" by the thousands without a second thought. The editorial wavered from indicting a people to indicting a system. The burning and exploding carrier *Franklin*, which survived, is shown. The idea of peace is supported by a portfolio of ideas for the home—24 pages aimed at the bourgeoisie and the advertisers. Details about "Hitler's Woman," Eva Helen Braun, are with a quote, "I think it was platonic." However, contraceptives were in the bathroom of her Munich house. Beautiful Okinawa and the gentle Okinawans are seen, with the note that Okinawa "may end up under U.S. trusteeship." The second installment on Churchill's career follows, correctly spotting September 15, 1940, as the climax of the Battle of Britain, but exaggerating the German losses. The research is excellent.

The cover of the following issue (June 4, 1945) was an appeal of the military commanders to invest in War Bonds, with their signatures. Seven pages of airviews of bombed German cities glorify the destruction. The "Picture of the Week" shows Lauren Bacall feeding wedding cake to the groom, Humphrey Bogart. The editorial says that America must feed Europe. (The Longwell joke may have been conscious but wasn't very funny.) The War Food Administration had cut back on meat production to avert a drop in U.S. farm prices. Further, even if food arrived in Europe, there was a great shortage of transport. More Nazi leaders caught, with some suicides, were shown. The closeup is of an ex-Armenian chef in San Francisco who feeds the conference delegates and thinks "America is wonderful." Paintings of the mating rituals of birds are by Roger Tory Peterson, a superb ornithologist but not considered a first-rate bird painter. The U.S. postwar plans in the Pacific are mapped to extend U.S. bases to a triangle from Truk, Guam, Okinawa to the Philippines with still other trusteeships, to prevent future attack from the Pacific. (This plan is being forgotten, for a necessity of politics is to forget history.) Richard Wright's autobiography, *Black Boy*, is seen as reenacted by black actors, mostly handsome mulattoes. This story justifies Longwell's literary bias. The final installment on Churchill, the man who truly respected history, quotes his great but mistaken line, "I have not become the King's First Minister in order to preside over the liquidation of the British Empire." Churchill (and the piece) correctly predicted history, including perhaps "a picture of the year 2000 when Europe and the U.S., depleted of their vigor, would be overwhelmed by the sheer power of the Eastern races" (including

presumably the Russians). He did not know that in the coming
election history would dispense with him, at the age of 70, preferring
nonentities.

Hell, history was also about to dispense with me, at the age of 41,
though I had recently (but before V-E Day) received this reassuring
letter:

March 27, 1945

Dear Dave:

I am very happy to tell you that the Board of Directors last week
confirmed your re-election to the Senior Group for 1945.

The Board also confirmed the election of two new members for 1945:

Joseph Kastner
Robert Sherrod

The enclosed list of Senior Group members for 1945 totals 47, but for all
practical purposes the Group is at its ceiling of 50, because three people on
leave in war service (two of whom were in the Group when they left) will be
"must" candidates on their return. Meanwhile, there are ten other men and
women who, at this moment, we think should be in the Group in 1946. With
the ceiling of 50 memberships originally set for the Plan now frozen by the
Stabilization authorities, the annual selection of the 50 members becomes a
more and more difficult job for Harry, myself, and the Board; and for
membership in the Group, current performance and responsibility become
increasingly important factors.

I think there is every reason to believe that, again this year, your
membership in the Group will mean a substantial extra compensation for
your efforts.

With best wishes, and with thanks for your part in Time Inc.'s progress
during the past year,

Sincerely,
ROY

A report from Craig Thompson in Moscow (June 11, 1945)
quoted Soviet correspondents in San Francisco as actually seeing the
American scene while still straining it through the usual abysmal,
invidious Communist ideology. The lead gives 13 pages to Middle
East oil. Here Britain and the United States had forced France to
stop suppressing a Syrian revolt. And "Russia has shown a bright new
interest in the area." Iran's Shah-of-Shahs goes to congratulate

Americans on V-E Day "on their tremendous job of slamming 4,500,000 tons of Lend-Lease across Iran to Soviet Russia. . . . This was one of war's greatest jobs and had nothing whatever to do with the matter of oil." The power of the editorial may have been indicated by its implied boast that the San Francisco Conference had included "a bow to justice and international law, equal rights and self-determination of nations and 'respect for human rights and for fundamental freedoms for all' [obviously not applicable to any Communist state]. To relative tyros in diplomacy like Americans, the educational value of such a conference is alone worth the price of admission." "Göring Art Treasures" were ironically displayed "by courtesy of the 101st Airborne Division," and three Germans caught in U.S. uniforms are seen being executed. A real exhibition of power, if it was read by President Truman, is a story on the formidable Japanese army and navy, saying, "Total war calls for total defeat." Japan had just "created a student army of 20,000,000 and an agrarian militia of everybody on the land over 14." The atom bomb is obviously indicated for any sensible U.S. president. Terrible paintings by Tom Lea of the battle of Peleliu September 15, 1944 (ranking with Tarawa, Saipan, and Iwo Jima "among the four bloodiest battles" of the marines) further support the point. John Chamberlain's piece on the obvious differences between Truman and Roosevelt mentions the military bureaucracy's "mighty effort to take over the country" with a compulsory labor bill or "total war," just as the victory was won. This little event might well be remembered. America in crisis is always on the brink of dictatorship. And by whom except the military? Highly as I regard a Patton in his function, I would not want him to progress from glory to power, as Caesar and Napoleon did, and so many others.

I have deliberately overlooked photographers, since this book is primarily a defense of word people, but *Life* photographer W. Eugene ("Wonderful") Smith writes the lead (June 18, 1945) in a way to rival Ernie Pyle. (There was another photographer called, probably unfairly, "Horrible" Smith.) "Wonderful" had photographed a full day of an infantryman on Okinawa, usually working ahead of the soldier, and was finally, inevitably, hit by a mortar shell in the hand and jaw. This man did not need to feel the ignominy of such reporters of great events as myself. His pictures are quite undramatic but in the context totally involving. I do not think I ever met "Wonderful." The editorial discussed the prospect of dead soldiers' families having their remains dug up and transported to American cemeteries. Robert Sherrod, *Life* correspondent in the Pacific, reported the men's overwhelming preference for lying where they had died, but of course the deciding vote would be their surviving families'. The murderous policy of Communist Russia was stripped clear, in Soviet pictures, as Russia gobbled Poland, East Germany, Czechoslovakia, Hungary, Rumania, Bulgaria (Latvia, Estonia, and Lithuania had already been consumed), and almost Austria and Yugoslavia and Greece (the last a racking failure). Stalin had already grabbed more territory than Hitler ever had under control. Would this great feast satisfy Soviet Russia forever? Modern men know the answer. The satiated conqueror is insatiable. My story was objective but I suppose I had enraged the Time Inc. Communists who, though Americans, were watching the seeding of World War III with perfect delight and did not recognize Cadmus, being essentially not wicked but stupid. They seemed like the oysters in Lewis Carroll's story of "The Walrus and the Carpenter." It was difficult for the Americans to transpose the great evil quickly from Berlin to Moscow. Longwell now has a story on Carl Sandburg's goats which love Sandburg. An essay on the Congress begins with the proposition that "for the first time since 1933 the Congress became again a full partner of the President in the formation of national policy." (This is a biased simplification of Chamberlain's piece on Truman, but typical of Longwell's frenzied desire to please Luce.) Generally impudent, the piece advises abolition of the seniority system.

An optimistic Churchill launching into an election campaign makes the lead (June 25, 1945). The editorial was a glowing tribute to Eisenhower, whom history was not to forget. Jinx Falkenburg is seen preparing to marry Tex McCrary. The closing of Ford's Willow Run bomber plant is seen. A text piece describes the impregnability of the Brinks armored car business (later the victim of the most spectacular holdup in history). "Harry Truman's Missouri" made a pleasant, small-town essay. The closeup by Charles Wertenbaker continues the hymn to Eisenhower.

The Eisenhower theme became the lead (July 2, 1945) as Eisenhower came home, met La Guardia, the Congress, Truman, and Mrs. Eisenhower. The editorial named the Fourth of July as the day Americans could feel proud but added "the purpose of American strength is to promote liberty and self-government throughout the human race" (not the purpose of Communist strength). Hitler's mountaintop house outside Berchtesgaden is seen with its awesome view. And France's Herriot, freed from his Nazi jail, is seen in his hilltop chateau with almost as good a view.

A response to the editorial on disinterring and returning the U.S. dead is a letter saying that, such is the confusion of battle burial, the grieving family might get back a German body (July 9, 1945). The lead shows the delegates of 50 nations signing the United Nations Charter, the Chinese first. The editorial gives credit for the charter to Edward Stettinius, Senator Vandenberg, and Australia's Herbert Evatt. Juxtaposed to a story on flamethrowers using jellied gasoline is one on bathing suits which "cannot go any further" in nakedness. Ha-ha. Good news is that the Japanese, trained never to surrender, are doing so.

The execution of three Germans who had murdered an American flier is the lead (July 16, 1945). The editorial asked, "What situation does the U.S. wish to bring about as the result of our inevitable victory over Japan? And how many Americans will be killed before Japan gives up?" (Another oblique plus for the use of the atom bomb.) The conclusion: wash our hands of responsibility for Japan. The "Picture of the Week" was Secretary General Alger Hiss bringing the United Nations Charter to Washington. (Later ruined by the magnificent liar-impostor, Whittaker Chambers, foreign editor of *Time.*) A lot of pages were given to paintings of "Paris 1945," one exhibiting the Time Inc. staff in Paris, perhaps indicating Longwell's yearning to be liked by the help. The trivia come in stories on saris and karakul furs. The essay on the University of Chicago's crash education theory exhibits one academic idiot from my college, Mortimer Adler. The closeup is on China's last emperor, Kang Te or

Henry Pu Yi. So quickly, pictures of fashionable French navels proved *Life* wrong on the nakedness bounds of bathing suits.

The fact that smashed Berlin was reviving made the lead (July 23, 1945), with more gossip of Hitler's cremation, to a thick Russian silence. Russia was acting like less and less of an ally, as might have been expected. The editorial noticed that prophecies of "disaster" and "chaos" seemed to have diminished, "even by Dorothy Thompson." American GIs were fraternizing with German girls, and the American jeep was amazing the Swedes. It was revealed that Germany had planned a sun-mirror to incinerate the Allies, but it would probably not have worked.

The story that about 4 million of 6.7 million displaced persons (figures obviously unreliable) had somehow been taken care of, East Europeans refusing to return to Communist puppet states, occupied the lead (July 30, 1945). The editorial focused on the democracies' disability, compromised by their Communist "fellow-travelers," to cope with the Communist doubletalk when the totalitarians described themselves as more democratic than the democracies. If Hitler had identified Nazism as a novel sort of democracy, history might have been different. Longwell inserted a bold departure from Time Inc. journalism, a decadence to corrupt Time Inc. for the next twenty-five years. This was a long essay on "American Songs": "Swanee River," "Home Sweet Home," "Home on the Range" et al., each illustrated by a sentimental picture of its scene. It told Americans something they knew, something that in reading *Time* and *Life* they were trying to advance beyond, and it buried Briton Hadden a mile deeper. But Luce allowed it. Doubtless, Longwell thought it was his masterpiece. Following this comes a piece on the Japanese kamikaze pilots by John Hersey in a masterpiece of miscasting. Hersey concludes that the Japanese code of Bushido is a carefully indoctrinated form of insanity. This theory would also make madmen of the men at Thermopylae, of the Americans who rushed to the Alamo to almost certain death, and Pickett's men at Gettysburg —all lunatics. While the Herseys sniffle, other men make history. He might note a Jew's ultimate comment on war: "There are worse things than war." A Hersey society would soon vanish. But Hersey was by then rich and celebrated, and Longwell was a literary toady. And I still did not realize what was going on, out of sheer pride of craftsmanship.

The Berlin Conference, with Stalin but without Roosevelt (dead) or Churchill (out of office) and with Truman and Clement (merciful) Attlee, was the lead. The editorial demanded "classic statesmanship" toward Japan. A nominal nod is given to Attlee and Churchill. There are seven pages of U.S. military insignia in color. Then comes a long account of her trip into Germany, courtesy of the U.S. Army, by Gertrude Stein and her companion. It is worthless. After this uncommon touch, the common touch is supplied by an essay on Coney Island.

The French trial of Marshal Pétain, "The Hero of Verdun," a satire on France, with an eyewitness account by Wertenbaker, was the lead (August 13, 1945). The editorial explained the British elections: "At a time when everyone was growing tired of 'indispensable' men, [Churchill] chose to campaign on one thing: his personality." He had no program except the preservation of the Empire. Good news was the fact that Stalin had promised "full freedom" to the democratic press in his Communist puppet states. (The wind blew this promise away.) Longwell's humanistic theory of journalism collapsed when it buried at the end of a story of the conventional bombing of Japan the mild statement that on August 5 "an American plane dropped the first atomic bomb on the Jap base at Hiroshima." Thus a new era leaked into history. August 5 is the Sunday after *Life* had closed on August 4 (August 6 in Japan). One endpoint of the Nazi lunacy was a chateau at Hohenhorst filled with bastard "super-babies" fathered by SS men.

"The War Ends—Burst of Atomic Bomb Brings Swift Surrender of Japanese" (no longer Japs) was the lead (August 20, 1945) and Longwell suddenly realized the significance of the atom bomb. On August 10 the Tokyo radio broadcast an appeal for peace. In the front of the magazine, Hanson Baldwin writes, "What is to come far transcends all man's experience in what has gone before. . . . Science does not appear to have it in its power to stop the rocket, once launched . . . a Frankenstein monster." He did not say while

America had this power it should use it against Russia to make a
decent peace. This omission was remedied in the editorial which
observed "the almost negligent manner in which he [Truman]
used—or rather failed to use—the atomic bomb as a diplomatic
weapon against Russia." It concludes that (American) morality was
the world's only hope. A picture of "The Graves of Iwo Jima"
contrasts with the correspondents' accounts of the celebration of the
final victory. Russia had declared war on Japan and entered
Manchuria in force. There is an explanation of the role of the
Japanese emperor as essentially a myth. A closeup of Princess
Elizabeth of England is singularly untimely. But in a summer stock
theatre at Stamford, Connecticut, Shaw's role of Candida is being
played by Clare Boothe Luce, of whom *Variety* says, "There have
been better and worse interpretations of Candida." A scientific
explanation of the atom bomb is appended, with a piece on the
Manhattan Project by Wickware.

The actual V-J Day came on Tuesday, August 14, at 7:00 P.M.,
when Truman announced that the Japanese had accepted the Allied
terms of surrender, General MacArthur to govern Japan with the
authority of the emperor (August 27, 1945). Longwell's journalism
was perfectly adequate to record a dozen pages of U.S. bedlam as
America celebrated the end of the war. The editorial was suspicious
of the peace. A story showed that Chiang Kai-shek's part of China
was totally exhausted, while Mao Tse-tung demanded a coalition
government under the threat of civil war. For the Communists had
conserved their strength, waiting for the Americans to win the war.
Chiang Kai-shek had made the grievous mistake of fighting; Mao had
cleverly saved himself for the final battle (against Chiang Kai-shek).
So much cleverness had to triumph. For poor Chiang Kai-shek had
thought his enemy was Japan. And America had made the same
mistake.

An essay on the estates of the Krupps asserted that Alfried Krupp
von Bohlen und Halbach's "power has gone and his fortunes are
uncertain . . . the history of the . . . dynasty of death may well be
ended." This was both extreme and wrong, in the event. A text piece
on "Russia and the U.S." by Joseph Freeman asserted that for over a

century there had been no real conflict of interest between them: John Paul Jones had helped build Catherine the Great's navy; Cassius Clay of Kentucky had been Lincoln's minister to Russia; and the Monroe Doctrine was largely directed at Russian colonization on the west coast. Seward bought Alaska from Russia in 1867.

Longwell journalism appeared in the "Speaking of Pictures" (September 3, 1945) on "the pleasures of a boy and his dog." The lead was "The Japs Get MacArthur's Orders," with more analysis of the Japanese character as essentially hysterical, this by Shelley Mydans. The editorial, on the need to reform the U.S. State Department, suggested the creation of a general staff. But nothing was ever to equip the United States to run the world as Britain had, probably for lack of the equivalent of the British gentry, and the attempt to substitute professors, lawyers, businessmen, and a few journalists. A story reported the mild crisis brought on by peace and demobilization. The Nazi war criminals arrived in Nürnberg expecting death, as I privately viewed these proceedings with misgivings. A text piece on world population predicted that Western nations' population would level off and decline while Russia in 1970 would be about 250 million. Actually, in 1970, Russia was at 241 million, the United States was up to 200 million, and France up to 50 million.

The American flag was seen flying over a Japanese airfield in the lead, "U.S. Occupies Japan" (September 10, 1945). Airborne troops and marines preceded MacArthur, who was smoking a corncob pipe. The Japanese signed the surrender September 2 on the battleship *Missouri*. Great airviews of Tokyo and other destruction were shown. The Japanese navy had one (damaged) battleship left to surrender. The editorial congratulates Chiang Kai-shek and Stalin for agreeing on everything. "Russian promises non-intervention . . . thus pulling the rug from under the Chinese Communists." Mao Tse-tung met with Chiang as his "younger brother." This was not a useful picture of the future. Russian soldiers are seen mobbing the Berlin black market. And William Walton describes the mad Nijinsky in Vienna, where he had begun to talk and dance again. The essay was on the Hudson River school of painters. "The French Look" was presented as sexier and less natural than "The American Look." There is a story on the discord in the United Automobile Workers' union. And Vannevar Bush correctly predicts machines that will "think."

On the developing Chinese event, it may be said that the modern evil in government is always a well-organized minority sworn to dedication and ambition who seize power and then terrorize the majority. This describes Lenin's Russia, Mussolini's Italy, Hitler's Germany, Mao's China (all adequately). The elite here are driven more fanatically by ambition and greed than any capitalistic tycoon's organization, which is relatively powerless and cannot really terrorize anybody, though sometimes it tries. Terror is easy in a peaceable society: witness the Boston Strangler. Any reasonably clever person could do far better than that. Tyranny has for several thousand years been the most effective form of government, and it still is. Democracy represents man at his best and is always vulnerable to him at his worst, which is often his dominant side. Tyranny has no such vulnerability, for it takes him at his worst, as both ruler and ruled. The tyrant learns how to use the mob (always a minority), which is man at barely the primate level, including the chimpanzee but not the baboon. It would be unfair to the Nazi, Fascist, Communist mobs to call them baboons. The other dictators are less dangerous, for they have only ambition.

At last the pictures of the Japanese signing the surrender on the *Missouri* and of the numerous allies signing became the extended lead (September 17, 1945). The Japanese premier attributed the surrender to the atomic bomb which "was likely to result in the obliteration of the Japanese people," Hiroshima's dead then being given at 125,000. The editorial frets about our intelligence preparations for World War III. An oddity was a condensation of an account of Commodore Matthew Perry's incursion into Tokyo harbor in 1853 to overawe the Japanese. Paintings show the destruction of Italy by the Americans and their allies. The beginning of American cities' self-destruction is underlined by a story on a plan (by Norman Bel Geddes) for a somewhat utopian Toledo, Ohio. A systematic analysis of Japanese society in all its forms is simple and straightforward (probably not by me). Noel Busch offers an acute closeup of John Maynard Keynes without going into his economic theories.

Each of Longwell's journalistic diddlings was followed in a subsequent Letters column by burbles of praise. Thus (September 24, 1945) the story on "a boy and his dog" brings: "If Mark Twain had chosen the camera as his medium, he could scarcely have done better than *Life*'s photographer did with Larry and Dunk." The lead was deadly serious, on the Japanese claim that Hiroshima and Nagasaki were still radioactive. A visit to the first atomic bomb crater at Alamogordo, New Mexico, showed it was still radioactive, but with the alibi of having been hit from only 100 feet up. The blast had turned the desert sand into green glass. William L. Laurence of the *New York Times* gives a classic account of the monstrous energies released over Nagasaki. The "Picture of the Week" showed Mao Tse-tung and Chiang Kai-shek smilingly toasting one another. The editorial, noting Lenin's advice to Bolsheviks to "confuse the vocabulary," tried to unscramble some definitions. It defined the heart, but not the system, of *fascism* in Hitler's words, "inner incoherence," or in Jack Jessup's words, "a denial of the obligation to be reasonable." *Democracy* was defined as majority rule with respect for the rights of minorities, thus removing the word from Lenin's vocabulary. It was pointed out that the liberal philosophy had been disintegrating since about 1880 but still retained the character of being "favorably disposed toward change." But the word "is losing its meaning." The bungled suicide by pistol of Japan's General Tojo is shown in aftermath. The fate he expected was awarded by the Norwegians to their traitor, Vidkun Quisling. The kind of essay for which Hubie Kay had been transferred by his friend, Billings, from *Life* to *Time* and later to *Fortune*, now appears: a roundup of U.S. secretaries of state, starting with John Jay and ending with Cordell Hull. Next came a story I still remember with affection, "The Incas": "It was the Roman empire of pre-Columbian America, where want was unknown and nobody worried about the passage of time. Most of all, the Incas loved the mountain stone. They worked with it as boys whittle wood and left their nearly imperishable granite towns and temples behind them, some impossibly massive, some wrought with exquisite fineness. They had no wheel, no sledge, no horses or oxen, though they used llamas as beasts of burden. But they moved 100-ton stones up precipices. . . . They sawed the hard granite and porphyry and limestone with copper wire in which were embedded diamonds and emeralds . . . [Here] lived the Sapa Inca, the One Inca, Son of the Sun, Lover and Benefactor of the Unfortunate, the god-on-earth whom no one could look in the face or approach without bare feet and a symbolical weight on his shoulders." The contrast with Longwell journalism is demonstrated in one caption: "This town is remarkable for having, among the usual one-storied buildings of the Incas, two houses of two-and-a-half stories at upper right. . . . The attic windows are visible toward the top of the gables. At upper left is the wall of the lookout platform with three deep embrasures. In the center is the town's small plaza. . . . Notice round stone pegs along roof edges to tie on thatch." In short, the picture was not just a reminder of a New England stone barn. It told something, a lot of things, and the reader was asked to look at it again and again. This was true picture journalism, certainly not very hard to understand, but with Longwell the picture part had overwhelmed the journalism, and Time Inc. had begun the long slide to its death, under the benign sanction of Henry R. Luce. Then, a remarkable piece by John Chamberlain almost saying that Roosevelt was delighted by Pearl Harbor (as I had exclaimed, "Thank God!"). The argument is complex, forked-tongued, and, much as I respect Chamberlain, futile and snide. Much is made of America's cracking of the Japanese code. Without knowledge of this, I had predicted a Japanese attack somewhere before Pearl Harbor. The irony of history is that America was committed to saving China from Japan. And we may soon be committed to saving Japan from China—or saving ourselves from China. It sounds like a joke, but of course it is not. And Pearl Harbor was the swing point of modern history up till now.

The welcoming home of a marine ace (26 Japanese planes), "Pappy" Boyington, was the debatable winner for the lead (October 1, 1945). The "Picture of the Week," on the other hand, was the departure, down a line of generals, of Secretary of War Stimson, and the editorial all but wept for his integrity. As a penalty of peace, the departure of 1.5 million war workers to unemployment compensation, and another 235,000 to the picket lines, was reported. Shirley

Temple and her $3 million are seen marrying an air force sergeant and his "sincerity." (The marriage turned out to be a disaster.) A Negro bishop revealed that in one of his frequent rides with God in his Packard he had arranged to end the war. The essay was on high fashion; the closeup on Henry Ford II, who had just become the "green" president of his grandfather's firm. Oddly, the *Life* party visits Erskine Caldwell and the wife who had replaced able *Life* photographer Margaret Bourke-White.

Frank Lloyd Wright exhibiting a model of his unique art museum for the Solomon R. Guggenheim art collection makes the "Speaking of Pictures" (October 8, 1945). A prophet who had predicted the end of the world for September 21, 1945, postponed the date a year. The petering out of great events was indicated by the extended lead on a photographer's train trip from Tokyo to Hiroshima. The editorial objects to the rebirth of "economic nationalism" with the end of wartime Lend-Lease and pleads for sharing our wealth with other nations. (This process had cost the United States $143 billion by 1971 and brought prosperity to most civilized nations—with fairly little gratitude.) The pleasant face of the woman who as head of the women's Waffen SS at Belsen prison camp had "surpassed the most bloodcurdling murderesses and sadists of previous history" is seen watching her trial. And in Berlin a few remaining Jews celebrated Rosh Hashana for the first time since 1938, as some must have wept. Surplus paintings of the Pacific war were unveiled in a long essay. The Americans are seen teaching the Hitler Youth how to live in a democratic world. After four months, they split evenly on describing Hitler as "an insane criminal." A story on New York's Waldorf-Astoria Hotel locates the rooms of several dozen famous patrons, for some reason excluding Herbert Hoover.

The new (ostensibly temporary) philosophy of *Life* was clearly expressed in Longwell's lead (October 15, 1945)—"The U.S. Relaxes"—culminating in the fad of bubble-blowing, a philosophy that Luce accepted. The impressive methodology of Time Inc. was thus officially diverted to the ends of frivolity. The editorial, after some preliminary persiflage, was quite serious about the futile Conference of Foreign Ministers in London. Historically, what Russia wanted and didn't get is of interest: (1) trusteeship of Italian colonies in Libya and on the Red Sea; (2) $600 million in reparations from Italy (would have been mostly U.S. relief money); (3) a voice in the control of Japan; (4) exclusion of France and China from the Balkan discussions. What the Westerners wanted and didn't get was a voice in control of the Balkans. It had become obvious at last what gulfs separated Russia from the West. An ominous map showed strikes in 38 American states. A story notes that the Berlin zoo animals unmoved by bombing were "the great cats, elephants, oxen, rhinoceroses, snakes, panda, goats and even the rabbits," while the baboons were paralyzed with fear. General Marshall's report on the war reveals the projected invasions of Japan, Operations Olympic and Coronet, negated by the atom bomb. He lists "seven German errors" which hold no surprises today. Impressions of Hollywood by the painter Doris Lee are at least odd.

The intellectual performance of some University of Wisconsin monkeys is diagrammed. "Shangri-La," Roosevelt's secret cabin in the Catoctin Mountains of Maryland, is unveiled. The essay shows the "Displaced Germans," now nearly as helpless as their victims were formerly. The navy is seen busy at Corregidor recovering from the bay bottom $8.5 million dumped by the Philippine government in 1942.

It appears that John Kenneth Galbraith was a *Fortune* editor on loan to the War Department (as it was then called). He contributes an amusing piece (October 22, 1945) on the Luxembourg spa Mondorf (code name Ashcan) where the top Nazi criminals had been dumped: "The waters are said to be excellent but I have forgotten, if I ever knew, whether one drinks them or bathes in them, or what they cure." His impression of the Germans is summarized by his pilot, "Who'd have thought that we were fighting this war against a bunch of jerks?" This contrasts unpleasantly with Liddell Hart's later assessment. The lead is another train trip—by President Truman, described as playing poker and having a wonderful time. His unmade hotel bed is given a full page. And here comes the Vietnam war under the guise of "Annam," an American officer quelling a native revolt with the help of Japanese troops which had in fact armed the

"Annamites." Two losers, Hirohito and the Duke of Windsor, are seen calling on, respectively, General MacArthur (tieless and ribbonless) and Queen Mother Mary. The essay is on the luxury of life in California at various caste levels.

Now, for a man who had often written over 20 pages of *Life*, I was not contributing much to these preponderantly absurd issues. I was grateful for the surcease and saw no change in my status. Who was producing this trivia? In the first issue in 1936 the masthead numbered 19 names. In this last issue the total staff numbered, by my count, over 150.

The October masthead follows, with the people I remember printed in italics:

LIFE

EDITOR-IN-CHIEF .... *Henry R. Luce*
PRESIDENT .... *Roy E. Larsen*
EDITORIAL DIRECTOR .... *John Shaw Billings*

MANAGING EDITOR
Daniel Longwell
EXECUTIVE EDITOR
Wilson Hicks
EDITORIAL CHIEF
John K. Jessup
ASSISTANT MANAGING EDITORS
Joseph J. Thorndike, Jr., Worthen Paxton
EDITORS: *Noel F. Busch, Fillmore Calhoun, John Chamberlain, Robert Coughlan, David Cort, John Field, Joseph Kastner, C. J. V. Murphy.*
ASSOCIATE EDITORS: *Lincoln Barnett, Herbert Brean, Dennis Flanagan, George Frazier, Richard Lauterbach, Lillian Rixey, Maria Sermolino, Margit Varga, Philip Wootton, Jr.*
ASSISTANT EDITORS: *Caroline Iverson, John Kay, Donald Marshman, Jr.,* Fred Morley, *Jean Speiser, A. B. C. Whipple.*
SENIOR RESEARCHERS: *Bernice Shrifte* (Chief), *Margaret Bassett, Earl Brown,* Gertrude Epstein, Shirley Herzig, *Elaine Brown Keiffer,* Betty Moisson, *Shelley Mydans,* Helen Peirce, *Jeanne Perkins, Jo Sheehan, Marion Stevens,* Burton Van Vort, *Joan Werblin.*
RESEARCHERS: Hudson Ansley, Peggy Bebié, Mathilde Benoit, Inez Buonodono, Madge Brown, Alice Crocker, Leota Diesel, Myron Emanuel, *Marietta FitzGerald,* Philippa Gerry, Zelda Gottlieb, Paul Griffith, *Phyllis*

Larsh, Geraldine Lux, Dorothy Marcus, Hildegard Maynard, Ethelind Munroe, Barbara O'Connor, *Rosemarie Redlich, Dorothy Seiberling,* Jeanne Stahl, Sylvia Todd, *Rachel Tuckerman,* Carol Welch.

STAFF PHOTOGRAPHERS: *G. W. Churchill* (assistant picture editor), *Robert Capa,* Edward Clark, Myron Davis, *Alfred Eisenstaedt, Eliot Elisofon, J. R. Eyerman,* Andreas Feininger, John Florea, Herbert Gehr, *Fritz Goro, Marie Hansen, Bernard Hoffman, Wallace Kirkland, Bob Landry, Tom McAvoy, Ralph Morse, Carl Mydans, John Phillips,* George Rodger, Walter Sanders, *David Scherman, Frank Scherschel,* William Shrout, *George Silk,* George Skadding, W. Eugene Smith, *Peter Stackpole, William Vandivert,* Hans Wild.

PICTURE BUREAU: *Dorothy Hoover* (Chief), *Mary Carr, Alma Eggleston, Margaret Goldsmith,* O. A. Graubner, *Natalie Kosek,* Gertrude Leahey, *Ruth Lester,* Maude Milar, Muriel Pitt, *Margaret Sargent,* Muriel Trebay, Grace Young.

ART DEPARTMENT: *Allan McNab, Charles Tudor, Michael Phillips.*

NEWS BUREAUS: *David W. Hulburd* (Chief); *Helen Robinson, Ray Mackland* (assistants); Suzanne Hammond, Jean Snow, Dorothy Sterling; Atlanta: William S. Howland; Boston: Francis E. Wylie; Chicago: Robert Hagy, *John Morris, Frances Levison, Don Morris;* Denver: Hugh Moffet; Detroit: Fred Collins; Los Angeles: *Sidney L. James, Bart Sheridan,* Helen Morgan, Jean Sovatkin, Richard Wilkes; San Antonio: *Holland McCombs;* San Francisco: Robert deRoos, Fritz Goodwin; Seattle: Richard L. Williams; Washington: Robert T. Elson, *John Purcell,* Ruth Adams, Stephen Herz, Rosamond Mowrer, Mollie Thayer, Elizabeth Watkins; London: *Walter Graebner,* John Boyle, Elizabeth Reeve, Eleanor Ragsdale; Paris: *Charles Christian Wertenbaker,* Elmer Lower, *Lee Eitingon, Will Lang;* Manila: William Gray; Chungking: *Theodore H. White,* Annalee Jacoby; Moscow: Craig Thompson; New Delhi: Peggy Durdin; Ottawa: Lawrence Laybourne; Rome: Tom Durrance.

GENERAL MANAGER
Andrew Heiskell
ADVERTISING DIRECTOR
Shepard Spink

The lead is on the campaign for New York City's mayoralty which La Guardia had abdicated (October 29, 1945). In a picture dominated by a portrait of an eighteenth-century gentleman, the subject is not identified: more Longwell picture journalism, which violated every precept. The editorial thought that the atom bomb virtually compelled world government and agreed that other nations would soon have it. The 24 top Nazis to be tried, including three generals and an admiral, are shown. A text piece by three atomic scientists can safely be ignored. (Don't blame them.) A story explains in color that plants change color in autumn. This news may have astonished somebody somewhere. The utter feasibility of anybody flying a Piper Cub plane is the theme of a closeup by Lincoln Barnett. The birth of a boll weevil is scrupulously photographed. At last comes my story on "English Country Homes"—"magnificent relics of a great age that is vanished." I used much of this material in a later book, but the subject seems fairly frivolous.

The readers didn't know how to take the story on displaced Germans who *looked* exactly as pathetic as their former victims. The letters were very confused (November 5, 1945). A piece is inserted on cute nicknames of shortline U.S. railroads. The lead on "New York Welcomes the U.S. Navy" includes a magnificent airview of part of the great fleet anchored in the Hudson River. The navy was fighting against being skeletonized. To my amazement, my boyhood friend Guy Richards, from the U.S. Marines, has a piece criticizing the navy's credo that an officer must be a gentleman born. In the army and the marines, the troops were always favored over the officers; in the navy the officers were pampered. The editorial charges that the United Nations Relief and Rehabilitation Administration can't do the job, partly because Northwest Europe won't let it in, partly because it has abdicated on long-range reconstruction, and partly because nearly all relief has so far gone to Communist Eastern Europe. A Czech Nazi is seen being tried, very correctly, and hanged. After a sound scientific story on germs comes one on hot-rod racing. The essay is a well-deserved tribute to *Life*'s 21 war photographers with their outstanding war pictures. Though photographers are not the focus of this book, no word or pay rate could do justice to their courage.

The prison of the Japanese war criminals in Tokyo harbor made the lead (November 12, 1945). Unlike the German war criminals, they seem remarkably merry. The others boycott Tojo who had bungled his suicide. The editorial, reporting the prospect of strikes, says that what America and the world need is hard work. Sukarno's rebellion against the Dutch in Java, with Japanese help, is shown, as also is the winner of the aircraft carrier *Yorktown*'s beauty contest. Frank Sinatra tried in vain to persuade Gary, Indiana, high school students to give some mild concessions to Negro students. This is followed by a remarkably intelligent horse which knows enough to press the foot pedal at drinking fountains. (Readers had protested an editorial calling horses stupid.) The closeup is on the couturier Hattie Carnegie. Dirty tricks in hockey are demonstrated. The essay is a sleepy exploration of New York's Mohawk Valley. A grand piece of wishful thinking, "China Reborn," headlines "Nationalist Armies Check the Communists." It points out, however, that the place for the Communists to wait for Russian arms was the Shantung Peninsula, where they were waging "undeclared" war. The superb Ingrid Bergman is shown in three movies. I suspect that the true story of Communist China has not yet been told for everybody involved—Russia, Mao, Chiang, Japan—and the United States was two-faced. As Longwell and Luce were "relaxing," the real problems facing the free world were terrifying.

An atomic scientist wrote in to say that the atom bomb should be in the control of the United Nations, without which "the United Nations Organization will eventually fail" (November 19, 1945). Right on schedule came letters lauding the idiotic story on how leaves turn red in autumn in the temperate zone. An amusing "Speaking of Pictures" shows eighteen people in civilian clothes and asks the reader to guess their military rank. I see on my copy of *Life* that I had guessed, roughly. The lead visualizes General Henry H. Arnold's vision of World War III in which an enemy (Russia then, of course) would deliver a rain of atomic bombs without warning, in a war "decided in 36 hours." Coincidentally, he also suggested giving the atom bomb to the United Nations. The "rockets" (ICBMs) are assumed to have been sent from secret bases in Africa. In response, the "potential aggressor" must know that "an attack on the United States would be immediately followed by an immensely devastating air-atomic attack on him." Public thinking has hardly progressed beyond this 1945 story. In the scenario the United States wins. The editorial is a little more worried about China than the "China Reborn" piece, pinning the problem on the American mothers' cry,

"Bring our boys home!" It is clear that we had a further job to do in China, for home front reasons did not do it, and are now about to reap the whirlwind. (Or, ironically, Russia may reap it, for history makes strange jokes, like that of the Western world's benefit from Franco's victory in Spain.) I seem to have written the ambivalent essay, "The New Poland": "Behind the facade of the government the will of Moscow was still decisive in Poland. . . . There was mysterious nightly shooting in the streets. . . . The Red Army was leaving Poland but it was taking great herds of cattle with it." It is noted that Poland has acquired the part of East Prussia which had been "the nursery ground for Prussianism and the 700 families who dominated the German officer corps." Here is a piece on the OSS (Office of Strategic Services), predecessor of the CIA. Columbia's "Wild Bill" Donovan, paged at the professional football game I attended on the day of Pearl Harbor, is the hero, a man of incredible courage and cunning. I have always been skeptical of the value of civilian underground organizations, but not of the need for a Central Intelligence Agency. John Chamberlain, the writer, confirms the latter and does not dissuade me on the former. A girl who did not become the heroine of the movie *Forever Amber* is picked by the magazine for the role, alas!

A host of readers applaud Guy Richards' attack on the navy's caste system and pose of gentlemanliness (November 26, 1945). John Chamberlain has a piece explaining that the political wolves are closing in on President Truman and, in his view, justifiably. It is not a very nice piece. The lead evaded the fact that "GIs acted more like conquerors than allies" in France by concentrating on the GIs' concentration on "Pig Alley" (the Place Pigalle) in Paris. The interesting line in the editorial, after glancing blows at control of the atom bomb and the need for a U.S. Navy, is that labor and management both seem interested only in power—"that nebulous goal whose quest is always a kind of somnambulism." It also notes H. G. Wells' observation of "a frightful queerness" in the air, some-thing again apparent in 1974, at least to me. A queer explanation of military and diplomatic ciphers is offered by Francis Wickware. I recall the essay with pleasure for it is "Hawaii: A Melting Pot," a story I had requested from the picture department. "There are so many races, pure and mixed, in Hawaii that prejudice for or against any one of them is simply impractical. Every race is a minority . . . the Chinese and Japanese are two of the best-behaved groups in the islands. (The worst-behaved are Puerto Ricans, part-Hawaiians and Filipinos.) . . . It is predicted that some day every inhabitant of Hawaii will be part Hawaiian . . . their carefree and tolerant tradition have had much to do with making a polyracial paradise." The closeup by Herbert Brean is on the United Automobile Workers' Walter Reuther. I think I was reduced to writing the story on Afghan hounds, as being "foreign news." Jackie Robinson is signed as the first Negro by the Brooklyn Dodgers (he had also been a brilliant halfback, basketball player, and broad jumper at college). There follows a text piece on the New York *Herald Tribune*'s saloon, Bleeck's (pronounced Blake's).

An extraordinarily banal lead (December 3, 1945) opens on the theme that the American people "were becoming absorbed again in familiar scenes, familiar objects, familiar emotions . . . 'normalcy,' " and proceeded to show everything going on in one city, Indianapolis, contrasted with small pictures of world events. Everything said was already known to every adult American. The editorial is still fretting over our Foreign Service and suggests that more individual responsibility be permitted, as in the superior British service. In the "Picture of the Week," about 300 of the bombers that pummeled the Axis are shown ready for destruction. The cartoonist Bill Mauldin is given two pages to be dubious about the American Legion. The battle of four dogs and a bobcat (which, with the mountain lion, "every year destroys $20,000,000 worth of livestock and game") is shamelessly detailed. Another version of "foreign news" is a story on "The Building of the Great Pyramid," which I wrote. The essay on "Life in Tokyo" told how MacArthur had given the vote to women, demobilized the home army, started bringing home 6 million Japanese troops overseas, and seized the army and navy's secret hoard of $250 million. With 10 million unemployed, the winter would bring some starvation.

An exaggerated account of the bad manners of American troops in France is contributed by one Joe Weston (December 10, 1945). The lead is "Civilization Tries 20 Top Nazis," with pictures of them in the courtroom pleading not guilty: "The trial is an ambitious attempt to forward human justice, an imaginative but risky innovation in international law. . . . The Nürnberg trial was making the profession of politics a responsible and dangerous one." I did not add that this was absurd. The special correspondent, John Dos Passos, superficially describes the scene. And then the "Picture of the Week" is of a hoggish man, Marshal Zhukov, dining with Eisenhower in Berlin. The editorial brilliantly proposed that the home of the United Nations be set in an internationalized Palestine. A young veteran suggested a rival organization to the American Legion.

A desperate housing shortage, estimated as an immediate need for 3.5 million new homes, is the lead (December 17, 1945). The editorial blamed the shortage on the contractors, subcontractors, craft labor unions, building codes, and licensing laws. In the "Picture of the Week," former ambassador to China General Patrick Hurley furiously tells a Senate committee that some U.S. career officers were helping the Chinese Communists against Chiang Kai-shek. A double page shows the Japanese emperor opening the Diet with a rescript dictated by MacArthur. The fascinating story of Nazi Production Minister Albert Speer first appears as told to John Kenneth Galbraith and George W. Ball. As virtually the only intelligent, brave, cultivated man in the Nazi regime, he rose slowly above the drunken clowns, fools, and poltroons such as Göring, Goebbels, Himmler, Funk, and Ribbentrop, who were grossly mismanaging the war. The authors thread the piece with heavyhanded indications that they had not been humbugged by Speer, and expected him to be executed. A most significant story on the Russian navy said: "Russia must always have four separate fleets, for the Arctic-Atlantic, the Baltic, the Black Sea and the Pacific. None of these fleets can make quick contact with another. . . . Furthermore, Russia owns no intermediate bases for refueling. . . . This fact makes intelligible and reasonable Russia's apparently insane desire for such remote spots as Tripoli, Eritrea. . . . In terms of ships, the problem is simply insoluble." Drawings of some very odd ships are shown: "No guess about the future of the

Red Navy is too fantastic to be possible." (Shouldn't this be "impossible"?) It is followed by an inane essay on college sororities. The mystery of what was to happen in China is partially explained by Charles J. V. Murphy's text piece "Crisis in China"—"a queer business." For the 1.1 million Japanese in China were still armed and holding North China in Shansi, Hopeh, and Shantung provinces, while two crack marine divisions in North China had become demoralized in two months by the "erroneous report . . . that even the *New York Times* wanted them out." After noble democratic promises, the Communists had begun to tear up the railroads, demanding total control of five provinces north of the Yellow River, in addition to Shensi, Kansu, and Ninghsia, vice chairmanships in six others, and an army of 48 divisions, separate from the Nationalist army. But "the Japanese had all the cities, ports and railroads (which were then running); they had the Yellow and Yangtze River Valleys. And the Russians were in Manchuria." A race for the Japanese weapons and the coast was in process. Then, after signing a pact with the Chinese in August, the Russians barred Chiang's army from Dairen. Chiang tried to take Manchuria, as the Russians left, for it held "tremendous stocks of weapons." The Communists were also enlisting Japanese troops. But, Murphy concludes, "in the absence of direct help from Russia, the Communist position is hopeless." Still, it is noted that "American apologists of the Chinese Communists have painted a picture of a prosperous, happy agrarian democracy," as against "the wholesale killing of village elders, the ruthless impressment of young men," and so on. Hurley's rage at the "American apologists" was matched by the usual murderous Communist duplicity. However, the villain in this piece may be isolated as the American mother; but for her, China might be a happy land today.

The escapism of Dan Longwell, supported and probably dictated by Henry R. Luce, was a reflection of an escapist reflex in the people. But the old Time Inc. had tried to lead, not follow. At the time I did not think along these lines but, if I had, it would have appeared that I was extraneous in this new landscape, for I was as worried about the foreseeable future as I had been in 1936. I should have been worried about *my* future.

The pre-Christmas dinner of one Kansas family is the lead (December 24, 1965), signifying nothing. The editorial begs Americans to send food abroad, even to the Germans. Britain's expenditures during the war having left her with a $3 billion deficit, the United States lent her $4.4 billion for fifty years. A picture story showed Communist destruction of railroads in Manchuria and assumed that Chiang would win North China. Another story has everyone apologizing for GIs' destruction of Japanese cyclotrons. The theatrical story points out: "Never in stage history have so many plays of Negro problems been presented simultaneously in one place as there are now on Broadway": *Anna Lucasta, Deep Are the Roots, Strange Fruit.* Another example of solvent religion is the colored essay of paintings of the Medicis, geared to Christmas. The death of Thomas Wolfe's mother occasions a view of his home town, Asheville, North Carolina. The essay is on the Japanese peasant returning home to sweet potatoes, buckwheat, tea, rice, and Shinto. The frivolous killer instinct in Longwell concludes with the slaying of a buck deer for the "party." But he was not really a killer; he just wanted to be one of the boys. *Life* was becoming more and more vulgar.

A justification for this book, and also a contradiction of it, is provided by a reader's letter (December 31, 1945): "No histories of World War II . . . will be of more educational value or more accurate than the *Lifes* I have carefully laid away," this from a newspaper editor. The lead is on the futility of Truman's first congress. The editorial, pondering the loan to Britain, advises against "economic nationalism," as before. Eighty million dollars worth of German art is brought to the United States, obviously in the naked fear that the Russians would grab it. As of this issue, I was extraneous.

The lead (January 7, 1946) was on the prospect of a winter of starvation for Europe: "blame will fall to the victor nations." Then came John Dos Passos on how the Americans were "losing the victory in Europe." The editorial picked apart liberalism, as defined by Harold Laski. The "Picture of the Week" is the suicide, Prince Konoye, long-time premier of Japan. The reverent funeral of General

George Patton, killed in an automobile accident, is shown. Chiang Kai-shek is seen on his first visit to Peiping in a long time, telling the Chinese to get to work. GI guards are shown peeking into the Nazi criminals' cells to prevent their suicide. (It didn't stop Göring.) The essay is an exhibit of Winston Churchill's rather flat paintings, weak in color, though he says, "I like bright colors. I rejoice with the brilliant ones." A bull market in stocks occasions a survey of Wall Street, including Alexander Hamilton's portrait several times, and the Stock Exchange governors.

A journeyman report on Japanese letters to MacArthur is contributed by Dick Lauterbach (January 14, 1946). The "Speaking of Pictures" is, incongruously, some drawings of Eskimo life documented by my research in Edward Weyer's book on the Eskimo. The lead tells of Canada's uranium mine near Great Bear Lake, making "Canada one of the world's most powerful nations." The editorial fumbles around with the idea of merging army and navy, and the "Picture of the Week" shows General Patton's apparently mourning bull terrier, Willie. A story on "the great electro-mechanical brain" is an early word on the computer, or "differential analyzer." But the really important thing in the issue was "Southern Resort Fashions": "the big postwar vacation which Americans have been promising themselves." For Longwell, history had taken an interregnum or recess.

Longwell passed the management of the magazine to Joe Thorndike, who had eliminated humanity from his personality (note my admiration), and either he or Longwell designated as "copy editor" (a new position leading to every sort of decadence) Joe Kastner, a hack whose mastery of the English tongue had been refined at least as far as junior high school. This latter had arrived early at Time Inc. as an office boy; he had mastered the jargon part of it, and that was all. But now, believe it or not, Joe Kastner was editing my copy. Also, Foreign News acquired new researchers, Lee Eitingon and Rosemary Redlich, the former at least a fellow traveler with the Communists, and also the daughter of a rich man. It was announced that pictures went first, not to me as heretofore, but to Lee Eitingon. I sent John Billings a memorandum protesting that this would injure the magazine. He replied that it was dreadful, but there was no action. (In the sequel Lee Eitingon married Ed Thompson, whose infirmity was not that he was a Communist but only that he was an intelligent honest hick who was to become managing editor of *Life*. In real life, anything can happen.) Occasionally, I have had to stand immobile, awaiting enemy action, and now I continued to do my assigned job impassively, even bowing to Joe Kastner's orders to rewrite my copy in ninth-grade terms of language and communication, as *Homo sapiens* deferring to the clever chimpanzee. Abasement as this was, I was resolved to play it out, but I may now lay a great curse on Joe Kastner, if he is still alive, may God have mercy on his soul.

A jocular piece by Guy Richards deplores the fact that men in saloons no longer stand tall and straight, possibly because bar heights have been lowered to accommodate women (January 21, 1946)—deliberate nonsense. Guy's appearance deserves a word. He had been a major (later colonel) of the First Division of marines, used primarily in New Guinea and the Solomons. With the death of Roosevelt, Luce was at last permitted to leave the United States and, encountering Richards in the Philippines, hired him. Guy was unhappy at *Life* because most of what he wrote was not printed—or so he now says. He left to write for the marines and the CIA, became city editor of the *Journal-American* (an aristocrat willing to compete with one and all), and exploded orthodox history with his book, *The Hunt for the Czar*, in which he proves that the Bolsheviks had not been permitted to murder and had not murdered the czar and his family. Since everybody "knows" they were murdered, our view of "history," as documented at some length in this book, must be amended. Lenin, begging for the Treaty of Brest-Litovsk, was holding the cousin of the man he was treating with, Kaiser Wilhelm. Another cousin was the king of England. The czar had the high cards, Lenin none, if he proposed to stop fighting. Russia was saved by the Americans, not for the last time, but the czar was by then long gone. Another irony of history which must shake any doctrinaire of any color: at last account, the czarevitch was living in Forest Hills, New York.

To return to the issue, the lead was on labor, headed by Philip

Murray of C.I.O., and strikes. Manfully, the editorial tries to put the best possible face on economic pessimism, GI looters and black marketeers, Congress and strikes. Richard Lauterbach comes up with a weird story on the "real" emperor of Japan, whose family's position has been "usurped" since 1392. Troops abroad are shown demonstrating in favor of going home. Of all people, James Thurber contributes a supposedly whimsical piece on what American animals had been doing during the war; it didn't belong in *Life*. The essay examines an American county (Adair County, Iowa), revealing nothing of consequence. The closeup on Cardinal Spellman is by Roger Butterfield. The cardinal's picture is the cover.

Now, incredibly, a selection of well-known limericks opens the issue (January 28, 1946). The lead is a reproduction of Winston Churchill's secret speech to the Commons April 23, 1942, first released. He said frankly, "From the beginning of our struggle with Hitler, I have always hoped for the entry of the United States," quoting Roosevelt as extremely happy about the course of events. These facts are the basis of the slanders against Roosevelt which can be extended to me. The editorial said that Germany could not and must not be disindustrialized—as Morgenthau, for example, passionately desired. The United Nations held its first meeting in London's Central Hall and elected Belgium's Paul-Henri Spaak president of the Assembly instead of Norway's Trygve Lie. A patriot is moved by the parade of the 82nd Airborne Division of Major General Gavin down New York's Fifth Avenue. Another absurdity is a set of paintings of Yugoslavia's "liberation"; they are nearly illegible. The August 1945 revolt of the Javanese is at last seen in pictures. The British were doing the imperialist fighting. The Dutch were in Japanese prison camps. It was a strange historical moment.

The great strike of steel workers, virtually paralyzing the United States, is the lead (February 4, 1946). The editorial sides with the workers. A drawing showed the almost empty Senate as the Southerners filibustered with endless trivia to prevent a vote on the Fair Employment Practices Commission favoring Negroes. An essay is on winter life in Florida. Another of Churchill's secret speeches, this as of December 10, 1942, is on the subject of French Admiral

Darlan of North Africa. His point was that the French obsession with legalism or legitimism made de Gaulle a rebel and Pétain the authority, and anyway it was the Americans who had elected to deal with Darlan to avoid some fighting. Darlan's order appeared to have stopped the fighting at Casablanca. A perfect Longwell story was on footling tricks with a three-foot plastic ball reconverted from a wartime solar still.

"From the sprawling empire they conquered and lost in the brief span of 50 years the defeated Japanese today are returning home by the million"—thus opened the lead (February 11, 1946). About 6.5 million remained abroad. The editorial worried about U.S. inflation and deficit spending ("Politicians can spend but cannot stop spending"). American Nancy Langhorne Astor, the wife of Viscount Astor, is seen visiting her family's Virginia estate. A perfect railway seat, an electronic blanket, and tassel stocking caps were eulogized. The essay is a superficial but grisly story on war surgery.

After readers have ridiculed *Life*'s limericks and art, the lead (February 18, 1946) is on the arrival of war brides, all British, in the United States. The editorial noted the absence of any long-range plan for Japan, despite the short-term merits of MacArthur's rule. A story on the United Nations tells how Russia (occupying northern Iran) and Britain (fighting in Greece) accused one another and backed down bilaterally. The UN tentatively picks a future home in New York's Westchester County and the rich natives protest. The Japanese tea ceremony, invented in about 1550, is meticulously described. In Bel Geddes' models the thrilling battle of Midway, which stopped the Japanese threat to Hawaii costing them four carriers, is diagrammed. The bodyguard of five presidents from Wilson on, Colonel Edmund Starling, tells his story. Nine movie starlets are seen at work and play. (Only one made it.) Longwell welcomed the return of bubble gum.

The nonsensical extension of war guilt to artists ("many of them embarrassingly great": Furtwangler, Strauss, Gieseking, Flagstad, Cortot, Gigli, Mengelberg, Lifar) is refereed by Winthrop Sargeant (February 25, 1946). The lead is the official U.S. denunciation of the fascism of Argentina's Perón, primarily, doubtless, because of its flagrant imitation of the European brands. Evita Perón first appears.

The editorial suggested we should send more grain to northwest Europe and perhaps less to the Communist satellites in southeast Europe. U.S. policy was castigated as "laggard . . . and lacking in bold imagination." In India, a parade of the Hindus who had fought beside the Japanese led to riots.

The "Speaking of Pictures" (March 4, 1946) showed the College of Cardinals in full, concealing the plurality (27) of Italian cardinals. Richard Lauterbach has a piece from Tokyo claiming that the Japanese decision for Pearl Harbor was not based on Secretary Hull's ultimatum of November 26, 1941, but had been decided just after November 20. This discredited my uninformed intuition before Pearl Harbor that a Japanese attack was coming, and was probably the chief credential for the Communist, Lauterbach, becoming my successor as foreign editor. More essentially, the primacy of people who had been in the field over a man who had sat in the Time-Life Building, thinking, was endorsed by Longwell, not so certainly by Billings, certainly by Luce. The current mood of the management is sufficiently revealed by the lead on high life in Palm Beach, Florida: "Several million Americans devoted themselves exclusively to the pursuit of pleasure." The whole piece toadies to the Beautiful People. The editorial reports the rest of the world's envy (not love) of the United States. The idea of getting to the moon is projected in drawings, based on the use of atomic energy. The essay is on games for parties, amusing but scarcely informative. John Dos Passos has a piece about Vienna displaying the tone of the literary snobs who hang around the edges of great events, unlike Descartes who actually fought at the battle of the White Mountain.

I think it was at about this time that Longwell called me in and said, "Dave, we all think you ought to be doing much more than you are doing here." I replied, "If you think I'm going to quit, Danny, forget it. You've got to fire me." He replied, "Nobody is thinking of that. I've never heard any criticism of your work. What I'm talking about is a year's sabbatical with full pay." I replied, "Danny boy, I could kiss you."

However, I was still the Time Inc. writer. Earlier, I had closed the color pages of an essay on the Holy Land, and I insisted on writing the black-and-white frontispiece before I left, for an issue to be dated April 1, 1946, a date that must add a smile to the event. I was working hard on this, getting into small compass the crucial dates in the history of the ancient Hebrews, when my friend the comptroller, Hugh Rodgers, told me the gossip of my departure was in the air. Therefore, I handed in my copy, took out a suitcase of documents (many used in this book), and let Rodgers transfer my furniture to my home. The color story read, for example, "But Joseph called them on into Egypt, where they become confused by some historians with the warlike Hyksos who ruled the Egyptians for hundreds of years. Moses led the Hebrews back to Palestine around 1450 B.C., long after they had adopted the invisible, one god of Abraham which they called Yahweh. They had great warriors and heroes: Joshua, Samson, Samuel, Saul, David and Solomon who built the Temple about 950 B.C."

Joe Kastner threw out my frontispiece copy. His substitution says very little except that "biblical Palestine is soaked in tradition" and the ancient Hebrews lived in tents. In this same issue is a presentation of one of Buckminster Fuller's round aluminum houses, anchored with a mast. After I left on sabbatical, I bought several thousand shares of stock in this house at a dollar a share. It rose to over $35 a share (or about $70,000 for me) but I was not interested in selling. Finally, I sold a few shares at less than a dollar. So it goes.

When I left Time Inc., I set up parting interviews with Henry R. Luce and John S. Billings. To the latter I said, "Did you know I was mad at you for several years because you laid down on Hubie Kay?" He replied, "I didn't lay down on Hubie. He laid down on me." I said, "That's not true." Then I went to Luce and said, "The magazine is just telling people things they already know. I thought we were in the business of telling people things they don't know." He told a story about (I think) the movie man Jack Warner who had been idealistically active during the war but now spent all his time at the race track. He said, "Give me another year, Dave." And at that the farewell ended.

I never again set foot in the Time-Life Building on Forty-ninth Street.

My failure to make overtures to Time Inc. is understandable for, after some difficulties, I had a satisfying career. But Time Inc.'s failure to make overtures to me must seem to the reader either mysterious or, if he has sophistication, obvious. Still, to me, there is something inscrutable about it, thinking, as I do, that I was the gold in the hills for Time Inc. For with me, or people like me, Time Inc. had credibility. Nobody could possibly believe in Dan Longwell, Joe Kastner, Joe Thorndike, and their successors, because they had no convictions or were too smart to expose them.

This part of the story can conclude with documentation. On February 14, 1946, Roy Larsen wrote: "So, around March 1st, you will receive a check totaling (again subject to final audit) approximately 70% of your 1945 salary." As of March 1 came the letter from Dan Longwell to me and his memorandum to the staff, both of which are reproduced:

March 1, 1946.

Dear Dave:

This note is to formalize our conversation of a few days ago.

You are taking a one year's leave of absence from *Life* starting March 1, 1946. Your salary will continue until March 1, 1947. By March 1, 1947 your relationship with *Life* will be terminated, and you are then to be given the limit of severance pay allowed.

By remaining on the payroll past January 1, 1947 you will receive all the benefits to which you are entitled under the company's annuity and retirement plan when you terminate your connection with *Life* on March 1, 1947.

So much for the purely business side. On the personal side, I and many others will miss you and wish you luck. As an editor who has watched you, with some awe, write whole great parts of complicated issues of *Life*, I cannot help expressing a profound sense of gratitude to you for our long association.

I hope you'll make the decision of trying to write some articles for *Life*.

Sincerely,
DANIEL LONGWELL

March 1, 1946.

To: The Staff
From: Daniel Longwell

Dave Cort, who has been with *Life* since Vol. I, No. I, is taking an extended leave of absence to undertake writing projects of his own.

Cort has written far and away more *Life* stories than anyone on the staff. I very much hope he'll find time on his leave to continue to add to the bookshelf of good writing he has already contributed to *Life*.

A review of *Life*'s subsequent issues shows an accelerating frivolity. My name remained on the masthead into the issue of May 13, 1946, as one of the "editors" who included Busch, Calhoun, Chamberlain, Coughlan, Cort, Field, Kastner, and Murphy. The assistant managing editors were Joe Thorndike and Ed Thompson. Worthen Paxton had left to rejoin Norman Bel Geddes.

The financial facts of life appear now in a confusion of documents, from which tangle I abstract the item "Your Cash Equity at December 31, 1945": $16,526.47, from three trusts—fair enough, if it had all reached me.

My tax records for 1947, as figured by L. Arnold Weissberger, show an income of $13,085.09, including $5,000 in severance pay. As of January 23, 1948, I was sent a final installment of $1,008.65, and one must always notice those nickels and dimes, by trustee David Brumbaugh, who had always addressed me as Dave (a familiarity) but now as "Dear Mr. Cort" (here a snub). In 1948 I elected to withdraw my contributions to the retirement fund, losing the Time Inc. contribution. This can be taken as one more financial lunacy but since I had some confidence in my productive potential (at the moment I overrated it), long-term assets under the control of Time Inc. lawyers did not have much reality.

THE SEQUEL

During the twelve months of my sabbatical leave, I wrote two books, a novel later published as *The Calm Man* and a philosophical work later published as *The Big Picture*, including chapters on Man, The Universe, Western Civilization, The Earth, and so on. These were being peddled by the agency of Harold Ober, Inc., and everywhere rejected.

It occurred to me that the New York literary world was bigoted about an ex–Time Inc. writer of my status. Yet various field correspondents were famous, headed by John Hersey, William Shirer, Theodore White, and so on. What in the hell was wrong with me? For I felt that I was a more capable, versatile, even Protean writer than these distinguished gentlemen, and I've never had occasion to change my mind.

Paranoia? I began to think so until an idiotic editor at Knopf returned a rejected manuscript with, by mistake, the house readers' reports on my earlier books. By then it did not matter. The minimum distinction I had deserved on Time Inc. and never received, that of being listed in *Who's Who in America*, and even in *Who's Who in the World*, had befallen me. And this came as a little reward for suffering for a few years, a price I would always have been willing to pay.

The first is by somebody named Ogden and dated as returned to me June 15, 1951, as follows:

This is a series of smart-aleck essays on Man, the Universe, Love, Current Events etc., proceeding from David Cort who served his novitiate with the Luce organization and has never discarded his belief that complicated issues can be capsulized and that problems are best viewed as opportunities for aphorism. His thinking has been enlarged in recent years by frequenting the salons of such uncrowned prophets as Bucky Fuller, but the habits of his youth remain. This is just a parade of vulgarization, impertinence and sciolism. The most injurious element of all is Cort's evident belief that a recital of atomic, uncriticized "facts" is decisive and denotes the mind operating at its fullest; such a view underlies the whole practice of the Luce publications, and in a hurried world accounts for their success. But I should be distressed if we gave it a foothold in our organization.

AO

By this time the admirable Don Congdon of Harold Matson, Inc., was my agent and he sent my novel to Knopf. It was, I am told, analyzed by a middle-aged homosexual: "This is a sort of biographical novel. The subject (I hesitate to use the words hero and protagonist) is an intolerable bounder—the old-fashioned word fits him—and a dullard. His adventures with the highly specified anatomies of several women, with the stock of a supersonics corporation, etc., etc., are about as childish as anything I've read in a long time. I looked up the reviews of his earlier novel (Liveright, 1932). They were decidedly adverse, and for the most part could be applied without change to this sophomore hash. Reject. H.W."

The reviews of the earlier novel, *Give Us Heroes*, were, as of the *New York Times*, "an obscene vitality," and the book was republished in 1971. I cannot imagine why the Knopf character thought the story was "biographical," meaning probably "autobiographical." I do regret his exposure to a dramatization of the female body, though in acceptable terms and with respect for that form.

The third Knopf account of my work was by Henry C. Carlisle. It no longer has the anti–Time Inc. bigotry but is still insane criticism, for this book too was published—and might have been published by Knopf.

I suppose I should examine the subsequent careers of these three critics who decided my life through an agonizing period. But they have too many replicas in the publishing world. Here is Carlisle's mystifying review:

This is an interesting novel. Scene by scene it is written with a grasp of the characters and background—America in 1938—which is both knowledgeable and imaginative.

These characters are H. B. Bohun, a foreign news editor; Marilyn, his wife, a night club singer, temporarily separated from him; Fiennes, an unemployed and rather wild young man, a friend of Bohun and Marilyn.

As Europe edges towards the brink of war (throughout the story the declining European situation is unfolded through Bohun's highly informed and critical analyses), Bohun discovers that Fiennes is (a) his own alter ego and (b) a rival for Marilyn's love. There follows an exciting game of cat and mouse, during which Fiennes and Bohun stalk one another, using as weapons at various occasions an axe, a shotgun, and a speedboat.

There are good scenes, good dialogue, and a definite *Zeitgeist* of America during the days of Munich. I wanted to like a novel of this kind but finally couldn't like this one. I simply didn't understand what Cort was trying to accomplish by means of the *doppelgänger* story, set against the gathering storm background. The novel is exciting to read by moments (esp. towards the end), never falls below the level of readability, but adds up to worse than nothing. Unless anyone else wishes to read, I suggest that we encourage Cort to submit anything else he does but reject this.

HCC

In this period I essayed almost every conceivable way in which a man of my equipment could be useful to society—in vain. I was useless. At last I surrendered and told Louis Dolivet of *United Nations World* (whose original dummy I had largely written) that I would work for him. This proved to be a maniac farm, Michael Straight having withdrawn, Dolivet (married to Straight's sister) being immured in Europe on suspicion of being a Communist in the Joe McCarthy period, another officer busy photographing Aly Khan and Rita Hayworth on safari in Africa, and the president, one Roger Phillips, a small-boy travesty of Luce, plus assorted neurotics and a genius Hungarian writer about food, Tibor Koeves. Publishing a monthly magazine seemed child's play; for some time I wrote a third of the magazine under various aliases, rewrote another third, and left the last hack third, mostly on the UN, untouched. I had come near solving the formula of a world magazine (probably insoluble) when Phillips fired me, to the shrieks of his attendant eumenides. I then tried to promote a real world magazine, without success, but with a charming letter of refusal from Albert Lasker.

I had acquired additional information, however, and had time to partially rewrite *The Big Picture,* now accepted by Hiram Haydn and Louis Simpson for Bobbs-Merrill.

I had long since resented the fact that Time Inc. did not review *The Big Picture,* favorably received elsewhere, but here is a letter from the Bobbs-Merrill publicity woman saying the *Time* reviewer wanted a copy. "Remembering my promise to you not to send any review copies to *Time* or *Life* until one week before publication, I have not sent one out but wondered if you might wish to reconsider this. . . . Cal Whipple telephoned again asking for another look at galleys, and I have stalled him off." In short, I was at fault.

This book attracted the notice of Carey McWilliams of *The*

Nation, for which I began to write regularly, with his splendid research, for he is an incredibly omnivorous reader, an open-minded thinker, and a great editor.

In view of the Knopf reader's sour view of *The Big Picture,* it is worth noting that *The Nation* picked it, together with Joseph Wood Krutch's *The Measure of Man,* for their Nation's Choice selection No. 4, and quoted some reviews. John Barkham for the Saturday Review Syndicate: "The publishers do not exaggerate when they call this a 'highly original' book about man and his place in the universe. It is all that and more. It is also a brilliant, exhibitionistic, sparkling, irritating, erudite and stimulating look at homo sapiens by one of the brightest young pundits to heave into sight in years." (I had not just heaved into Barkham's sight.) E. B. Garside in the *New York Times:* "Mr. Cort analyzes love, marriage, the psychology of corporation hierarchy, the emotions of prehistoric man and many other topics that swarm into his fertile mind. Even the specialist must admit that what Mr. Cort 'really knows' is very much worth knowing." Two other comments may be noted. Hiram Haydn told me Harlow Shapley had said that the description of the universe was the best he had yet seen. An old friend, Philip Wylie, to whom a copy was sent, wrote: "Dave doesn't know enough to write a book like this." So it goes.

In view of Luce's authorizing wildly contrary points of view in his magazines (note only Chambers versus Cort), one must look long at his statement in a speech at the University of Oregon on February 20, 1953: "The fashionable and convenient and profitable doctrine is that, in order to amuse the reader or in order 'to give readers various viewpoints,' the owner-publisher has the right, even the duty, to print what personally he deplores or detests. In my view that is a childish evasion of a man's responsibility. It is worse than that: it is cynicism at the heart of American life."

The Luce performance, as against the doctrine, has been fully documented, and the reader must make the judgment. It is enough to make one weep. For Hadden had projected a magazine that hoped to rise above "various viewpoints" into the stratosphere of "facts." The effort is doomed if it is not dedicated. But Luce believed he had been responsible and virtuous, even as he protected and supported Whittaker Chambers until the moment the real Jay Vivian Chambers (stand up) revealed himself as a Communist agent. (Now a further surprise: this too may be a lie.) For Luce was that truly pitiable character: a decent responsible man who cannot distinguish between honest men and impostors, and finally, in despair, opens the door to the reliable mediocrities such as Joe Kastner, Ed Thompson et al.

Such men cannot tell the difference between good sources and bad sources, and they are fatal to a communications operation. However the Howard Hughes "autobiography" turned out, somebody at Time Inc. should have had the antennae to sense something a little peculiar—in short, not exactly a good source. Luce eliminated all such people, with whom Time Inc. was once fully endowed. A really good journalist has to be a little paranoiac about his sources. Faith in liars is the shortcut to destruction. Longwell did not care whether they were liars, only whether they were interesting and immediately profitable. He, like the present editors of Time Inc., hungered for the slam-bang sensation right now, the jackpot, instant celebrity. He is not really dead.

And here, probably in 1952, when I was being sued for a pittance by a restaurant where I had provably spent at least $5,000 a year, is a letter to my dear friend, Roy Larsen:

> My lawyer in a civil suit tells me he wants some proof of my literary abilities over the years. I'm emphasizing my books and signed stories and articles, but would like to make some note of my journalistic experience. Would you care to write a brief note recalling my record on *Time* and *Life* and, if you like, your recollection of its quality? The lawyer tells me that if you can notarize the signature, it's an affidavit but he can do with an ordinary letter. . . .

I have no record or recollection of any reply from my friend.

On Carey McWilliams' research, I wrote a piece on water, long before this had been generally recognized as a national disaster. But *The Nation* was slow to print it.

Carey asked me to write a piece about Time Inc. I answered, "You mean, you want me to cash in all my chips there for the pittance you pay?" (That is, I still felt some tie to Time Inc.) He still had not published my piece on water. Finally, I told him that if he would print the water story, I would write a piece on Time Inc. and Luce. And he did.

The piece, called "Once Upon a Time Inc." (*The Nation*, February 18, 1956), is reproduced in a book, *Is There an American in the House?* and caused much amusement. But I was amazed to discover that this single publication mysteriously lifted from me the Time Inc. curse and relegitimized me, more or less, in the literary world.

I must acknowledge one error. The new publisher of *Life* (Andrew Heiskell) is described as having been born in France, whereas he was born in Naples, Italy, and educated in Switzerland, Germany, and France. I will omit the intramural scandal which makes me think him a silly man. His elevation lies on the record of H. R. Luce.

Buckminster Fuller's brother-in-law whom I had helped to get a Time Inc. job (which he deserved) told a friend of mine, "Dave shouldn't have written that piece." This must have meant that I still owed Time Inc. something.

Somewhat later *The Nation* ran a back cover ad saying, "Who writes for *The Nation*? David Cort writes for *The Nation*," adding that I was working on a certain subject for a book. (Because I would still like to do the book, I omit the subject.) This brought me a friend, Emile Capouya, an editor at Macmillan, who wanted to see the manuscript. I told him at lunch there was no manuscript on that subject but I had a novel (later published as *The Minstrel Boy*). I had received permission from C. D. Jackson at Time Inc. to use my own writings in *Life* as part of a dramatization of the year 1938, the year of Munich, as a demonstration of the pragmatic morality toward the assassin. I had written Larsen for permission, but Jackson had answered that the material was in the common domain. This book was rejected by Macmillan. Capouya then accepted the collection of essays published as *Is There an American in the House?* expressing my astonishment that a real American could be embarrassed by Senator Joseph McCarthy or Nixon or Whittaker Chambers. Under our law, the individual is the sovereign power, a majestic person, though personally he holds only a splinter of the power. His powers can never be alienated from him, but only delegated to representatives. The idiot children do not seem to know this. When they riot, they are essentially rioting against their own sovereign power. An odd thing, indeed.

My increasing interest in Whittaker Chambers is evidenced by two astonishing documents I find—projected letters to Edward Skillin, editor of *Commonweal*, and Chambers. I do not know (but doubt) whether they were sent. I had written a story, clearly based on Chambers, which *Commonweal* had rejected. Now hear this:

I think this is a whole view of such a man as Chambers, and of all the people who hate their fathers and try to be clever. I submit that the most revealing job to be done today is to understand this sort of man. I happen to know, at enormous length, about this particular man. I take a poor view of him, not because of anything he has said recently, but because I took a poor view of him over 30 years ago—and he has not yet said or done anything that surprises me.

Chambers says that he believes in God and adjures America to believe in God also. Why? Because America is on its deathbed—and deathbed conversions are easy. Such evil, so patent a revelation of Satan rationalizing, almost staggers me, but not to the point of being speechless. Mr. Skillin, you cannot continue to separate yourself from this evil, which protects itself with a belief in God. You are in a war, as I feel myself to be in a war. I have sworn to myself that I will finish off Chambers and McCarthy, and the last time I so swore was in regard to Hitler. I acknowledge that this great threat has no apparent substance, but because my people have been here for several centuries I think I am obliged to stay with it. I have tried only to suggest that a jehad is in force. I believe it is restricted to the "old Americans" who are supposed to be all rich, reactionary and impotent. I only await, with a vast optimism in all mankind, the reaction of the new immigration.

The faith of the founding fathers is about to be tested. What does the new immigration think, not about the "old Americans," but about itself? Does it feel dignified? Does it fight for its dignity? Do those outlandish first ten amendments convey anything? Or is it all just a silver sty, where one eats well, rattles around in one's car to no purpose, groans at the income tax, sends money or parcels back to Italy or Ireland, stocks the beer cans in the icebox and might as well be dead?

Luckily there is a majority of us who have no European country to look back to, as has McCarthy. I am stuck with the United States, with my life list of 247 *American* birds seen and identified. If I wished to be a traitor to everything I love, I would be hard pressed to know what country I should be a traitor *for*. And so it is with all people like myself, of whom the Kremlin and McCarthy are in agreement: we are fools, they say. 160 million people slowly forming an opinion is an awesome thing. If the opinion is imposed on them, as the McCarthy wants to do, it is nothing.

The other letter:

Dear Whittaker, I do owe you a letter of sincere thanks.

May I first remind you of my identity: I was first a growing child in Woodmere while you had your appalling childhood in Lynbrook; I was next a classmate of yours at Columbia; and finally while you contributed your distinguished touch to world events as foreign editor of *Time*, I was the opposite number on *Life*—although I honestly do not remember hearing about your functions on *Time*, which I had long since ceased to read. I have the same queer feeling toward you that I have toward Mrs. Luce: you are following me, but upside down.

To return to my first theme: I am in your debt. I read your book carefully and had great trouble convincing such a magazine as *Commonweal* that you are still fundamentally, in the company of McCarthy, a traitor to this country and all its ancient traditions and founding fathers. You are not technically guilty of treason.

But I was not believed, at first. I am perhaps not as perfect a propagandist as you, in the matter of throwing loaded dice. I am immensely superior to you as a propagandist at throwing honest dice. Put the honest dice out and I will take your last dollar. But I do know that poor Luce is a sucker for the crooked dice. . . .

It would seem that the subject of Whittaker Chambers is in some strange way (anything involving Chambers is strange, including his hypnosis of William Frank Buckley, Jr.) integral to the subject of Henry R. Luce. I did a piece (unpublished) on Chambers' book *Witness*, listing his five assumptions as follows:

1. Western civilization is "sick unto death." However, there is one man (Chambers) who, even knowing it to be sick, will die with it.

2. Communism is a faith far more heroic and inspiring than Freedom, and produces more ascetic and dedicated saints and heroes, such as Chambers.

3. This faith is shared, perhaps unconsciously, by all scientists and those who seek "to reduce the meaningless chaos of nature by imposing on it [the] rational will to order, abundance, security, peace" and "the rigorous

exclusion of all supernatural factors in solving problems." "The vision is shared by millions who are not Communists (they are part of Communism's secret strength)."

4. The Communist's superior courage is all that differentiates him from "those miscellaneous socialists, liberals, fellow travelers, unclassified progressives and men of good will, all of whom share a similar vision, but do not share the faith because they will not take upon themselves the penalties of the faith."

5. "Communism is the central experience of the first half of the 20th Century." "A common force of character" sets both Chambers and Hiss and all Communists apart from the mass of free men.

No. 3 seems to abandon to Stalin all the world's scientists, scholars, and technicians. No. 4 surrenders a good many of the 10 million Americans of the independent vote and possibly a clear majority of the electorate. No. 5 claims for Stalin anybody of spirit who has really lived. Nos. 1 and 2, however, give the whole world to communism. A troubled soul reading the book would probably elect for communism.

With explicit quotations from *Witness,* I documented all five assumptions to the hilt, but this work need not be repeated here. (I have it.) The consumption of assumptions is best taken neat. The whole essay might be included here but it would repeat material the reader has seen. I believe that Chambers deserves fame, as a true monster who simultaneously fooled the American Right, Left, and Center.

The documents reveal my peculiar relations with Time Inc. A letter from Larsen's secretary, Doris Smith, dated February 24, 1956, acknowledges receipt of *The Nation* piece on Time Inc. but says that he is off on an extended trip. (Fifteen years later, when I wrote him that he might see this manuscript and make an adversary reply, I got the same answer from another secretary. No imagination.)

Dated March 14, 1956, comes a letter from one Alex Groner at work on the history entitled *Time Inc.* He wants to interview me in room 1725, using a tape recorder. I refused the interview but said I would answer written questions. Dated March 20, he repeated the request. Apparently, I was unmoved for, dated April 9, a letter opens: "I couldn't quite tell from your note whether you are agin me or dead set agin me." However, he submitted some questions, to which I gave answers.

Q. When you joined company and why.

A. I came from *Vanity Fair* on a letter from Frank Crowninshield. My reason was that though I wrote well I knew nothing. I came to learn something. The date was about March, 1932.

Q. What was it like to write for *Time* under Billings? Martin? Luce? What kind of writing was appreciated, what deprecated? Was any *Time*-style in the ascendant or decline during your writing period?

A. Martin was the most provocative, Billings the most consistent, Luce interesting for short stretches but giving the impression that he doesn't really know what he is doing. Martin, however, was often tight on Saturday noon. Billings was dull and pig-headed. He would refuse a raise he planned to give if the man asked for it. (Explaining that this was what he was doing.) Half the writers wanted to kill Martin; the other half whom he liked laughed at him. Billings' closest friend was Hubie Kay. He fired Hubie from *Life* because Kay suggested that *Life* ought to do what it is now doing in the Man-Universe-Culture series. When I left *Life*, I reproached Billings for this.

Q. Coming of the Guild to Time Inc. and how it reflected or affected right-left political consciousness. Sharpness or lack of feeling about it. Signs of company or magazines changing their drift of political sentiment in the mood of the times.

A. You must know by now that I ignored the Guild; I was called the "parlor fink" (if I try, I can think of the name of the man who coined this) because I got a list of signatures opposing the closed shop, but the labor boys did not realize I was also opposed to management. I delivered a written speech at a Guild meeting over the dead body of Cameron Mackenzie, the Communist president and a cousin of old friends of mine. My checker, Ruth Berrien (Fox), whom you should interview, headed the fight against the Communists. Some of them are still there. Insofar as I was concerned, it is wild understatement to say that Guild policy had no effect on my handling of foreign news. Kay told me, "You're a fool. It's either too little to fool with or too big to buck." I disagreed then, and disagree now. However, it should be added that I was the only overt Roosevelt man in the place, though 80% of the staff actually voted New Deal.

Q. When and what first heard of *Life*? When began working on it? Excitement of new venture.

A. September, 1936.

Q. Kinds of stories thought about, talked about, worked on, prior to publication.

A. Life of Stalin. Spanish civil war—an attempt at a sequence. (I think it was published.) I was also art editor at that stage. All this is in the published magazines. Martin was still managing editor but in an ominous euphoria. Billings was brought up at the last minute to get out an actual first issue.

Q. Starting publication; first stories worked on; shift from experimental to working feel; people worked with in early period.

A. I only remember fighting for a picture of a back-country small town in Brazil. (See issue.) At first we worked in big room over picture bins. I remember having a very hot political fight with a homosexual Communist (though both features were unknown at the time) at the bins. The layout department will remember. I think the man actually wept.

Q. How *Life* shaped up into a magazine. What it discovered, invented. Who responsible for what?

A. Obviously I invented the handling of foreign news, as Luce wrote me at the end of the first year. I don't understand what I invented in that sense but I do think I first began the real study of the picture in the caption. (But *Life* has now abandoned this, so it is unimportant.) I also invented Gary Underhill.

Q. Was there early consciousness of journalistic opportunity present in great events that led to war?

A. No.

Q. *Life's* change in tone from off-beat, quaint and cute things that could be done with pictures to urgency of news during the war years.

A. I deduce from this question that you know nothing.

Q. War's end and Thorndike moved into Billings' job. What this meant in terms of changes in magazine.

A. No comment.

Later, I wrote an (unpublished) piece about Groner's requests, in the dishonorable voice of a corporation, to me, an individual, committed by his honor to any statement he made. This can be forgotten.

Absolutely no intimation of anything I had given Groner peeped into the book finally produced, called *Time Inc.* (which I reviewed for *Commonweal*). In fact, its sole mention of my existence at Time Inc. is contained in the sentence: "There were three associate editors (writers): Joseph Kastner, drafted from *Fortune*; Thorndike who had been with the experimental department from the beginning; and David Cort, transferred from *Time*." On the basis of this credential, I am unqualified to have written this book. I am nearly a phantom.

However, I have a friendly letter, dated December 24, 1956, from somebody on *Life* whose signature I cannot decipher. He was enjoying my *Nation* pieces, "especially on autos and highways," and wanted to have lunch. Except for my continuing friendships with Hubert Kay and Busch, it is a unique recognition of my existence. (Postscript: it was Roger Butterfield.)

Two letters from Gary Underhill appear. That in July 1956, when he had eight more years to live, is about the Soviet air force, and the reader is asked to decipher his use of initials, for I cannot.

7 July 56

Dear Dave:

It's hard to tell who if anyone is looked up to these days. Aviation's command got worked over by Stalin, with arrests and changes since 1945, so that like the present political rulers it doesn't appear that anyone can seem very clean.

The original Chief Marshal of Aviation, Alex Novikov, got a good war reputation, but by the end was drinking so hard that though Stalin kept him around he was relieved of command; regarded as good man but far from tops. Was CinC of Avn of Soviet Army N's Dpty Marshal of Avn Vovosheikin, and C of S,M of Avn Sergei Khudyakov, all were arrested with Novikov in '45;

Then Vershinin was tops, with Col Gen Pavel Fedorovitch Zhigarev, who had been C in C Far East AForce, as Deputy; with Col Gen Vladimir Sudets as C of S;

Then 1948 C M of Avn Alesandr Golovaney, who had been wartime Long Range AF cdr, who got arrested for maladministration resulting in crashes;

Zhigarev succeeded him; also kept deputy post;

Then Aug 49, Vershinin, Sudets & Lt Gen Kolokov were arrested for maladministration and poor training policies.

Zhigarev came to the top, with Col Gen Sergi Rudenko as C of S, with Lt Gen Vladimir Aladinski as cdr Long Range Air Army;

From all I can find out, the airmen never did well for themselves in the war, and hence with that record, and with the lack of any combat proof since, and with the Stalin business, there aren't any great heroes in the ops end.

The Army of course dominates the Air Force, which doesn't exist separately—there's a Chief of Avn, like the days when the US Army had a Chief of Artillery; then the Cdr of Army Aviation, and of the long range aviation. But it's all under top Army leaders—and these are the WW II marshals who did beat the Germans and are known and respected as good fighters—esp. Zhukov, who's been known to knock a subordinate general's teeth out to put him in his place.

It's the design engineers who are revered—old Tupolev above all; Mikovan and Gurevitch, and Sergei Ilyushin; and the jet engine designer Klimov. They've done well and been above politics, put Soviet avn (so many think) 1st. For increasingly the Reds come to worship technology—about which they know far more than we. In fact, they've come to be "technically cultured" while we regard technology as for technicians. Hence Aid is vital in that the Russians take a real interest and concern in the advancement of technology and of the t. of an area—we really don't take such real interest.

You get the idea—that in Soviet aviation it isn't the military leaders who enjoy the admiration—but the engineers, with proven record—and the kind of mind generated in Russia fits into this, and all is significant if Russia is going to try a cold war of technology with the allied and neutral nations the stakes.

Best,
Gary

P.S. Pat lacks Catharine's address, sends her best to you, and we both enjoyed the piece on *Time*.

The other is dated July 4, 1955. I had probably written him about my thoughts on atomic war, published in *The Nation*, I believe, in 1959. Later, I sent him my thought that the Soviet air force could take over Russia by circling over the Kremlin with an atomic bomb. His remarks have a formidable authority.

Dear Dave:

Yours is quite a thought—and of course that's how things might well work out. Actually one outfit here has figured total destruction of the 97 cities making H-bomb targets would leave 100 million people and over half the industrial resources, and the bulk of the transport, communications, etc net left—which is plenty to fight on with.

But then the aggressors never have had the sense about these things one tends to credit them with—and they'll start a fight they haven't much of a chance of winning, if any. Good defense then is a matter of showing them we mean business, and that we are good—know what they're up to, and can take them. Dolts in the govt and military only invite the scorn of aggressors, and thus help start wars.

Best,
Gary

As a postscript he wrote:

What's more to be feared than bombs are the forms of radiological war, which don't necessarily kill anybody, and certainly don't destroy things. They could get everybody so weak that airborne troops could easily take over—if we aren't set for such things. *One* U-bomb blown off the Pacific coast would radiate the whole US—fatal dose about up to the great Plains but only prolonged weakening East of that. Etc. We're preparing for the wrong thing.

To verify the date of Gary's death, I wrote the brilliant author of *We Give to Conquer*, Asher Brynes, who discovered Gary's body. His answer follows:

October 30, 1971

Dear David Cort,

Although I was involved in the incident, I don't find, unfortunately, any note of the exact date of Garry's death in my papers. It was midsummer of 1964, about two months after I had emerged from the hospital following a serious illness.

He had been coming to see me about weekly. When he missed a week-end and then some I walked over to his place on M Street.

His door was at the top of a flight of stairs.

When there was no response to my knocking I tried the lock and found it unbolted. One could see without crossing the threshold that he was apparently asleep. This was late in the afternoon, but he was a man of irregular hours, so I backed out, hoping the door would close silently.

Since I was myself still convalescent and not working, I returned the following day. He still appeared to be asleep, from the doorway.

On the next day following I tried his door and this time walked into his bedroom for a closer look, because he still seemed to be sleeping in the same posture. He was lying on his side with his face pressed into the pillow. I didn't see the wound. The weapon was one of his pair of Belgian revolvers—the model with recessed chambers for rimmed ammunition.

I throw in this detail because he would have noticed and mentioned that, had he been in my place.

He was a wonderful person. Oh yes, the date: it was June, about, 1964. The *Washington Post* carried his death as a small news item; no mention of suicide.

Finally, you say you have a note from him on the Soviet Air Force. I dare say he knew more about it than most of the certificated experts in the Pentagon. What interested him wholly in that final year of his life, however, was the mystery of the Russian missiles in Cuba. He insisted it was a mystery, so far as U.S. knowledge of them was concerned. He never believed the official story.

In a manner of speaking he was a casualty of McNamara's war gamers, the operations research pedants who stole the show away from the generals with whom Garry—despite their occasional stupidity—could have discussed the future of the military. He was full of the future. He kept reminding me and other military outsiders that it grew, that is, everything usefully novel in it grew out of the past. Now that the military mathematicians have fallen out amongst themselves (the Wohlstetter-Weisner-Rathjens-Lapp-Weinberg quarrel which has just been refereed by the Operations Research Society of America), we'll have need for Garry's kind of intelligence in the present "future."

> With all good
> ASHER BRYNES,

Here we have not only a corroboration of my opinion of Underhill's importance, but also an indication that history is less what happens than what people *think* has happened.

I may have been a little manic in those days and, I think, with sufficient reason. I might wish to modify these communications but it would be wrong to do so. Like everything else in this book, they are the real thing, and thus have some historical value. For there are some situations in life which must occasion only pure rage. My opinion of that great historical figure, Jay Vivian Chambers, has not changed in fifty years, except to clarify. And, remember, he was a darling of Henry R. Luce.

An unfocused rage, for I did not aim it at Time Inc. or at anything I could define, probably possessed me for a decade or so. I became, once again, a fighting drunk. If the word reached Henry R. Luce, Dan Longwell, Joe Kastner, Ed Thompson, or the other mediocrities, I am sure that they thought all's right with the world, the hillside dew-pearl'd. Jim Parton, Thorndike's partner, saw a brother of mine at a Loomis School reunion and said, "I saw your brother on the street and he looked terrible." My admirable brother, six feet four and distinguished, replied, "I had lunch with him today and he looked better than I do." (Paul had been voted the best football end ever to play at Loomis up to his time.)

However, I am still here and probably still look terrible. I do not know what shape Parton is in.

This book is not about my entire career.

The theme is that Henry R. Luce once had an organization of people who wrote what they believed and had the talent to know what they believed. In consequence, his readers believed in the Time Inc. magazines. In this sense journalism resembles religion, requiring the enlistment of the communicant's faith—but not a blind faith, an earned faith based on continuous performance.

The ancient truth is that the medium's strength is based on its credibility. And this must always be a communication from one mind to one mind. The reader is one mind; the medium addressing him had best speak from one mind, an authentic individual human being.

Hacks do not know what they really think, and could not express it anyway. The audience senses this very quickly.

For some time, the magazines have been trying to compete with television, not on their home grounds of credibility, but on television's grounds of numbers. The mass magazines have been disappearing and, while this was written in September 1971, *Look* vanished, with a story by Gardner Cowles that television had destroyed him.

Television cannot compete with the printed word; it is supported by advertising which compels the audience to look and listen. Subliminally, the advertising destroys the credibility of television, for it is all transparent, including insulting lies. As of this moment in time, let me cite a few examples, though I imagine that everybody knows what I mean.

Only idiots would believe any of it. "It's great to be alive. New buckwheat high nutrition cereal. . . . Makes you feel like a million bucks." "If anything goes wrong we will fix it free. American Motors. Before I put my name on it, everything's got to be just right. . . . I promise, you'll get action, not a run-around." "Salada teas—great teas." "Absorbine Jr. . . . penetrating heat gets deep in the muscles." "Texaco—you can trust your car to the man who has the star." "Rice Chex—doesn't leave a lump in your stomach." "A tummy-warming breakfast—Aunt Jemima's real French toast." "The greatest fried chicken in America—frozen food department. Very stirring old home recipe." "If our loan man says no, you get a different loan man." And so on, infinitely.

Some of these products may be worthy. The point is that various people are trying to *sell* you something when you thought you might be about to *learn* something. You are forced to accept the selling spiel, much of it accompanied by music, by deliberately subliminal suggestion. If you have the wits of a baby, you know somebody is trying to seduce you.

But in the magazine nobody is obliged to read the advertising. This is the crucial advantage of the printed word over television. But the printed word must achieve credibility—if possible passionate, almost religious, faith.

The loss of *Life*'s credibility is illustrated in the masthead. Thorndike was managing editor under Longwell and Luce until 1949, and one day revolted and walked out. Ed Thompson, a decent human being but not one who belongs in my profession, succeeded him, and the magazine was dead.

The sin of Luce is signaled by the fact that John S. Billings one day in 1954 walked out without saying goodbye to anyone. Repeatedly, Luce wrote him at his South Carolina plantation but never got a reply. The betrayal that I have gone to so much trouble to pin on Luce was evidently flagrant to people closer to Luce than I ever was. For all the people who understood what Time Inc. was all about, what Briton Hadden had meant in the first place, disappeared. The survivors were Luce's minions.

Here let me note an amazing fact. This project, subsidized by the John Simon Guggenheim Foundation, was publicly announced. Yet Time Inc. has not communicated with me in any way. I can interpret this as only a highly ill-advised contempt for me. The people on *Life* had said that "picture journalism" and *Life* would soon be extinct. But they were not even trying picture journalism (which is two words).

I made a small effort to get random recollections of the old Time Inc. but soon gave it up. From the highly knowledgeable, trustworthy Hubert Kay I got the following:

Mary Fraser said that "Dan's ideas are 95% screwy and 5% wonderful."

Bourke-White ran into a Time Inc. person and asked, "Are you still with *Time*?" and he replied, "Well yes, I'm supposed to be president." This would be Linen.

John Hersey quit his job over a review by Roger Hewlett of a William A. White book.

John Martin once told Kay, "Don't sit down," and on another occasion said, "Never open that door without knocking."

Billings thought Kay's greatest story for *Time* was about pigs, for its ingenious synonyms.

When Kay left Time Inc. everyone told him, "I wish I had the nerve."

This is "inside" information but seems fairly useless in building a history. Every individual in this story was in his own personal situation (in every direction) and his own point of view (in every direction). Many of the characters are dead. In one sense, this is the voice of a drowning man, seeing his whole life in one last flash; he sees it as it really was, not as he wished it had been.

The degeneration set in train by Luce, working most conspicuously through Longwell, is best examined by synopsizing a late issue of *Life* (as I write). (I did this in a book called *Revolution by Cliché*.)

But, before I do, I must introduce evidence that, almost mystically, Hadden's journalism has not yet entirely vanished. A gifted young man on Time-Life International, Paul Trachtman, invited me to write a book on the first year of World War II, not knowing who I was. I noticed that the research and checking of his staff and his editing were as rigorous as in Time Inc.'s golden age. His superior was Cal Whipple, a survivor whom I respected. The old lamp still flickers in odd corners. The book was arbitrarily taken over by Time-Life books under Maitland Edey (whom I had ridiculed in public print) and, as far as I know, never published. The lamp is feeble under Edey, I suppose, but much of the research for that book has surfaced in this one.

Another disclaimer. Money men regard Charlie Stillman as the savior of Time Inc. for his financial manipulations. A look at Time Inc.'s current net worth is therefore required, though it is hardly my line of work.

I must rely on the data given in *Moody's* of this moment. If we exclude brief jugglings, Stillman has wrapped Time Inc. in a tortuous skein of manipulations, having nothing central to do with true communication. These would include about 600,000 acres of Texas timberland (Eastex), distribution of TV and educational films, folding cartons and milk containers, a Louisiana paper mill, real estate (including six Time-Life buildings around the world), and (against his opposition, according to the money men) TV and radio stations in Denver, Indianapolis, Grand Rapids, San Diego, and Bakersfield (now being sold off), foreign broadcasting chiefly in Latin America, the publishing firm of Little, Brown & Co., Time Inc.'s own book division, 26 small newspapers in the Chicago suburbs (Pioneer Press), art books, and so on.

To Briton Hadden, this maze of irrelevancies would have seemed insane.

Boring as they are, the rest of the figures must be given. Since 1941, when I had my stock, the stock has been split 24 for one. Outstanding shares are 7,257,000, of late years selling in the thirties, in 1970 between 25 and 44. Retained earnings at the end of 1970 were $211,209,000. Total current assets were $223,409,000; total assets were $545,616,000; net current assets were $140,555,000. In that year net ad revenues were $231 million, and net income $20,627,000. Circulations (in millions) were *Time* 5.5, *Life* 8.5, *Sports Illustrated* 2.0, *Fortune* 0.5. In 1971 Time Inc. earned $2.81 per share and paid a $2.30 dividend.

This is the world of the Belshazzars, to the original of whom the great threat was given, mene, mene, tekel, upharsin, which he could not read without Daniel, the somewhat unhistorical Jew. The last word means "the others will divide" and this process is now in course. Stillman and Larsen and Heiskell would not understand this; they would prefer to buy some more wood pulp and milk cartons, even some TV stations, while *Life* went down the drain, for lack of any elementary grasp of what picture journalism is. To this imminent sequence, I respond with a keening howl of protest, the terrible song of the hunted wolves in the last of the Arctic night, for some poetry is evoked by so great a death.

And so, the net worth of Time Inc., the figure as of 1970, is $202,479,000, but the sophisticated will deduct from this $30 million in "unexplained assets," an expression that means nothing to me. The estimated figure for 1971 (without the sophistication) is $212 million, and the book value $29.20 per outstanding share. Multiplying this by the number of shares comes out at about $212 million. This latter figure is common knowledge on Wall Street.

Time Inc.'s net worth, for all the magic with the wood pulp, seems shockingly trivial. Had more devotion been given to *Life*'s credibility with the reader, it might have been four times that by now. But then Stillman, Larsen, and Heiskell would have missed all that fun with the contracts and the lawyers. Mene, mene, tekel, upharsin.

The issue reviewed is that for October 1, 1971, costing 50 cents (but an enclosure offered a 25-week subscription at 12 cents an issue). The magazine has abandoned the hard-working, factual journalism shown in such massive detail in this book. Yet the masthead has 184 names, excluding company officers. How they occupy the week is beyond my imagination. The aim of the magazine seems to be wit or sophistication or being "with it" or something. A regular feature called "Gallery" offers two American Gothic elders, and the issue ends with a mystifying department called "Parting Shots"—a defense of the radical lawyer William Kunstler, a Russian astronaut's little girl, a picture of ranks of row houses, and one of a skier on grass. These open up a sort of whimsy. A signed page attacks stripmining. The "lead," if one may call it that, is on the aftermath of the famous Attica Prison massacre. It adds nothing to what the papers had told, and ignores the three white convicts killed by the black convicts. A good airview of the prison should have been heavily labeled. Then comes a long competent text piece on life in New York's Tombs prison. The two editorials are for a female Supreme Court justice and in favor of getting along with the European Common Market. (This latter is the only foreign news in the issue at a time when the world situation was complex and tragic.) The editorial content is overpowered by a four-page Plymouth Fury ad. The issue is really devoted to an 18-page "essay" on "The Brain," meaning, without saying so, the human brain only. (The fascinating area of other brains is never opened. However, four more installments are promised.) This first installment makes the mistake of thinking that the whole can be understood by giving a list of the parts. In consequence, it is confusing while telling much more than I want to know. That the human brain is ultimately mysterious to the human brain does not disqualify the project, but it might have been more effective to describe its evolution from the lower animals, starting with the simplest. A "new" kind of teaching is treated so superficially as to make it seem silly. There is a story about a homey woman columnist, Erma Bombeck, who is like everybody else but funny. Body-surfing on the California coast is shown without illumination. Then come "Parting Shots." Eighty pages in all. And yet worth fifty cents, at least in inflation.

The hidden infirmity of the present Time Inc. is that it doesn't know what it is doing. The brain story, for example, is bound to make the reader self-conscious and nervous: hardly a service to him. The old Time Inc. self-assurance has evaporated, and the Knopf reader would doubtless now forgive Time Inc. Certainly nobody today can be so ungracious as to hate Time Inc., for Time Inc. is trying to be "where it's happening." This is a mistake. Time Inc. must be "square."

The absolute truth may not be available about anything this week, but all journalism has a date stamped on it, and a great deal is true as of this week, no matter how it turns out twenty years from now. What is happening is what people *think* is happening, not what *happens*. Those three Attica convicts killed by the convicts are what happened, and Time Inc. should say so, instead of bowing to the fashionable belief that they did not happen. The other killed convicts were military casualties in a declared war, and the killed hostages were homicides.

The present Time Inc. does not dare ask the reader to believe anything.

Henry Robinson Luce died in 1967, and probably never recognized, much less diagnosed, the decadence into which he had slid his journalistic empire. And yet is not his sin epidemic in all human affairs? The managers want an organization not dependent on fallible human beings, on talent and heart and honor, for these are "temperamental." They prefer dull "reliable" cogs. It is a form of automation.

Narrowing the point down to Time Inc., the change in *Life* may have been dictated by the executive decision that *Life* was competing with *Time* and that such competition was cannibalistic. Certainly I felt that *I* was competing with *Time*.

But if *Life* was not competing with *Time* as a reporter of all the news, it had to become a piece of nonsense, a hubris, as it has done. After all, *Time* reports business and sports (both very carelessly, I am told), but Time Inc. embraces a business magazine, *Fortune*, and a sports magazine, *Sports Illustrated*. Longwell was incapable of doing Billings' journalistic job on *Life*, and so he convinced Luce that it was not worth doing, that he knew a greater and more profitable magic.

Luce's acceptance of this story is the final proof that he did not understand Time Inc. Its perpetuation shows that Briton Hadden's invention has fallen into the hands of zombie executives who do not even care. So it goes.

A marvelous satire caps the story and confirms the point of this book. For Time Inc.'s newest magazine is named *Money*. At last it has a communication that the executives may understand more perfectly than the writers.

Time Inc. once spoke to people with the recognizably human, opinionated voice of a certain kind of real human being, who had heart and guts and honor and did not care who hated him (such as the Knopf reader). Time Inc. today speaks as a corporate entity, ex cathedra, out of a sound-effect machine, and hence into a vacuum. It wants large numbers of subscribers—not readers, much less believers. Incredibly, the executives have decided that credibility is too bothersome to try for, and that the human voice is something that can be bought and sold. Thus Andy Heiskell and Charlie Stillman and the rest, may God have mercy on their shriveling souls in the bitter wind of obsolescence, as their portfolios also shrivel. They had their time; this is mine. Dear God, my cry for mercy on them is purely ritual. As on the soul of Henry R. Luce: Mene, mene, tekel, upharsin. For all the executives are Belshazzars. And the talent and honor are being counted and weighed. But God and the lions weighed Daniel differently, for he did not smell like an executive.

And so, as the golden anniversary of the glory men's Time Inc. approached in 1973, the victorious power men brought to birth the magazine *Money* and conferred death on the magazine *Life*.

Index